Commitment and Compassion in Psychoanalysis

Selected Papers of Edward M. Weinshel

Edward M. Weinshel, M.D.

Commitment and Compassion in Psychoanalysis

Selected Papers of Edward M. Weinshel

Edited by
Robert S. Wallerstein

THE ANALYTIC PRESS
2003 Hillsdale, NJ London

Published by
The Analytic Press, Inc., Publishers
101 West Street, Hillsdale, NJ 07642
www.analyticpress.com

Designed and typeset by
Christopher Jaworski, Bloomfield, NJ
qualitext@earthlink.net

Index by Leonard S. Rosenbaum

Frontispiece photograph by Kent Marshall © 1992
www.kentmarshall.com

Library of Congress Cataloging-in-Publication Data

Weinshel, Edward M.
Commitment and compassion in psychoanalysis : selected papers of
Edward M. Weinshel / edited by Robert S. Wallerstein.
p. cm.
Includes bibliographical references and index.

ISBN 0–88163–379–8

1. Psychoanalysis. 2. Weinshel, Edward M., 1919–.
I. Wallerstein, Robert S.

Printed in the United States of America
10 9 8 7 6 5 4 3 2 1

Contents

Commitment and Compassion in Psychoanalysis:
Selected Papers of Edward M. Weinshel
Edited by Robert S. Wallerstein

(Continued)

Acknowledgments

The creation of this volume of selected papers by Edward M. Weinshel has been spurred by the collaborative intent of his wife, Jenny Weinshel, and two long-time friends and collaborating colleagues, Leonard Shengold and myself, to fix in an accessible and enduring place the full measure of Ed's contributions to the mainstream American ego psychology paradigm within which he was educated and lived and worked lifelong psychoanalytically. The 14 papers selected for inclusion here do represent well the spread of his clinical and theoretical interests and the specific contributions, both to the praxis and the theory of psychoanalysis, by which we expect Ed will be remembered. Basically, the papers comprise the span of Ed's thinking and writing over the two decades from the early 1970s to the early 1990s.

Both clinically, and also organizationally within the affairs of the American and the International Psychoanalytic(al) Associations, Ed was quintessentially a team player, and four of the 14 papers in this volume were coauthored with his closest lifetime professional collaborator, Victor Calef. Calef actually participated as coauthor in approximately a quarter of Ed's entire psychoanalytic output, and Ed wrote collaboratively with a range of others as well, including myself. But the literary voice in this volume in both the solo and the collaborated papers is truly Ed's own. And it is a very lucid voice that reflects the clarity of Ed's thinking, and a modest and tentatively put style that reflects Ed's real character propensities.

In addition to the statements in this volume by Leonard Shengold and myself, we are also including brief notes by Ed's daughter, Julie Weinshel Tepper, by Jenny Weinshel's daughter, Dena Marshall Sorbo, and by Ed's granddaughter, Caitlin Pittel Stark. Julie and Dena are now both also part of our psychoanalytic world, in Los Angeles and in San Francisco, respectively; Caitlin is a clinical psychologist in Boston. Others have also played important contributing roles. I note especially the ever-invaluable help of Barbara Lehman, who prepares my manuscripts with meticulous and diligent attention, and Dr. Harvey Salans, whose very substantial contribution from the Salans Patient Care Fund at Mount Zion Hospital in San Francisco has made this undertaking possible. My gratitude goes as well to Paul Stepansky, Managing Director of The Analytic Press, whose strong belief in the effort to maintain access to the work and thinking of significant contributors to the historical development and evolution of psychoanalysis has ensured this publication, and to Nancy Liguori, Senior Production Manager of The Analytic Press, who has carefully monitored the production process and maintained the productive working liaison with me that has so facilitated my editorial responsibilities.

* * *

I am grateful to the following publishers and periodicals for permission to republish these articles.

Part 1: Chapter 1, "On Certain Neurotic Equivalents of Necrophilia" (1972), *International Journal of Psycho-Analysis*, 53:67–75. Chapter 2, "'I Didn't Mean It': Negation as a Character Trait" (1977), *The Psychoanalytic Study of the Child*, 32: 387–419. New Haven, CT: Yale University Press. Chapter 3, "Some Observations on Not Telling the Truth" (1979), *Journal of the American Psychoanalytic Association*, 27:497–531. Chapter 4, "Some Clinical Consequences of Introjection: Gaslighting" (1981), *Psychoanalytic Quarterly*, 50:44–66. Chapter 5, "Perceptual Distortions During Analysis: Some Observations on the Role of the Superego in Reality Testing" (1986), in *The Science of Mental Conflict: Essays in Honor of Charles Brenner*, ed. Arnold D. Richards & Martin S. Willick. Hillsdale, NJ: The Analytic Press, pp. 353–374. Chapter 6, "On Inconsolability" (1989), in *The Psychoanalytic Core: Essays in Honor of Leo Rangell, M.D.*, ed. Harold P. Blum, Edward M. Weinshel & F. Robert Rodman. Madison, CT: International Universities Press, pp. 45–69.

Part 2: Chapter 7, "The Ego in Health and Normality" (1970), *Journal of the American Psychoanalytic Association*, 18:682–735. Chapter 8, "The Transference Neurosis: A Survey of the Literature" (1971), *Journal of the American Psychoanalytic Association*, 19:67–88. Chapter 9, "Reporting, Nonreporting, and Assessment in the Training Analysis" (1973), *Journal of the American Psychoanalytic Association*, 21: 714–726. Chapter 10, "The Analyst as the Conscience of the Analysis" (1980), *International Review of Psycho-Analysis*, 7:279–290. Chapter 11, "Some Observations on the Psychoanalytic Process" (1984), *Psychoanalytic Quarterly*, 53:63–92. Chapter 12, "Further Observations on the Psychoanalytic Process" (1990), *Psychoanalytic Quarterly*, 59:629–649. Chapter 13, "How Wide Is the Widening Scope of Psychoanalysis and How Solid Is Its Structural Model? Some Concerns and Observations" (1990), *Journal of the American Psychoanalytic Association*, 38:275–296. Chapter 14, "Therapeutic Technique in Psychoanalysis and Psychoanalytic Psychotherapy" (1992), *Journal of the American Psychoanalytic Association*, 40:327–347.

5, 6

Edward M. Weinshel

A *Mensch* for All Seasons

Leonard Shengold

> Belief in the existence of other human beings as such is love.
>
> —*Simone Weil, quoted in Auden and Kronenberger (1962)*

Edward Weinshel has been a moral as well as an intellectual force in his roles as political leader, as teacher, and as author in psychoanalysis. Good character is an indispensable quality for a true psychoanalyst. But Ed has all the other prerequisites: intelligence, empathy, a gift for humor, tact, patience, a flair for original ideas and insights. Ed's goodness is a positive force and has a radiant quality. With all his benevolence (I realize that I am making him sound like the Saint Francis his hometown is named for), he has known how to be firm; like a good parent, he has been able to say "no" when it was appropriate. As those who remember his term as Chairman of the Board on Professional Standards of the American Psychoanalytic Association will attest, he could also be tough. He has fought for what he felt was right—and, above all, against the current trends in and out of psychoanalysis toward dehumanization and deindividualization.

The qualities of a writer's personality—his conflicts and his character—are evident both in how he writes and what he writes, in his style and in his content. His moral convictions can furnish and influence the motivation for his writing. Therefore I want to evoke the kind of person Ed Weinshel is as well as to describe his accomplishments. I can do this from the perspective of a close friendship that has lasted for more than 35 years.

Part 1 of this book, organized and edited by another of our close friends, Robert Wallerstein, consists of Ed's clinical papers, based on the analyst/writer's records of his psychoanalytic work. (Ed's preponderantly theoretical papers in Part 2, when given, at times contained clinical examples also, which were, however, deleted in the published version because of space constraints or issues of confidentiality.) Freud wrote somewhere[1] that "all records are lies." This is of course a statement of exaggeration. I think Freud was, although specifically referring to analysts and analysands, expressing the difficulty that besets us all as human beings of fulfilling his ideal goal—of standing for the truth, no matter what. This is an impossible goal never to be arrived at by those of us in what Freud called an "impossible" profession, yet it is a goal that all analysts need to strive for. W. H. Auden (1939) wrote about Freud: "All that he did was / To remember like the old, / And to be honest, like children" (p. 165).

We try, bearing in mind the impossibility of attaining historical truth and the vagaries and unreliability of narrative truth (see Spence, 1982), to examine and use what the patient tells us to pursue and, if the patient does not remember, to approximate and help reconstruct what may actually have happened. Memory (even, and sometimes especially, contra Auden, for the old) is too malleable and distorted ever to be more than relatively reliable, but analyst and patient can make a mutual effort to explore the past and connect it to the present. We may never discover or authenticate "the facts," but we can critically examine with the patient how his or her mind has registered the past. The imprint[2] is revealed in the repetitive emotional and intellectual patterns that emerge in the interplay (transferences and resistances) between the patient's attempt at free association and the analyst's listening and commenting. In the course of this mutual exploration, both the analyst and the patient are obliged to try to be "honest like children." One must be aware that children are not always honest; this is true of analyst and patient alike especially when motivated by transferences and resistances (which, paradoxically, furnish the grist for our psychoanalytic mill). But the analyst's reliably good moral character is essential for earning enough trust to enable the patient to expose, accept and struggle to modify the

[1]I think it is somewhere in the *Minutes of the Vienna Meetings* book, but I have not been able to find it in those poorly indexed volumes.

[2]The "imprint" has both changeable and "permanent" (compulsively repetitive) qualities.

burden of conflict-ridden impulses and defenses—ridden with the hostility and distrust of the neurotic past. This struggle requires a controlled moral passion from the analyst, skillfully used so that it can be evoked in, and tolerated by, the patient. The analyst must be able to care with an intensity that is employed with tactful empathy, according to awareness of the needs and vulnerability of the individual patient. For this vital and difficult function of the analyst, central to the art rather than to the science of psychoanalysis, Ed Weinshel was superbly equipped.

Everyone calls him Ed or Eddie. Ed has almost everything that is excellent in human qualities. These still shine through even now that he has, tragically, become subject to the declining vicissitudes of old age. He is no longer, alas, able to write his brilliant papers. From boyhood on he has been a natural leader. He has had a soaring intelligence, flavored by a marvelous sense of humor that still can make its appearance despite the decline of his health. His wit is frequently accompanied by the sudden flash of sparkling eyes and a wicked, delighted and delightful smile that reveals the child in the man. His most powerful and admirable trait is what the *New Testament* in the King James version calls the greatest of man's characteristics: "charity,"[3] a mistranslation in my opinion from the Latin *caritas*. In more modern translations (e.g., the Revised Standard Edition) the term is rendered as "love." This is not sexual love, but love in the sense of caring for and about another human being. *Caritas* as love is what the great religious philosopher Simone Weil is referring to in her definition, quoted in the epigraph to this Introduction. (Lionel Trilling, in a statement that complements Weil's, writes that the essence of morality is "making a willing suspension of disbelief in the selfhood of somebody else" [1951, p. 95]—appreciating the separate existence of another person.)

Ed not only cares about others, he cares *generously*. In this he is like his grandfather. Every Friday afternoon (*erev Shobiss*) in Milwaukee, where Ed was born and raised, it was his grandfather's pleasure and nourishing mission to bring a chicken for the Jewish Sabbath to each household of his close friends and of his extensive family. Young Ed often was taken along during these charitable excursions. (Anyone who has seen Ed confronting one of his grandchildren needs only one glance at his dimpled face, beaming with benevolence, his whole countenance

[3]St. Paul says: "And now abideth faith, hope, charity, these three; but the greatest of these is charity" (King James version, Corinthians 13:13). The Revised Standard version does substitute "love" for "charity."

exuberantly concentrated in his characteristic smile, to know what kind of grandfather *he* is.) Many of Ed's students, colleagues, and patients have been the recipients of psychological equivalents of his grandfather's chickens. Ed has not been a saint—he cares too much for that, and, as he can love with passion, he can hate and fight with passion for what he thinks is right as well as against what he thinks is wrong (as readers of these papers will note). As a result of his richness of emotion, Ed's psychic world is full of real others about whom he feels intensely. This makes Ed a profoundly moral person.[4] He has been our psychoanalytic Thomas More, not a saint but a *mensch* for all seasons.

He has an impressive list of accomplishments. But the key to his influence on psychoanalysis is to be found less in the important things he has done than in the kind of person he is. (This will be sensed by the readers of this book.)

Ed was born in Milwaukee, Wisconsin, and went to college and medical school at the University of Wisconsin. He served as Army psychiatrist in the Philippines during World War II. For the past 50 years he has lived and worked in San Francisco. He has been a great teacher and has influenced the lives and careers of generations of psychiatrists and other mental health workers, and not only in psychoanalysis—I am thinking particularly of his service as Chief and Director of Training of the Department of Psychiatry at Mt. Zion Hospital during its halcyon years as a psychiatric training center. (There has been a bountiful distribution of weekly and daily Weinshellian chickens at Mt. Zion.) Ed has had decades of service as a Clinical Professor of Psychiatry at the University of California School of Medicine in San Francisco. He has filled many of the main administrative positions in the San Francisco Psychoanalytic Institute, where he trained and became a Training and Supervising Analyst. He is a master editor; he has been on the Editorial Board of the *Journal of the American Psychoanalytic Association, The Psychoanalytic Quarterly*, and had 10 years of dedicated and wise leadership as the North American Editor of the *International Journal* and *International Review of Psycho-Analysis*. He has chaired many important Committees at both the American and the International Psycho-Analytical Associations. Most notably, he was the Chairman of the Board on Professional Standards of the American, and the Program Chairman and

[4]In this he was joined by one of his dearest friends and a frequent coauthor, Victor Calef—each a stalwart knight of psychoanalysis, as Ernest Jones once characterized Karl Abraham.

Secretary of the International Psycho-Analytical (serving as second in command to his friend Bob Wallerstein who was President). Ed has demonstrated his devotion to psychoanalytic education and educational standards in his many administrative assignments. He has tackled all of his jobs with characteristic enthusiastic dedication. It has been hard work tempered by his great capacity for friendship.

He has never been too busy to be a loving and lovable husband, father, grandfather, and friend. When I worked as his Secretary of the Board, I was wont to make bets on the length of time it would take him to cross a crowded room to exit from a meeting. There were so many friends to stop and exchange some words with that it became part of my duty to start him toward the door with at least a 20-minute lead time. No Chairman is supposed to be a hero to his Secretary, but I ended my years as number two man with the same love for and awe of Ed that started when he picked me—a complete stranger to him (I was his second choice, recommended by a mutual friend). He made my acquaintance by giving me a bear-hug. Ed's bear-hug has since become a customary greeting among his friends and colleagues and for a while threatened to become a ritual greeting in institutional psychoanalysis.

Ed's eminence as a psychoanalytic author has been recognized in his having been selected as the Freud Lecturer at both the PANY–NYU and the New York Psychoanalytic Institutes and as the Rado Lecturer at the Columbia Institute. He has written over 40 publications on his own, and another dozen in partnership with Vic Calef (as well as several with Owen Renik and Bob Wallerstein). One always knows where Ed Weinshel stands. He has written clinical and theoretical papers of wonderful variety and quality, full of wisdom, compassion, humility, with appropriate attention given to his own failings and countertransferences. His clinical descriptions feature his self-observations and negative self-criticisms (see, e.g., the paper "On Inconsolability" in this book). There is no great dramatic revelation; there is no spectacular success or failure. We are left with many mysteries. He knows what he does not know, and the accounts ring true.

The subjects he has written about include: inconsolability, negation, tinnitus, the role of the superego during analysis and in reality testing, the functioning of the ego in health and normality, on not telling the truth, homosexuality, brainwashing (called "gaslighting"), regressive states in psychoanalysis. He has given us critical surveys of the borderline diagnosis, the overuse of the concept of development; he has published comprehensive presentations of transference neurosis, the psychoanalytic process, training analysis, affects and moods, of structural change in psychoanalysis. The characterological thread of caring—about people and ideas—runs through all his written work. This book presents a selective sampling; I hope there will be a *Collected Papers* to follow it. One of his papers written with Vic Calef, included here, is titled, "The Analyst as Conscience of the Analysis." In his distinguished career, Ed Weinshel has served as the caring and steadfast conscience (ego-ideal as well as superego) of clinical and organized psychoanalysis.

I want to pose a question about the therapeutic influence of the patient's awareness of the kindness and benevolence of the analyst (so obvious in Ed and his work) in contrast to the traditional goal of the analyst's emotional neutrality. In several of his publications, Ed has presented cases that have told a story of patients who have suffered child abuse and deprivation, usually at the hands of a parent. For a terrified child who has suffered abuse or deprivation, there is an enhancement of the danger inherent to every child's feeling intense anger toward the parent on whom the child is dependent. Children feel that their rage, inevitably present due to frustration as well as part of human instinctual endowment, can have murderous magical power. One can see or sense in every victim of child abuse the presence of an urgent (conscious and/or unconscious) wish to kill the parents while feeling he or she cannot live without them—a terrible psychic double-bind that is there to some extent in all of us. We all need good parenting to protect us from insult, injury, and one's self-destructive impulses. But there is an especial need for the traumatized child to preserve the mental image of the parent by what are sometimes idealized delusions of being cared about and loved. Yet being loved and rescued is contradicted when the child repeatedly experiences that opening itself up to love and then to seduction will lead[5] to traumatic overstimulation. Rage is intolerable; and the love that leads to it becomes intolerable. It can surprise the analyst to find that often for the abused child love seems to have become even more frightening than the murderous rage. And yet only by being able to feel love can the child or the former child-victim modify the terrible emotional consequences of the abuse and alleviate the cannibalistic intensity of the anger.

[5]Alternatively, the child who is beaten needs to sexualize this and becomes subject to masochistic compulsion. Beating is equated with being loved, as Freud (1919) observed.

One of the great difficulties of working with abused children or with adults who were abused as children is their distrust. It is an understandable and even an adaptive distrust, but it comes at a great price. It specifically can mean distrusting loving feelings both in oneself and in others—a terrible burden for an abused child who so desperately needs love and rescue. I recently began a supervision of a beginning candidate who was assigned his first analytic case. He learned a lot about his patient in the first session on the couch when she, while describing her traumatic childhood at the hands of a depressed and cruel mother, broke down and began to weep. The neophyte analyst "found himself" handing her some Kleenex. The patient refused his offer. She first took them, then threw them to the floor, looked back at him in disdain, fumbled in her purse for her own tissues, used some and then said, emphatically, "*Now* I feel better!" Being comforted apparently (and so it turned out) led this woman to expect danger. Of course, not only abused children have such bad expectations in relation to parent figures, but I have found that all the patients I have seen who were abused as children do have them.

When feeling and caring has led to torment, emotional responses must be dampened. This requires massive isolation: joy-killing, rage-suppressing, life-inhibiting defenses. Love and longing are suppressed along with rage; sometimes this deadening of feeling exists alongside sporadic losses of emotional control. Where there has been frank sexual abuse, the child was often initially motivated to it partly out of the need for love for, and from, the parent.

So the obvious and basic loving nature of an analyst like Ed Weinshel can, if not patiently and carefully controlled, constitute a specific danger for some patients. It is often necessary for the analyst to begin with a long period consisting of passive benevolent listening with an occasional empathic comment. The intensities of contradictory affects and impulses, and specifically the intensity of the longing for love, can make the promise of loving and caring more than the patient can bear. Anger, terrible as it is, is for some patients a lighter load. And yet the patient must eventually be able to bear to keep both the love and the hate (toward the parents transferred onto the analyst) together in consciousness if there is going to be any modifying positive change. Only the painful emotional simultaneous revival in responsible consciousness of both love and hate can make possible the acknowledgement and the modulation of the primal emotions. This can connect the past meaningfully with the present, and undo brainwashing (which Calef and Weinshel [1981] call "gaslighting"; see this volume, chapter 4).

And here is the paradox. The psychoanalyst's power to effect change depends not only and not primarily on the correctness of interpretations, but on those interpretations effecting and being able to release the patient's ability to love. The patient must learn to tolerate loving the analyst as part of the achievement of being able to come to some bearable terms with rage and murderous impulses. Murder is part of our animal instinctual nature and murderous impulses are made to burgeon by actual torment and deprivation in childhood.

The task of learning to remember rather than to repeat the traumatic past takes much time and patience on the part of both partners in the analytic process. Did the perception of Dr. Weinshel's goodness help or hinder his "soul murder" (my term for children who have been abused or deprived) patients? It is of course not easy to generalize here. Of course the analyst's good character must be there for the patient to become able to tolerate it. But goodness, although essential, is not enough, and at moments especially early in the treatment of some cases it can be a frightening burden if thrust upon the patient. Here the analyst must operate with patience, empathy and tact. Edward Weinshel has these qualities as well as wisdom and benevolence. He once said that in his view relentless self-observation is what constitutes proper psychoanalytic neutrality. Ed has been a magnificently talented clinician. I want to end this essay with a characteristic quotation from a speech Ed gave on "Freud and His Legacy" in 1991. (I don't believe that it has ever been published.)

> One of the mixed blessings of becoming an older psychoanalyst and accumulating more and more clinical experience is that you begin to experience just how difficult and demanding psychoanalysis *really* is and what a *tour de force* Freud's conception of psychoanalysis and the mental apparatus *really* is. Hanns Sachs once said, "Our deepest analyses are no more than scratching the earth's surface with a harrow." Not long ago I observed with some indignation and some sorrow the hubris of a colleague who claimed that "anything is analyzable." That this is a fantasy I try to tell to anyone who will listen.

Edward Weinshel in his person and in his papers shows his ability to feel "caritas." He has demonstrated in his papers that what we can do for our patients is better regarded as amelioration rather than cure, and still it can make for a crucial change for the better. He is wise and modest about how much psychoanalysis can succeed in helping the patient cope with the human condition and yet has a fervent belief in its therapeutic as well as in its heuristic value. Freud (1895, p. 13; 1920, p. 64) has quoted at least twice: "Was man nicht erfliegen kann, muss man erhinken. . . . Die Schrift sagt, es ist keine Schande zu hinken" ("What one cannot fly to, one must reach by limping. . . . Scripture says that limping is no sin" [my translation]).[6]

REFERENCES

Auden, W. H. (1939), In memory of Sigmund Freud. In: *The Collected Poetry of W. H. Auden.* New York: Knopf, 1966.

_______ & Kronenberger, L. (1962), *The Viking Book of Aphorisms.* New York: Viking, 1966, p. 29.

The Bible (Authorized King James Version). London: Oxford University Press, undated.

Calef, V. & Weinshel, E. (1981), Some clinical consequences of introjection: Gaslighting. *Psychoanal. Quart.,* 50:44–69.

Freud, S. (1895), Letter to Fliess of 10/20/1895. In: *The Origins of Psycho-Analysis,* ed. M. Bonaparte, A. Freud & E. Kris. New York: Basic Books, 1954, pp. 129–130.

_______ (1919), "A child is being beaten": A contribution to the study of sexual perversion. *Standard Edition,* 17:179–204. London: Hogarth Press, 1955.

_______ (1920), Beyond the pleasure principle. *Standard Edition,* 18:7–64. London: Hogarth Press, 1955.

Shengold, L. (1989), *Soul Murder: Child Abuse and Deprivation.* New Haven, CT: Yale University Press.

Spence, D. (1982), *Narrative and Historical Truth.* New York: Norton.

Trilling, L. (1951), *Freud: Within and Beyond Culture.* New York: Viking, 1965.

Weinshel, E. (1981), On inconsolability. In: *The Psychoanalytic Core,* ed. H. Blum, F. R. Rodman & E. Weinshel. Madison, CT: International Universities Press, pp. 44–66.

[6]The quotation comes from the 19th-century poet/Orientalist Friedrich Rückert.

PART 1: CLINICAL PAPERS

Introduction to Part 1

Clinical Papers

Of the half of Edward Weinshel's literary corpus that is properly labeled clinical papers, six have been selected for this volume. Of those, two are from the quarter of his output that was coauthored with Victor Calef, his closest long-time professional collaborator and one of his closest personal friends. Actually, their constant intellectual discourse is implicated as well in the majority of each of their papers that was separately authored over the more than two decades of their close professional collaboration; but those that appeared in the literature as actually coauthored were the product of their being jointly talked through idea by idea, and word for word, though from a close knowledge of the writings of each of these two colleagues of mine. I would tend to assign the actual language construction, the writing style, of each of these joint creations, primarily to Weinshel.

As was true of the propensities of both men, these clinical papers stand squarely in the British, more than in the American, psychoanalytic tradition, that every clinical paper should carry a theoretical proposition, should try to make a point widely applicable to the clinical work of the psychoanalytic reader, and that, conversely, every imputed theoretical advance should derive solidly from within the matrix of clinical experience, should not reflect just abstract (armchair) theorizing.

And in distinction to all too many of the clinical contributions that fill our literature, where the clinical descriptions—whether an extended case report or a succession of briefer vignettes—agglutinate into a homogenized mass of "average expectable patients," meaning with properly traumatized upbringings and properly neurotic (or deeper) illness structures, where each patient blends into the common mass without distinguishing characteristics, the patients in this Weinshel collection are each described felicitously enough and distinctly enough as to emerge as clearly individually recognizable case histories—and life histories. They come alive in the reading.

The six selected here span two decades of writing. The first, written with Calef, published in 1972, "On Certain Neurotic Equivalents of Necrophilia," was presented at the International Psychoanalytical Association Congress in Vienna in July 1971. It deals with common enough fantasies—both the attractions and the fears—of sexual involvement with the passively receptive, even masochistic, helpless and inert, perhaps sleeping, and even (psychologically) dead sexual object—dead in the same sense as in André Green's signature article on the dead mother. It is the common neurotic equivalent of the extremely rare perversion of actual necrophilia, active sexual involvement with the physically dead. The fairy tale of Prince Charming and Sleeping Beauty is the mythic embodiment of the marker theme. The article comprises a whole panoply of possible psychodynamic meanings of this fantasy structure, and is built around an extended case report of a married woman who relatively early in her analysis described a lifelong fantasy of making love to a dead man, as well as briefer accounts of several other patients with widely varying manifestations of this organizing fantasy, in more or less disguised versions.

The next paper, "'I Didn't Mean It': Negation as a Character Trait" (1977), by Weinshel alone, had actually been presented at a special meeting of the San Francisco Psychoanalytic Society in 1959 with Anna Freud as the formal discussant, and Edith Buxbaum, Kurt Eissler, Merton Gill, and René Spitz contributing from the floor. It deals with negation, or denial, or disavowal as a replacement at a higher level (within consciousness but with its accuracy or meaning denied) for a failed repression. The article is built around one long case description where this phenomenon—negation—was built in as a pervasive and deeply enduring character configuration, a married woman who came to define herself during the analysis as "living with the brakes on," a constant inhibition of content and affect, a life of enforced self-denial and self-control, of offering almost everything in terms of uncertainty, ambiguity, of not realizing its context or meaning, and so on, altogether a (very generalizable) example of how a particular defensive propensity could embrace and dominate an entire character structure. It is all encapsulated in the title phrase, "I didn't mean it."

The third paper, again by Weinshel alone, "Some Observations on Not Telling the Truth" (1979), was presented at the Association for Psychoanalytic Medicine (the Columbia Society) as the 21st Sandor

Rado Lecture in March 1977. It is a many-sided discussion of the ubiquitous issue of lying, from which no one is immune, at least not on certain occasions or in certain contexts, let alone the universal phenomenon of "white lies," social lying, etc. One of the cases described here is of a young woman, given very frequently to the not uncommon statement from the couch, "I have nothing to say," and tracing the various meanings of this statement within the analytic discourse, centering around repressed sexual fantasies and secrets, often transferential in nature—with the defensive charge often made against the analyst that he would withhold from the patient his own (in keeping with her father's own) sexual interest in her. Over several case descriptions Weinshel describes (and gives particularized meaning to) small or trivial lies as well as outrageous lies, and by and large in the context of morally upright individuals who were not characterological liars. As can be expected, the plea is to not equate lies with moral lapses, but rather to see them as screens to be used as sources of informative analytic data. The ironically felicitous title of "Lying on the Couch" had been suggested to Weinshel as apt for this article.

The fourth in this series of clinical papers, "Some Clinical Consequences of Introjection: Gaslighting" (1981), this one again with Victor Calef, was presented at a September 1978 meeting in San Diego in honor of Leo Rangell, under the sponsorship of all the Western psychoanalytic societies within the American Psychoanalytic Association. It is justly probably the best known (and most cited) of Weinshel's clinical contributions. The first of the four patients described is prototypically a woman whose dynamics as they unfolded psychoanalytically consisted of the manipulation, often in a sadomasochistic manner, of herself and her children by a coldly controlling husband, and usually in ways of which she was consciously not aware. The title, "gaslighting," comes of course from the very popular Broadway success in 1939, "Angel Street," and has by now become part of our colloquial lexicon. What is of particular interest in the description of this phenomenon by two deeply committed adherents to the ego psychological paradigm, architected by Heinz Hartmann and his collaborators, is how as early as 1978—long before it became widely known and popular within mainstream American psychoanalysis—Calef and Weinshel delineated the very Kleinian concept of projective identification, albeit not by that name, embracing it under the rubric of the vicissitudes of introjection. Within the analytic situation, "gaslighting" can of course work in both directions and across almost the entire spectrum of psychopathological disorders. Indeed, since it is a matter of influencing and being influenced, it can be—at least to some degree—ubiquitous and inevitable in every close interpersonal relationship.

The fifth paper in this clinical sequence, "Perceptual Distortions During Analysis: Some Observations on the Role of the Superego in Reality Testing," appeared in 1986 in a volume (Richards and Willick, eds.) published in honor of Charles Brenner. Three patients are described, all women, and all three with a generally phobic-hysterical character structure, who each in different ways, in the course of the analytic work developed an illusional perceptual distortion, in each instance a reflection of a fantasied threatened sexual advance by the analyst. Although these women could generally be described as avoidant, inhibited, and even "mousey," the florid underlying exhibitionistic-voyeuristic conflicts could well be brought to light in the analytic work. The fear of being crazy surfaced with the uncovering of awareness of the illusional distortion of reality testing that was involved, as well as of all the imbricated ego and superego interdictions. In all three instances, there was a difficulty, going back to childhood problems, in separating ego injunctions against dangerous impulses from superego injunctions against (morally prohibited) "bad" impulses.

And the sixth and last of this series of clinical papers, again by Weinshel alone, "On Inconsolability" (1989), was actually presented in different versions on a number of prior occasions, as the Freud Anniversary Lecture at the Psychoanalytic Association of New York, at the Cleveland Psychoanalytic Society, and as a keynote address at the Annual Scientific Colloquium of the Anna Freud Centre, in London. It was published in a volume of essays honoring Leo Rangell (Blum, Weinshel, and Rodman, eds.). This paper deals with another common enough clinical condition, those patients who stubbornly hang on to their lifelong feelings of misery, their seeming enduring inconsolability in the face of whatever—and however mild—adverse circumstance. This was manifest in the described patient's constant distress and inconsolable status in the face of whatever misunderstanding arose in the course of the analytic process, this together with her lifelong difficult relationship with her spoilsport mother. And she was constantly fearful of her inevitably disconsolate reaction to whatever in the analytic interaction could be construed as a broken (even if only implied) promise. Dynamics of oral greed and of penis envy were implicated throughout the course of the case. In this last of the clinical cases, as in the whole array of them, a particular dynamic is highlighted and proved central to the analysis, that to a lesser degree is so widely prevalent here in the whole array of pessimistic characters who so regularly gravitate to the conception of the glass as half-empty.

Altogether the entire sequence of six clinical papers to follow (two of them coauthored with Victor Calef) present a kaleidoscope of common personality organizations and characteristics, exacerbated in these particular patients to a discomforting enough prominence in their personality organization to play significant roles in their decision to seek the help of psychoanalytic therapy.

Note W's helpful 2 intro
discussions p. 1-5, 141-147

Chapter 1

1972

On Certain Neurotic Equivalents of Necrophilia

Victor Calef and Edward M. Weinshel

The theme of the 'Sleeping Beauty' who is brought back to life, as it were, by the love of a Prince Charming is one which has fascinated both story-tellers and listeners for hundreds of years. It is our impression that not infrequently we hear, from our analytic patients—primarily via various denials—this same theme and its disguised wishes. We are referring to those patients who complain that their spouses go to sleep before them and before sexual activity can be initiated. It is our experience that, at least in many of these individuals, this complaint is an attempt to hide the fascination and attraction for the sleeping sexual object and the wish to make love to that object.

Further, it is our hypothesis that this wish is the central organizing force for a group of fantasies which involve a series of necrophilic equivalents and which play a not insignificant dynamic role in a variety of behavioural patterns. We are not concerned with necrophilia as a perversion *per se*; we have not had any first-hand clinical experience with this clinical entity which we believe to be relatively rare and probably is observed only in relation to extremely severe psychopathology. The neurotic equivalents and derivatives of necrophilia,[1] however, we believe to be quite ubiquitous and do not necessarily denote the same kind of

[1]We would emphasize that in our use of the term 'necrophilia', we are not referring to an object that is literally or corporeally dead. As we stress throughout this paper, we are dealing with the psychological aspects of the 'idea' of a sleeping (dead) object in terms of both conscious and unconscious fantasies, associations, equivalents and derivatives.

malignant psychopathology. We will attempt to describe some of the dynamic and genetic aspects of these fantasies and to illustrate at least some of their clinical manifestations. Perhaps one such illustration will best permit us to delineate some of these factors.

Relatively early in her analysis, Mrs L. described a life-long fantasy of making love to a dead man. Mrs L. was in her mid-20s when she began analysis because of a severe agoraphobia, and the necrophilic fantasy could be traced to some point between the ages of four and five, at least roughly parallel with the time that her mother was pregnant with the patient's younger sister. As might be expected, Mrs L.'s memory of the childhood fantasy was a rather diffuse and amorphous one; her concept of what constituted 'love-making' was vague, but the idea of a dead man (later the object could also be asleep, drugged or otherwise helpless) was from the beginning vivid and central. As the fantasy-imagery crystallized, fellatio became its most conspicuous and consistent erotic activity. Somewhat later—although the patient has never been absolutely certain of this, she feels that it began in mid-adolescence—the necrophilic fantasy became commingled with an equally vivid voyeuristic fantasy in which an unidentified man carries on violent sexual activity with some woman.

Limitations of space preclude anything but the briefest résumé of the pertinent dynamic and genetic factors in this complicated and fascinating case. It will come as no surprise to the analytic clinician that an essential root of the patient's agoraphobia was connected with her very strong and conflicted exhibitionistic impulses; throughout her life she struggled with intense sadomasochistic wishes which gradually emerged in the course of the analytic work; she demonstrated what at times appeared to be a sexual insatiability and at the same time an intense fear of being damaged during the sexual act; her fear of not getting enough sexual gratification was paralleled by a comparable anxiety in regard to being deprived of food and oral gratification in the broader sense. She was exposed to frequent primal scene situations, a good deal of precocious sexual enlightenment, and an inordinate amount of highly-sexualized physical abuse from a two-year older brother. The birth of the patient's sister proved to be one of the critical events in Mrs L.'s psychological development; the devastating impact of the disappointment she experienced *vis-à-vis* both the mother and father played a crucial part in Mrs L.'s subsequent neurosis and in her particular character formation.

The principal constituents of Mrs L.'s necrophilic fantasy can best be delineated by sketching out in a rather schematic and fragmentary fashion some of the clinical material which came up in the course of her analysis. Although these data will be presented as if they emerged in a linear, chronological fashion, we should point out that what we are presenting has been systematized for convenience and emphasis; nevertheless, our editorial licence has resulted in only a partial distortion of what actually occurred. For a long time she bemoaned the fact that she must be such a dull and lacklustre patient. She could not imagine the analyst would in any way find her interesting or attractive, particularly as a sexual object. Time and again, Mrs L. condensed her complaints in the phrase that the analyst must be 'bored stiff'. It also became clear that this repetitive lament was a defence and a resistance against her wishes to be interesting and to be attractive to the analyst and to be the object of his sexual love. As this resistance was exposed together with her frustration and anger at being the woman-scorned, the 'You are bored stiff' rather quickly changed into the almost obsessive thought that the analyst was 'a bored stiff', with the emphasis on the 'stiff'. This could readily be analysed in terms of her angry wish to have the analyst dead, a 'stiff', who, because he was dead, could not attack her sexually. Again, as the analytic work progressed and her fears of sexual attack and penetration could be dealt with, a third adage entered the lists. (The very complex and admittedly delightful facility of utilizing these 'plays on words' obviously were in themselves a source of considerable gratification and resistance for the patient. It can only be stated that very early in her life, she became entranced with words, became an omnivorous reader, and derived a good deal of hidden scoptophilic pleasure from her reading. One of the relatively early and obvious manifestations of this was the preoccupation with finding so-called 'dirty' words in the dictionary. She also developed a rather extraordinary facility with languages, a gift she could not 'show off' because of the inhibition of her exhibitionism.) She now perceived the analyst as a 'stiff board', whose phallic qualities she admired and desired as an instrument of sexual satisfaction, albeit never without a good deal of anxiety.

Gradually there was a shift in the material; and, particularly, what could be observed was a return to the 'bored stiff' phase. At this period in the analysis, it was the patient who was bored stiff, or more often 'a bored stiff'; and it was during this period that we were able to recover and understand a good many of her primal-scene experiences and the impact that these experiences had exerted in the patient's development.

The central element in these experiences was the patient's tremendous feeling of excitement and her playing dead, being the 'stiff', as a means of both hoping to be ignored by the active participants of the sexual activity and hoping to be able, by her own deadness, to ignore her own frightening excitement. The final phase in this series of 'headlines' came with the recognition of her identification with the male and with the male organ. It was an identification which was the complicated product of various defensive processes (primarily a kind of identification with the aggressor), of her own aggression towards the male related to the envy of the phallus of both her brother and father, and of her wish for an instrument which would permit her to do what her father had supposedly done—enter into and explore the interior of her mother's body. The latter wish, in turn, had both libidinal and aggressive components; the former was manifested by the desire to return to and be close to her mother almost in a primal reunion, the latter by the desire to get into mother's body and destroy the intrauterine sibling and rival. During this period, the key phrase was 'I am a stiff board'.

During this latter period it was possible to analyse more clearly the meaning and significance of the necrophilic fantasy, especially as elements of that fantasy were involved in the transference and the transference neurosis; and it was also possible to discern a number of different levels in the composition of that fantasy. Most immediately, by dint of role-reversals and the identification with the aggressor, the patient was now able to do actively what she feared (and wished) would be done to her; the fellatio was not only an oral-incorporative means of gaining the phallus but also of assuring her that the phallus would not be used against her.

A deeper level of the fantasy also was based on a shift of identifications and of roles. The patient, now the possessor of a fantasied penis, became the male partner in the sexual act; and the 'dead' male was the passive, helpless mother in the love-making. The ostensible link from the manifest content of the fantasy to its unconscious element was, of course, the sucking on the penis and the penis–breast equation.

But at an even deeper stratum, the patient was also the sister (child-phallus) who was to be evicted from and replaced in the mother's womb. This element in the fantasy involved the destruction of the intrauterine rival; and, as a result, this patient's 'rebirth' or even 'change' fantasies and wishes were heavily tinged with this kind of aggression and its consequent guilt. For Mrs L., furthermore, the idea of becoming pregnant was a terrifying prospect; she was concerned that either she would in some way harm the baby or that she herself might be damaged by the foetus within the womb.

Condensed as this case summary is, nevertheless we feel that it permits the following generalizations about the necrophilia fantasy:

1. It reflects a specific form of the genotypical wish to return to and re-enter the mother's body (see Ferenczi, 1933). We recognize, of course, that not all of the fantasies expressing such a wish necessarily include a 'dead' love object. We also recognize that this genotypical wish and its specific necrophilic variant are part of a genetic continuum which is rooted in the even more primitive wishes and fantasies for the 'oceanic' reunion with the maternal object. However, the particular fantasies with which we are concerned are essentially verbal rather than preverbal and their special content is the product of particular vicissitudes of the more general wishes. (Although the description, of necessity, stresses the content of these fantasies, our central interest is the recognition of the multiple determinants, the phase-specific events, both internal and external, which determine the end products of development and maturation.)

2. The necrophilic fantasy includes, in addition to the wish for reunion with and re-entry into the mother, the more particular emphasis on the wish to explore the interior of the mother's body and its contents.

3. We feel that the principal, more immediate determining factors for the formation of this fantasy are two-fold. First, there is the need to master the primal-scene trauma, especially by overcoming in an active manner the helplessness attendant on the passive experience of overwhelming anxiety and excitement as well as the need to master the terror of the paternal phallus (both in the male and the female). Second, there is the trauma and the rage connected with mother's pregnancy, the jealousy and aggression directed at the intrauterine rival, and the desire to replace that rival within the womb, if need be, by destroying it.

4. What distinguishes the necrophilic fantasy from the other varieties of a 'return to the mother' fantasy is that the love object (the mother) is 'dead'—or asleep, bound, drugged or otherwise helpless and immobile. From the data we have accumulated, it is our conviction that this distinctive element derives from the destructive wishes directed toward the object (mother, intrauterine sibling, paternal phallus) and the fears of retaliation emanating from such destructive fantasies. The immobility and the helplessness of the sexual object provide reasonable assurance that such reprisals cannot and will not occur.

5. Although this may not be sufficiently clear from the very truncated case-summary presented above, the central role of the scoptophilic impulses in this group of fantasies should be underscored. We are not suggesting that these are the only—or always even the principal—instinctual tendencies involved in such fantasies. However, we do feel that the vicissitudes of the scoptophilia (and we would include here, of course, its exhibitionistic counterpart as well), and particularly the sadistic components and derivatives of that scoptophilia, provide one of the fundamental nodal points around which such fantasies are elaborated. The most obvious basis for the mobilization of the scoptophilic impulses would appear to be its relationship to primal-scene experiences and the preoccupation with the visual perception of the pregnant mother. (See Fenichel, 1935, for a very comprehensive and insightful delineation of this topic.)

6. We realize that other explanations (or other combinations of dynamic factors) could be invoked to explain these phenomena. However, in our own clinical material, we have been impressed with the way in which this concatenation of psychological forces have presented themselves.

What has been equally impressive in the course of our investigations has been both the frequency and the diversity of the clinical material in which some aspect of the necrophilic fantasy has been a significant component, especially in its derivative or equivalent forms. Parenthetically, we should also point out that comparable themes have appeared in many works of literature. Time does not permit more than a perfunctory mention of some of these, and a comprehensive review of the literary sources of the necrophilia theme would entail a full-sized monograph. We would merely note, however, such varied works as Faulkner's *A Rose for Emily*, Fowles's *The Collector*, Shakespeare's *Romeo and Juliet* (we are referring chiefly to the last act death scene in the tomb) and Kawabata's *The House of the Sleeping Beauties*. And we have already made mention of the whole repertoire of 'Sleeping Beauty' stories. All of these fictional works portray, in varying degrees of disguise and distortion, one or more aspects of the making love to a 'dead' (i.e., sleeping) sexual object which we have described. We would hazard the speculation that similar literary productions can be found in each and every language!

It is impossible to spell out in detail all of the protean clinical situations in which some of these equivalents can be demonstrated; however, in the remainder of our paper, we would like to outline a number of such situations which will at least depict the range and broad spectrum of these manifestations. In the opening paragraph of this essay, we have already alluded to one of the more common—and more important—necrophilic equivalents: the fascination and resentment that many individuals demonstrate towards a sleeping sexual object.

A patient complained of his wife's sexual indifference. She frequently managed to go to bed and fall asleep before he did. He fought with himself and his fantasies about whether and how to wake her and how to stimulate her interest in sex. At one point in his analysis he reported an episode in which he succeeded in arousing his wife from sleep which culminated in a successful sexual experience. Suddenly, he heard the door of his bedroom squeak. He called to his son, angrily asking what he was doing there. The patient's immediate impulse to scold and punish the boy very quickly gave way to compassion and understanding. It was quite apparent that he had identified with the child who had been witness to the primal scene.

This compassionate understanding led the father and son to indulge themselves in a midnight snack. It may be added that the patient frequently followed his sexual exchanges with his wife by a raid on the refrigerator. The associations which accompanied the scene of the midnight feast left little doubt that the patient, in identification with his son, recaptured his own fantasies of the primal scene and its attendant thoughts of an oral–anal theory of conception and birth. For reasons which become clear only retrospectively, his compassionate identification with his son served to eliminate his anger. The evidence of a defence against aggression permitted the analyst to remind him of the intense sibling rivalry which had occupied so many previous analytical hours. He then recalled his mother's pregnant body silhouetted against the light of the refrigerator as she stood in front of it in a transparent gown. He recalled the explorations of his own body and the curiosity regarding his sibling's birth, as well as his own.

In our experience the complaint is not infrequent that a wife's disinterest in sexual matters is manifested in her falling asleep, leaving the resentful husband wide awake, frustrated, lonely and angry. He will at times culminate this vigil in an attempt to stimulate his wife's sexual interest by masturbating her while she is asleep despite the fear of disapproval, anger and rejection should she awaken. Although not without ambivalence, he wants his sexual partner to become sexually aroused while she is asleep or semi-conscious. He feels that he is doing something clandestine and forbidden, although the sequence of behaviour is easily rationalized by the culprit on the basis of his wife's sexual disinterest. These defensive distortions hide the unconscious desire and solicitation of such behaviour by one of the partners while the other submits as the passive victim.

On the theoretical grounds alone the manifest behaviour, with its component modes of activity and passivity constantly reversed, suggest a sadistic conceptualization of sexuality, while clinical data reveal that the concept of parental intercourse is conceptualized as a sadistic oral exchange. Some of the patients describe bondage fantasies as a part of their sexual life; and we believe that the sadistic sexual fantasies may be related dynamically to the necrophific fantasies with which we have concerned ourselves in this essay.

The patient's identification with his son in the above-mentioned clinical example suggested the reconstruction that as a child he was stimulated by the activities in his own parents' bedroom and that he identified himself with them. After the parents were asleep, he assumed that they had given up their vigil; then he could permit his fantasy free rein and could be 'active'. With the reversal in which the parents were asleep and 'passive' and he was awake and 'active', the patient was no longer prohibited from pursuing and exploring his ideas about the parents' sexual activities; this in turn produced a change in aim (from passive to active) and permitted an active scoptophilic participation instead of an uneasy feeling of being the passive outsider awakened by disturbing noises.

However, his participation in the sadistic primal scene is in itself not sufficient to produce the specific fantasy of making love to a 'sleeping beauty'. The conviction of conception as oral and birth as anal in the presence of an intense sibling rivalry would appear to be necessary ingredients for the production of the specific fantasy. These clinical experiences suggest that specific aspects of fantasy life are stimulated in certain psychosexual phases of development (perhaps also out of specific stimulating experiences)[2] which are then retrospectively and regressively incorporated into the oedipal fantasies while simultaneously representing an attempted solution of the oedipal conflicts.

More generally, it is well known that different individuals have quite different preferences in regard to the ideal degree of activity or passivity

---

[2]This is not to imply that the specific stimulating experiences are necessarily reproduced in the fantasies. The latter are only specific elaborations which arise out of the particular erotic zones stimulated.

of their sexual partner. It is also well known that many men—in spite of their openly espoused desire for an active, 'passionate' bed partner frequently demand that their sexual object be relatively passive during the sexual act. The degree of passivity which is demanded can be satisfied, in some instances, simply by the 'feeling' of being in control of the love-making; in others, however, it becomes important, and even imperative, that the woman be almost completely inert and, for all practical purposes, be inanimate. These men function best sexually when, psychologically speaking, they are having intercourse with a corpse. We realize that this preference for an inert and immobile sex partner is multiply determined; and that more often than not some aspect of castration anxiety is operative in these situations. However, it is our observation that in some cases the necrophilic fantasy also plays a significant role, a role which need not exclude the importance of the castration fears and other factors. An abbreviated clinical example will perhaps be illuminating:

A 30-year-old obsessive-compulsive teacher, the eldest of four children, described in the course of his analytic work—in a rather scattered, piecemeal fashion—his insistence on having a passive, inert sexual partner. In fantasy—or in the foreplay 'games'—his wife would become a slave girl who had to quietly submit to any of his wishes (the reverse could also be true, where he became the slave). In intercourse, he rarely could make any actual sexual advances until he had received permission to have intercourse; and even then the sexual activity was approached obliquely in a specific sort of ritual as if 'sex' was not the intention of that activity. He preferred his wife to be, for a good part of the sexual act, 'like an inanimate object . . . like a fruit or vegetable . . . a juicy plum . . . an obedient beast of burden'.

The implementation of these wishes not only provided him with a sense of power and guaranteed that the relatively helpless woman could not hurt him, but also offered him the opportunity for gratifying very intense scoptophilic impulses. He was enthralled with the prospect of looking, of inspecting his wife's body and especially her sexual organs, and particularly of looking 'into her . . . of getting inside of her vagina'. The latter phrase was used interchangeably to describe both his voyeuristic activities and the actual sexual penetration. Voyeurism had been a preoccupation from early boyhood; he seized every opportunity for gazing up women's skirts, hoping to steal a glance at the genital area, particularly the pubic hair. He had been aware for many years of the almost obsessive curiosity of what went on inside a woman's body—and this included that of his mother as well as his wife. It should also be noted that in addition to the scoptophilic tendencies, he was also aware of numerous sadistic impulses which often became difficult for him to manage.

The patient was obsessed with a very painful screen memory which he dated from his fifth year (during the time that his mother was pregnant with his sister); in that memory, his mother is very upset, crying and unhappy—and there is the implication that all of this has taken place because of some kind of serious misbehaviour on the patient's part. It was not until the fourth year of analysis that the meaning of that memory could be captured. What had occurred was that some time late in the pregnancy, the patient had come home and found the back door closed; when his mother did not immediately respond to his call, he became furious and kicked in the panel of the door. It seems likely that the 'unhappy mother' imagery does not derive directly from this episode and probably is related to one of the frequent explosive—and often violent—arguments which took place between the mother and the father, who could at times become quite brutal. However, what did emerge in the course of analysing this memory was his anger with the pregnant mother, the jealous rage with the baby *in utero*, and his wish to destroy his rival. For him, kicking in the door-panel of the house (the symbolism here is so clear that it needs no elaboration) was the same as kicking in his mother's belly and destroying its contents. During the period of several weeks that this material was being worked over, the patient had a number of dreams in which he was trying to get through a tunnel which was blocked by the presence of a huge obstacle. It was only later that the patient remembered that the day on which he had presented that material which permitted the analysis of this crucial screen memory was also his sister's birthday.

One consequence of the impact of the mother's pregnancy and the sister's birth together with the deprivations and feelings of deprivation associated with these events was a character trait which he labels as 'never have enough'. The multi-level manifestations of this attitude cannot be sketched out in this report; but those expressions of the 'never have enough' related to his sexual activities deserve adumbration inasmuch as they involve certain aspects of the necrophilia. A crucial residuum of the whole pregnancy experience was the unresolved wish to replace the sister-rival in the womb, to enjoy this particular closeness and oneness with the mother which he had imagined his sister had enjoyed. This set of wishes became incorporated in the overall gestalt of what sexual intercourse meant for him and what gratifications it could provide. For this man each act of intercourse was an opportunity not only for sexual gratification but also an opportunity to re-enter the mother, explore the interior of her body, and to satisfy many primitive wishes within that body; further, it was always the opportunity for another chance to get that which had been denied in the past. Sexual intercourse, therefore, involved his own special 'oral triad' which came up with impressive regularity. First there was the need to have the sexual object be inert and inanimate—but also something edible, 'a fruit, a vegetable, a juicy plum'. Secondly, oral sexual activity was a prerequisite for his feeling that the overall act was really gratifying; if he could not participate in fellatio and, especially, cunnilingus, he felt that he had been cheated and deprived. The cunnilingus involved not only oral satisfaction *per se* but also the fantasy of 'getting into' the sexual object, ultimately the maternal body. Thirdly, after the completion of the sexual act, there was usually the feeling of something 'incomplete' and not entirely satisfied. This feeling could be managed by a ritualistic 'raiding of the ice-box', usually with a cup of warm milk or other snack. It became evident that this post-coital dissatisfaction was the consequence of the recognition that the aim of entering and exploring the maternal body was not 'really' achieved—and could not. The symbolic raid on the ice-box was a partial compensation for the frustration of this archaic wish.[3]

Mention should also be made of the role of the necrophilia theme in that group of sexual perversions which, loosely, are considered together under the label of 'bondage' fantasies and practices. Here too the helplessness of thc sexual object is the crucial dynamic element: most frequently the object is tied-up or bound in some other fashion; but the numerous variations include the object's being a slave, being drugged or anaesthetized, asleep, hypnotized or paralysed. Sexual gratification for these individuals is often possible only when the object is in this helpless condition, for practical purposes—dead! We recognize that no one single determinant is responsible for such fantasies and behaviour, and both the products of regression from an oedipal conflict and more primitive pregenital fixations play some role in the formation of these tendencies. Further, it is our experience that at least in some of these cases the wish to re-enter and to explore the interior of the mother's body may be an

[3]Although we do not have definitive clinical evidence for it, we have conjectured that the apparently widespread oral rituals after intercourse (the snack, the cigarette) may have somewhat similar dynamic and genetic roots.

important dynamic ingredient; and it is our further impression that the more immediate causal element is related to the traumatic impact of viewing the paternal phallus together with a defensive identification with it. It should be added that in all of these fantasies the mechanism of turning passive into active is a crucial factor.

What warrants special notice in these cases is the importance of the scoptophilic impulses and particularly their sadistic-intrusive components (the latter being reinforced by the identification with the 'aggressor' phallus). These patients may often be preoccupied with a highly erotized examination of their sexual partner's body, especially the genitalia. Not infrequently this activity must be carried out quite furtively because of the fear of the object's retaliation. This feared retaliation centres on the object's 'looking' or staring. These patients report fantasies of 'eyes' that can annihilate with a glance 'of penetrating sarcasm' (one patient reported the fantasy of such a visual attack while the woman scathingly asked, 'Are you afraid mother will hurt you?'), shoot daggers or extrude X-rays. Two patients have mentioned almost identical preoccupations with the stories of the cobra snake that spits venom into eyes of its victim. One patient found it necessary to blindfold, as well as to bind, his bondage-partner; with this precaution, he felt much more secure against the potential danger of the retaliatory attack from the woman's eyes. At times he would read pornographic literature to a helpless, blindfolded woman, relishing her increasing impotent excitement along with his own feeling of mastery and domination.

The analysis of these fantasies was closely connected to the emergence of material dealing with his hatred of babies, particularly the intrauterine ones. He justified this hatred by the projection that the babies could kill the mother. His scoptophilic activity with the bound and helpless women included the fantasy of getting inside the woman and of losing himself inside of her body. He divided women into two groups: there were the 'innocent ones', who had never had babies; and there were the 'dangerous' ones, who had given birth to a child. It was only the latter whose eyes and whose glances could harm him and who, therefore, had to be blindfolded during the sexual act.

Only very perfunctory mention will be made of three other necrophilic equivalents. Lewin (1946) has very beautifully and convincingly sketched out the part which such fantasies play in the development of the physician's attitude towards his patients. He has suggested that because of the doctor's aggressive impulses towards the patient and the fear of the latter's retaliation, the passive helpless patient also is the ideal one. Such an attitude is buttressed by the experience which every medical student has with his first 'patient'—a cadaver. In this vein, therefore, we would also suggest that such fantasies may represent one of the constellations of motivations which go into the choice of medicine as a profession and even more in the selection of specific subspecialties such as obstetrics-gynecology, radiology, or psychiatry (see Pomer, 1959). Obviously this is an area which deserves much more intensive investigation. We have also been impressed with the way in which the unconscious derivatives of necrophilia may influence the attitudes of some physicians (including psychiatrists) in the recommendation of therapeutic abortions. We have noted in a number of such instances a tenuously sublimated or rationalized wish to eliminate an intrauterine rival by vicariously entering into the mother's womb and removing its contents. We need hardly add that the reaction formation against this wish can, conversely, be one of the factors that lead to a physician's taking a categorical stand against such abortion procedures.

A second area which warrants consideration involves a group of learning difficulties which depend on the inhibition of 'really getting into a subject'. There are individuals who, ostensibly free of other learning problems, are unable to get deeply involved in a given subject. Some of our observations suggest that for these individuals 'getting into a subject' is connected with the fantasy of exploring the interior of the mother's body, a fantasy which in turn is responsible for the inhibition in question.

The third set of situations revolves around a fantasy which is not infrequently encountered in the course of analysis, namely the fantasy that the analyst is asleep. It is well known that the inaudible or monotonous delivery of free associations may sometimes be activated by the wish to put the analyst to sleep (which sometimes is successful). One patient's monotone seemed to imply a sleepy indifference and distance from his analytic environment as he spun his associations. Actually, he was very far from being asleep. All his senses were alert to every breath taken by the analyst in an effort to determine the analyst's state of consciousness. While he appeared asleep and almost dreaming in the analysis, he was in fact wide-awake; and, so far as he was concerned, it was the analyst who was asleep and dreaming He was investigating and exploring the analyst much as he examined his mother's undergarments; much as he explored pornographic literature; and much as, in fantasy, he explored his mother's pregnant body while she slept. In this way he participated in the primal scene, and kept alive the source of the intense jealousy of his younger sibling.

Another patient came to analysis because of a work inhibition which threatened his professional career and which manifested itself in a recurrent retreat to his quarters where he would remain incommunicado (sometimes for as much as a week at a time) and most of which time he spent sleeping. It will come as no surprise that late in the analysis his tardiness became marked; frequently he would become suddenly sleepy in the middle of the analytic hour, barely able to fight off his urge to sleep. It is not entirely accurate to say that he wished to put the analyst to sleep; because, on the contrary, he managed to keep the analyst constantly alert, amused and entertained by associations which were studded by long quotations in a variety of languages (including Latin). Despite his lively involvement in the analysis and the analytic work, he would from time to time express the fear that the analyst was bored and even asleep. Here too, as with the previous patient, his apparent indifference to the analyst constituted only a thin veil for his constant vigilance over the analyst's mood and his state of consciousness. He never ceased the exploration of the analyst who was supposed to be lulled by the various amusements which the patient supplied.

In another context, it might be possible to detail more satisfactorily the manner in which the ego functions of consciousness and unconsciousness were split in both these patients; in which consciousness, reality and wakefulness would be guarded by the patient; while unconsciousness, unreality, sleeping and dreaming could then be assigned to the analyst. Alternatively, the functions assigned to each could be reversed. Here we are concerned only with the fact that these alternations in consciousness, duplicated during the analytic work, were the concomitants of a powerful interest in the exploration of the mother's pregnant body stimulated by primal-scene experiences in combination with intense sibling jealousy. In this case the patient's rivalry was stimulated not only by the numerous castration threats issued by both parents in regard to any show of exhibitionism, but also by the specific and recurrent banishment of the child from the home during the last trimester of each of the mother's pregnancies. Later this banishment was reenacted when the patient became old enough to be sent away to boarding school and then high school.

We will not attempt anything approximating a comprehensive review of the literature on necrophilia and related topics. Actually, there is a real paucity of psychoanalytic papers dealing with necrophilia; and this paucity is even more marked in respect of its neurotic equivalents and derivatives. However, 60 years ago Ernest Jones (1911, 1912) contributed two brief, but remarkably insightful, articles on the subject of 'dying together'. Basing his observations on literary and folklore sources in addition to clinical material, Jones (without making a definite, organized formulation in regard to necrophilia) alluded to many of the ideas which we have presented in our paper. He suggested the dynamic contributions of the wish to effect a reunion with the mother; the sadistic elements involved in such a wish; the central role of the 'helpless resistlessness' of the love object in these fantasies; the part played by curiosity, exploration and the wish for discovery of forbidden secrets; and the 'desire to beget a child with the loved one'.

Fenichel's (1935) extensive study on 'The Scoptophilic Instinct and Identification' provides us with a thorough survey of the vicissitudes of scoptophilia, particularly with the aggressive elements in that part-instinct and with the defences which can be noted in reaction to such impulses. His paper presents bountiful evidence for the fears of reprisal which are associated with such wishes and the concomitant need to have a passive, helpless sexual object who is unable to retaliate. Although he does not deal directly with necrophilia or with necrophilic equivalents *per se,* he makes numerous references to ostensibly 'dead' love objects in relation to these wishes and fantasies. Hanna Segal (1953) also emphasizes the aggressive aspects of the necrophilia; and she too views the choice of a helpless object as a means both of denying the subject's own sadism and of nullifying the risk of retaliatory aggression on the part of the object. One of us (Calef, 1968) has contributed a study on infanticide which takes up some of these same issues, although not in terms of necrophilia as such.

Lewin's classic paper (1933) on 'The Body as Phallus' offers the material and ideas for the understanding of that element in the necrophilic fantasy which has to do with the 'entering into' the interior of the mother's body, especially in identification with the paternal phallus. His later paper (1946) on 'Countertransference in the Technique of Medical Practice' deals more directly with necrophilic fantasies and their derivatives. Lewin's point of departure is also around the aggressive and sadistic wishes directed towards a love-object and the defensive measures utilized in warding off the dangers associated with these impulses. The short monograph by Ferenczi (1933), which he entitled 'Thallasa: A Theory of Genitality', develops his hypothesis of the universality of the wish to return into the interior of the mother's body and the role which sexual intercourse (and its attendant fantasies) plays in effecting this wish.

SUMMARY

We have attempted to delineate the principal features of the necrophilic fantasy and the equivalents and derivatives of such a fantasy. We have emphasized the pivotal role of the wish to return into the maternal body and to explore its interior. We have similarly stressed the relationship to the wish to remove—and replace—an intrauterine rival as well as the wish to replace via identification the paternal phallus (the latter, we feel, is especially significant as a consequence of primal scene experience and traumata). We have also pointed to the very crucial role which scoptophilic impulses play in the elaboration of such fantasies. We have attempted to demonstrate the manner in which such fantasies may play a significant part in the structure and content of a variety of clinical situations. Finally, we should make more explicit what we have tried to keep, at least, implicit throughout the body of this essay: we are not suggesting that any of these clinical entities is dependent directly or completely only on the necrophilic element; nor are any of the constituent elements which we have described limited in its effect and impact only to the necrophilia. Any one fantasy, let alone a complex piece of manifest behaviour, must represent the final common confluence of a large number of interacting determinants; and each of these determinants, in turn, can find quite different means of expression. We have tried to show how certain impulses, certain experiences and certain defensive configurations can come together and contribute to a specific fantasy and specific forms of behaviour.

REFERENCES

Brill, A. A. (1941), Necrophilia. *J. Crim. Psychopath.*, 2:433–443, 3:51–73.

Calef, V. (1968), The unconscious fantasy of infanticide manifested in resistance. *J. Amer. Psychoanal. Assn.*, 16:697–710.

Ehrenreich, G. A. (1960), Headache, necrophilia, and murder: A brief hypnotherapeutic investigation of a single case. *Bull. Menn. Clin.*, 24:273–287.

Fenichel, O. (1935), The scoptophilic instinct and identification. In: *Collected Papers,* 1st series. New York: Norton, 1953.

Ferenczi, S. (1933), Thallasa: A theory of genitality. *Psychoanal. Quart.*, 2: 361–403.

Jones, E. (1911), On 'dying together.' In: *Essays in Applied Psychoanalysis,* vol. 1. London: Hogarth Press, 1951.

_______ (1912), An unusual case of 'dying together.' In: *Essays in Applied Psychoanalysis,* vol. 1. London: Hogarth Press, 1951.

Lewin, B. (1933), The body as phallus. *Psychoanal. Quart.*, 2:24–47.
_______ (1946), Countertransference in the technique of medical practice. *Psychosom. Med.*, 8:195–199.
Pomer, S. (1959), Necrophilic fantasies and the choice of specialty in medicine [abstract]. *Bull. Phila. Assn. Psychoanal.*, 9:54–55.
Segal, H. (1953), A necrophilic fantasy. *Internat. J. Psycho-Anal.*, 34:98–101.

Chapter 2

1977

"I Didn't Mean It"

Negation as a Character Trait

Freud's paper on negation (1925) provides us with an excellent example of his concise, richly packed psychoanalytic writing. In 5 pages he covers a variety of seemingly diverse topics ranging from the role of perception in reality testing to the manner in which an intellectual function (judgment) acts as a substitute for repression. Characteristically, Freud begins his discussion with clinical material. He mentions patients who in the course of their analytic work may say, "Now you'll think I mean to say something insulting, but really I've no such intention." Or: "You ask who this person in the dream can be. It's *not* my mother" (p. 235). Freud offers these as typical examples of negation; and he states that through the use of this mechanism patients can bring certain subject matter of a repressed image into consciousness while concurrently holding that "I don't feel inclined to let the association count." In a footnote added in 1923 to the Dora case (1905), Freud made a similar observation: "There is another very remarkable and entirely trustworthy form of confirmation from the unconscious . . . namely, an exclamation on the part of the patient of 'I didn't think that' or 'I didn't think of that.' This can be translated point-blank into: 'Yes, I was unconscious of that'" (p. 57).

Freud describes negation as a "way of taking cognizance of what is repressed; indeed it is already a lifting of the repression, though not, of course, an acceptance of what is repressed" (1925, p. 235f.). This is accomplished by allowing the ideational representation of repressed instinctual drive to reach consciousness, but only on condition that its

---

An abbreviated version of this paper was presented at a special meeting of the San Francisco Psychoanalytic Society and Institute in 1959. I am indebted to Anna Freud, the formal discussant, the other discussants (E. Buxbaum, K. R. Eissler, M. M. Gill, and R. A. Spitz), and W. Barrett, V. Calef, and N. Reider for their very helpful suggestions and criticisms.

impact be canceled out by the negation. Thus negation does away with only one aspect of the consequence of repression. It permits the thought content to become conscious; but the affective component is kept out of awareness, and the initiation of voluntary muscular activity is prevented. In substance, then, negation results in "a kind of intellectual acceptance of the repressed, while at the same time what is essential to the repression persists" (p. 236; see also Lewin, 1950, p. 69). As Freud says elsewhere (1915), "Negation is a substitute, at a higher Ievel, for repression" (p. 186).

The acquisition of negation represents a "momentous intellectual gesture," according to René Spitz. In *No and Yes,* Spitz (1957) traces the phylogenetic and ontogenetic roots of the process of negation with special emphasis on the role that this process plays in the evolution of abstract thinking, communication, and socialized behavior. The development of negation is intimately connected with the development of the function of judgment; and this, in turn, represents a decisive step in the development of the thinking process both from the viewpoint of the child's psychic economy and from that of psychic structure. Basically it is through the utilization of the process of negation that thinking is enabled to escape many of the limitations which are imposed on it by repression and "enriches itself with material that is indispensable for its proper functioning" (Freud, 1925, p. 236; see also Rapaport, 1951, p. 343, n. 15).

There is some ambiguity, however, as to how to categorize most effectively the process of negation. Freud (1925) states, "Thus the content of a repressed image or idea can make its way into consciousness, on condition that it is *negated*" (p. 235). It is not clear if Freud meant to use the concept of the mechanism of denial as part of the process of negation. Actually he did not clarify his concept of the mechanism of denial until his 1927 paper on fetishisn, and the *Outline* (1940). Fenichel (1945) implies that denial is a considerably more archaic mechanism which becomes relatively unfeasible as reality testing becomes increasingly prominent. He acknowledges, however, that "these tendencies toward denial try to remain operative." Fenichel interprets Freud's concept of negation as "a compromise between becoming conscious of the data given by the perceptions and the tendency to deny" (p. 144).

Part of this ambiguity is related to the uncertainty which exists in our thinking in regard to the precise nature of denial (or disavowal) as well as the interconnections between denial and repression. Freud (1940) delineated the process of denial as one where the ego wards off some "demand from the external world which it feels distressing and . . . this is effected by means of a *disavowal* of the perceptions which bring to knowledge this demand from reality" (p. 203f.). By and large Freud's concept of denial has persisted in psychoanalytic thinking, although Waelder (1951) argues that denial can act against an instinct as well as against external perceptions. Nevertheless it is consistent with these above-mentioned formulations to view the mechanism of denial as operating against the ideational representation of instinct when the idea becomes conscious. When this occurs, the idea, in effect, becomes an external perception and can be treated as such by the ego, utilizing the process of denial. This would seem to be the way Freud handled the matter in the paper on fetishism (1927) and in a somewhat more preliminary way in the Schreber case (1911). It would appear, then, that the process of negation acts against an unwelcome thought in a manner which is comparable but not identical with the manner in which the process of denial acts against an unwelcome external perception.

There is also the question of whether or not it is proper to consider negation—together with denial—as one of the true mechanisms of defense. Anna Freud (1956) did not include denial among the basic defense mechanisms, but set it aside under the heading of the "Preliminary Stages of Defense." Jacobson (1957) claims that denial does not involve "a true defensive struggle." Hartmann (1956) and Sperling (1958) both stress the necessity of distinguishing between what is conscious or preconscious "avoidance" (which is akin to Freud's "repudiation") and the "countercathectic activities of the unconscious ego," i.e., the defense mechanisms in the stricter psychoanalytic sense. (See also Brenner, 1957, p. 36.) It is, then, of some significance that negation operates on a conscious or preconscious level rather than on an unconscious one.

Rapaport (1951) stresses the relationship of negation to isolation. His remarks stem from Freud's statement, "the intellectual function is separated from the affective process" (1925, p. 236). By the "denial" of the truth of an assertion, the process of negation vitiates or removes the meaningfulness of that assertion. The potential affective impact of such an assertion is then "cut off," and the ideational representation of the instinct has lost its emotional connections. The "patient has not forgotten his pathogenic traumata, but has lost trace of their connections and their emotional significance" (Fenichel, 1945, p. 155). Fenichel continues his description of isolation by saying, "here again countercathexis is operative; its operation consists in keeping apart that which actually belongs together. . . . The most important special case of this defense mechanism is the isolation of an idea from the emotional cathexis that originally was connected with it" (p. 155f.).

In effect, then, the process of negation brings about a split in the ego. Consciously there is a denial of the validity of an assertion. Preconsciously the assertion is accepted. This kind of "split in the ego" can also be conceptualized in terms of "keeping apart" the affect-shorn idea in consciousness from the affectively meaningful idea in preconsciousness. Sperling (1958), in evolving his concept of the defense mechanism of neurotic denial, comes to somewhat similar conclusions, although without resorting, at least not by name, to the concept of isolation. He says, "In denial, the affectively cathexed, repressed image, stimulated by the corresponding conscious, external image, was 'becoming conscious' . . . The consciousness of this image . . . is denied, which is obtained by maintaining the repression of the affective cathexis" (p. 28f.).

Earlier I stated that negation operates primarily on a conscious or preconscious level. This statement, however, glosses over the significant relationship between the negated idea, which becomes either conscious or preconscious, and the repressed unconscious idea. In "The Unconscious," Freud (1915) describes the topographical and dynamic interconnections between such a pair of related ideas.

> If we communicate to a patient some idea which he has at one time repressed but which we have discovered in him, our telling him makes at first no change in his mental condition. Above all, it does not remove the repression nor undo its effects, as might perhaps be expected from the fact that the previously unconscious idea has now become conscious. On the contrary, all that we shall achieve at first will be a fresh rejection of the repressed idea. But now the patient has in actual fact the same idea in two forms in different places in his mental apparatus: first, he has the conscious memory of the auditory trace of the idea, conveyed in what we told him; . . . he also has—as we know for certain—the unconscious memory of his experience as it was in its earlier form. Actually there is no lifting of the repression until the conscious idea, after the resistances have been overcome, has entered into connection with the unconscious memory-trace. It is only through the making conscious of the latter itself that success is achieved [p. 175f.].

The crucial point in this regard is that the process of negation serves to prevent these unconscious memory traces from effectively coming into connection with the conscious idea, thereby facilitating the maintenance of repression. Both Jacobson (1957) and Sperling (1958) postulate a similar interrelationship between denial and repression in which the former aids in the reestablishment of the latter.

Although it is difficult to distinguish between denial and negation in an absolute way, there are a number of features which suggest basic differences between the two processes. First of all, negation entails the utilization of words; it is a verbal activity. This is not true in respect to the process of denial, which probably always acts independently of verbal expression. Secondly, in the process of negation, the ego is able to meet the instinctual demands at least "halfway." The ideational representative of the drive can be accepted in a conditional manner. The process of denial is much closer to a complete flight; the external perceptions related to the instinctual drive cannot even be recognized. This distinction can be illustrated by Freud's hypothetical patient quoted at the beginning of this paper, who stated, "You ask who this person in the dream can be. It's *not* my mother." Freud points out that this patient did think of his mother in regard to the person in the dream, but he did not want the association to count. Hence it was negated. However, it would have been possible for that same patient not to have taken any cognizance whatsoever of the perception of the person in the dream insofar as it related to his mother. This failure of recognition would constitute a denial. It is clear, then, that negation tends to be a more efficient, mature, and reality-oriented mechanism than denial.

Thus far I have examined negation primarily in regard to its defensive functions. However, we cannot ignore the fact that negation constitutes a negative judgment and that the process of judgment represents an intricate activity of the ego. Therefore, negation cannot be viewed as a simple psychological process which can be neatly pigeonholed as a denial, as an isolation, or even as a defense mechanism. Rapaport (1951) considers Freud's statement, "A negative judgement is the *intellectual* substitute for repression" (my italics), as the major implication of the paper. Rapaport then goes on to categorize negation as a "re-representation of repression on a higher level of integration" (p. 343, n. 13).

Freud concludes his 1925 paper, saying,

> The study of judgement affords us, perhaps for the first time, an insight into the origin of an intellectual function from the interplay

> of the primary instinctual impulses. . . . But the performance of the function of judgement is not made possible until the creation of the symbol of negation has endowed thinking with a first measure of freedom from the consequences of repression and, with it, from the compulsion of the pleasure principle [p. 238f.].

These statements clearly imply the basis for the concept of secondary ego autonomy. Judgment is a function which derives from instinctual drives and instinctual conflict, but gradually achieves independence from the drive and acquires motivations of its own, and which follows "autonomous laws of the emergent higher levels of integration" (Rapaport, 1951, n. 28).

The recognition that the process of negation operates both autonomously and in response to instinctual pressure is particularly cogent when we consider the manner in which the process of negation might be incorporated into the character structure of a given individual.[1] In this context the view expressed by Margaret Brenman (1952) is relevant. She points to the "necessity" for trying to "place" various highly organized pieces of clinically observed behavior within a coherent theory of psychological organization. She demonstrates that a piece of a patient's "*behavior . . . is a complex configuration resulting from the interplay of: (1) primitive unconscious drives with (2) defensive processes and (3) adaptive implementations*" (1952, p. 264).

In my own case presentation I would like to offer some clinical material to illustrate some of these theoretical problems. I shall describe portions of an analysis of a young woman who presented a constellation of defensive reactions which were so pervasive as to impart a very specific cast to her entire character structure. Further, I shall attempt to demonstrate how these particular defensive reactions were elaborated at a specific point in her development in relation to a specific set of traumatic events. Finally, I shall try to indicate how these particular defensive systems played a crucial role in this woman's analysis. The essence of this defensive constellation is best reflected in the phrase, "I didn't mean it." I have considered this phrase as a form of negation, as one of its

---

[1]Although the recent literature on negation (Abend, 1975; Altschul, 1968; Basch, 1974; Katan, 1964; Lichtenstein, 1971; Modell, 1961; Podvall, 1970; Stewart, 1970) contains many clarifications of this concept, I have made no attempt to discuss it in detail because it has no direct bearing on the main thrust of this essay—negation as a character trait.

"hierarchy of re-representations." This phrase or one of a large variety of similar expressions signified in a verbal fashion how this patient's ego attempted to cope with unacceptable and potentially painful impulses, thoughts, and feelings.

I

Mrs. Jane S. was 29, married, and the mother of two young children when she began her analysis. Her overall appearance suggested such words as "lady," or "patrician"; but at times this characteristic effect was diluted by a number of somewhat incongruous girlish features. Her manner, though gracious and sincere, frequently had the perfunctory ring of a child saying, "Thank you for the lovely time."

The patient's patrician quality was reflected in her speech. Her voice was soft and well modulated; her diction was clear; her vocabulary impeccable. For almost two years Mrs. S. produced no profanity stronger than an exasperated "Damn." She was punctilious in matters of protocol, and she scrupulously observed all the social amenities. Superficially she appeared to have exquisite control of herself, but it was soon clear that this was much more apparent than real. The patient was quite aware of her own tight constraint and the exertion necessary to maintain even this superficial appearance. One of her chief complaints was that her "tightness" produced a lackluster personality and that she always thought of herself as "plain Jane."

The patient was the second of five children in a wealthy and prominent Eastern family. Between the patient and her eldest sister there had been a stillborn boy; after Mrs. S.'s birth, a sister, a brother, and then another sister had arrived, at approximately 18-month intervals. The patient's mother was part of a large, closely knit family, which had always been cognizant of good manners and social responsibility. The mother was described as an extremely maternal woman who had devoted an inordinate amount of her energy to her children and husband. The consequence of this unselfish dedication, the patient felt, was a blurring of her mother's own personality; and this blurring was accentuated by the mother's close dependency on the patient's maternal grandmother, Granny, an austere, uncompromising matriarch who ruled her whole clan with a benign rigorousness.

The patient's father—whom she always referred to as Daddy—was a self-made man who became one of the top executives in a large corporation. He was described as quiet, reserved, and somewhat cold. Mrs. S. charged that her father was afraid of his own feelings and had never been close to the children. The patient had always been involved in rather tense rivalry with her brother and sisters, This was most clearly expressed in regard to the sister, Marian, 18 months younger, and the brother, Lawrence, not quite 3 years the patient's junior. Marian was born with a congenital hand defect which did not prevent her becoming a most accomplished pianist, through which she was able to "show off" quite successfully. Lawrence was the fair-haired boy in the family; and the patient had always nurtured a very protective and idealized image of Lawrence in which the blatant denials of her envy and hostility were quite evident. Consciously Mrs. S. always felt closest and most positively toward her younger sister, Kathy; but here too this protective role could not be separated from the intense feelings of rivalry which sprang from the fact that Kathy "arrived in place of" the patient's own fantasied oedipal child.

Mrs. S. always felt herself to be on the periphery of things. In the family circle she saw herself as being "accepted on sufferance." When she went away to boarding school, she identified herself with the less desirable girls rather than with the more popular clique. She always had friends, but never felt secure in these relationships, fearing that the other girls would tire of her and find other more interesting friends. Instead of going to one of the more fashionable Eastern girl's schools, the patient—apparently in identification with Granny—chose one of the more progressive colleges where the emphasis was on scholarship and on social consciousness. College was essentially uneventful during most of her freshman year. She got along reasonably well with her fellow students, her studies, and the usual array of Ivy League undergraduates. Near the end of her second semester, however, she inexplicably did something which resulted in her being asked to leave school. Although she had both the time and the ability to write a required paper for one of her courses, she copied an entire article verbatim from a well-known textbook. She was apprehended and asked to leave school not because of the enormity of her crime, but rather, as she was told by the dean of women, because the patient could not comprehend that she had really done something wrong. It was felt that such an attitude reflected an immaturity which precluded continuation of her college work. The patient was more or less dumbfounded; she insisted that "I didn't mean it," and since she had not really intended to do anything wrong, she could not see why she was treated so harshly.

The patient returned home and devoted herself to "good works" under Granny's tutelage. She described her attitude in this period as one of the "princess waiting for the knight in shining armor to drop in her lap." The knight soon presented himself in the person of Stan, who became her husband, and who at that time was one of her older sister's excess boyfriends. Up to this point the patient had never been closely involved with a man. She had enjoyed the usual modicum of dates with the eligible males of her set. As a rule, however, she was more concerned with being seen at the proper places by her peers than with the relationship of the young man who was escorting her. Her sexual experience had involved no more than a perfunctory good-night kiss.

Stan was handsome, wealthy, charming, and considered to be the catch of the season. They were married after a relatively brief courtship, which was marred by a short period of anxiety several days prior to the wedding. The anxiety obviously was connected with the imminence of sexual relations. The first few years of marriage were quite stormy; the patient felt lost without her mother, and she described her initial sexual experience as "horrible." Sex remained a problem throughout her marriage; orgasms were infrequent; in the typical pattern of intercourse she experienced increasing excitation to a point where she felt orgasm was possible, only to find herself tightening up. Mrs. S. usually accepted this in resignation. She was aware that she was as concerned with Stan's pleasure and response as with her own; and she derived a good deal of vicarious enjoyment from his gratification.

II

Mrs. S.'s first pregnancy and delivery (of a daughter) were quite uneventful, and the patient was quite eager to have another child. During the latter part of her second pregnancy 3 years later, Mrs. S. became uneasy and anxious; and these symptoms were accentuated by a series of severe upper respiratory infections, which finally ended in a stubborn case of sinusitis. The delivery of her second child, a son, Warren, was in itself extremely traumatic; but it was not until well into the second year of her analysis that she recounted some of the details of what had occurred.

When Mrs. S. was first admitted to the hospital for this delivery, there was some confusion as to whether or not she was having false labor pains, and she vaguely recalled some comments about the possibility of the cord's being "wrong." Her husband was sent home; and soon afterward the patient's obstetrician left. She felt upset and humiliated, as if she had been chastised for doing something wrong. Shortly after the doctor left her pains became extremely severe; she did not know how she could tolerate these pains; she felt she would lose control and "burst." After the birth of her son she experienced a mixture of relief and shame. She was conscious of wanting to forget the whole thing as quickly and as completely as possible.

The patient's mother had come from the East to help with the new baby. Mrs. S. was aware of a strong feeling of dependence on her mother, but at the same time also recognized a vague uneasiness in her mother's presence. Nevertheless she looked forward to returning to her usual domestic and social routine. Soon afterward, however, the patient's mother caught a severe cold which led to a recurrence of the mother's chronic sinusitis. The patient was concerned about this, and her anxiety became more marked when the new baby also developed a number of minor difficulties. Mrs. S. suffered considerable overt anxiety, which then crystallized into an increasingly severe agoraphobia. Her symptoms became more marked when her mother returned to the East; and the morning after her first social night out—about a month after Warren's birth—she awoke with a hangover which threw her into a panic. She called her mother, saying that she wanted to come home—to mother. The patient was hospitalized in a private sanitarium near her parents' home, and the symptoms gradually waned in intensity so that she could return to San Francisco for the Christmas holidays. On doing so, however, her symptoms came back in full force, particularly the agoraphobia; and she was hospitalized in the psychiatric ward of a local general hospital. While there she began psychotherapy with Dr. X., which continued after the patient left the hospital. Dr. X. referred her for psychoanalysis, which seemed appropriate in spite of the strong regressive coloring in the recent history. When I first started to work with the patient, she no longer complained of her agoraphobia, nor did she suffer inordinately from feelings of anxiety.

She did complain of sexual difficulties and the fear of losing Stan to another woman, but mostly Mrs. S. was concerned with the lack of real pleasure in her life—more specifically, she spoke of living "with the brakes on." She could not really permit herself to enjoy a big meal because she might get indigestion; she was afraid to fondle her children because she might spoil them; she was afraid to have sexual intercourse because she might be upset by not having an orgasm; she avoided skiing because she was afraid that she might fall and injure herself. All these activities she declared could be carried out only if she forced herself to participate in them; and then she tended to do so without enthusiasm or real pleasure. One aspect of this multidetermined "living with the brakes on" emerged early in the analysis. As Mrs. S. described these situations in more detail, it was increasingly clear that not only was it difficult to permit herself to enjoy these activities, but even more it was crucial that she experience them as if they had been forced on her either by external authority or by her own sense of duty. Thus she tried to disclaim any real responsibility for what were for her essentially forbidden but desired activities. This was accomplished by some variation of the "I didn't mean it."

Therefore, what she tried to express was this: "I don't really want to eat an elegant, luxurious meal—one has to be a good guest at a dinner party; I don't really enjoy close physical contact with my children—one has to be a good mother; I don't really enjoy sex—one has to submit to a forceful husband; I don't really enjoy the excitement of a successful ski run—one has to be a good sport when one is on an outing." As long as she was able to maintain the myth that the pleasurable aspect of these activities was not really desired—that she didn't mean to enjoy these things—the patient could permit herself some participation and some gratification in these activities. It became apparent that these "I didn't mean it" attitudes pervaded her entire psychic life. A poignant example of this was the manner in which she approached the possibility of a third pregnancy. Since she experienced pregnancy as forbidden, she fantasied that she would become pregnant as the result of an accident. She facilitated the possible materialization of such a fantasy by forgetting to obtain spermicidal jelly or by permitting her husband to have intercourse without the use of contraceptives; and then, if perchance she would become impregnated, she could readily maintain that "I didn't mean it." Later in the analysis she repeatedly goaded me to instruct her to become pregnant; then her pregnancy would result not out of her own desires but from a need to please me.

The patient's attitude in regard to sexual intercourse was equally striking. Until the end of the second year of her analysis, Mrs. S. never openly initiated sexual activity with Stan. She would never insert her diaphragm until after her husband had made unmistakable and insistent overtures in the direction of intercourse. If she had taken the initiative in the sexual act, she was certain that her husband would think that she was wanton and whorish. Later she expressed the fear that he would find her "a vampire, greedy, rapacious, sapping him." As long as Stan "forced" her to submit to sex, she could eschew the responsibility not only for her sexual desires but also for the underlying oral-sadistic and incorporative impulses.

Her behavior in the analytic situation reflected the same pattern. If Mrs. S. was late for her appointment, she would say, almost automatically, "I didn't realize it was so late," or, "I forgot what time it was." Such statements settled the issue for her; since she had not come late on purpose, there was no reason for her to feel guilty and no need to discuss the matter further. In her relations with her friends and family she would demonstrate the same kind of attitude and behavior. She readily explained away minor lacks of consideration for others with the stereotyped "I didn't mean it," and she was frequently genuinely perplexed when people were annoyed with her.

The facility with which this patient could negate her own responsibility and intent is nicely illustrated in a dream which she reported early in the analysis.

> I was picking the kids up at school. Teacher asked me to take this large, dark, oversized 10-year-old "juvenile delinquent." Then I was sitting on the character's lap. I'm not sure if I was driving or not . . . somehow his penis was in my vagina . . . since it was enjoyable, I thought I might as well let it stay that way. There were no movements, but I thought there might have been an orgasm because of the fiendish look on his face. I wondered if I might become pregnant by this oaf, and I kept saying, "But you didn't move." It seemed so unfair—a stab in the back.

In her associations to the dream, the patient stressed a feeling of being duped—that it wasn't fair. She referred to the possibility that she might be punished (become pregnant) for forbidden activity (intercourse) in which she had been only a tacit—and therefore innocent—participant. To Mrs. S., the crucial phrases in the dream were "there was no movement" and "but you didn't move."[2] The lack of movement meant

[2]"No movement" could be considered the motoric equivalent to negation. The developmental line from "movement" and motility to a sense of responsibility and guilt on the one hand and from "no movement" to innocence and blamelessness on the other is one which deserves a much more detailed and careful explication than is possible here. Suffice it that these motoric concepts and metaphors played a significant role in many areas of her psychological life and were concepts which were ready foci for sexualization.

a lack of activity, and this, as far as this patient was concerned, was equated with a lack of responsibility. These phrases expressed in motoric terms her ubiquitous "I didn't mean it."

III

In the first few months of the analysis, Mrs. S. approached the work with great trepidation and anxiety. She insisted she had nothing of any consequence to say. She feared that I would belittle whatever she might bring forth. These attitudes seemed particularly significant inasmuch as the patient obviously had a great deal to say, and she did not appear to be unduly uncomfortable about saying it. When this discrepancy was pointed out, the material shifted a bit. The patient then emphasized that she didn't like coming to the analysis; that she hadn't wanted to come; that she, in effect, was coming against her will. It was apparent that she wished to disassociate herself from any real responsibility for the analysis and what she said there.

Throughout the larger portion of the analysis she produced dreams in voluminous quantity, insisting that the dreams "really aren't me." Frequently in the course of her associations she would insist that a certain thought or idea was "real psychiatric, intellectual, from the psychoanalytic books" (Lossy, 1962). Invariably such comment occurred in connection with painful, anxiety-ridden material; and by ascribing her associations to these "artifacts," she could reject both the responsibility for the material and the extent of its impact. In a similar vein she would insist that she said certain things to please me or because it was expected of her. It was true that Mrs. S. was compliant in the analysis and produced a good deal that was intended to please or placate me. It was likewise true, however, that she utilized the awareness of these tendencies to negate the significance of a good deal of material whose primary source was not compliance with the analysis. Her saying, "I didn't mean it; I said it only because you wanted me to," was a way of paying lip service to the repressed material without really lifting the impact of the repressive process.

It was apparent that the patient was involved in a real dilemma in regard to the analytic situation. On the one hand she was convinced that she had to speak freely and openly and had to spew forth all of her feelings in an unbridled way. If she could not produce in this exemplary fashion, she was certain that I would not approve of her and that the analytic work would end in humiliating failure. Simultaneously, however, the prospect of such unbridled production was quite frightening. The patient looked upon the "basic rule" with considerable suspicion, seeing it as a device whereby the analyst could encourage or cajole her to speak freely, but then hold her culpable for what she said. Her "letting go" would also result in my belittling or humiliating her; so that whether she did what I asked for or whether she held back, the results would be some narcissistic blow. The same dilemma was especially poignant in the patient's relationship with Granny. This was the woman whom the patient could never please. Mrs. S. had resigned herself to the fact that no matter how she acted, Granny's reaction would always be a negative one. If the patient was shy and retiring, Granny was critical and charged that "Jane does not have the milk of human kindness in her veins." If the patient was active and effusive, the grandmother coldly pointed out that such behavior was not ladylike. This same conflict as to whether she should give forth freely or hold back cautiously played a significant role in her sexual behavior. For Mrs. S., the sexual act was a kind of melodrama where performance was the crucial factor. If she performed well, she virtually expected her husband to applaud. If he failed to do so, she was hurt and angry. If she had an orgasm, this meant that she had trusted him—because she had really "let go"—and she waited for him to show how impressed and pleased he was. His failure to demonstrate his approval in a very explicit fashion led not only to disappointment but to a tremendous anxiety that Stan might be disgusted with her, think of her as dirty, and even be contaminated by her. Not infrequently, after intercourse, she would examine the sheets for evidence of such contamination. On the other hand, when Stan's virtually fulsome approval was present, she felt exhilarated and satisfied; this was obviously the source of greater satisfaction in the sexual act than orgasm itself.

As might be predicted, this woman was tremendously concerned with problems of control. There was the fear that once she started something she could never stop. This was true in regard to the expression of emotion, of an orgasm, or of crying. One of the early themes of the analysis was a plea for the analyst to assist her in the control of dangerous impulses. These pleas, however, were intermingled with constant doubts as to my dependability and the fear that I would be no more consistent than her parents. Not infrequently, after doing something she regretted or which turned out badly, she would bitterly reproach me for not warning her or of not preventing the action which had caused her regret. When she was confronted with her tardiness in paying her bill, she insisted that it was not her fault since I had not specifically warned her in advance about promptness in this regard. The patient took the stand that the absence of my specific prohibition was tantamount to permission.

Early in the analysis, the fear of loss of control was manifested by the fear that she would soil me or the office. She detailed the fear that I would find her dirty, slimy, greasy, or "ugly." She was concerned that she might dirty the couch and was relieved that there was a napkin to protect the pillow. Her need to produce enough to impress me, on the one hand, and her fear that such a production would get out of control and lead to humiliation, on the other, were gradually crystallized and fused into the apprehension that her exhibitionism in the analytic work would end up with her "making a mess." Just as sexual intercourse became a melodrama, wherein her overzealous performance might result in her soiling Stan, the analysis also became a kind of play where a performance for my benefit might be climaxed by being "messed up." At the same time, she kept reminding me that she was in the analysis against her real wishes, that she was talking only because it was required of her, that the reprehensible thoughts and words which emerged were not really her property—she was doing all this because I had, in effect, forced her to. In short, she seemed to be giving me fair warning that if there was a mess, it was not going to be her fault.

This was more clearly expressed in an hour during the tenth month of the analysis. She had canceled several hours a number of weeks in advance because of a ski trip. I filled the hours; and when she postponed the holiday, I was unable to see her. She was obviously furious with me, but clearly unable to express this anger. When I pointed out her discomfort, she did not respond directly, but after a brief pause recalled the image of a mangled finger of a little girl who had caught her hand in a dishwasher. This imagery made her nauseated. She feared she might get sick to her stomach, and throw up before she got to the bathroom. She then mused about the consequences of such an event. What would my reaction be? What would I say? Do? Think? Would I get on my hands and knees and clean it up, or would I say, "It's your mess. You clean it up."

The aggressive, retaliatory aspects of this vomiting fantasy are quite evident. Also, the vomiting is something which is ostensibly beyond her control, and again she has the ready rationalization of "I didn't mean it." The concern over my reaction to the vomiting is quite indicative of the manner in which Mrs. S. tries to reexternalize the superego function. If

I clean up the mess, this would mean that I did not hold her responsible or guilty, and this represents the hoped-for absolution. If, on the other hand, I were to insist that she "clean it up," this would be the same as accusing her of "meaning it," of doing it on purpose, and she would have to feel responsible and guilty.

Her image of herself as dirty and grubby became accentuated with each menstrual period. At such times she was concerned with the possibility of contaminating others, together with all the humiliating consequences of such an event. This attitude was much more marked when the menstrual period was accompanied by severe cramps. During the whole analysis there was only one session that she deliberately missed. This occurred on the first day of a menstrual period, at a time when she had been discussing her fears of coping with strong feelings which arose during intercourse. On the day of the missed hour, she was preoccupied with the possibility of suffering "writhing cramps" while on the couch. She was so apprehensive that these cramps might cause her to be sick to her stomach that she canceled her appointment. In discussing this on the following day, she spoke of her fears of contaminating me and the office with "words—things I've never said before." Similarly, when she was expecting her menstrual period, there was a tendency to avoid sexual intercourse; and here too it was possible to demonstrate to her the fear of contaminating Stan and her concern with "holding back something evil" associated with the cramps.

Gradually, Mrs. S. began to bring more and more anal material into the analysis. She described an operation for rectal polyps which had occurred when she was about 3. She also told of the repeated infestations with intestinal worms which necessitated frequent rectal and anal manipulations. She "confessed" for the first time a long-standing history of constipation. From the age of 4 she remembered a severely traumatic experience in which the "town bully" had pinned down the sister of the patient's girlfriend and forced sand into her "fanny." Mrs. S. recalled how this incident had impressed and frightened her and how she had repetitive traumatic dreams involving this event for a number of months. After this material had been revealed by the patient, the "bully" became a frequent character in her dreams, invariably cast in the role of scapegoat.

She spoke with considerable fervor of her fear of enemas; how they invariably produced the sensation of bursting, which in turn evoked tremendous terror. Gradually she recalled that when she first learned the glimmerings of sexual intercourse, she imagined it as an anal and destructive act. Her first thought at the time was, "Did Daddy go to the bathroom in Mother's rectum?" As could be expected, she manifested considerable confusion between rectum and vagina (as well as rectum–vagina–mouth), and this in turn was connected with fantasies of anal impregnation and delivery. Fantasies involving the equivalence of feces and baby and feces and penis were frequent. She recalled a particularly vivid memory from age 7 when she witnessed a somewhat older girl having a huge bowel movement. At that time she thought it was as if this girl were having a baby, and she remembered her concern about the prospect of such a big mass coming out of herself. Dreams of making a mess with feces were frequent, and for a long time the mess was produced by someone not actually in the dream. It was not until relatively late in the analysis that she could accept the responsibility for the hostile, soiling tendencies reflected in these dreams.

IV

Even in the necessarily sketchy summary of the material in this case, the extent of the "I didn't mean it" constellation can be observed. While the whole spectrum of the "I didn't mean it" mechanisms can be seen most sharply in relation to the vicissitudes of the exhibitionistic and anal drives, the same defensive and adaptive configurations operate in respect to the other drive derivatives as well.

It is also apparent that the ego syntonicity of this group of reactions fluctuates tremendously. For instance, Mrs. S.'s ladylike appearance, her excellent taste in clothes, her careful speech and diction can all be viewed as character traits which are relatively ego-syntonic and which operate primarily within the conflict-free sphere of the ego. These character traits subserve defensive, gratificatory, and adaptive functions. If we examine these traits from the vantage point of their defensive activity, we can state that they arose as countercathectic organizations in opposition to exhibitionistic and anal-sadistic impulses. One segment of this countercathectic organization includes negation. These habitual modes of behavior represent a constant negation of her wish to exhibit herself or to soil. Her appearance says, in effect, "I don't mean to exhibit myself; it is not true that I wish to show off. I am just Plain Jane." To this extent these currently ego-syntonic traits involve defensive attitudes and patterns which were derived from instinctual conflicts and which play a significant role in maintaining in effective repression the involved drives.

However, at the level at which we now observe these character traits, they have achieved considerable independence from the instinctual conflicts and reflect a significant degree of autonomy.

On the other hand, the manner in which Mrs. S. incorporates the "I didn't mean it" attitudes into her pregnancy fantasies is much closer to the instinctual conflicts and much more ego-alien. The negation of the intent of her wish to become pregnant is, in this instance at least, directed against the affective representations of both the id and the superego. As long as she is able to maintain that she becomes pregnant by accident, she is able to reject her intention and responsibility and thereby avoid the anxiety and guilt she fears, inasmuch as the pregnancy wishes are contaminated by her oedipal conflicts. Here the "I didn't mean it" mechanism enjoys relatively little autonomy; its defensive efficiency is limited; and there is constantly a "return of the repressed."

Numerous ways in which this patient describes her "living with the brakes on" provide an excellent opportunity to observe the synthetic functioning of her ego. The particular manner in which she utilizes the "I didn't mean it" patterns in regard to forbidden pleasurable activities involves not only defensive activity directed against the forbidden impulses but simultaneously permits an appreciable degree of impulse discharge and a useful vehicle for social and interpersonal adaptation. Here too the negating defensive operations have become relatively automatized and rationalized, but nevertheless the stamp of the original instinctual conflict is evident in her limited gratification, the cramped and rigid patterns of her activity, and the sporadic breakthrough of the derivatives of the underlying repressed impulses (Fenichel, 1938). In this group of activities the isolating tendencies of the "I didn't mean it" mechanism can be seen. When she does something because it is her duty to do so rather than because she really wants to, the patient has effectively isolated the idea from the affect; and at the same time some motoric discharge of the drive is permitted.

In the analysis, the "I didn't mean it" patterns became most prominent in the evolution of the transference and the defenses against it. As the wishes to exhibit herself to the analyst and to soil him anally began to emerge, they were countered by the negation of her intent. Mrs. S. was then able to express the ideational representation of the drive by keeping the affective component in abeyance and isolation. What was noteworthy in this connection was the way in which the whole defensive configuration was drawn back into the matrix of the drive and erotized. The libidinization of the "I didn't mean it" in terms of her being coerced to perform in the analysis provided the patient with considerable gratification and enhanced the resistance value of these patterns.

The thesis of this case presentation is not that Mrs. S. was in any way unique in manifesting this particular kind of defense. The process of negation is obviously a universal one, utilized by all individuals in varying degrees. What is unique about this woman is her readiness to utilize the "I didn't mean it" patterns in all aspects of her psychological life. Thus far I have not presented any material which might explain this preference. In the remainder of this paper, I would like to review a portion of her analytic work which might give some hints as to the genetic roots of the "I didn't mean it" configuration as well as the economic basis for its preeminence in her defensive armamentarium.

V

In mid-November of the third year in her analysis, Mrs. S. announced that for income-tax purposes she planned to pay her December bill before the end of the year. This was certainly a deviation from the usual procedure, where I presented her with a statement for the previous month's work shortly after the first of each month. She hurriedly assured me this was really Stan's idea; but she supposed that I would feel that this was in some way shady or illegal. Then she shifted ground and asserted that my attitude was holier-than-thou, high-handed, and critical. She became angry and insisted that she could not stand my refusing what was a simple request. She mentioned the fantasy of "wheedling" this out of me, as she used to wheedle certain concessions out of Daddy. At the end of the hour, I merely told her this was something we should discuss further.

She left the office in a huff, something quite foreign to her usual mode of behavior; and after this there occurred several weeks of maneuvering to get me to permit this bit of acting out. At first she tried to bribe me with good behavior, with spectacular dreams, or with confessions. She alluded to my Jewishness in a somewhat condescending, protective fashion. She found it difficult to abandon her scheme to have me involved in what she recognized was a forbidden transaction; and experiencing my reluctance as a narcissistic blow, Mrs. S. tried to bolster her damaged self-esteem by asserting that she really didn't need me. As she became more aware of her own guilt in regard to the fantasy, she tried to shift these feelings onto Stan or me. It was evident that a crucial part of her fantasy was that I had promised her some special dispensation and now had reneged on implicit promises. She dreamed:

> I was coming to see you, together with a group of seven or eight people. We were going to play tennis. No one knew you were my psychiatrist. You had told me that we could use the tennis court, and I had told the other people about it. When I got to the back gate I was very cagey as to whether or not to enter. There was a tiny tennis court, and a Japanese gardener who was acting like a policeman. Also there was someone looking out the back window. Then the Japanese gardener said that we were doing something wrong. At this point, you came out, surrounded by a big bunch of people. You looked like Al Capone—shady and underhanded—or perhaps you were just busy. I pointed out that you had said it was okay for me to play tennis. You acted in a very perfunctory way, just saying rather coolly, "All right. All right." You then brushed me off and went to the car. I felt snubbed and felt that I had been put in a bad situation when it wasn't necessary. I had expected you would be apologetic and friendly. I felt like saying, "To hell with you."

She recalled that the evening before, while at bridge, she had been unduly upset by some quip her opponent had made when she reneged in the playing. It was as if he had accused her of cheating. Her associations then shifted to the matter of the December payment. She harangued me for making a big issue out of nothing. She felt that I was a dirty dog. I had shown her up, just as I had done in the dream in front of all of her friends. She identified the woman-at-the-window as my wife, and associated her with her own mother.

Gradually she could recognize that she was trying to inveigle me into a forbidden activity, as well as attempting to shift the feelings of guilt from herself to me by making me into "a dirty dog" and "gangster." As her feelings were being slowly worked out, her behavior changed. She began to come late to the sessions; her excuses for this were flimsy and flippant; there were many long pauses in her associations; what she spoke about was clearly anal in emphasis; there was an absence or paucity of dreams. In alluding to the early payment, the focus was on "I didn't mean it." She reiterated that it was Stan's idea. The whole thing was innocent. There were no ulterior motives. She was tardy about paying the November bill and was indignant and anxious that I might accuse her of doing this on purpose. She became disinterested in sexual intercourse and took considerable pleasure in withholding sex from Stan, just as she was withholding her associative material from me. She became quite constipated. During this period I attempted to show her how she wanted me to beg or force her to produce, just as she was trying to get Stan to beg her or force her into intercourse.

During this period Mrs. S. brought up the operation for rectal polyps, and she connected this with a fantasy of originally possessing a penis that was given to her younger brother, who was born several weeks before she had the surgery. Several sessions later she reported a dream:

> Bill [a boy she had known since childhood and who had always been effeminate] was at a party with a number of girls. He was there in a pink maternity outfit. Bill was married, and there was considerable concern as to why he was pregnant. Bill had taken over his wife's role. The reason for this was that, as a child, he had some kind of kidney trouble. Because of this he had gotten something from his mother like a transfusion. Something had gotten into him, and he was now pregnant. It was a dirty, lousy trick.

What impressed Mrs. S. most about the dream was her own anger as she told me about it. She quickly recognized her own identification with Bill, her own confused sexual identity, and her blaming her mother for this. She again referred to Lawrence's birth, his penis, and the feeling that this was incontrovertible evidence of her mother's favoritism. For the next few sessions she presented herself as a helpless little girl who is completely dependent and unable to care for herself. She was afraid that I expected too much of her in insisting that she "take the reins in her own hands." She warned me that this would bring dire consequences.

Now the material became overabundant; dreams came in waves; the patient referred to the "hodgepodge" she was presenting. It then became clear that she was, in effect, saying, "Okay, if you want me to produce I will, but you will have to clean up the mess yourself." She had warned me of this in earlier sessions and thereby felt relieved of any real responsibility for the consequences of her productions. On the contrary, it was evident that the patient was deriving considerable gratification from making a mess and my discomfiture in not knowing what to do with it.

During the "hodgepodge" period, attempts to interpret these various aspects of her behavior and defensive attitudes were seemingly quite unsuccessful. However, a dream she reported at this time afforded an opportunity to point out to the patient—in essentially this order—her current feelings of humiliation; that her behavior toward Stan and me represented a way of defending herself against these feelings; and that her making a mess in the analysis was her method of doing to me what she felt I had been doing to her. The dream in question was a relatively accurate replica of a life situation of a decade ago. Shortly after she had met Stan she went with him to his sister's wedding, where he wandered off, leaving her alone and infuriated. She ran home and felt she might "go berserk," but shortly afterward Stan came after her, contrite and repentant; and in a few weeks they were engaged. The dream itself did not contain the "happy ending" of the real-life situation; and it was evident that this was a typical "examination" dream where the manifest content was a cover for the wished-for happy ending. When I pointed this out to the patient, her immediate associations were situations in the past which had "not turned out so well," particularly the polyp operation. She felt that up to this point in her life all of her relations with Granny had been "sweetness and light," but after she had gone to stay with Granny following the operation, the latter was "disenchanted" with her. The patient told of the enemas and suppositories she had received after the operation and how terrible and painful they had been. Then she remembered that her mother had taken her to the city where the operation was performed, but had left her behind with her grandmother in order to care for the infant brother.

I then further interpreted her recent behavior in the analysis in terms of "Will you love me, even if I make a mess, or even if I don't produce anything at all?" She was able to recognize the various ways in which she was testing me as well as attempting to master a painful past situation. As the old feelings of humiliation became more distinct, the first reaction was again an accentuation of some of the defensive patterns. Her attempts to belittle Stan and myself became more insistent. She dreamed that I attempted to seduce and rape her—and she spurned me. On a ski trip she took great delight in besting Stan on the ski slopes—and avoiding him in bed.

For many years Mrs. S. had known that she had a deviated nasal septum, and a corrective operation had been advised. The patient precipitously—and quite secretively—made plans for immediate surgery. The operation was to undo the damage and castration that had been done to her in the previous rectal operation. She harbored all kinds of extravagant ideas in regard to the effects of this operation; but at the same time she was convinced that Stan, Daddy, Granny, and I would strongly disapprove of such a venture, and she expected some kind of "catastrophic punishment."

For several sessions the patient continued on her highly salutary expectations of the operation. I did not directly prohibit the operation, but pointed out the clandestine character of her plans, the highly unrealistic expectations, and the fear of dire consequences. She immediately postponed surgery and was extremely angry with me, accusing me of withholding pleasure just as her parents had prohibited sexual activity as a child. As she became more aware of the fantasy nature of the operation, she became morose and depressed; and she reverted to all kinds of withholding in the analysis—and outside as well. She described herself as a "balky child," and there was an exacerbation of her constipation.

Gradually Mrs. S. began to wonder if she were doing this on purpose, whether or not she could really "help it"; and it was evident that she was not certain as to whether or not she had control over her behavior. I repeatedly interpreted this confusion to her. In response the patient poured out a wealth of material connected with the rectal polyp operation. She recalled, first of all, how she had been promised that the operation would not hurt. Strictly speaking, her mother and grandmother had not lied; but Mrs. S. felt deceived because she had been abandoned. Even worse was the fact that she had been hurt so badly by the enemas and the suppositories during the period of convalescence. She was bitter about being held down by the nurses and about her mother's leaving. She began to see some glimmerings into the fact that her need to please and to placate me was a recapitulation of her need to please her mother and Granny. She reenacted in the transference her fears of being too demanding of me as she felt she had been of her mother—because such greediness would lead to her rejection.

Sessions when the patient poured out this highly charged material alternated with hours when she relapsed into being the balky child, complaining again of her being forced to come to the analysis, and performing against her will. She railed at the way I expected so much of her and how I was waiting to laugh at her ineptitude. She alluded to secrets which she would not give up. I suggested that she wanted me to cajole and beg and, if this was not successful, to force the secrets from her as the enemas and suppositories had forced the fecal material from her in the past. The day after I made this interpretation she reported the following dream:

> I was having an operation. The doctor was probably Dr. X [her previous therapist], but it might have been Dr. C. [the surgeon], and there were a number of people around. First they pretended the operation was nothing, but then they became concerned as if it were a real important thing. There was no anaesthesia until the last minute. Then at the climax there was a whiff of gas and they took it out. Then I went onto a boat, as if the last part of the operation was to be done there.
>
> Nothing happened except that I got sick to my stomach. I had the feeling of being in some danger but also of being in good hands, with all the doctors and nurses. I'm not sure if I threw up on the boat or over the side. I wondered what their reactions might be.

She spoke first of how the dream must be connected with her polyp operation and the imminent nose operation as well as with having a baby. She then had a period of great difficulty in saying anything; this was accompanied by anxiety that I would become disgusted. She then spoke of having been her father's favorite and of having lost this special position. This was also how she might have felt when her mother was pregnant with her three younger siblings. She then mentioned how lonesome she had been when she had gone off to boarding school in her teens and her intense feelings toward her mother when she returned home, which produced exaggerated emotions and an "overflow." This same theme returned in a dream several weeks later. "I was about to have a baby, and the doctor told me to push down as the baby was ready to come. However, I didn't trust the doctor. It was as if they really weren't ready to catch the baby."

She awakened from the dream with severe cramps. Her first thoughts were, "As if the grownups were saying, 'Do it,' but I was concerned about making a mess and then being blamed for it."

The following day she was in a foul humor which she ascribed to being angry with Stan because of an unsatisfactory sexual experience. As she spoke, however, it became evident that a large portion of her irritability was directed toward me because she felt she had to tell me the details of the previous night. She insisted I was forcing her to humiliate herself; and when I questioned this, she became more rebellious. She enjoyed, she said, tantalizing me; and when she finally gave up her secret, which related to fellatio fantasies, she felt "real good" about confessing, as if she had been a good girl and done what was expected of her. At the same time, she felt that I had deceived her. Even though I had said it was all right to talk about all these "grubby and dirty things," I would hold it against her, and she regretted that she had let out too much. When I reminded her of the dream she had reported on the previous day, she was taken aback. She's not sure if what she is doing is really safe. Do I really want her to do this? Do I really know what it entails? Then, as an afterthought, she said that she was not sure that she honestly regretted saying these forbidden things. "I've done what you asked me to do; but did you really expect the mess?"

The next day she felt "useless, trapped, depressed." She had nothing to say, fearing she would become embarrassed and make a fool of herself. Mrs. S. then "confessed" that when she had walked into the room that day, the thought had come to her that she might vomit and mess up the place. She related it to the feeling of wanting to keep down what she felt should stay down. She felt hopeless because "I can't do what I'm supposed to do—I can't erupt." She then recalled that, in reality, she has rarely thrown up and that it had always been important for her not to do so. The patient remembered that when she was a child, her entire family was accustomed to ride on a ferryboat, and it was not unknown for many members of the family to get seasick and throw up; but she never did. Even when she became violently nauseated, Mrs. S. resolutely refused to vomit, and she could recall her grim determination in the face of appeals from her mother and aunt to "Throw up, and get it over with."

At this point I suggested that she was afraid that if she did get sick in the office, I would think she was doing it on purpose. Her reaction was quite dramatic. She could not say anything for a few moments. She blushed and was obviously quite agitated.

The next day Mrs. S. could hardly wait to tell me a dream of the previous night:

> I was in the waiting room, and the woman patient who preceded me walked down the hall. In a few moments, you angrily strode in, saying, "Why didn't you come in?" I was angry. I knew I hadn't done it on purpose to be mean. I thought perhaps you wanted to make a phone call or just rest. I was upset that you had suddenly turned against me.

Mrs. S. spoke of how upset she had been the previous day because she felt that I was displeased with her. She did not like what I suggested about her "doing it on purpose." I had no right to accuse her of this. She was doing what I had asked her to do and doing it for my benefit. She felt that this was the gist of the dream she had reported at the beginning of the session. She was not keeping me waiting on purpose. She was just doing something to please me, and so forth.

At this point, however, it was not difficult to demonstrate to the patient how she was using the dream to disown the underlying intent. It was clear that the repressed was returning via a negation; and through this mechanism, she could permit the forbidden, repressed thought to gain access to consciousness, free of its strong affective component. The latter was isolated from the ideational representation through the disclaiming action of the "I didn't mean it"—more specifically here in terms of "I didn't do it on purpose." Mrs. S. could then observe how she derived gratification from the prospect of keeping me waiting, just as she derived even more gratification from the prospect of soiling me and making a mess of my office.

After this dream material was worked through, the patient's "I didn't mean it" attitudes by no means magically disappeared, but their frequency greatly decreased, their defensive effectiveness was greatly vitiated, and the patient independently became increasingly cognizant of their significance in her psychic activity.

VI

It is difficult not to be impressed with parallels between the current "I didn't mean it" attitude and Mrs. S.'s polyp experiences. Obviously the polyp operation and its sequelae do not in themselves completely explain the evolution and prominence of this construction. It is reasonable to assume that there was a readiness to react to the polyp experience in a striking fashion; it is also not unlikely that, had this particular patient afterward faced somewhat different life situations, the "I didn't mean it" configuration might have provided a less useful vehicle for coping with some of her instinctual conflicts.

The operation occurred at a crucial period in the patient's development when she was vulnerable to certain traumas. The relationship with her mother had been strained for the second time in 18 months by the birth of a new sibling; and the more recent arrival was a male child whose penis she fantasied had been taken from her and was thus evidence of her mother's partiality and undependability. She had only recently gained control of her sphincter activity; and the concomitantly achieved feelings of autonomy could hardly have been well consolidated. Then came the crucial blow of her mother's deceiving and abandoning her when the patient discovered that she was being subjected to a terrifying surgical procedure instead of enjoying a pleasant holiday. The operation had special meaning because of the enforced restrictions—being taken to the operating room, being given anaesthesia, being held down in bed; to these were added the even more significant passively endured experiences with being given enemas and rectal suppositories. The fact that the latter events were associated with the loss of autonomy in regard to her painstakingly won bowel control was particularly meaningful. Not only did she suffer a series of serious narcissistic blows, but in addition there was the mobilization of significant quantities of aggression which this child could, at best, discharge only with difficulty.

Yet the particular concatenation of events as they occurred constituted not only a trauma for the patient but in other respects became a focal point for defensive and adaptative development. I am referring especially to the psychological effects of the administration of the enemas and suppositories. Because of them she lost control of her sphincters, of her anal impulses, of her aggressions. In *reality* she couldn't help it—"she didn't mean it." At the same time it is clear that she wanted to make a mess, to soil her mother and grandmother, to discharge her aggressions. But the specific external reality facilitated her negation of the intent and affect. Furthermore, there is considerable evidence that these tendencies were reinforced by the attitude and reactions of nurse and grandmother who, after their initial censure and disgust at the mess, relented—and probably overreacted out of guilt—in a rather solicitous fashion, and reassured the patient, "You couldn't help it," and "You didn't mean it."

It is reasonable to assume that, at this point, the patient took over the attitude of Granny and the nurse, elaborated on it, rationalized from it, and used it as a model and point of departure for defensive patternings. Via this identification, she not only could ward off fears of retaliation in respect to her aggressive and anal-sadistic drives, but she could bolster her highly deflated self-esteem. Mrs. S. learned, therefore, that the process of negation, couched in the particular elaborations and variations of the "I didn't mean it," permitted her to cope with the demand of her forbidden instinctual drives in an effective manner; and later she frequently responded to the demands of the superego with this kind of negation.

At this point we should examine the same set of phenomena from another direction, namely, in regard to the role which Mrs. S.'s object relationships played during this crucial period in her life. Here the ideas of Spitz (1957, 1958) were pertinent to an understanding of the "I didn't mean it" construction. He points out that one of the significant roots of the process of negation is its connection with the anlage of object relations in the earliest feeding experiences. A more immediate root is the fact that the "No" of the infant arises out of a defensive mechanism, the identification with the aggressor. When the infant is first able to comprehend the significance of these prohibitions of the adults (between 9 and 12 months), he can counter the frustration and aggression produced by the prohibitions only by a very limited motoric activity. By 15 to 18 months, the child has acquired the function of negation; in doing so he at first imitates the "No" of the significant frustrating adults, and later identifies with it. This identification, together with the others being formed at this time, plays a significant role in the formation and maintenance of object relationships. An important element of this complex process is that via this identification the child is in a better position to handle his aggressive impulses toward the love object.

It can now be seen that Mrs. S.'s identification with the negation of her grandmother and nurse (behind whom, of course, was her mother) expedited her handling of a most difficult psychological situation. Not only did the negation in the "I didn't mean it" provide an admirable vehicle for the discharge of aggression, particularly because of the dynamic and economic advantages of the identification process; but by virtue of the same process the negation also facilitated and strengthened the relationships with these early objects. The latter was critical in that during this period of overwhelming stress the object relations, as it were, served to neutralize the danger of undue regression and the loss of ego-object differentiation. The "I didn't mean it," as a symbol of a relationship with the love object, acted as an anchor in the real world and as a deterrent to further regression.

I would go one step farther in this reconstruction. During the postoperative enema-suppository period, Mrs. S. did indeed experience a limited regression, one which might be conceptualized as a "regression in the service of the ego." I would suggest that the regression was to the period in her ego development when the identification with the aggressor and the formation of the process of negation initially occurred. This must have represented a strong point of psychological development, a haven, so to speak, to which she could retreat, and where she could remobilize her forces in order to handle the tumultuous conflicts within her. In so doing, she could lean not only on an effective method of dealing with undesirable tensions, but also on the strength of those toward whom so many of her unacceptable impulses were directed.

Although these formulations may not explain every facet of the phenomena described, I believe they have merit in the attempt to understand the patient's predilection for a certain defensive constellation and its evolution from a relatively concrete reality experience to a highly abstract internalized construction.

REFERENCES

Abend, S. M. (1975), An analogue of negation. *Psychoanal. Quart.*, 44:631–637.

Altschul, S. (1968), Denial and ego arrest. *J. Amer. Psychoanal. Assn.*, 16: 301–318.

Basch, M. F. (1974), Interference with perceptual transformation in the service of defense. *The Annual of Psychoanalysis*, 2:87–97.

Brenman, M. S. (1952), On teasing and being teased. *The Psychoanalytic Study of the Child*, 7:264–285.

Brenner, C. (1957), The nature and development of the concept of repression in Freud's writings. *The Psychoanalytic Study of the Child*, 12:19–46.

Fenichel, O. (1938), Ego disturbances and their treatment. *Internat. J. Psycho-Anal.*, 19:416–438.

_______ (1945), *The Psychoanalytic Theory of Neurosis.* New York: Norton.

Freud, A. (1936), The ego and the mechanisms of defense. *W.*, 2.

Freud, S. (1905), Fragment of an analysis of a case of hysteria. *Standard Edition*, 7:3–122.

_______ (1911), Psycho-analytic notes on an autobiographical account of a case of paranoia. *Standard Edition*, 12:3–82.

_______ (1915), The unconscious. *Standard Edition*, 14:159–215.

_______ (1925), Negation. *Standard Edition*, 19:234–239.

_______ (1927), Fetishism. *Standard Edition*, 21:149–157.

_______ (1940), An outline of psycho-analysis. *Standard Edition*, 23:141–207.

Hartmann, H. (1956), Notes on the reality principle. *The Psychoanalytic Study of the Child*, 11:31–53.

Jacobson, E. (1957), Denial and repression. *J. Amer. Psychoanal. Assn.*, 5:61–92.

Katan, M. (1964), Fetishism, splitting of the ego, and denial. *Internat. J. Psycho-Anal.*, 45:237–245.

Lewin, B. D. (1950), *The Psychoanalysis of Elation.* New York: Norton.

Lichtenstein, H. (1971), The malignant no. In: *The Unconscious Today*, ed. M. Kanzer. New York: International Universities Press, pp. 147–176.

Lossy, F. T. (1962), The charge of suggestion as a resistance in psycho-analysis. *Internat. J. Psycho-Anal.*, 43:448–467.

Modell, A. H. (1961), Denial and the sense of separateness. *J. Amer. Psychoanal. Assn.*, 9:533–547.

Podvall, E. (1970), On negation and the structure of paranoid thought. Read at annual meeting of American Psychoanalytic Association.

Rapaport, D., ed. (1951), *Organization and Pathology of Thought.* New York: Columbia University Press.

Sperling, S. J. (1958), On denial and the essential nature of defence. *Internat. J. Psycho-Anal.*, 39:25–38.

Spitz, R. A. (1957), *No and Yes.* New York: International Universities Press.

_______ (1958), On the genesis of superego components. *The Psychoanalytic Study of the Child,* 13:375–404.

Stewart, W. A. (1970), The split in the ego and the mechanism of disavowal. *Psychoanal. Quart.*, 39:1–16.

Waelder, R. (1951), The structure of paranoid ideas. *Internat. J. Psycho-Anal.*, 32:167–177.

Chapter 3

1979

Some Observations on Not Telling the Truth

My title, I must confess at once, is somewhat misleading. I am not prepared to examine all aspects of "not telling the truth." A comprehensive survey of such a subject should include an analysis of the topic from the philosophical, the theological, the legal, and the ethical-moral points of view; I shall limit myself to some psychological, especially psychoanalytic, aspects of this particular human frailty. Not telling the truth is a most complex and heterogeneous matter, encompassing a host of phenomena which range from essentially organic conditions to the at least ostensibly conscious and deliberate telling of a falsehood. An attempt to delineate an acceptable definition of The Truth would very quickly become a Talmudic exercise, and the comparable task of spelling out what is meant by "knowing the truth" risks traversing a semantic and epistemological mine field. Even a very abbreviated catalogue would have to take cognizance of such diverse conditions as the Korsakov psychosis, the Ganser syndrome, obsessional doubting, malingering, the impostors, plagiarism, the schizophrenias, pseudologia phantastica, the "white" lie and—for want of a better term—the "plain" lie.

My paper is primarily a clinical one, and will be limited to one special instance of the "plain" lie. Arbitrarily, I will paraphrase Fenichel's (1939, pp. 130–131) definition of the lie as an "untruth in which the subject himself *did* intend to deceive others with his assertion and *did not* believe that assertion himself." However imperfect such a definition may be, I believe that it will serve the purpose of the subsequent discussion. The

---

Although I have written and am responsible for the material and the formulations in this essay, I am indebted to Dr. Victor Calef for his help in clarifying some of my thoughts on the subject. Because we regularly discuss our work together, it is sometimes not altogether clear if the initial stimulus for a given line of thought came from him or from myself.

"special" instance of the lie with which I will concern myself is that of a *particular* type of lie that I have encountered in the analytic situation. I am indebted, by the way, to Ms. Rosalind Chambers, the Executive Secretary of the Columbia Institute who, without having any knowledge of the specific content of my paper, made the uncanny suggestion that its subtitle should be "Lying on the Couch." Her title is more accurate and certainly more felicitous than the one I submitted.

It is difficult to ascertain just how frequently the analyst is confronted with lying by his patients, and little is said about it in the contemporary literature. I believe that we anticipate that patients with definite psychopathic traits, those who are inordinately grandiose, and those who are more severely disturbed (Kernberg, 1975, pp. 139, 142) are more likely to demonstrate lying in the course of their analytic work; however, there is a paucity of data about the frequency of this type of falsification and the circumstances in which it may occur. There is a comparable "expectation" that the so-called neurotic, the healthier patient, will not lie deliberately to the analyst; and the idea that the patient will be assiduously "truthful" with the analyst is a more or less commonly accepted element of the analytic relationship. Again, although the topic has not been discussed widely or explicitly in the articles on analyzability, the implication exists that an individual prone to lying would not be a particularly good candidate for analysis (for instance, see Waldhorn, 1960, p. 501). Although Ruth Mack Brunswick states (1943, p. 462) that "In the analysis of the neuroses, periods of lying in otherwise truthful individuals are of *frequent* [italics mine] occurrence," my impression is that Brunswick is alluding to the consequences of denial and comparable mechanisms rather than a deliberate falsification. Similarly, I assume that most analysts accept as inevitable the fact that patients, as a product of defense and resistance, will distort various elements of truth and reality; and, further, I assume that most analysts are less prepared for *conscious* deception, though recognizing that the latter must also be determined by a host of unconscious motivations.

The case material I present comes from the analyses of patients I considered to be essentially "neurotic" and analyzable, although the dynamics I describe may well be applicable in comparable instances to more disturbed individuals. Further, the patients I present all demonstrated a more than adequate level of superego functioning. The episodes of lying that I have selected all took place after the patient had shown evidence of involvement in a transference neurosis. I propose to demonstrate that these episodes all represented a re-enactment within the analysis and the transference neurosis of a particular aspect of the oedipal conflict, and that while it was evident that pregenital elements were present and significant, these were not the *essential* features of these reactions. It is my intention to show how these lies served multiple functions: permitting the partial recovery of old memories and the perceptions—real or distorted or both—connected with these memories; attempting to reveal certain unconscious fantasies and wishes while simultaneously continuing to protect those wishes by a variety of mechanisms which collectively are most effectively conceptualized as "screen" functions; and expressing in a form that is defensive—but not only defensive—the hidden resentment over being lied to by one or both of the oedipal objects and of confronting the oedipal object with the latter's own residual incestuous tendencies. Finally, without detailed elaboration, I point to the connection between the oedipally determined lie and an infantile primal-scene trauma. It will be apparent, as the clinical material unfolds, that not all of these elements will be manifested in an equally clear and convincing fashion in all of the cases.

CLINICAL ILLUSTRATIONS

The first case is that of a 22-year-old graduate student in English literature who came into analysis because of vague phobic symptoms, sexual problems, and an inhibition in her seminar work wherein she was unable to express herself freely, especially when convinced that she had something worthwhile to say. She was bright and competent and, in spite of her inhibition, successful in her academic work and obviously well regarded by her professors. She felt a bit guilty about this and could not rid herself of the feeling that her academic achievements were at least in part related to her attractiveness and her "way with men." This may have been partially correct, but she glossed over the fact that she was equally successful with her women teachers. She was the middle of three children, having an older sister and a younger brother. Her parents were both professionals; sophisticated, and sympathetic with the children and their needs. For a long time the patient presented her family life and her own development in a somewhat idealized fashion with the repeated comment that she could not possibly understand why *she* should have the emotional problems that brought her into analysis. In the first eighteen months or so of the analysis she displayed the usual resistances, but it was evident that she was psychologically minded and, as she became more accustomed to the analytic work, was learning to free associate. The two things that struck me as a bit incongruous were her somewhat distant, guarded dealing with me as a person and her seeming inability to follow up on trains of thought that seemed at the moment to be potentially very productive.

In the middle of her second year of analysis, there was a gradual but definite change in her overall demeanor. She was demonstrably more ill-at-ease with me and more self-conscious at the beginning and the end of the sessions when we had some face-to-face contact. Later, she described with some embarrassment the emergence of a new symptom. Her vague phobic fears became crystallized, and she became aware of the fear of a sexual attack. Even though she attributed this fear, in part, to the reality of the danger of such an assault on her college campus, she was also aware that the thought about such a misadventure was accompanied by a trace of excitement; and she recognized that the latter fact caused her as much discomfort as the fear itself. I pointed to the possible linkage between the new symptom and the shift in her attitude toward me, and although she appeared to concur with my observation, the only new material was her recognition that in recent months she had become more curious and more aware of me. In the third year of the analysis, the patient introduced another new symptom. She intermittently began her session—usually after a brief period of silence—with the statement "I have *nothing* to say." Early in the analysis, she had made similar remarks. However, those disclaimers appeared to be either a genuine reflection of what she felt was "nothing to say" or a somewhat stubborn and provocative refusal to do what she felt was expected of her; and, at times, it represented the reaction to feeling pushed or prodded by some intervention on my part (Olinick, 1957). These rebellious gestures had previously been very short-lived, but at this point even the tone of voice in which she uttered her "I have *nothing* to say" was distinctly different. It was clear that she was both very uneasy and *not* telling the truth—a fact she eventually confirmed. It took some time to recognize the amount of anxiety connected with relating these "lies" to me, but finally I was able to focus on the fear of revealing certain things to me, a fear which she handled by insisting that she had nothing to say. Her reaction to this was, for her, an unusual outburst of anger. She accused me of being the one not talking, of withholding from her; and she insisted that since I was the one who really "knew," why didn't I talk and tell her "what it was all about." She claimed that even if it were true that she did indeed have things on her mind, the thoughts that *she* had withheld were so trivial and so prosaic that telling them would be truly humiliating; and since I would be the one who would be the agent of her humiliation, she was perfectly justified in lying to me. In fact, she argued, my not telling her what I knew was just as much of a lie as her telling me that she had nothing to say.

Gradually, she was able to "confess" the thoughts that she had lied about not having had and, in a sense, she was quite correct about their ostensibly pedestrian character. They had to do with various items in the office: the patterns in the plastered ceiling, the knick-knacks on my mantel piece, the color of the rug, the various doors in the office and her speculations about where those doors led, etc. It was not difficult to make the connections between these thoughts and her curiosity about me, especially those with a sexual connotation. The "big" secret which was covered by these "screen" associations about the office was the fantasy that I had a crush on her, that she was my favorite patient, and that I desired her sexually. She herself made the connection between these fantasies and the fantasies that her professors were attracted to her and had given her preferential treatment because of this. Further, what emerged was that her "anxiety" about revealing these apparently innocuous thoughts and which led to her lying was the fear that in telling me about such prosaic thoughts she would inadvertently reveal her knowledge of sexual matters.

These "lies" became the point of departure and the organizing focus for extensive analytic work around the inhibitions of her letting people know what she really "knew" in class and related character traits. We learned more about her resentment that mother had not shared confidences and secrets, especially sexual ones, with her. As she became aware of the multiple meanings of this resentment, she also began to bring in pieces of material from her childhood relationship with her father when she was around five years old. She and her father had a special "ritual" each evening before her bedtime: he read her stories or they played some games. The family joked about it being "their time." The patient recalled an evening when this ritual had been interrupted by the necessity of her father and mother to talk together. It was an interruption that the little girl did not take in good grace, and what stood out most sharply in her memory was her asking the parents what they were talking about and the mother's replying "nothing." She acknowledged that it must have been a situation that had been repeated many times, mostly with her being the one who said "nothing." However, what we were able to reconstruct in the ensuing work was her anger at having the special time with her father taken from her, her helplessness at not being able to do something about it, the humiliation that she must have felt in revealing how much she cared for her father, and the conviction that her parents were sharing some forbidden sexual secrets. She felt that her mother had lied to her at that time, just as she had experienced her mother telling her nothing about sexual matters as a lie, and just as she had felt about my silence and general anonymity. Finally, we could recognize that the memory of the "nothing" episode served as screen for much earlier primal-scene experiences and their derivative fantasies.

Our withholding sexual secrets from her was, as far as she was concerned, a justification for withholding her sexual secrets from me. In the analysis, her lying about having nothing to say was also her particular way of revealing a secret. The secrets that she withheld were innocent ones, but displacements which served as screens for the much more highly charged secrets about her oedipal feelings in the transference. At the same time, her lie and her behavior provided her with a vehicle for exposing my lie and her father's lie—our sexual interest in her. It was not difficult for this young woman to see how she had utilized this "projection" as a means of denying her own oedipal strivings; but, for her, it also represented reliving a piece of painful reality which, however distorted it had become, was indeed a fateful one for her. I should add that this was a young woman who, as best as she could recall, rarely lied. Her inhibitions about letting others know what she really knew served the same purposes; and it was only under the pressure of the transference regression that she revealed via these lies her old secrets, secret knowledge, and secret traumata.

My second example concerns what at first glance appeared to be a very trivial lie related by a 33-year-old married housewife and mother who came to analysis for a variety of hysterical complaints, a florid snake phobia, depressive feelings, and dissatisfaction with her marriage. She had a four-year-older brother with whom she had a most tenuous relationship, and her parents were both successful teachers with whom she enjoyed very close but stormy relations. She was extremely bright and attractive and had almost invariably achieved whatever goals she had set for herself. She started analysis with the declaration that she was going to have the best and the shortest analysis on record.

During the fourth year of the analysis, she was very much enmeshed in an intense transference neurosis and attempting to deal with strongly negative feelings toward me and her mother. She had already recognized that she was not likely to achieve the fabulous analysis in a strikingly short time, and she was also aware of the unconscious basis for that fantasy, obtaining a penis from the analyst. These frustrations and resentments also brought to the fore angry feelings toward her mother, feelings that were complicated by the mother's illnesses during the patient's childhood and the vivid recollection of many details of the mother's miscarriage when the patient was somewhere between four and five. We were able to delineate various elements of her wish to castrate men, her furious feelings at having lost out in the oedipal struggle, a good deal about the meaning of the snake phobia, the relationship between her wish for the father's baby-penis, and the trauma connected with the mother's miscarriage. What had also begun to emerge during this portion of our work were some of the pregenital roots of the depressive constellation which related to a number of separations from the mother and which later became intertwined with the disappointments of her oedipal loss.

As this occurred, the phobic symptoms returned in greater force, and she became more openly resistive and stubborn. Instead of pursuing the reconstructive work within the analysis, she sought out her mother and other relatives and tried, with great vigor and ingenuity, to fill out the details of her earlier life by eliciting the "real facts" of what had happened. It was not difficult to point out to her how she was not only depreciating me by doing the work "all by myself," but also defending herself against me by not permitting herself to be "surprised" (a crucial aspect of her snake phobia) by any potentially traumatic revelation. She was convinced that unless she procured all the necessary information in advance, I could confront her with an interpretation that would panic her. Her overall attitude toward me oscillated between being the righteously indignant and justifiably vengeful woman-scorned and the frightened little girl who was about to be overwhelmed by some unspeakable catastrophe.

Over a period of several months, she confessed a series of what she labeled "little lies" *about* me. These were not extraordinary fabrications: that I never said anything, that I said too much, that I always laughed at her jokes (which at times I had done), that I told her funny stories (which I had not done), that I had begun to wear rather outlandish clothes, and so forth. Her reasons for doing so were somewhat unclear, but she did connect these episodes with getting even with me, and she did bring in a considerable amount of material about her father's lying, most of which was not so much deceitful as self-aggrandizing. About six weeks after reporting the last lie she had circulated about me, she rather matter-offactly mentioned that she had developed a genital itching over the previous weekend. We (including her personal physician) were never able to determine with certainty if the itching was caused by an infection, by psychological factors, or both; but it was evident that as far as the patient was concerned, the itching was directly related to her masturbatory activities, past and present, and their attendant fantasies. Further, she revealed—and the parallel with her frenetic search for childhood data was striking—that for the first time in her life she had examined her own genitalia. She was shocked, disgusted with what she felt was a "freaky ugliness," yet pleased and proud with herself in that she had mustered the courage to look. However, she also related with a mixture of anger and uneasiness that a friend of hers who had recently completed a long analysis had told the patient that even though she was very satisfied with the results of her analytical experience, she also felt that "in some ways things were harder since the analysis." The patient had (not without reason) interpreted her friend's remarks to mean that since the analysis she *had* to be more honest and that it was harder for her *not* to "look."

At this point, I began a series of interpretations whose central thrust was to demonstrate that her lies about me, her spirited quest for the "real facts" of her early life, and the belated examination of her own genitals were all motivated by her need to distract us from really looking at and seeing what she had felt had really happened and that her attempts to do so had been only partially successful. I further offered the suggestion that what was being enacted currently in the analytic relationship was probably a reasonable facsimile of what had taken place at an earlier period of her life.

The patient's reaction to my version of the analytic scenario was not exactly a docile one. Her initial response of disdain and contempt gradually gave way to a somewhat grudging willingness to consider the interpretations. Then one day she began her session with the contrite confession that she had lied to me about her genital itch. The fabrication consisted not in the essential description of her symptom but in dating its onset ten days later than the time she had related; and she had done so with the deliberate intention of deceiving me and of hiding from me the real date of the beginning of the itching. She could not understand why it was difficult for her to make this confession, and she was genuinely mystified as to the reason for her lying in the first place. A few days later, she recalled an incident from the age of six-seven, an incident which she had not alluded to in the analysis, although, she insisted, it was certainly not an unconscious memory. It was, rather, something she just didn't *think* about. She related, with increasing affect, about waking up one night and getting out of bed. She was not sure whether her intention was to go to her parents' bedroom or to the bathroom which lay between that room and her own. Just as she was about to go into the hallway, she saw her father clearly (in spite of the dim light), naked and obviously headed for the bathroom. She was content that he had not noticed her; she said that she does not remember being particularly upset by what she had seen; she went back to bed and to sleep. At breakfast the next morning, she was briefly tempted to report to the family the highlights of the previous night's drama, but she was too uncomfortable to do so. Instead, she rather cheerfully told what she designated as her "very first real lie." She related a dream, a dream which she asserts she made up in its entirety, wherein the only action consisted of her watching a big monkey swinging from the chandeliers.

Space does not permit a detailed replication of the next month's analytic work. Suffice it that we considered the possibility that she had, in fact, dreamed about viewing her naked father and that the dream she had labeled as a falsehood could well have occurred (Calef, 1972). She accepted the possibility of both of these alternatives, but she doubted whether such distortions had taken place. What did emerge, gradually, was that in all likelihood she had seen her father's erect penis, that she had the thought at that time that her father was going to the bathroom just after the parents had completed intercourse, that she had suppressed her very strong emotional reaction to this unexpected perception; and that her next morning's fabrication was not just a "lie," but her special version of one aspect of the sexual act as distorted by her own fantasies, both conscious and unconscious. In this case, the connection with the primal scene and primal-scene fantasies was even more striking and conspicuous.

The point most germane to this essay, however, was her own connection between the postdating of the time of the inception of her genital itching and her postponing confronting her father with his—albeit unwitting—exposing himself to his daughter. Both events required looking at things that were painful and frightening, both involved her unwillingness to accept the differences between the sexes, and both had to do with her dealing with incestuous wishes toward her father; and although the two situations were not identical, the overall configuration of both lies represented attempts at displacements and the establishment of "screens." The lie that she told me could not be isolated from the inspection of her own genitals (and of her past life) which, in addition, had the quality, not of the "command to remember" (Fenichel, 1927, p. 114), but the "command to look." As long as she could scrutinize her own genitals and convince herself that nothing was there, she could at the same time avoid thinking about and looking at the phallus that was so threatening to her. In what she called her "first real lie" she could focus on the fabricated dream-image rather than deal with the traumatic perception of the night before. Both lies, then, served in the denial and eventual repression of painful memories. Later, she came up with her own explanation of the function of her lies, and, although I cannot quote her precisely, her words were amazingly similar to the ones Fenichel used (1939, p. 133) in his formulation of pseudologia phantastica: "If it is possible to make someone believe that untrue things are true, then it is also possible that true things, the memory of which threatens me, are untrue."

The third case is that of a 29-year-old married biochemist whose complaints were vague and who in our preliminary interviews stated blandly but quite sincerely, "I want to find the truth." Further discussion, however, revealed that this very intelligent and psychologically sensitive man was really very unhappy. His life was dull and bleak; his friendships were unsatisfying; his work was congenial enough but he could not put it behind him at the end of the day; his relations with his wife were, to him, pallid; he enjoyed his daughter but found her an intrusion. It was as if he were trying to tell me that in some way his whole life was a lie.

He was the younger son of middle-class parents who worked in the business world. The father was a big, quiet, kind, scrupulously honest man, devoted to his family and to a low-level executive job, which he held for many years. He did not seem to be perturbed that his wife was the ostensibly dominant member of the household, nor upset when the other members of the family mocked his reticence, his lack of competitiveness, and his incorruptibility. The mother, on the other hand, was a much more outgoing, decisive, and verbal person. She was opinionated and contentious; she denigrated her husband, but was extremely loyal to her sons, watching over their material comforts and capable of becoming a real lioness in defending her not always well-behaved cubs. The brother was portrayed in much the same brush-strokes as the father and had often served the patient as a substitute for and link to the father.

The patient, therefore, viewed his mother as an ally on whom he could rely whether he was good or bad, right or wrong. In addition, he experienced the alliance as a collusion wherein forbidden activities could be carried out in a surreptitious, unspoken way. This was reinforced by their participation in a series of games, the essence of which was to demonstrate that he was blameless and need not fear punishment. The mother was careless about exposing herself and otherwise behaved seductively. This environment produced in the patient considerable excitement and anxiety, on the one hand, and facilitated the externalization, denial and the repression of the derivatives of his oedipal fantasies and fears, on the other.

After a number of months of relatively perfunctory, low-key attempts to describe himself, his difficulties, and his past life, the patient gradually drifted into a behavior which much later we could recognize as a replication of childhood patterns. At that time, however, it was confusing, inexplicable, and very disconcerting; and for long periods of time, I had only the vaguest idea of what was happening. He spoke very rapidly, often in a manner which left me with an image that his last words had just erased the preceding ones and, at times, those verbal productions sounded very much like a contrived doubletalk. Whereas in the early weeks of the analysis, he had presented himself as a sophisticated, introspective individual, there were now long periods wherein he appeared to be naïve and simple-minded. He would bombard me with series after series of rationalizations and externalizations that were so patent that it was hard to imagine that these statements did not contain a significant element of challenge and provocation. He was constantly looking for judges and for witnesses to pass judgment or to bring in evidence. At times this virtual compulsion to turn my consulting room into a courtroom verged on the bizarre; sometimes it was necessary to assume that he was playing a joke on me. And, in a sense, he was!

In addition, the patient presented a repeated offer to "make a deal" with me, to have me collude with him in his not being analyzed, in his not saying whatever came to mind. (What is ironic, of course, is that in *his* way he was saying what came to mind; and, in *his* way, he was producing the only material that would permit the analytic process to operate.) He very candidly suggested that if I would not pursue my analytic work with him, not "give him a hard time," then he would behave himself and not cause me any trouble in the time we spent together. I confess it was an offer I was sorely tempted not to refuse!

All of this behavior, any of which appeared at a given moment to be capable of precluding any real analytic progress, was, of course, a replication in the transference of various aspects of his earlier object relationships, especially with his mother, and constituted both significant resistances and most helpful sources of information which were necessary to understand this complex man. Gradually, however, what had for long periods of time appeared chaotic and senseless, became more and more meaningful and interrelated for both of us.

After this long introduction, we come to his lying in the analysis. For prolonged stretches, my patient would make all sorts of exaggerated and deceptive statements about his financial condition. Some of these statements reflected, in a distorted way, what at that moment he believed to be the true state of his finances; others were deliberate, albeit also the product of defensive alteration, attempts to misrepresent that status. In reality, his income was always more than adequate; and he had been able to accumulate a considerable investment portfolio and other savings. Most, but not all, of his concerns and complaints about money (and one of his justifications for both his exaggerations and his lies) derived from the resentment of having to pay me and the insistence that my fees were depleting his financial resources. He related these resentments to elements of a personal myth that he had been materially deprived in his childhood. As we worked on these various distortions it was possible to demonstrate not only their projective character but also their relationship to his resentment at having been excluded from his parents' sexual secrets and to his fantasies of stealing and incorporating father's penis and power.

His lying about his money was an attempt to deny his oedipal victory over father and to disclaim an adolescent promise to provide financially for his mother. He recalled, now, the times, as a little boy, when he crept into his parents' bedroom and stole money from his father and searched for condoms in his father's bureau. On the transference level, the lies about the money represented his attempted denial of the fantasies of stealing my knowledge-power and penis. His poverty was proof-positive that he indeed was innocent in this respect, just as his pseudo-stupidity was evidence of his not having taken in any of my interpretations and ideas. Further analysis of these themes revealed the extent to which his alliance with his mother had served as a protection, not only against the punishment for real depreciation and provocation of his father, but even more significantly against the much more terrible retaliation for his unconscious fantasy of stealing the father's penis.

A much more complex and perplexing kind of lie was what we eventually labeled the "outrageous lie." With varying frequency during the first years of the analysis, the patient would make a statement more or less out of the blue and superficially senseless. Often these remarks were presented as somewhat pompous pronouncements, and there was much to suggest that they were a more specific elaboration of the type of speaking I described earlier as "contrived doubletalk." He might calmly walk into the office, lie down on the couch, and announce that he wanted to shoot me or, conversely, that he knew that I was going to hit him. Or, he might—without any preparatory remarks—declare that he had finished his analysis. On one occasion, he confided dramatically that he now understood what was the real source of his current problems: his car needed repairs. Not only were such declarations bizarre and quite surprising, but he made it clear that he was aware that these statements were not true and represented a kind of nonsense and an attempt at deception. However, it became evident to both of us that these remarks were by no means as nonsensical (Fenichel, 1939, pp. 132, 135; Greenacre, 1966) as they might sound; and that what he planned to present as lies were, in fact, distortions of very important fantasies.

A special variation of the "outrageous" lie was particularly helpful in understanding the structure and economic aspect of these phenomena. From time to time, the patient would, again quite histrionically, declare, "I can't believe it—I just *can't* believe it!" The "negation" could apply to any of a large number of topics with which he was dealing at that moment, but most frequently in relation to some intervention I had made. However, he said these things in a voice whose tone, timbre, and quality were quite at variance from the one I usually heard; it was a feminine "voice," which represented an imitation of and identification with his mother's when she became exasperated with his behavior. The more important aspect of this was that both the patient and (he was convinced) his mother "knew" that the "it" was true, that they did believe "it"; and that, therefore, the disclaimer was a lie. What he really wanted to say was that "I *won't* believe it" or "I don't want to believe it." What he didn't want to accept (at least at this stage of the analysis) was the recognition of his fear of me and the fear of a homosexual submission to me. The identification with his mother's "I can't believe it" was a reaffirmation of the fateful alliance with her as well as support for his wish not to believe what was real and dangerous. The detailed analysis of this material facilitated an understanding of his shifting identifications with mother and father and also the way in which that material served as a screen for and a link with earlier primal-scene experiences.

If (and this was especially so earlier in the analysis) I offered no response at all, his subsequent associations reflected his sense of satisfaction and relief that the "lie" had not been questioned. He felt safe for the moment, reassured that the analyst-mother was his ally and a witness to the fact that he was not "really lying," that he did not have forbidden fantasies, especially the oedipal ones—that he "had gotten away with it." The ostensible collusion in accepting the lie as the truth facilitated his denial and repression of the forbidden fantasies and the dangers associated with them.

If, however, I reacted in any way—even an innocuous clarifying question or a gentle comment—he became quite upset. At first, my failure to completely "ignore" the lie produced a mild anxiety and a vague feeling of being "caught." This was transitory, however, and what was much more conspicuous was an angry and righteous indignation as if I had violated a pact[1] by my intervention. He claimed that he was being criticized and he counterattacked with some variation of the "analyst is not supposed to be critical" theme.

A second group of reactions is best described by his statement, "I feel that I have been hit on the head." My not going along with his lie not only represented an exposure but also a punishment, the concretization of which was the sensation of my hitting him on the head. This was followed often by a period of quiet sadness and bleakness. It was a complicated affect state compounded by the humiliation of his exposure and the partial loss of his feelings of omnipotence, a feeling of helplessness and vulnerability, an identification with his humiliated father, and by a sense of guilt and remorse connected with his memories of maltreating the father.

The third category of reactions became clearer and more explicit after we had been able to deal with many of the elements in the lies and their underlying fantasies. He would become anything from quite anxious to almost panic-stricken. In this state, his associations were neither new

[1]This reaction of "righteous indignation" together with the allegation that I had violated a pact of some kind by failing to turn a completely deaf ear to his lies was, in one way or another, observed in all of these patients. It is a phenomenon that deserves a more detailed exposition than is possible here; but the analysis of this "violation of a contract" revealed that it was a repetition in the transference of the memory of the patient's "perception" that a forbidden relationship had been established, and would not be spoken about or otherwise revealed by either party. Because I have observed comparable fantasies in patients who did not lie, I have concluded that it is a product of the oedipal struggle rather than being more specifically related to the issue of lying.

nor extensive. Most explicit was the intensity of the "feeling" (often portrayed in visual images) of being caught and wanting to run. The fourth category was characterized by a specific symptom, produced *in situ* and an extension of the feelings of intense anxiety. At certain times, he would develop the sensation of being very far from me (or, conversely, that I was very distant from him). He felt strange and uncomfortable (but less anxious than when he had to cope with the feelings of incipient panic), was definitely aware of thoughts of being altogether trapped, fearing that I would hurt him, that he might harm me, that he would in some way lose me. This complex depersonalization-derealization symptom being repeated in the transference neurosis had its earliest roots in primal-scene fantasies; it was connected with oedipal conflicts and fears and subsequent phobias and an obsessive preoccupation with being "exiled," and included the memory of his father "discovering" his adolescent masturbation. You will realize, I am sure, that I have not attempted to present a complete exegesis or comprehensive formulation of all of the elements of this case or even of the various lies. I want to stress, however, that the analytic work around these "lies"—the resistances, defenses, fantasies, and reconstructions associated with them—comprised a very large part of this man's analysis and the key to understanding his life and personality. Before concluding the description of the case, I want to describe one other lie, the working through of which led to a mild depression and the termination phase of the analysis.

In the sixth year of his analysis, he reported an episode in which he had "overreacted" to a lie that his by-now oedipal age daughter had told her mother and which was coupled by speaking to her mother in a very insolent manner. He lost his temper, reprimanded her harshly, and quite uncharacteristically spanked her. He was terribly upset and ashamed of himself, but even more disturbing was the awareness of his intense fury and wish to hit her ever harder. During the course of our working over this event, a good deal of which involved a review and integration of much of the previous material in regard to his own lying, he produced a dream. In the dream, the patient was reading the stock market quotations in the financial section of a newspaper, and he was concerned with two items on the page. The first was something that stood for a lie; it was not very important but printed in large, bold-faced type. The second was an item that stood for the truth—but very important and quite dangerous—and printed in tiny type in an unobtrusive part of the page. However, that faintly visible item also had an asterisk along side of it! The subject matter of the two items was the manifest content for the patient's conflicts and fantasies deriving from his own oedipal drama. The formal aspects of the dream were, I believe, a most interesting replication of the structure of a "screen" as formulated by Freud (1899) and Fenichel (1939). The asterisk, however, can be seen as the tendency for the repressed to return and/or the patient's wish for the truth to come out.

Shortly after the patient presented this dream, he "confessed" what I think was his last lie in the analysis. A few days after telling me the dream, he had mentioned very casually a report he had to submit to his superior at work; and he had elaborated in some detail some of the content of that report—and I confess that the material had not made much of an impression on me. In that report he had committed a minor—one might say symbolic—falsification, and he repeated that lie to me. Although the fabrication was of no real significance, in terms of the patient's psychic reality it represented both textually and in his associations a condensation of the whole oedipal conflict and his desire to keep it out of awareness. Further, he recognized this deception as a last-ditch effort to re-establish old defenses and that he wanted urgently the analyst's participation in this deception; but, even though he had succeeded in the latter, he also realized that the deception gave him no comfort and no satisfaction. With considerable poignancy, he explained that if he were going to tell the truth, the responsibility for doing so would now have to be his own.

DISCUSSION

We still have much to learn about "not telling the truth" and about the "plain lie." Honesty and the capacity to tell the truth are highly venerated moral virtues in our society, but like so many of the moral virtues, our relation to them is both inconsistent and paradoxical. While we respect those who demonstrate these virtues, it is not infrequently a respect commingled with some cynicism and mistrust. The feeling that the truly honest man is somewhat gullible and naïve is not a rare attitude limited to the antisocial fringes; and a modern-day Diogenes is likely to be viewed as a quixotic figure open to condescension or gentle ridicule. The Catholic Church looks upon overscrupulosity as a sin; and H. L. Mencken (I believe) created the provocative oxymoron "pathological truth-telling," a phrase that doesn't even strike one as particularly incongruous. Psychoanalysts tend to talk about overcompensation or reaction formations.

We find it difficult to suspend disbelief at the claim of always telling the truth; and as Stein (1972, p. 238) points out, "This is hardly to be expected, and it is by no means certain that it would be altogether desirable. . . . The compulsion to tell the truth in every situation, without exception, is by no means a criterion for mental health. But the capacity to do so certainly is."

Outside of the analytic situation, if someone does not have the capacity to tell the truth, his communications and his relations with other people will soon be undermined. The same is true in analysis, at least up to a point; but in the analytic situation, the analyst is likely to have a somewhat different reaction. As analysts, we would of course be concerned with the overall capacity to tell the truth, but we would be less inclined to see it only as a moral issue (Calef and Weinshel, 1980). Rather, the analyst would probably accept these "lapses" as part of the analytic work. We may, of course, decide that the patient's thinking or his reality testing is so disturbed that he is unable to know the truth let alone report it, or that his need for self-aggrandizement is so imperative that the reporting is, in effect, governed by the pleasure principle rather than by an adherence to the needs of reality, or that his superego is so defective that there is the incapacity to understand and/or acknowledge the significance of the truth; and, if our assessments are such that we do not believe that these deficiencies will yield to analytic work, we may conclude that the patient is not analyzable and terminate the analytic efforts.

Moreover, in our accepting the patient's "lie" as a piece of at least potential analytic material, we view that material as having meaning, and distorted and idiosyncratic as it might be, as part of the patient's psychical reality. (See Arlow, 1969, p. 43 for an excellent conceptual definition of "psychic reality.") When a patient provides us with a memory which clearly must be a falsified rendition of the facts as they *occurred*, we would acknowledge the "general practice of using memory so earnestly as an instrument of mendacity" (Kempton, 1976, p. 22), but we would also hold that those mendacious fabrications reflect, on the other hand, the psychic realities of that patient and ". . . in the world of the neuroses it is psychical reality which is the decisive kind" (Freud, 1917, p. 368). Further, we assume that both the patient's distorted memory and his deliberate lie contain at least some trace of the historical truth (Avenburg and Guiter, 1976, pp. 13, 17; Freud, 1913a, p. 161; 1917, p. 367; 1937, p. 267; Deutsch, 1923, p. 159), just as we recognize the presence of the "grain of truth" in the confabulations of the Korsakov psychotic (Betlheim and Hartmann, 1924; Rapaport, 1950, pp. 226–231), the complaints of the malingerer (Eissler, 1951), the delusions of the paranoiac (Freud, 1937, p. 267), and the simulations of the imposter (Deutsch, 1955; Greenacre, 1958). And, finally, we see our task as "liberating the fragment of historical truth from its distortions and its attachments to the actual present day and in leading it back to the point in the past to which it belongs" (Freud, 1937, p. 268). Thus, the lies our patients tell us are viewed not primarily as moral lapses but as sources of potentially useful analytic data and as likely focal points for the reconstruction of critical, traumatic events.

I believe that these generalizations are applicable to the "lies" I have described and, taking into account the reservations I have outlined above, I would suggest that they may have validity, as well, for *all* of the lies (not just cases of pseudologia) our patients bring to us.

In my case discussions, I have stressed a number of central elements. Structurally, the lies represent a special instance of the "screen" functions (Freud, 1899, 1937; Arlow, 1969; Greenacre, 1949, 1975; Greenson, 1958; Fenichel, 1927, 1928, 1939; Reider, 1953)—wherein the screen serves as a vehicle for both revealing and concealing an oedipal secret, a secret that contained not only oedipal fantasies but earlier primal-scene components which had become integrated into the overall oedipal structure. As a relatively specific repetition of a much earlier screen experience, the lie is a particularly useful source of information about pivotal traumatic events and important unconscious fantasies and well suited for pursuing the reconstruction of those events. Dynamically, the lie represents one by-product of the interaction between the component forces in the patient's oedipal struggle. In my cases, the pregenital material was not the immediate precipitant for the production of the lies; but I am not prepared to state that in other cases, the pregenital factors may not be more central. I have also attempted to demonstrate that these lies were the means of expressing aggressive feelings toward one or both of the parents—and in the transference toward the analyst—particularly as a retaliation and revenge for lies told to the patient, and it is my impression that the angry focus on the parental deceptions was in itself a displacement and a screen for the oedipal frustrations. I have also tried to show that these lies constituted a highly condensed accusation of and exposure of the parents' own incestuous strivings toward the child, a topic which is somewhat murky in my own data and one worthy of further analytic investigation (Fenichel, 1939, p. 135; Freud, 1913b; Rangell, 1955). Economically, the lie functions primarily to maintain the repression and denial of painful unconscious material (Fenichel, 1927, p. 113; 1939, p. 133). Blum (1976, p. 168 and especially p. 180) has some pertinent and perceptive observations on "conscious lying" in analysis. Although he approaches the phenomenon from the point of view of acting out, he too stresses its role in "denial and other unconscious defenses." Lying is a disguise which subverts verbal free association, and Blum noted that what is not verbalized may also be enacted.

We know that everyone—or at least just about everyone—lies at some time and under some circumstances, but I confess that I am not able to spell out that specific concatenation of the "minimal and necessary" ingredients which would explain why some individuals would lie more often than others or why my essentially neurotic patients would lie in the analysis rather than utilize some other defensive configuration. My patients all focused on the fact that they had been lied to by at least one of their parents, and they very much wished to maintain the conviction that the parental lying had exerted a significant and lasting impact, which played a critical role in their fabrications. I found that these experiences represented a secondary—albeit not insignificant—rather than the primary factor in their own lying. I have already mentioned that my patients were individuals who, by and large, were people of "conscience" and integrity whose superegos functioned quite effectively and with reasonable autonomy. My patients' allegations that their analyst had, in effect, lied to them is a charge that cannot be dismissed lightly.

The lies my patients told me came up when highly-charged oedipal fantasy material was emerging in the transference (case 3 is somewhat more complex; but, essentially, the statement fits this instance as well) and the sense of dangers associated with the fantasy—both external and internal—produced anxiety, the need to maintain repression, and a search for "screen experiences" (Fenichel, 1927, 1939; Greenson, 1958; Reider, 1953), for something in the real world that could be used as a screen and as an object for projection. This search included a meticulous scrutiny of the analyst in order to rediscover some indication in what I said or did that could be seen as a replication of a childhood experience where the patient had felt the parent had lied; and I believe that this mechanism has its earlier roots in the attempt to cope with primal-scene excitation, a topic which cannot be pursued here.

The revivification of such a scene in the analysis appeared to be a necessary part of the process of forming a screen and an overall defensive configuration that had represented a critical element in dealing with a traumatic situation in the past. Under such psychological conditions, it was impossible for the patient *not* to find something in regard to the analyst which could be fitted in with his particular needs. I do not believe that I lied to my patients; but when the analyst is involved in the working through of these intense oedipal transference fantasies, the possibility of some regressive countertransferential manifestation and an unwitting collusion with the oedipal strivings of the patient cannot be discounted. Such a collusion might well serve as the "mote in the analyst's eye" and provide the basis for the patient's feeling that he is being lied to or otherwise deceived.

It may be that we could learn more about the nature and genesis of lying by understanding better its relationship to two, in themselves, related phenomena: fetishism and negation. In some respects the fetishistic paradigm is the unconscious formula "As long as I insist that 'A,' which I know is not true, is true, then I do not have to believe that 'B,' which I do not want to be true because it frightens me, is really true." Further—and again this is a topic about which my own data is fragmentary—as these patients described the childhood traumata associated genetically and dynamically with the lying, their reconstructions emphasized a specific perception: in the first patient, the mother's saying "nothing"; in the second, the sight of the naked father; in the third, the sound in adolescence of hearing his father come into the house while the patient was masturbating (in this case the adolescent memory was a screen for earlier trauma which cannot be detailed here). In many ways, those descriptions and emphases were most reminiscent of what Freud (1927, p. 155) called the "last impression" in the formation of the fetish.

The relationship between lying and negation is much more complex; and inasmuch as the subject of negation is such an important and, as yet, very vexing one, it is more appropriate to talk in terms of hoping that a fuller understanding of the phenomena of lying may contribute something to a better comprehension of the negation phenomenon (Freud, 1923, 1937, p. 262; Olinick, 1957, p. 319; Greenson, 1958, pp. 113–114; Arlow, 1969, p. 31; Weinshel, 1977 [chapter 2, this volume]). A lie could be defined as a "negation with conscious deception," but certainly the negating aspect of the lie is a significant one. Secondly, like negation, the lie (at least so I believe) is a "watershed" (or Janus-faced) concept: in one direction, the lie moves toward avoiding reality and concealing the truth, but in the other direction, it moves toward affirming a piece of reality and exposing a portion of the truth. Since most of my clinical data were collected during the phase of a regressive transference-neurosis, it was relatively easy to see the ways in which the lie was being used to deal with the perception of a particularly unpleasurable reality, and it has also occurred to me that the lie may represent one specific kind of regressive sexualization of the process of judgment. I raise these speculations in the anticipation that other analysts may have comparable observations and hypotheses about these clinical phenomena, which very much need further elucidation and elaboration.

I want to say just a word about the technical aspects of dealing with the lies. I do not believe that one can handle the lie *primarily* as a moral issue. I have been most successful in utilizing this material and bringing it into the analytic work (whether it involved a lie to the analyst or a lie to anyone else) when I treated it as a specific kind of resistance, i.e., of resorting to the fabrication as a means of not dealing with otherwise painful or potentially traumatic material. Using this approach in these cases, I found the lies to be extremely helpful in revealing data, and that without any additional effort on my part, "what is moral became self-evident" (a slight alteration of a statement by V. T. Vischer [in Hartmann, 1960, p. 14]) to the patients. In two other cases where patients have told me lies, I was not able to obtain relevant analytic material and not able to utilize productively the falsehoods in the analytic work. In these latter instances, I tended to deal with the lies from the point of view of superego lapses; and, empirically, the resistances increased, and the material was—at least at this level—lost to the analytic work.[2]

SUMMARY

Lying, in the analytic situation of essentially neurotic patients, is proposed to represent a re-enactment within the analysis and transference neurosis of a particular aspect of the oedipal conflict. These lies permit the partial recovery of old memories and perceptions; the emergence of

[2]This experience may be related to the statements Freud made at the beginning and at the end of his *Two Lies Told by Children* (1913b): "These lies occur under the influence of excessive feelings of love, and become momentous when they lead to a misunderstanding between the child and the person it loves" (p. 305), and "We should not think lightly of such episodes in the life of a child. It would be a serious mistake to read into childish misdemeanors like these a prognosis of the development of a bad character" (p. 309).

certain unconscious wishes and fantasies, while simultaneously continuing to protect those wishes by a variety of mechanisms which are best conceptualized as "screen functions"; and the expression of resentment over being lied to by one or both of the oedipal objects. Connections are also made between the oedipally determined lie and an infantile primal-scene trauma.

REFERENCES

Arlow, J. (1969), Fantasy, memory, and reality testing. *Psychoanal. Quart.*, 38:28–51.

Avenburg, R. & Guiter, M. (1976), The concept of truth in psychoanalysis. *Internat. J. Psycho-Anal.*, 57:11–18.

Betlheim, S. E. & Hartmann, H. (1924), On parapraxes in the Korsakow psychosis. In: *Organization and Pathology of Thought*, ed. D. Rapaport. New York: Columbia University Press, 1951, pp. 288–307.

Blum, H. (1976), Acting out, the psychoanalytic process and interpretation. In: *The Annual of Psychoanalysis*, 4:163–184. New York: International Universities Press.

Brunswick, R. M. (1943), The accepted lie. *Psychoanal. Quart.*, 12:458–464.

Calef, V. (1972), "I am awake": Insomnia or dream? *Psychoanal. Quart.*, 41: 161–171.

_______ & Weinshel, E. M. (1980), The analyst as the conscience of the analysis. *Internat. Rev. Psycho-Anal.*, 7:279–290.

Deutsch, H. (1923), Pathological lying [abstract]. *Internat. J. Psycho-Anal.*, 4:159.

_______ (1955), The imposter. *Psychoanal. Quart.*, 24:483–505.

Eissler, K. (1951), Malingering. In: *Psychoanalysis and Culture*, ed. G. B. Wilbur & W. Muensterberger. New York: International Universities Press, pp. 218–253.

Fenichel, O. (1927), The economic function of screen memories. *Collected Papers*, First series. New York: Norton, 1953, pp. 113–116.

_______ (1928), The inner injunction to "make a mental note." *Collected Papers*, First series. New York: Norton, 1953, pp. 153–154.

_______ (1939), The economics of pseudologia phantastica. *Collected Papers*, Second series. New York: Norton, 1954, pp. 129–140.

Freud, S. (1899), Screen memories. *Standard Edition*, 3:301–322.

_______ (1913a), Totem and taboo. *Standard Edition*, 13:1–162.

_______ (1913b), Two lies told by children. *Standard Edition*, 12:305–309.

_______ (1917), Introductory lectures on psycho-analysis. *Standard Edition*, 16:243–463.

_______ (1923), Negation. *Standard Edition*, 19:234–239.

_______ (1927), Fetishism. *Standard Edition*, 21:149–157.

_______ (1937), Constructions in analysis. *Standard Edition*, 23:256–269.

Greenacre, P. (1949), A contribution to the study of screen memories. In: *Trauma, Growth and Personality*. New York: International Universities Press, 1952, pp. 188–203.

_______ (1958), The imposter. In: *Emotional Growth*. New York: International Universities Press, 1971, pp. 93–112.

_______ (1966), On nonsense. In: *Emotional Growth*. New York: International Universities Press, 1971, pp. 592–615.

_______ (1975), On reconstruction. *J. Amer. Psychoanal. Assn.*, 23:693–712.

Greenson, R. (1958), On screen defenses, screen hunger, and screen identity. In: *Explorations in Psychoanalysis*. New York: International Universities Press, 1978, pp. 111–132.

Hartmann, H. (1960), *Psychoanalysis and Moral Values*. New York: International Universities Press.

Kempton, M. (1976), Witness review of *Scoundrel Time* by L. Hellman. *New York Review of Books*, 22:22–25.

Kernberg, O. (1975), *Borderline Conditions and Pathological Narcissism*. New York: Jason Aronson.

Olinick, S. (1957), Questioning and pain, truth and negation. *J. Amer. Psychoanal. Assn.*, 5:302–324.

Rangell, L. (1955), The return of the repressed "Oedipus." *Bull. Menn. Clin.*, 19:9–15.

Rapaport, D. (1950), *Emotions and Memory*. New York: International Universities Press.

Reider, N. (1953), Reconstruction and screen function. *J. Amer. Psychoanal. Assn.*, 1:389–405.

Stein, M. (1972), A clinical illustration of a moral problem in psychoanalysis. In: *Moral Values and the Superego Concept in Psychoanalysis*, ed. S. C. Post. New York: International Universities Press, 1972, pp. 226–243.

Waldhorn, H. (1960), Assessment of analyzability: Technical and theoretical observations. *Psychoanal. Quart.*, 29:478–506.

Weinshel, E. M. (1977), "I didn't mean it": Negation as a character trait. *The Psychoanalytic Study of the Child*, 32:387–420. New Haven: Yale University Press.

Chapter 4

1981

Some Clinical Consequences of Introjection

Gaslighting

Victor Calef and Edward M. Weinshel

In April of 1978 a cartoon by William Hamilton, the creator of the popular "The Now Society" series, depicted a man and a woman glaring at each other. Their facial expressions and bodily postures reflect surprised anger and uncompromising indignation. The caption reads, "I am not pushing your buttons. You are pushing my buttons."

The broader concept of gaslighting is suggested in the "button" cartoon of William Hamilton, while the more limited aspects are suggested in Patrick Hamilton's (1939) play, *Angel Street,* later adapted into the popular movie, *Gaslight,* starring Ingrid Bergman and Charles Boyer. Most readers are probably familiar with the main elements of that story. A thirty-one-year-old innocent, newly-wedded woman is driven to the brink of madness by the deliberate machinations of her criminal husband. His intent is to make her uncertain of her hold on reality in order to commit her to an institution. He is plotting to retrieve some jewels (suggesting a thieving acquisitiveness, i.e., greed) hidden in the house in which the couple are living. It was because of the jewels that the villain, now posing as hero, had years earlier murdered an old woman. One of the ways in which he was able to shake his wife's confidence in her own perceptions was to alter the brightness of the gaslights in the house; hence the title of the movie and our paper. During the play, it develops that the villain-husband is the one who is mentally disturbed, perhaps psychotic.

The work of both Hamiltons portrays the confusion of the victims who struggle with the feeling that their minds are being "worked over," their thoughts influenced, and the validity of their perceptions undermined. Meanwhile, the victimizers perpetrate these distortions, disavowing them and even claiming that they themselves are the victims.

Our paper, the cartoon, and the play all deal with one human potential: the ability to disavow (with the help of a variety of defenses) that which has been introjected and/or the ability to incorporate and to assimilate that which others externalize and project onto them. The ubiquity and the diverse permutations of these phenomena encompass so many areas of interpersonal behavior that we cannot possibly describe all of the varieties of gaslighting. We will sketch out some examples and present some hypotheses in regard to dynamic and genetic factors. We are aware that we merely present old wine in a somewhat different bottle and that the phenomena we describe have been known to all under different labels; for example, we describe some of the ways in which sadomasochistic exchanges between people are manifested. Our report is a preliminary one which contains a number of issues requiring further study and more extensive elaboration.

SOME REFLECTIONS ON THE LITERATURE

There are a number of British papers (Barton and Whitehead, 1969; Smith and Sinanan, 1972) which have applied the term gaslighting primarily to those situations in which one individual has attempted to make others feel that a second individual is crazy so that the latter will be taken to a mental hospital. These authors, who do not have a psychodynamic approach, imply that such occurrences are by no means rare. In a number of the cases, the "gaslightee" became increasingly uneasy and even symptomatic.

A related phenomenon is the attempt to drive someone actually crazy. This is a topic which has attracted the interest of those who work with schizophrenics and other psychotics. It is a theme which runs through some of Laing's (1960) work. Arieti (1955), in the first edition of his book on schizophrenia, speaks of "acted-out" or "externalized" psychosis. Without much elaboration he refers to persons who "often create situations which will precipitate or engender psychoses in other people whereas they themselves remain immune from overt symptoms" (pp. 142–143). Comparable observations have been made by those who work with the "double bind" concept (Bateson, 1962; Jackson, et al., 1956; Sluzki and Vernon, 1971), especially in regard to the impact of the family on the identified schizophrenic patient. Revitch (1954) has some interesting data and ideas on what he calls "conjugal paranoia," in which the truly psychotic mate manages to appear healthy while the marital partner is judged to be mentally sick.

Searles (1965) concerns himself with a number of issues which bear on the theme of our essay. He points out, for instance (pp. 32–34), the significance of the differences between the intrapsychic and the interpersonal processes in working with schizophrenic patients. Searles writes about mental states such as confusion and perplexity and argues that the emergence of a delusion may represent the attempt to find relief from the anguish associated with these states of mental uncertainty (pp. 70–113). He suggests that in interaction with other factors, "the individual becomes schizophrenic partly by reason of a long-continued effort, a largely or wholly unconscious effort, on the part of some person or persons highly important in his upbringing to drive him crazy" (p. 954). Searles raises the possibility that "the inexperienced or unconsciously sadistic analyst" who makes many premature or otherwise inappropriate interpretations might drive a patient psychotic. He points to a number of modes of driving another person crazy, stating that "each of these techniques tends to undermine the other person's confidence in the reliability of his own emotional reactions and his own perceptions of outer reality" (p. 260).

The British school of psychoanalysts, especially the followers of Melanie Klein, have been interested in some of these questions. The concept of projective identification, although considered to be an intrapsychic mechanism, needs to be carefully compared with what we here consider as gaslighting, since the clinical phenomena may be similar, if not identical, while our formulations may differ (Bion, 1956; Klein, 1946 [especially pp. 8–12], 1955; Rosenfeld, 1950; Segal, 1964). Bion (p. 344) defines projective identification as "a splitting off by the patient of a part of his personality and a projection of it into the object where it becomes installed, sometimes as a persecutor, leaving the psyche from which it has been split off correspondingly impoverished." Segal (p. 126) writes: "Projective identification is the result of the projection of parts of the self into an object. It may result in the object being perceived as having acquired the characteristics of the projected part of the self but it can also result in the self becoming identified with the object of its projections."[1]

[1]For a careful critique published after this paper was written, see Meissner (1980).

Freud's (1909) monograph on the Rat Man contains a number of statements on doubt and doubting mania, and in *The Future Prospects of Psycho-Analytic Therapy* (1910) he alludes to the role of suggestive influences (pp. 146–148). Fenichel (1945) also takes up the subjects of obsessive doubting (for instance, pp. 297–300), perplexity (pp. 418–420), and the role of introjection (p. 428). Niederland (1960, 1963) has written extensively on the "influences" which may have contributed to Schreber's psychosis; and Shengold (1975a, 1975b, 1977) has focused on the subject of soul murder.

CLINICAL ILLUSTRATIONS

Case 1

A wife described her husband as a handsome, prominent, professionally successful young man, forceful, articulate, and quietly domineering. He appeared to be solid and normal, in many ways the epitome of the All American Boy. His wife was a quiet, retiring, but intelligent woman who was at her husband's beck and call. Although she had done extremely well at college, she appeared to be content to submerge her own interests and talents and to devote herself to her husband's needs and career. She was considered to be nervous and neurotic, a typical "scatterbrain." The children, one boy and one girl, exhibited a series of psychological difficulties which brought them under the care of child psychiatrists. It was the consensus of the family that the wife was the sick individual whose problems had been responsible for the children's difficulties.

One typical example of the family's behavior follows. The husband is driving through the city streets at fifty or more miles per hour. He drives calmly, with his arm resting in comfort upon the window ledge; and, with an air of nonchalance, he does not indicate any concerns for the family's safety. He does, however, repeatedly warn his wife and children to keep an eye out for the police. His wife and his children are in a state of near panic as he ignores their pleas for him to slow down and drive more carefully. He demeans them for their anxiety. He is content that he is behaving normally and that the rest of the family are overly emotional and irrationally concerned. Fortunately, no catastrophe occurs.

Both husband and wife considered the wife to be a disturbed, illogical woman whose actions appeared to verge on the psychotic. This is why she first consulted a psychiatrist. She and the children presented florid fears and strange behavior; and for a long time the nature of their difficulties did not become clear to their respective psychiatrists. The situation continued over a number of years with relatively little change, especially in regard to the relationship of the husband and wife. He was coolly tolerant of her illness, but at the same time made it evident that he was displeased and misused in having to put up with such chaotic and irrational behavior.

Gradually, however, first the children and then the wife responded to therapy; and in doing so, their relationship to the father-husband changed, first subtly and then more strikingly. She began to ignore his dictatorial behavior and to question his omniscience. She began to separate herself from his domination and to develop a life of her own. She became active in community affairs and, for the first time, spoke up in social situations. At first her husband seemed pleased; but after a while he became annoyed and openly disparaging of her "new personality." When no one responded to his criticisms and to his attempts to undermine the improvement in the rest of the family, he began to withdraw, to become despondent, and to develop a series of psychosomatic conditions. His mental state deteriorated; and within a relatively short time, he manifested a series of bizarre actions which disrupted his professional life. He went through a brief psychosis, after which his marriage dissolved. He married a much younger woman who seemed content to accept the role which the previous wife had rejected. The wife remarried and functions efficiently and quite happily in a different atmosphere. The children are doing well both socially and academically and have not received psychiatric attention for many years.

We are not able to reconstruct all of the detailed dynamics of this complex case; and we have virtually no first-hand data in regard to the husband. However, one aspect of the wife's history is extremely pertinent. She was the only child of parents whose relationship in many ways was like that in her own marriage. The father was a driving, self-made, domineering man who treated his wife with contempt and condescension. For years, he flaunted a sexual relationship with his secretary. When her mother protested, he would insist she was "crazy" or "paranoid." Her protestations were weak and perfunctory; she retreated into the role of the servile handmaiden to the father, and she would timidly confide to her daughter that he must be correct, and that there was, indeed, something wrong with her. The daughter, later the wife in our original family, was confused. She felt on one hand that there was something wrong with her mother; but she was also reasonably sure that the father was involved in an illicit affair. Further, the father quite openly favored the daughter over the mother, a situation which the daughter found both gratifying and guilt producing, clear indications of oedipal victories from which she was forced to retreat. In the daughter's subsequent treatment, the identification with the mother, especially in respect to those elements which were central to the whole gaslighting process, were explored quite exhaustively. It was the clarification of these areas of her personality which permitted her to become free of her husband's gaslighting proclivities. Although the data are from a remote source, there was reason to believe that this wife's father harbored paranoid propensities. Just as her husband had been able to "transfer" his psychotic tendencies and his underlying fears of those tendencies onto his wife and children, her father had been even more successful in perpetrating the same kind of manipulation with her mother.

Case 2

Less dramatic examples of gaslighting are seen frequently in clinical practice. An intelligent, attractive, middle-aged woman reluctantly came to consult one of us at the behest of her somewhat older husband. He had urged her to see a psychiatrist because of her inability to accept his brief affair with a much younger woman. As far as the wife knew, there had not been any previous infidelity, but she was not able either to accept her husband's assurances that there would be no repetitions or to stop her anxious ruminating over what had taken place more than a year before. She was troubled by the conviction that she had been betrayed and felt that she had lost that comforting sense of trust in her husband. Even more troublesome, she had lost the sense of trust in her own judgment. Following his initial confession, the husband directly and through subtle indirection changed his position of guilty defensiveness to one of shifting the blame and responsibility to his compliant wife. He exerted a considerable amount of pressure on her to "forget about the past and start afresh" (which she tried to do but just could not) and argued that his affair was essentially her fault because their sex life had been unsatisfactory. He insisted that he had repeatedly told her about his dissatisfaction; and since there had not been any "real response" on her part, he felt that his taking up with the younger woman was really "for the good of both of us." The patient was not able to recall such discussions—which only added to her discomfort. Later, on questioning her husband about his alleged earlier warnings, she got him to acknowledge that he had not really discussed his dissatisfaction with her except in a vague and indirect way. Even after this admission the patient was unable to shake off completely the concern that she had not heard, not listened, not remembered, what he had allegedly said. Consequently, she was burdened with feelings of shame and inadequacy in respect to her sexual role and concerned with the adequacy of her mental functioning. She worried that perhaps she was losing her mind "a little bit," and this uneasiness was accentuated by the husband's pressure to have her see a psychiatrist. It was only later that she was able to understand and to accept that, at least in part, her husband's infidelity, as well as his allegations of her inadequacy, related to his increasing anxiety about his growing older and his waning sexual potency. Although we did not have first-hand data about the husband's conflicts and modes of coping with them, we believe that he needed to disavow and externalize his own sexual conflicts and fears onto his wife. She had immersed herself in her husband's life and work. Her sense of self-esteem was dependent on a vicarious participation in her husband's personality and activity. For her to question, let alone reject, her husband's statement entailed a significant psychological loss.

DEFINITION AND CHARACTERISTICS

Perhaps these brief examples will permit us to sketch out a conceptual definition and some general characteristics of gaslighting. It is, first of all, a piece of behavior in which one individual, with varying degrees of success, attempts to influence the judgment of a second individual by causing the latter to doubt the validity of his or her own judgment. The motivation may be conscious, although it is usually unconscious; and almost invariably the conscious motives are rationalizations and/or distortions of deeper, more complex, and less acceptable motives. The victim becomes uncertain and confused in regard to his or her assessment of internal or external perceptions and the integrity of his or her reality testing. Schematically, at least, gaslighting should be differentiated from those phenomena in which there may be comparable experiences of doubt and uncertainty about one's perceptions primarily because of intrapsychic difficulties, such as in severe obsessional doubting, psychotic impairment of reality testing, and organic conditions in which the whole process of judgment is impaired. We say "schematically at least" because in practice internal conflicts always play some part.

Gaslighting generally involves one person, the victimizer, who tries to impose his judgment on a second person, the victim. This imposition is based on a very special kind of "transfer" ("dumping" is a less elegant and more accurate term [see Langs, 1976]) of painful or potentially painful mental conflicts. Any kind of mental content or function may be transferred, such as affects, perceptions, impulses, resistances, fantasies, delusions, conflicts. The basic motive for such an activity is the removal of the attendant anxiety.

The experience of the victim is more complex and less clear. Such individuals have a tendency to incorporate and to assimilate what others externalize and project onto them. We do not have a precise, overall formula which would explain why some individuals respond with a nonconflicted refutation, others with an angry rejection, and still others with what appears on the surface to be a docile, uncritical acceptance of such an attempt.

One variant of the latter group is the patient who is concerned with internal changes which are the harbinger of a real psychosis. Such an individual in effect says to herself, "He says I am crazy; but even though I believe that he's right, it can't be right because he is saying that to make me feel I'm crazy. Therefore I'm not really crazy." This complex form of negation and magical undoing is in many ways reminiscent of some cases of malingering wherein the fear of real psychosis is allayed and denied by making believe that one is psychotic.

In our own experience a second variant frequently occurs. We are referring to those individuals who are constantly afraid that if a secret fantasy (often some variation of a hidden penis fantasy) were exposed and known, others would consider them to be crazy. These are the patients who are convinced that their fantasies are so unduly bizarre as to be crazy. When the gaslighting attempts include other allegations of craziness, these individuals are all too eager to accept the allegations which they know to be erroneous and unfounded because they cover and keep secret that which they feel to be the true craziness of their fantasies.

In the gaslighting partnership some individuals, by their characterological make-up, seem to be predisposed to playing the role of either victimizer or victim. The roles, however, may oscillate within a given relationship; and not infrequently, each of the participants is convinced that he or she is the victim.

GASLIGHTING IN THE THERAPEUTIC SITUATION

The psychology of gaslighting is of considerable significance for all psychotherapists. The psychotherapeutic situation puts the therapist in a position of great influence vis-à-vis the patient, and all the therapist's interventions take on a more than ordinary importance. Moreover, the transference with its mobilization of previous object relationships and forgotten memories can produce a feeling of ambiguity and uncertainty. The formal structure of the analytic interchange, the use of the couch, the anonymity of the analyst, his relative silence, the decreased sensory input to the patient, the analysand's not infrequent feeling of helplessness, and the patient's inevitable uncertainty as to whether he is dealing with external or psychical reality—all contribute to the burden with which the patient must cope in differentiating inner from outer, self from object. All of this is accentuated in the intense atmosphere of those periods in the analysis which we designate as the transference neurosis, in which we can frequently observe transient episodes of altered consciousness. And perhaps most important of all, there is the whole array of countertransference reactions in which the analyst may facilitate the distortion of the patient's perceptions or impose his own perceptions on the patient.

On the other hand, many of these same considerations may operate in the other direction; that is, analysts may become the victims of gaslighting maneuvers. Analysts are also prone to transference reactions, with the mobilization of old memories, conflicts and feelings. They too must be prepared for the impact of reduced sensory input and for the regressive consequences of "freely suspended attention." They serve as objects for the patients' feelings and desires; and they daily face a barrage of emotional pressures and a variety of complaints and accusations. They may be told that they are cold, uncaring, distant, hostile, seductive, unsympathetic, dishonest, incompetent, stupid, and sadistic; and at times, they will not be sure that the patients are not correct. Analysts inevitably become the targets for the patients' disavowals, defenses, and externalizations. Patients try to "transfer" their unacceptable feelings and conflicts onto analysts. Since those feelings and conflicts are often universal, analysts may not always find it easy to separate what the patients wrongly ascribe to them from what truly belongs to them. We would add, therefore, to the long list of our professional hazards that of being gaslighted. In the transference, ironically enough, analysts may be accused of being gaslighters. It is, after all, anything but a rarity for patients to complain that analysts are using suggestion, influencing their thoughts, putting words into their mouths, and driving them crazy. And one of the classical signs of the onset of the transference neurosis is a patient's insistence that "everything would be fine if I weren't in analysis." What needs to be differentiated in all these psychological occurrences is that which is externalized or projected from that which is simply an introjection of a fantasy about the analyst that serves the function of a disavowal and is not a projection at all.

These interactions in the therapeutic situation are commonplace and by no means limited to the more disturbed patients. The following vignettes come from reasonably healthy "neurotic" analysands.

FURTHER CLINICAL ILLUSTRATIONS

Case 3

A young woman argues that the analysis is a "typical catch-22 situation." She alludes to her passivity, a topic which has been in the center of the analytic work for many months. She concedes, with some self-satisfaction, that it is true that she tends to be helpless; but what can she do about it? She recognizes that she waits for others to take care of her and take responsibility for her, but isn't that the reason for her being in analysis? If that passivity is her trouble, how can the analyst expect her to do the analytic work? Isn't it reasonable for her to wait for someone else to do it for her? Isn't the analyst being unreasonable, and isn't he being unreasonably uncaring, expecting her to do something which is more than she can do? There is little doubt that she experiences a degree of triumph as she presents her brief to the analyst.

The intent of her presentation is quite clear. On the one hand, if the analyst is silent, and does not agree with her position of helplessness, he is unfeeling, unempathic, and sadistic. On the other hand, if he does intervene—and virtually no matter what he says in this context will be experienced as his concession and her victory—he is gratifying a variety of neurotic wishes and, in effect, colluding in her current resistances. In a sense, then, it is the analyst who is helpless. The fact that this is true only in a sense does not alter the intent or the dynamic interaction, which must be dealt with for the analytic work to resume. Indeed, she wants the analyst to make clear which of his values and ideals she might incorporate and identify with—without being considered hostile, evil, aggressive, destructive, etc.

At the same time, it is important to realize that in some respects the patient is quite correct in what she is saying; and her behavior can be understood in that light. Most immediately, the patient is correct in that the analyst did say that she was passive and that she avoided responsibility. However neutrally those observations were conveyed, they carried with them critical overtones and a feeling of impatience. Moreover, the interaction in the transference touches on old memories and conflicts. She was the youngest of five children, and the whole family treated her as weak, delicate, and helpless. In fact, there was a definite premium in her behaving accordingly. This took on particular significance in her being a girl as well as the baby in the family. We cannot go into all of the interesting details of her development and how she tried to adapt to these external patterns and her own internal reactions (particularly during and after the oedipal conflicts). One of these adaptive mechanisms was the emergence of a special and specific identification which became a kind of caricature of how she felt she was viewed by the family. The exaggeration of her helplessness, passivity, and ineptness served many functions: it provided her with the opportunity of being treated as a special pet (rather than a failure in the oedipal conflict); it provided her with a vehicle for justifying her hostile, vindictive feelings about the infantilizing and about her own sense of inadequacy in regard to being little and being a woman (and doing so in a manner which made counterretaliation difficult); and it provided her with a defensive configuration which covered her more painful disappointment in not having a penis. She presented herself as a passive child rather than a castrated woman. As long as she was passive she did not have to deal directly with the derivatives of her sense of castration and her penis envy. Yet in her own mind (and not always completely unconsciously) her very behavior was a thinly disguised, exhibitionistic accusation about being deprived of a penis; and at a deeper level it also diverted her and others from her fantasy of really possessing a secret phallus by means of an aggressive orality. We cannot pursue the topic here, but it may well be that such a fantasy is an integral part of many gaslighting ploys.

Case 4

The analyst was, for periods of time, reduced to a state of impatient frustration and the feeling of "I'm losing my mind." The patient was a bright, compulsive lawyer in his mid-twenties who came to analysis with feelings of depression, primarily in relation to his sexual problems. The analysis proceeded quite smoothly until there were manifestations of a transference neurosis. Gradually, the patient stopped bringing in significant analytic material; and he would talk endlessly of what seemed to be pointless complaints about trivial matters. Although he had previously demonstrated an excellent facility for moving back and forth from, and seeing connections with, his external life, his past, the transference, dreams, and fantasies, now he was absorbed in the minutiae of everyday living. Although he had previously used his dreams as a point of departure for solid analytic work with an abundance of associations, now he would relate a dream and make no effort to work with the dream material. Never had the analyst felt that his interpretations were so ineffective and so useless; and never had he felt, with a patient whom he believed he understood and with whom there existed an empathic harmony, so left out and so disconnected. The interpretations were met with a kind of annoyance (because the patient did not enjoy being interrupted) or with an unenthusiastic "yes, I was thinking about that." When queried about why he had not said "that," the patient became vague and evasive and quickly wandered off the subject. Sometimes the "yes, I was thinking about that" response would be followed by a whole series of confirmatory associations which very rapidly radiated out centrifugally from himself and the analysis to all sorts of external events, movies, books, etc. For many months there was hardly a session in which the patient alluded to anything the analyst had said.

The only clues as to what was going on (other than the analyst's despair and a kind of "what am I doing wrong" feeling) were that the patient obviously wanted to talk, even though it did not appear that he wanted to say anything; that he wanted the analyst to listen rather than talk; and—this came through only faintly—that he wanted to be complimented and admired.

Finally, there were a number of sessions in which the patient complained of often trivial situations in which he had been with someone (business associate, old friends, woman friend) and had felt left out, although he never stated this quite clearly. Moreover, his feeling of being left out always had to do with interchanges in which he had said something and there had not been what he felt to be an appropriate response. It was not clear what he considered to be an "appropriate" response. Without being entirely aware of what he was saying, the analyst commented that perhaps the patient felt that these people weren't listening to him. This clearly touched the right chord. For the first time in months, the patient responded with a restrained "aha" reaction. (The analyst had many times brought up the patient's concern about the analyst's really listening, without any apparent response.) He went on to explain how sensitive he was to people really listening, adding "even if I'm not saying anything important." In the next week, he told for the first time of how, as a child, he had tried to attract his parents' attention and how they invariably ignored him or sloughed him off with a perfunctory reply. When he was between five and eight years old, the family would frequently have adult guests to dinner. The conversations were invariably weighty and intellectual. This very bright boy wanted to participate, but virtually no attention was paid to his questions or comments. It is likely that many of the occasions the patient could recall were those in which the adult group was fairly inebriated. To these felt rejections he reacted not only with frustration, anger, and the feeling of intense inadequacy, but with the vague, amorphous feeling that he was losing his mind. It was never clear whether the latter sensations were transient depersonalization-derealization states or whether they were replications of how he had experienced the primal scene as a much younger boy; subsequent data from the later stages of the analysis support the latter hypothesis, i.e., he could not trust his perceptions of the primal scene.

At some time during this period, probably when he was around seven years old, he started to talk more and became a "chatterbox." He recalled being chided for talking a lot and not making much sense; however, later it was also true that people listened. Actually, as he entered adolescence, he became an excellent speaker and debater and was feared as a devastating opponent in an argument. There is a parallel line to this story which can be summarized only briefly. At about the same time that these dinner parties were going on, the patient's father had to be away from home a great deal. The patient spent an inordinate amount of time with his mother, who was also moderately depressed. For the boy the period was an extremely difficult one. He very much enjoyed in a sexualized way the attention from his mother, but he felt that it was not enough. She would drop him to be with the other children, her friends, and probably her lover. He developed the fantasy that the rejections by mother were the result of his sexual inadequacy, his small penis. He felt cheated and felt that he deserved mother even though he did not have the wherewithal to please her. He developed strong sadistic fantasies about women. His sexual problems with women in later life reflected these sadistic fantasies, together with a wish that he, and even more his penis, be admired even if he did not function well sexually. If this admiration was not forthcoming, he would become depressed and angry and withdraw in one way or another. One of the things that impressed him in his relations with women was how often they would complain that his sexual behavior was driving them crazy. Later in the analytic work, it was reconstructed that as a boy he had felt "crazy" trying to deal with his mother—with her seductiveness, his own sexual feelings, and his helplessness because of his inadequacy. However, it was not simply his biological inadequacy as a child that was involved. It was rather that, just because of his inordinate insatiability, he ascribed to his mother the notion that he was inadequate and then introjected (identified with) that view of himself, thereby disavowing both his greed and his inadequacy. This is not the same as projection or externalization, although from a purely behavioral point of view, it resembles those defensive techniques.

It seemed reasonable to the patient that the analyst had somehow "snubbed" or disparaged him. And this triggered the mobilization of these old conflicts. In the analysis the patient reverted to being a chatterbox who had to be listened to even though he was not saying anything, and his words—his symbolic phallus—had to be admired even though they were not effective. For the sake of revenge, and as a magical kind of communication, he wanted to make the analyst feel as he had felt as a child: helpless, impatient, confused, and crazy. In the re-experiencing of these feelings in the transference neurosis, he tried with some success to "dump" or transfer those feelings onto the analyst.

THE PERVASIVE NATURE OF GASLIGHTING

Our incomplete survey of the literature indicates that the majority of those contributions which deal with what we consider to be the clinical phenomena of gaslighting concern themselves predominantly with psychosis, especially with schizophrenia. While we are very much aware of the importance of these considerations in both the possible etiology and the treatment of these conditions, our own interest and experience is with the neurotic or the "normal" patient. It is our contention that gaslighting phenomena are both ubiquitous and inevitable; we believe that they play a significant role in human relationships, exert an important influence in the marriage relationship, and exercise a sometimes overlooked impact on the course of psychotherapy. The "bridges" from the intrapsychic and the interpersonal to the broader social areas are numerous, already well known, and are combined in our everyday idioms. Brainwashing, credibility gap, and subliminal perception advertising techniques are among the more obvious examples. The whole question of political manipulation and the ways in which advertising exercises control over our taste, purse strings, and lives are intertwined with the questions we have raised in regard to clinical gaslighting.

Where, then, does gaslighting fit in this diverse array of psychopathology? Is gaslighting merely a somewhat more colorful term for the traditional mechanism of projection? Although we have acknowledged that those phenomena which we call gaslighting have already been described many times in many ways, we do not think that gaslighting can be equated with projection or is determined by that defense mechanism. It may be both appropriate and necessary to think about a whole spectrum of defense mechanisms, in which introjection is the first and foremost line of defense for purposes of disavowal of the instinctual-impulse derivatives. In regard to gaslighting, we are dealing with a very complex, highly structured configuration which encompasses contributions from many elements of the psychic apparatus and from a number of levels of consciousness. Although both the gaslighter and the gaslightee may have considerable awareness of what is transpiring, this awareness is only a partial one. Often the ostensible explanations are rationalizations and other defensive distortions. Further, while projection is essentially an intrapsychic phenomenon, gaslighting is a process which involves two people. And as Fenichel (1945) suggested in his formulations of pseudologia fantastica, "the denying effect is intensified if other persons (as 'witnesses') can be made to believe in the truth of the denying fantasy" (p. 529). (See also, Wangh [1962] in his "Evocation of a Proxy.") When there is no available victim onto whom the unacceptable mental conflict can be transferred, it is our impression that the potential gaslighter becomes more pressured and anxious and may regress. This is an area which needs further study. One of us (Weinshel, 1986) has described a number of cases in which, during the transference neurosis, regressive perceptual distortions occurred that involved the incorporation of the analyst's phallus. The patients' relinquishment of reality testing and perceptual judgment seems to have been related to a regressive reaction of old (and corrupt) superego introjects who—in these instances—served as the gaslighters.

SOME DYNAMIC CONSIDERATIONS

We have already suggested that the basic motive for the gaslighting is to rid oneself of unacceptable mental content or functions, not by a random expulsion and externalization, but by "transferring" that content to another individual. The gaslighter may demonstrate many of the characteristics of the paranoic, but paranoid breaks with reality are avoided, and fears of craziness are kept at a distance. Here we are referring not only to certain relatively realistic concerns in regard to poor reality testing or the fear of loss of control over various impulses, but also to a more idiosyncratic anxiety about the significance of various conscious or less-than-conscious fantasies which are felt to be bizarre, terrible, perverse—hence, crazy. We feel that the latter concerns, rather than the manifestations of an actual or threatened psychotic process, are responsible for most of the gaslighting attempts.

As we have reviewed our clinical data from material which goes back more than fifteen years as well as that related in this paper, we have become convinced that what we are encountering in the gaslighting are the specific outcomes of *greed* which have their origins in early oral, cannibalistic impulses. We are not suggesting that this is the only possible outcome of the need to deal with greed; rather, it is a very important group of ways which the psychological apparatus has available to control and to manage the greed. The emphasis here is not simply on the greed (especially oral greed, with all of the implications of aggression) but much more importantly on the control aspects of the behaviors involved.

Greed is an affective state, a fusion of instinctual forces, that has been of much greater interest to the Kleinlan analysts than to ourselves. We have not found the Kleinian formulations in regard to greed (and to projective identification and its technical handling) to be convincing or congenial. In part, this is because of their emphasis on primitive instinctual forces and projective defense, an emphasis which does not adequately recognize other control mechanisms which reject or struggle against the introjects. Greed is not a particularly acceptable feeling; it is one which conjures up frightening fantasies. Further, its connection with orality and with oral sadism make it likely that greed may be one of the earliest mental contents which has to be eliminated, and care has to be taken that it not be directed toward another individual. We have a number of observations indicating that one of the earliest ways in which even a well-intentioned parent may gaslight a child may be in connection with eating and with incorporative impulses in general. Even more convincing to us are the clinical examples in which the penis-envy configuration in men and women involves both feelings of greed and the gaslighting mechanism.

One important concomitant of gaslighting phenomena is that the victims are invariably unsure of their own perceptions and motivations. That insecurity seems to arise originally from some biological given, bolstered by a childhood environment that shakes the child's faith in her/himself and the world about her/him. It appears that not all individuals will predictably react in the same fashion to a given gaslighting attempt or to the same gaslighter. If in the victim the gaslighting impinges on an area of internal conflict involving greed, guilt, or shame, the chances of that attempt being successful will be enhanced considerably. This appears to be especially so when that conflict comes closer to consciousness and if the person has not been capable of managing it successfully in the past.

SUMMARY

By "gaslighting" we refer to the behavior of two individuals, victim and victimizer. The latter, disavowing his or her own mental disturbance, tries to make the victim feel he or she is going crazy, and the victim more or less complies.

We describe a ubiquitous, if not universal, human potential: the ability of individuals to disavow that which has been introjected and/or the ability to incorporate and assimilate that which others externalize and project onto them.

Reflections on the literature and a study of our own clinical material have led us to suggest that we are dealing with the outcome of an introjective defense in which victim and victimizer join in expressing and defending themselves against oral incorporative impulses (greed). The behavior permits the judgments and perceptions of one individual to be shaken by another and functions for the disavowal of anxiety by the latter. The accomplishment is an intrapersonal one (although instituted interpersonally) to rid the perpetrator of all manner of mental functions and contents, in his or her attempt to avoid anxiety and breaks with reality.

The dynamic core of gaslighting is an effort to control and manage greed. The genetic core is the concatenation of circumstances (including maturation, development, and reality) which shakes the child's faith in his/her perceptions and motivations, i.e., he or she feels the victim of his/her parents, whether this was so in fact or in fantasy, as a defense against oral impulses. Since greed and its control are necessarily universal, the varieties by which control is established over such impulses are of interest to analysts in the treatment situation as they observe them not only in their patients but also in themselves.

REFERENCES

Arieti, S. (1955), *Interpretation of Schizophrenia.* New York: Robert Brunner.

Bateson, G. (1962), A note on the double bind. *Fam. Process,* 2:154–161.

Barton, R. & Whitehead, J. A. (1969), The gas-light phenomenon. *Lancet,* 1:1258–1260.

Bion, W. R. (1956), Development of schizophrenic thought. *Internat. J. Psycho-Anal.,* 37:344–346.

Fenichel, O. (1945), *The Psychoanalytic Theory of Neurosis.* New York: Norton.

Freud, S. (1909), Notes upon a case of obsessional neurosis. *Standard Edition,* 10.

_______ (1910), The future prospects of psycho-analytic therapy. *Standard Edition,* 11.

Hamilton, P. (1939), *Angel Street.* New York: Samuel French, 1942.

Jackson, D., Bateson, G., Haley, J. & Weakland, J. (1956), Towards a theory of schizophrenia. *Behav. Sci.,* 1:251–264.

Klein, M. (1946), Notes on some schizoid mechanisms. In: *Envy and Gratitude and Other Works, 1946–1963.* New York: Delacorte, 1975, pp. 1–24.

_______ (1955), On identification. In: *New Directions in Psychoanalysis: The Significance of Infant Conflict in the Pattern of Adult Behavior,* ed. M. Klein, P. Heimann & R. E. Money-Kyrle. New York: Basic Books, pp. 309–345.

Laing, R. D. (1960), *The Divided Self: A Study of Sanity and Madness.* Baltimore: Penguin, 1965.

Langs, R. (1976), *The Bi-Personal Field.* New York: Jason Aronson, Inc.

Meissner, W. W. (1980), A note on projective identification. *J. Amer. Psychoanal. Assn.,* 28:43–67.

Niederland, W. G. (1960), Schreber's father. *J. Amer. Psychoanal. Assn.,* 8: 492–499.

_______ (1963), Further data and memorabilia pertaining to the Schreber case. *Internat. J. Psycho-Anal.,* 44:201–207.

Revitch, E. (1954), The problem of conjugal paranoia. *Dis. Nerv. Syst.,* 15:2–8.

Rosenfeld, H. (1950), Note on the psychopathology of confusional states in chronic schizophrenia. *Internat. J. Psycho-Anal.,* 31:132–137.

Searles, H. F. (1965), *Collected Papers on Schizophrenia and Related Subjects.* New York: International Universities Press.

Segal, H. (1964), *Introduction to the Works of Melanie Klein.* New York: Basic Books.

Shengold, L. L. (1975a), An attempt at soul murder: Rudyard Kipling's early life and work. *The Psychoanalytic Study of the Child,* 30:683–724.

_______ (1975b), Soul murder. *Internat. J. Psychoanal. Psychother.,* 3:366–373.

_______ (1977), Child abuse and deprivation: Soul murder. Presented at the December meeting of the American Psychoanalytic Association. In press.

Sluzki, C. & Vernon, E. (1971), The double bind as a universal pathogenic situation. *Fam. Process,* 10:397–410.

Smith, C. G. & Sinahan, K. (1972), The gaslight phenomenon reappears: A modification of the Ganser syndrome. *Brit. J. Psychiat.,* 120:685–686.

Wangh, M. (1962), The "evocation of a proxy": A psychological maneuver, its use as a defense, its purposes and genesis. *The Psychoanalytic Study of the Child,* 17:451–469.

Weinshel, E. M. (1986), Perceptual distortions during analysis: Some observations on the role of the superego in reality. In: *The Science of Mental Conflict: Essays in Honor of Charles Brenner,* ed. A. Richards & M. Willick. Hillsdale, NJ: The Analytic Press.

Chapter 5

1986

Perceptual Distortions During Analysis

Some Observations on the Role of the Superego in Reality Testing

I am reporting on segments of the analyses of three women in their mid or late twenties, all of whom had been in analytic treatment for at least three years. None were psychotic or "borderline," and none had manifested gross disturbances in their reality testing capacities. However, all three reexperienced a perceptual distortion that involved their seeing or being convinced that they would or might see the analyst's penis. Further, their subsequent associations indicated that they also suspected that their perceptions were erroneous. Nevertheless, they insisted that they had "decided" to maintain the distortion even if that decision meant that they were "crazy." In what follows, I focus on the analytic data connected with these events rather than presenting a comprehensive review of the patient's history or of the analysis as a whole.

Mrs. A walked into my office and stopped at the door for a second or two before proceeding to the couch. She seemed considerably agitated and promptly informed me that what first had caught her attention as she entered was a small Japanese print that hangs on the wall adjacent to the couch. She quickly added that she had noticed the picture many times before and that it had never made enough of an impression on her to warrant any comment. (In fact, it was a rather innocuous, muted, unobtrusive decoration.) But on this day, looking at the picture, she was absolutely convinced that a definite protuberance emerged from its surface. She was further convinced that the bulge was due to an erect penis that was covered by the print. At the same time, she realized that this could not be so; nevertheless, even after glancing again at the print while lying on the couch, she could not completely rid herself of the perception of the protuberance. Mrs. A went on to say that the whole thing was "crazy" and that she must have had an hallucination of some sort. Only later, in her associations, and in a manner that revealed a definite reluctance to share it with me, she mentioned another thought that had passed through her mind very rapidly and virtually in the same split-second as she had become aware of her perception of the bulge. That thought can best be summarized—although, obviously, it did not come to her so coherently—as, "If I recognize that protuberance as real, then I would be crazy, because I *know* that there is no such thing on that painting. But my 'decision' is still that there *is* such a protuberance."

The second vignette, concerning Mrs. B, occurred two years later, shortly after I had returned from the midwinter psychoanalytic meetings with a bad cold and a very stuffed head. Somewhere in the middle of the analytic hour, Mrs. B accused me of having fallen asleep. She was hurt and angry; she insisted that she could tell I was asleep because of my deep breathing. My falling asleep was evidence of my indifference, my being bored with and not caring for her—even as a patient. I had not been asleep, but she had been correct in her perception of the somewhat troubled breathing. As we were discussing her feelings and fantasies about this event, she suddenly broke off in the middle of a sentence and told me that it was not really true that she thought I had been asleep. She explained that at the moment that she had become aware of my labored and noisy breathing what had actually occurred to her—and again this was very brief and transient—was that I must be masturbating. For a moment at least, she was convinced that I was masturbating. She tried to dismiss this unwelcome idea, and then "I made up the business about your being asleep even though I knew you would think that it sounded crazy." She explained that she would prefer to be crazy than to face up to the possibility that I was masturbating. What was so threatening to her about that possibility was that she would have to turn around and look at me and my erect penis.

The incident with my third patient, Mrs. C, took place about a year later. Mrs. C was my first afternoon appointment, and it was necessary for me to pass the waiting room, from which she could readily observe me. It had been a typical San Francisco day with intermittent showers, so I was carrying my black raincoat. Folded over my arm, it covered the area of my crotch. A few minutes later, when the patient was lying on the couch in the office, she began to muse that it was most interesting that I would have a *white* raincoat. She went on at considerable length about how strange it was for a *man* to wear a *white* raincoat. Wasn't this evidence of some kind of "problem"? However, after a spate of these somewhat forced associations, she acknowledged that she had not told me the whole story even though, she insisted, that what she *had* told me was genuine and reflected what she had been thinking. The reader can surmise what it was that Mrs. C had omitted from her original version of what had gone through her mind as I passed her in the hallway. She had looked at my crotch and was for a moment convinced that she had seen my penis. She consciously repudiated the perception and the thought. These were replaced by the conviction that she had seen a white raincoat. She knew the perception was distorted but "preferred" that what she saw was a white coat. Even though Mrs. C did not articulate a preference for being "crazy" to an acknowledgment that she might see my penis, there was no question that this was implied.

Before I present additional clinical material about each of these patients in order to provide a clearer understanding of these phenomena, let me sketch a number of qualities and characteristics shared by all three patients:

1. All were neurotic, essentially hysterical characters, who demonstrated phobic symptoms, although only one (Mrs. C) offered a phobia as a presenting complaint.

2. None had exhibited gross or consistent difficulties in reality testing or had significant perceptual distortions. However, all three, in varying degree, had noted at times a striking and inexplicable lack of faith and confidence in their assessment of reality. This difficulty was especially conspicuous in situations when their own estimation and judgment of what they had perceived was in conflict with the assessment made by another person, particularly when that person was meaningful to them. In such circumstances, the patients tended to lose confidence, to question their own judgment, and, usually, to accept the judgment of the other person. What all three expressed in somewhat different terms was a vague feeling of remorse and of not having done the right thing. They felt, in effect, that in order to stay on good terms with the other person, they had temporarily relinquished their own confidence that they could perceive reality correctly.

3. All three patients manifested strong exhibitionistic and voyeuristic conflicts. These tendencies had undergone considerable inhibition, which was reflected in their character structures. Both Mrs. A (the Japanese print) and Mrs. C (the white raincoat) came to analysis as quiet, mousey, almost achromatic persons. They were shy and withdrawn, and explained that it was important for them to be unnoticed

and inconspicuous. They spoke in almost muted voices, and their clothes were inappropriately drab and unflattering. They did nothing to enhance an intrinsic and potentially marked attractiveness. They were scrupulous in avoiding their curiosity about me, especially my private life; and they found it very difficult to look at me at the beginning and the end of the analytic hour. A great deal of analytic work had focused on these conflicts, their attendant anxieties and depressive affects, and the resultant defenses and inhibitions; and, as the analysis progressed, definite changes occurred. Prior to the "perceptual distortion" episodes, both Mrs. A and Mrs. C had become more openly and comfortably curious, attractive, and outspoken.

Although Mrs. B (who accused me of falling asleep) was outwardly almost the obverse of the other two, her inner situation was quite similar. Until marriage in her late teens, she had behaved in a very quiet, "tight," and colorless manner. After her marriage, and especially after the birth of her daughter, Mrs. B became loud, seductive, almost a caricature of the "life of the party." In fact, one of the conscious reasons Mrs. B sought psychoanalysis was her discomfort at being such a "show off" despite her husband's undisguised disgust with the exhibitionistic behavior. She had become markedly overweight; but instead of grooming herself and wearing clothes that might minimize her heaviness, Mrs. B went out of her way to dress, talk, and act in a fashion that would make her and her defects the center of attention. At times, the overall effect bordered on the grotesque.

4. In all three cases, the episodes described were preceeded in the analyses by considerable work on the manifestations in the transference of the exhibitionistic/voyeuristic drive derivatives. It was not difficult to demonstrate fantasies (partly conscious from the beginning) of exposing themselves to the analyst and to have him find them sexually attractive. Also it was possible to deal with their fantasies of seducing the analyst into exposing and exhibiting himself.

5. These patients presented a number of other common experiences that appeared to be of significance in understanding the perceptual distortions. As so often happens in the course of analysis, additional information both clarifies and complicates our understanding of the patient and the analysis. The material in question deals with "ambiguous" incestuous activity in childhood. I say "ambiguous" because in spite of careful analytic work, it was never possible to determine with certainty whether or not actual physical interchange with the father had occurred. The patients could never be sure—and neither could the analyst—that

what they were recalling was a real event, a distorted elaboration of an ambiguous event, or the product of a sexual fantasy. Within the analysis following the perceptual distortion, all three recalled particular sexual traumas during the latency period and their recognition that their parents were somewhat corrupt in regard to reality testing and their consciences in general.

Mrs. A's concerns about ambiguous sexual contact with her father centered around a number of experiences between the ages of five and six. Her memories of close physical contact were vague in detail but strong in regard to the associated belief that her father's behavior may have exceeded the limits of paternal propriety. Beyond this, nothing more definite could be established. However, these suspicions and concerns were reinforced during adolescence, when she observed her father making clumsy advances towards her girl friends. She was aware of sexual feelings towards her father; she had always displayed a penchant for older men, and early in the analysis some of her acting out had involved affairs with considerably older men of prominence in the community. Also, around the age of five and six, there had been a number of instances of sex play with her brother four years older than she. She had strong memories of fascination and awe at the sight of his erect penis, and these memories had not been repressed.

In the period after the protuberance-on-the-Japanese-print event, Mrs. A recaptured the memory of an incident that had occurred when she was nine years old. One Sunday, after a strenuous (and apparently sexualized if not sexual) afternoon of play with her brother and some cousins, the patient was sent off with an older man, a close family friend, to get some refreshments. While enjoying an ice cream soda, she became panic stricken that this man (who as far as could be determined was behaving appropriately) might make some sexual advance and expose himself. Then she had the thought (and again this is in "translation"), "If I can act like my grandfather did, then everything will be all right." The panic subsided almost instantly, and the rest of the outing went off uneventfully.

Mrs. A's maternal grandfather, who had been an important figure in her life, had died not long before this event occurred. He had been warm, protective, and considerate toward his granddaughter (in many ways more than her mother), and there was nothing to indicate that he had in any way abused her sexually. In the last years of his life he had become psychotic, most likely as a result of advancing senility. She could not remember clearly all of the details of his disturbance; but it *was* clear to her that because of his mental illness, the grandfather was permitted special license and special privileges. She recalled that many aspects of his behavior, which ordinarily would have been considered peculiar and offensive to her family, were tolerated and accepted with, "Well, that's grandpa and his mishagas." Even though Mrs. A did not have a precise idea of what "craziness" involved, she evidently associated it with the general concept of diminished personal responsibility and with the specific idea of diminished adherence to reality. As we reconstructed this episode, what emerged was the patient's notion that if *she* were crazy, then she would not have to look, not have to see—and whatever else happened, it would not be her fault. In that portion of the analytic work, Mrs. A volunteered the speculation that in the play that had preceded the outing with the older family friend there may have been some mutual exhibitionism among the various children and that her sexual excitement may have carried over into her thoughts about the older man later that day. It was my impression that she had feared the repetition of an earlier traumatic event associated with the perception of the male genitals, and that to avoid reexperiencing this trauma, she had adopted a new set of defensive patterns, one of which included being able to "decide" that she should be "crazy."

At various times in the analysis, Mrs. A complained about the consciences of both of her parents and of her husband. The mother lied to the father about money she had received from her parents and involved the patient in these deceptions. The mother would also insist that something the patient "knew" to be true was not true, or vice versa. My patient had a vague notion that her mother had been aware of the sex play between her brother and herself but that she preferred not to notice it. Mrs. A's father was repeatedly involved in obviously foolish business ventures that always failed, in part because he had siphoned off money for his equally foolish personal expenditures. I have already related the patient's concern over his behavior with her and even more with her adolescent girl friends. The patient's husband, though successful in business, achieved a certain notoriety for shady financial dealings and lied regularly to his wife about these matters. When confronted with his fabrications, he insisted that she had misperceived and misconstrued what he had said and done—even in the face of incontrovertible evidence to the contrary. Mrs. A, like the two other patients, did not have a good deal of faith in the integrity of either the reality testing capacity or the honesty of her parents, her husband, or herself. After the analysis, Mrs. A divorced her husband, primarily because of irreconcilable differences associated with these issues, to which she was no longer so vulnerable.

With Mrs. B, the "ambiguous incestuous sexual activity" was considerably less ambiguous. Her father was an alcoholic. When she was about five years old (and just before the father left the home; after the parental divorce) her father had "quite likely," while intoxicated, attempted to play with her genitals. This was an exceedingly traumatic event, which led to a several-month period of phobic disturbance and nightmares. Mrs. B was never sure whether her father had exposed himself during this episode or on other occasions; yet it always remained clear in her mind that her mother had known of her husband's behavior but had chosen not to do anything about it.

In the weeks after her perceptual distortion in the session, Mrs. B reintroduced memories that had appeared earlier in the analysis under quite different circumstances and without either the affective charge or the specific connections that characterized the current recounting of the material. A number of years after the divorce, the mother remarried. When Mrs. B was around eight or nine years old, the family was living in a flimsy, jerry-built house not far from the San Francisco airport. Her mother and stepfather carried on an active and rather noisy sexual life, which both excited and frightened the patient. She knew, even then, that the noises were reminiscent of comparable disturbances that had aroused and bothered her before her parents had been divorced. During the same period, the patient's sleep was also disturbed by the noise of the planes from the nearby airport, noises she later recognized had a definite sexual significance for her.

The particular episode that Mrs. B connected with the perceptual distortion in analysis (in reaction to my noisy breathing) occurred when she was nine years old and already having difficulty in her relationships both at home and at school. She recalled being awakened from her sleep by unusually loud sounds from the parents' nextdoor bedroom, especially by piercing and sexually explicit cries of encouragement from her mother. Not long before, the patient had tried to talk to her mother about these nocturnal disturbances and had, indirectly, asked her mother to tone down the activity. But the mother had flippantly and from the daughter's point of view rather callously dismissed the girl's concerns and entreaties. On the occasion in question, the patient became more and more excited and increasingly anxious; she feared (and wished) that she would be able to see what was going on, and she feared that she was going to lose her mind.

While this was taking place, the patient was simultaneously aware of the noises coming from the planes that were landing and taking off. The sounds were experienced as assaults. Then, in the midst of all this turmoil, Mrs. B had the thought that if she concentrated on the sounds of the airplanes and that if those sounds drove her crazy, then somehow she would be able to tolerate this seemingly overwhelming experience. This is precisely what happened for her, and the patient was able to go back to sleep. Furthermore, the remainder of the time that the patient and her family remained in this inadequate house, she invariably dealt with the discomfort over the sounds of sexual intercourse by invoking—almost as an incantation—the formula that she had created that night. Mrs. B's latency age solution featured, first, the selective perception and displacement of her perceptual activities from a more to a less emotionally charged stimulus and, second, the determination that she would be "crazy" on a more or less active and conscious rather than passive and unconscious level. Mrs. B had constructed a "new" set of defenses.

Her defensive configuration also involved an identification with a psychotic object, her mother, who as far as the patient was concerned tended to behave in a crazy and unrealistic fashion. Mrs. B's mother was a naive, superstitious, and gullible woman, who constantly and consistently lied to her daughter whenever it appeared easier to lie than to face the truth. She turned a deaf ear and a blind eye to the patient's pleas and concerns and was promiscuous in relationships with men and unfaithful in three marriages. She was careless in these and other ways in regard to the care of herself and of her household.

Mrs. B's father was an irresponsible alcoholic who abused both his wife and children physically and verbally. The patient's maternal grandmother and her first stepfather, however, seemed to have been responsible, solid individuals with whom she had relatively close relationships. Mrs. B was an excellent student and a talented writer, who was "adopted" by many of her teachers. These relationships, which were crucially important in her later development, probably permitted reasonably effective superego functioning in her adult life in spite of the impact of her parents' pathology.

Mrs. C, shortly after the black-white raincoat incident, recalled a traumatic episode from the age of eight. While she sat alone at a Saturday afternoon movie, an older man sat next to her and made sexual advances, including a surreptitious exposure of his penis. At first she sat there more or less paralyzed; eventually she was able to get up and change her seat.

The man attempted to follow her; and, when the usher asked Mrs. C if the man was bothering her, she lied and said no. The reason for doing so, she remembered, was the feeling that if she accused him of sexual wrongdoings, there would be counteraccusations and she would end up the guilty one. (She expected, of course, that the same would take place in the analysis.) She could not even imagine that the usher would believe her story. In fact, when the patient returned home and related the harrowing incident to her mother, the mother was unsympathetic, pooh-poohing the whole affair, and insinuating that her daughter had either made it up or if it really happened, it must have been her fault. It is difficult to reconstruct the overall ego state in effect at that time; but, on the basis of comparable situations in the transference, the patient could not be entirely sure if she was lying, denying, or merely stating the facts as she had experienced them. And, even though Mrs. C explains that episode as if she were deliberately lying in order to protect herself, I am not convinced that the dynamics at that moment were so clear cut.

However, in the context of the movie memory, the patient related an experience from the age of six or seven. She awakened in the middle of the night ostensibly to go to the bathroom. Noticing some light coming from the living room, she walked into it and saw her mother together with her current boyfriend. Mrs. C then, as she recalled it, turned around, closed the door, and went into the kitchen to get a snack—she could not remember whether or not she ever went to the bathroom! In her associations to this event, she insisted that her mother and the boyfriend were not engaged in any sexual activity; at the same time, she realized that this was probably not correct and that she had peremptorily shut the whole thing out of her mind (her shutting the door behind her is probably a symbolic screen representation of the attempt to repress and deny her perception of sexual activity). When Mrs. C first told me about the memory, most impressive about it (and the focus of the work) was the way she glossed over, both in her perception of what had occurred and in her recounting of it, that part of the memory relating to seeing her mother in the living room. At the same time she overemphasized those portions of the memory having to do with going to the kitchen and enjoying a snack. It seems, therefore, that even at that early age, the patient utilized selective perception, with a hypercathexis of the relatively innocuous and regressive oral element as a means of diluting the potential impact of the more frightening sexual perception.

Mrs. C reported, as had Mrs. A and Mrs. B, disconcerting parental attitudes toward "moral" issues and an inappropriate lack of responsibility.

Her mother was a childish, ineffective dreamer, who neglected her household and other caretaking chores whenever the prospect of more immediate pleasure was available. She made her daughter a precocious confidante and made no effort to protect her from noxious sexual stimuli and experiences. The mother was flamboyantly unrealistic in regard to her own talents and insisted that, even in middle age, she could still become a world famous ballerina. The father was a tyrannical, unstable (and possibly paranoid) person, who would shower his children with overly expensive clothes and take them to exorbitantly priced restaurants. After the exotic meals, which he selected, he would rail at them for spending so much money. Although we could not be absolutely certain, it is likely that Mrs. C's father had been involved in some kind of sexual activity with her.

It is, of course, impossible to reconstruct precisely the dynamic factors that led to such behavior by the parents of these patients. What is of importance is that—whatever the actual source of pathology—these women understood a good part of their parents' behavior in terms of defects of conscience and reality testing.

When I presented this clinical material to various analytic societies, the diagnoses offered by the discussants ranged from overt psychosis to "a hoax" to neurosis to psychopathy. Different analysts will view and understand this material in somewhat different fashions. The focus here is on the perceptual distortions reported by my three patients. For the sake of brevity, I will discuss the material in a composite manner. Although the three cases are hardly identical, the issues involved are sufficiently similar to justify such a blending.

As for the perceptual distortions themselves, I am confident that the material presented by the patients was genuine. The patients experienced transiently and vividly what could best be described as illusion. That is, each reacted to a stimulus in the external world, but the perception of that stimulus was distorted by internal wishes and conflicts, anxiety and depressive affect, and the products of defensive operations. These reactions occurred during periods of intense transference involvement with considerable anxiety and evidence of both instinctual and ego regression. The patients were struggling with frustrated wishes to possess the analyst's penis (breast, baby). These frustrations and the underlying wishes were either conscious or close to consciousness and were related to thoughts and fantasies of getting the analyst to expose himself so that the penis could be incorporated visually or by way of intercourse. These fantasies involved both libidinal and aggressive drive derivatives, the content of which included the wish for her *own* penis; for taking the penis from the analyst-father; for taking the penis from the analyst-father for the mother; and for revenge.[1]

At the time that the perceptual distortion took place, the balance between the drives and the defenses had been altered sufficiently (resulting in increasing pressure from the drive derivatives and decreased effectiveness of the defensive structures opposing them) so that the heightened cathexis of the forbidden wishes could be attached to an external percept. It is not surprising, of course, that the external percept so cathected was intimately related to the person of the analyst (the picture on the wall of his office, the sound of his heavy breathing, his raincoat), a fact that facilitated the process of displacement. For the moment at least, the faithful testing of reality and the fidelity to the reality principle were abrogated; the hitherto repressed or partially repressed forbidden wishes emerged in the distorted perception of the analyst's penis. We can view the product—here presented as a schematized version of a much more complex series of compromise formations—as a symptom providing transient and partial gratification for the patients.

Such a solution, however, cannot be tenable for a nonpsychotic person. These patients were not altogether convinced (in spite of some of their disclaimers) that they had really seen either a penis or its symbolic distortion. Neither were they convinced that they had *not* done so. The result was a mixture of doubt, confusion, and uncertainty connected to the memory of comparable ego states in the past, when they had been confronted with similar difficulties in dealing with a potentially threatening reality.

In addition, the patients *felt* vaguely that in acceding to the break with reality, they had done something wrong. This incipient feeling of guilt involved more than the recognition that the gratification of the underlying wishes was "bad"; there was also the realization that rejecting a realistic appraisal of reality was contrary to the precepts of their own conscience. In opposition to this set of superego demands were those introjects and identifications within the superego with certain elements of the behavior and superegos of their parents, who had been egregiously unconcerned about respect for reality and reality testing.

[1]It is interesting to look back at Freud's (1910) pioneering contribution, "The Psycho-Analytic View of Psychogenic Disturbance of Vision."

At this point in the analysis, the regressive process impinged on the superego as well as the ego. The integrity and stability of each had been further compromised. As a result, in addition to the various intersystemic conflicts, the patients were struggling with intrasystemic ego and superego conflicts. One of the compromises that emerged from those conflicts was the identification in action with the behavior of parental objects who flouted the demands of the recognition of reality and the acceptance of self-responsibility. Further, the patients "preferred" to surrender their superego in order to retain the tie to and/or the love and approval of those objects. This was reenacted in the transference with the analyst. Such behavior is reminiscent of Freud's statement in "An Outline of Psychoanalysis," "if the patient puts that analyst in the place of his father [or mother] he is also giving him the power which his super-ego exercises over his ego, since the parents were, as we know, the origin of his super-ego" (Freud, 1940, p. 175).

Particularly striking in these three incidents is the insistence of each of the patients that even though she "knew" she had distorted a piece of external reality, she would not unequivocally repudiate the distortion. Each "decided" that she preferred to appear "crazy" or "a liar" rather than surrender the compromise-distortion-symptom; and each made it abundantly clear that the reason for doing so was to avoid acknowledging the possibility of seeing my penis. That possibility evoked intense anxiety and was experienced as preliminary to a full-fledged trauma. Somewhat less intense were concerns about being punished for the misdemeanor (the forbidden looking) and mild depressive affect at the prospect of losing a loved object or the love of that object. It was not until later that it became evident that these reactions were repetitions of earlier traumatic experiences connected with seeing a penis or the wish or possibility of seeing one.

This complicated series of psychological events illustrates the multidetermined, interdigitating activities that occur in a situation of psychological conflict, the necessary participation of all three psychic agencies, and the resultant compromise formations (see Brenner, 1982, especially pp. 7, 75, 89, 91, 125, 136–137). There is no way that *all* the elements involved in these events could be teased out and understood. For instance, it is not clear to what extent these patients utilized denial or counterphobic mechanisms as defenses in their insistence that they preferred to lie or to be crazy rather than unequivocally renounce their distorted perception. Masochistic tendencies were conspicuous in all three women, particularly in regard to their superego functioning (Brenner, 1982, pp. 126–128). In the analytic work, material came up that had many parallels with lying (see Weinshel, 1979 [chapter 3, this volume], where the close relationship between lying and the vicissitudes of the oedipal phase conflicts is examined), with fetishism (Freud, 1927, p. 155), with negation (Freud, 1925; Weinshel, 1977 [chapter 2, this volume]), with "screens" (Freud, 1899, 1937; Fenichel, 1927, 1939; Greenson, 1958; Reider, 1953) and with "gaslighting" (Calef and Weinshel, 1981 [chapter 4, this volume]). All of these topics touch in one way or another on the problems of reality, reality testing, and the superego; and all of them warrant considerably more investigation.

We cannot be satisfied with only the partial understanding of many aspects of these phenomena now available to us. It is particularly difficult to tease out of the analytic data what should be attributed to the superego and what to the ego. Often the task of translating the "sense" of superego activity into ordinary language seems awkward. There is an aura of mild confusion about this material; the responsibility is not mine alone. (See Greenacre, 1973, in regard to the role of primal scene memories.) My patients felt confused and readily acknowledged their confusion during these portions of the analysis; they were also *confusing*. Their own sense of reality and the sense of themselves vis-à-vis that reality were somewhat disturbed; and, sometimes, they complained that they felt they were not telling the truth, lying, or just a bit befuddled, even when they *knew* otherwise. Part of the "confusion," the feeling of uncertainty, that I experienced when listening to my patients reflects the nature of the superego, its development, and its somewhat unstable—if not capricious—relationship to the ego.

Stanley Goodman, in his opening remarks on the 1965 Panel, "The Current Status of the Theory of the Superego," explained that the urgent reason for a reevaluation of the superego was that there are still so many unanswered questions and still so many aspects of unclarity in regard to superego functioning. Part of the problem, reported Goodman, was that so many of our "relatively precise" theoretical formulations appear inadequate when we apply them "broadly to our clinical data" (Panel Report, 1965). Twenty years later, most of the same questions and problems remain unclarified.

Although it has not been a crucial or vigorously debated issue, there has never been a consensus about the role of the superego in the testing of reality, either inner or outer. Even after the publication of "The Ego and the Id" (Freud, 1923) where Freud seemed to have assigned the function of perception, especially the perception of the external world, to the ego, there were lingering doubts about the locus of the testing of reality, especially of internal reality (self-observation). Perhaps an extract from "The New Introductory Lectures," which contains a resume of the pertinent material, will give a hint of why some of this doubt persisted:

> We can best arrive at the characteristics of the actual ego insofar as it can be distinguished from the id and from the superego by examining its relation to the outermost superficial portion of the mental apparatus, which we describe as the system *Pcpt-Cs.* This system is turned towards the external world, it is the medium for the perceptions arising thence, and during its functioning the phenomenon of consciousness arises in it. It is the sense organ of the entire apparatus; moreover it is receptive not only to excitations from outside but also to those arising from the interior of the mind. We need scarcely look for a justification of the view that the ego is that portion of the id which was modified by the proximity and infiuence of the external world, which is adapted for the reception of stimuli, comparable to the cortical layer by which a small piece of living substance is surrounded. The relation to the external world has become the decisive factor for the ego; it has taken on the task of representing the external word to the id—fortunately for the id, which could not escape destruction if, in its blind efforts for the satisfaction of its instincts, it disregarded that supreme external power. In accomplishing this function, the ego *must* observe the external world, *must* lay down an accurate picture of it in the memory-traces of its perceptions, and by its exercise of the function of "reality-testing," *must* put aside whatever in this picture of the external world *is an addition derived from internal sources of excitation.* The ego controls the approaches to motility under the id's orders; but between a need and an action it has interposed a postponement in the form of the activity of thought, during which it makes use of the mnemic residues of experience. In that way it has dethroned the pleasure principle which dominates the course of events in the id without any restriction and has replaced it by the reality principle, which promises more certainty and greater success [Freud, 1933, pp. 75–76, italics added].

I will not review the history of Freud's vacillations on this subject; excellent summaries can be found in the Panel Report (1965) and in Stein (1966). However, the foregoing extract from Freud raises two questions. The first has to do with the three italicized *musts* in regard to the ego's "accomplishing this function." It is possible, of course, that these imperatives are merely stylistic or linguistic coincidences, but we should also recall that the function of the superego is "to observe and to criticize, approve, disapprove, or punish the ego or the self as we would say today" (Loewenstein, 1966, p. 302). Later Loewenstein adds, "We call the superego that organization within the mental apparatus which becomes a systematic third independent variable in the intrapsychic conflicts, and which exercises control over drives and some essential tendencies and functions of the ego, e.g., individual self-interest and even self-preservation" (p. 302). Freud, discussing the various functions of the superego, speaks of its "keeping a watch over the actions and intentions of the ego and judging them, in exercising a censorship" (Freud, 1930, p. 136). A few years later, Freud (1933) argued that "it is more prudent to keep the agency [the superego] as something independent and to suppose that conscience is one of its functions and that self-observation, which is an essential *preliminary to the judging activity* of conscience is another of them" (p. 60, italics added).

Freud, in describing the activity of the ego-ideal and the shift from ego-ideal to superego, utilized imagery and metaphors having to do with watching and observing. As mentioned earlier, the observation was merely a preliminary step in evaluation (measuring the ego against the ego ideal), judgment, criticism, and punishment. Although evaluation and testing of external reality does not at first appear to be a "moral" issue derived from the conflicts of the oedipal phase, a closer examination indicates that it is more complex.

Not only does observation entail all the conflicts about looking and forbidden looking, curiosity, knowing (and not only in the Biblical sense), responsibility, truth ("Face the truth even if it hurts"), and so forth, but the very process of the renunciation—relinquishment of the oedipal object—depends on varying degrees of observing and accepting the facts of reality.

The superego, I suggest, does play a significant role in the testing of reality in the external world. That role is in partnership—albeit a junior partnership—with the ego. Among its functions is to keep watch over the actions and intentions of the ego, judge them, and exercise censorship over them—including the monitoring of the ego function of reality testing. Stein (1966) asks: "Does the superego, like an ideal policeman, ever prompt the ego in the direction of more adequate reality testing?" a question he answers in the affirmative (pp. 281, 288; see also Blum, 1981).

The second question suggested by the extract quoted earlier has to do with the other quintessential task of reality testing; the ego "must put aside whatever in this picture of the external world is an addition derived from internal sources of excitation," that is, the differentiation of outside from inside, object from subject, reality from fantasy. This junction has to do with more than the "musts." It deals with an equally important area of the superego's contribution to reality testing and the sphere of the most useful aspect of the ego–superego partnership vis-à-vis reality testing. Freud's caveat refers to the synergistic interdependence between self-observation and the observation of the external world.

There is a reasonable consensus among analysts who have studied self-observation that this function is the domain and responsibility primarily of the superego, with the ego playing a secondary role (e.g., Freud, 1933; Hartmann, 1956; Kris, 1956; Hartmann and Loewenstein, 1962; Gitelson, 1964; Jacobson, 1964; Loewenstein, 1966; Stein, 1966; Schafer, 1968; Calef and Weinshel, 1980 [chapter 10, this volume]; Blum, 1981). Stein's observation in the 1965 Panel Report is particularly enlightening. "The closer to the clinical level," he notes, "the more likely it is that self observation will be treated as a superego function and vice versa" (Panel Report, 1965, p. 180).

In his definitive 1966 essay, "Self Observation, Reality, and the Superego," Stein states: "Self observation is an essential element in the process of reality testing . . . self observation and self evaluation are inextricably linked, and are intimately involved with superego functions. Therefore, the superego functions play an essential, if indirect role, in reality testing and reality adaptation" (p. 275). The very nature of reality, however, argues Stein, is dependent on "that which is determined by the inspection of one's own mental processes" (p. 276), that is by self-observation and the superego. Quoting Hartmann, "In a broader sense, reality testing also refers to the ability to discern subjective and objective elements in our judgments on reality" (Hartmann, 1956, page 256), Stein concludes, "It is reasonable to assume that reality testing as applied to the outer world, and that which is directed toward one's own mental processes, are interdependent" (p. 276). Stein suggests that self-observation plays a ubiquitous role in reality testing and that "the latter would be subject to serious limitations or impairment *were there not a constant flow of stimuli from the inner world and were the capacity lacking to perceive and evaluate these inner stimuli*" (p. 276, italics added). For these reasons, Stein maintains that self-observation "is a necessary, although not a sufficient or sole determining factor in the adequate evaluation of reality"

(p. 276; see also Freud, 1936, for example, of the role of the superego interference with adequate reality perception).

It is true, of course, that the pressures from the outer world can disrupt the processes of self-observation and interrupt the proper perception and evaluation of the internal stimuli. Thus, there is an ongoing interdependence between those processes that regulate the functions of testing external and internal reality.

In addition to its crucial heritage from the id and the instinctual drives, so much of the superego and its contents come from the external world. The most important of these contributions are from the parental and other early significant objects. These objects not only become the basis for the pivotal superego identifications during the oedipal phase conflicts in the formation of the superego structures, but the content of some of those identifications may relate more specifically to the external world and reality testing. The parents of each of the patients described in this paper had a cavalier or grossly corrupt attitude toward the exigencies of reality and reality testing. Hartmann (1947) talks about the individual "who constantly emphasizes the matter-of-fact view of life he has, his realistic attitudes, and the high degree of rationality he has reached . . . ." (p. 64). These individuals have a specific relation to reality in that "while parts of reality are emphasized, other parts, mainly of inner reality are scotomized." Hartmann (1956) describes people whose "values" about reality and reality testing are often passed on from generation to generation. The children of such parents will hear admonitions and/or exhortations like (and these are all familiar ones with all sorts of variations) "You must face the facts," "You have to realize that we live in a cold, hard world," "Be a man and stand on your own two feet." These remarks are internalized to some degree and become a part of the superego's relationship vis-à-vis the external world. The impact may be to enhance the tendency towards more stringent reality testing; it may also, for a number of reasons, result in defiance of such admonitions and a reluctance to follow other parental precepts. The tremendous importance of the early objects to the child also entails dependence on the object's values, even including dependence on parents' atypical, idiosyncratic, and grossly distorted pictures of reality (pp. 255–256). Greenson's (1958, p. 259) epigrammatic "Parents who deny create children who lie" could be said equally well in the reverse order (Parents who lie create children who deny) since the young child cannot differentiate with any accuracy between denial or overt lying. It is the realistic importance of and dependence on the parents, and the fear of losing the parental objects and/or the love and approval of those objects, that intensifies the possibility of the child's incorporating those parental "manipulations" of reality and reality testing.

In a similar, but (usually) less critical way, culture and society exert their influence on the values that eventually become part of the overall superego structure, particularly, the contents of the structure. These influences are important elements that account for the diversity of superego content; and as Brenner (1982, pp. 137–138) warns, variations in superego functioning should not be mistaken for superego pathology.

The role of culture in the formation and maintenance of the superego, particularly in establishing what may be called "the conditions for repression" is noted in Freud's (1917) rendition of Nestroy's "In the Basement and on the First Floor," the Viennese version of England's TV series "Upstairs–Downstairs." In this well-known portrayal of the consequences of sex play between two "invented" six-year-old girls, the daughter of the caretaker of the apartment house (in the basement) has already witnessed adult sexual activity and had access to sexual knowledge. As a result, the childhood play did not have any deleterious effect, and the girl grew up free of sexual problems and neurosis. Her partner, the daughter of the landlord (on the first floor), however, "came under the influence of education and accepted its demands." Therefore, while still a child (because of the "tendency to conflict, arising from the development of the ego, which rejects these libidinal impulses") she will feel that she had done something wrong, will give up masturbation after considerable struggle, turn away from adult sexual intercourse, prefer to remain sexually ignorant, and suffer from neurosis (Freud, 1917, pp. 352–354). In spite of its somewhat Victorian, melodramatic tone, Freud's depiction of the impact of the social-cultural milieu is a vivid one.

Hartmann (1956) dealt with these more general issues of the role of the superego in the creation of the conditions for repression in his *Notes on the Reality Principle.* He pointed out that with the advent of the superego, the question of what is pleasurable and what is not becomes much more complicated. He said, "The aspect of structure formation under scrutiny now has changed also the conditions for pleasure gain; it has not only limited them but also newly defined what is and what is not pleasurable or less pleasurable" (pp. 247–248).

The superego, like the other principal agencies of the mind, is not a fixed structure, certainly not with the "sharp frontiers" that might be inferred from the diagrams of the psychic apparatus. Freud warned that the divisions of the personality are essentially artificial ones and that

> after making the separation we must allow what we have separated to merge together once more. . . . It is highly probable that the development of these divisions is subject to great variations in different individuals; it is possible that in the course of actual functioning they may change and go through a temporary phase of involution. Particularly in the case of what is phylogenetically the last and most delicate of these divisions—the differentiation between the ego and the superego—something of this sort seems to be true [1933, p. 79].

We see this blurring most conspicuously in regressive states and dissolution of the superego structures and functions, but the reverse is also true. Freud implies that with maturity of superego development, there may be an ongoing integration of the superego activities into the ego, especially when there occurs a gradual diminution of the "moral" elements of a particular superego function and pattern. (Comparable views are expressed by Arlow, 1982; Loewenstein, 1966; Loewald, 1959, and Stein, 1966.) This blurring of ego–superego boundaries and the merging of the superego with the ego are, in part, reasons why, on the clinical level at least, it may be so difficult to ascertain whether a particular activity—including the testing of reality—is governed by the ego or the superego.

Two other aspects of superego development deserve comment. First, as the child becomes more active motorically and begins to explore the outer world, the child's behavior often evokes responses from the parents that are simultaneously frightened and angry. These responses occur in reaction to behavior that is potentially or actually self-destructive, or even life threatening: events like crossing the street alone, climbing up to high places, playing with matches, opening bottles containing dangerous substances—the list is long. For the child, a certain degree of uncertainty and confusion ensues, the distinction between what is related to self-preservation and what is related to something "evil" is neither altogether clear nor convincing. It takes a long time for the child to be able to distinguish moral conflicts from other conflicts; and, although with the gradual development of the superego this distinction becomes more evident, "we are never completely free of this equation of danger with 'evil'" (Loewenstein, 1966, p. 302). Similarly, the analyst will have problems in differentiating those functions which are closely dependent on the influence of the ego, those of the superego, and those which are the product of their collaboration.

Part of this "joint venture uncertainty" is reflected in the double meaning of certain words. For example, "good and bad," "right and wrong," "straight and crooked," "correct and incorrect" can have either a moral connotation or one that reflects the ego's adaptive functioning. "Judgment" can pertain to a particular assessment of reality, but the phrase "passing judgment" raises images of judges, juries, and punishment. Even the innocuous word "observation" carries with it not only the ordinary meaning of looking but also the morally tinged idea of "observing" the rules and the laws.

A second important role of the superego is the way in which we see and relate to the external world has to do with moods. This is especially true in regard to those moods in which the superego has exerted a significant influence, although to some extent the superego plays a part in all mood formation. Depression and mania are the most conspicuous examples, but a comparable distortion of reality to fit the mood can also be noted in paranoid and masochistic conditions. To see the world "through rose colored glasses" is more than a figure of speech. The outside world as viewed by a severely depressed patient and by one who is hypomanic is hardly the same world. The whole area of moods and their influence on relations with the external world is one that has not been pursued carefully by analysts (see Jacobson, 1957, and Weinshel, 1970).

The civilized person may not always be moral, but at least our so-called civilized world is one of morals, of rules, and of regulations and limitations; and in spite of all-too-frequent horrendous and egregious exceptions, human beings must maintain a certain minimal degree of morality in order to exist in that world. In that sense, a reasonable degree of effective superego functioning is essential for adaptation and survival. We know all too well, however, that the constancy and reliability of the superego and its various activities are considerably less than ideal. One of the outcomes of a reasonably successful psychoanalysis is the enhancement of the autonomy and the fidelity of those superergo functions, but we recognize that these changes are only relative. An additional vignette involving Mrs. A, the patient whose story began this essay, is illustrative.

Several years after the completion of what we both considered to be a gratifying analytic experience, Mrs. A sent a UNICEF Christmas card with a report on her current life and progress. After detailing a series of satisfying events and changes in her work and her personal life, she wrote:

> . . . And I enjoy it, and my logical powers have sharpened—you would not recognize me, so different from the old fuzzy-headed, don't dare look-under-the-Japanese hanging me I used to be. In fact, I now look under everything, as well as around, up, down, beneath. And I look at every question imaginable, and no one is a wizard anymore— which is kind of sad in a way. . . . I send you my card—to show you that I even advertise myself (in quite good taste of course)—and when the occasion demands it, I can be self assertive like anything. . . . I have thought several times of coming in to see you in spite of my super-positive tone—then changed my mind because a certain amount of sadness is existential . . . .

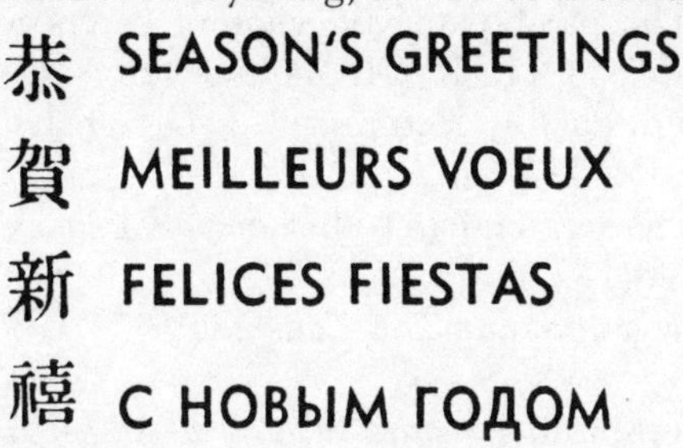

The note was, of course, gratifying to me. I was, however, also intrigued: the image on the card was almost identical to the image of the Japanese print: The familiar UNICEF "logo" served as the "protuberance" that instigated the perceptual distortion described and discussed earlier.

Neither my explication of these cases nor my presentation of the role of the superego in reality testing is complete. Just as in analysis, much remains unclear and unfinished—and the power of the unconscious is undiminished!

REFERENCES

Arlow, J. (1982), Problems of the superego concept. *The Psychoanalytic Study of the Child,* 37:229–244.

Blum, H. (1981), The forbidden quest and the analytic ideal: The superego and insight. *Psychoanal. Quart.,* 50:535–556.

Brenner, C. (1982), *The Mind in Conflict.* New York: International Universities Press.

Calef, V. & Weinshel, E. M. (1980), The analyst as the conscience of the analysis. *Internat. Rev. Psycho-Anal.,* 7:279–290.

_______ (1981), Some clinical consequences of introjection: Gaslighting. *Psychoanal. Quart.,* 50:44–66.

Fenichel, O. (1927), The economic function of screen memories. In: *Collected Papers,* First Series. New York: Norton, 1953, pp. 113–116.

_______ (1939), The economics of pseudologia phantastica. In: *Collected Papers,* Second Series. New York: Norton, 1954, pp. 129–140.

Freud, S. (1899), Screen memories. *Standard Edition,* 3:301–322. London: Hogarth Press, 1962.

_______ (1910), The psycho-analytic view of psychogenic disturbance of vision. *Standard Edition,* 11:210–218. London: Hogarth Press, 1957.

_______ (1917), Introductory lectures on psycho-analysis. *Standard Edition,* 16:243–463. London: Hogarth Press, 1963.

_______ (1923), The ego and the id. *Standard Edition,* 19:3–66. London: Hogarth Press, 1961.

_______ (1925), Negation. *Standard Edition,* 19:234–239. London: Hogarth Press, 1961.

_______ (1927), Fetishism. *Standard Edition,* 21:149–157. London: Hogarth Press, 1961.

_______ (1930), Civilization and its discontents. *Standard Edition,* 21:59–145. London: Hogarth Press, 1961.

_______ (1933), New introductory lectures on psycho-analysis. *Standard Edition,* 22:3–182. London: Hogarth Press, 1964.

_______ (1936), A disturbance of memory on the Acropolis. *Standard Edition,* 22:239–248. London: Hogarth Press, 1964.

_______ (1937), Constructions in psycho-analysis. *Standard Edition,* 23: 256–269. London: Hogarth Press, 1964.

_______ (1940), An outline of psycho-analysis. *Standard Edition,* 23:141–207. London: Hogarth Press, 1964.

Gitelson, M. (1964), On the present scientific and social position of psychoanalysis. *Internat. J. Psycho-Anal.,* 44:521–524.

Greenacre, P. (1973), The primal scene and the sense of reality. *Psychoanal. Quart.,* 42:10–41.

Greenson, R. (1958), On screen defenses, screen hunger, and screen identity. *J. Amer. Psychoanal. Assn.,* 6:242–262.

Hartmann, H. (1947), On rational and irrational action. In: *Essays in Ego Psychology.* New York: International Universities Press, 1964, pp. 19–36.

_______ (1956), Notes on the reality principle. In: *Essays in Ego Psychology.* New York: International Universities Press, 1964, pp. 241–267.

_______ & Loewenstein, R. (1962), Notes on the superego. *The Psychoanalytic Study of the Child,* 17:42–81.

Jacobson, E. (1957), On normal and pathological moods. *The Psychoanalytic Study of the Child,* 12:73–113.

_______ (1964), *The Self and the Object World.* New York: International Universities Press.

Kris, E. (1956), On some vicissitudes of insight in psychoanalysis. In: *The Selected Papers of Ernst Kris.* New Haven: Yale University Press, 1975, pp. 252–271.

Loewald, H. (1959), Internalization, separation, mourning, and the superego. In: *Papers on Psychoanalysis.* New Haven: Yale University Press, 1980, pp. 257–276.

Loewenstein, R. (1966), On the theory of the superego: A discussion. In: *Psychoanalysis: A General Psychology,* ed. R. M. Loewenstein et al. New York: International Universities Press, 1966, pp. 298–314.

Panel Report (1965), S. Goodman, Reporter. The current status of the theory of the superego. *J. Amer. Psychoanal. Assn.,* 13:172–180.

Reider, N. (1953), Reconstruction and screen function. *J. Amer. Psychoanal. Assn.,* 1:389–405.

Schafer, R. (1968), *Aspects of Internalization.* New York: International Universities Press.

Stein, M. (1966), Self-observation, reality, and the superego. In: *Psychoanalysis: A General Psychology,* ed. R. M. Loewenstein et al. New York: International Universities Press, pp. 275–297.

Weinshel, E. M. (1970), Some psychoanalytic considerations on moods. *Internat. J. Psycho-Anal.,* 51:313–320.

_______ (1977), I didn't mean it: Negation as a character trait. *The Psychoanalytic Study of the Child,* 32:387–420.

_______ (1979), Some observations on not telling the truth. *J. Amer. Psychoanal. Assn.,* 27:503–531.

Rx at least 3 yrs — (45)
(re: reporting from incomplete Rx)

98 – new info clarifies & complicates

104 differing explanations

107 topics: reality & S.ego

This 1986 paper was
in the Brenner Festschrift

(107) Superego functions 109, 113

Danger restrictions
become confused c̄
moral restrictions

114 mood

115 incompleteness
of his findings

Chapter 6

1989

On Inconsolability

At the first class on the morning of my very first day of my first year in college, the professor arrived promptly, walked briskly to the blackboard, and wrote the following:

> I am Dr. Jones.
> This is Biology IA.
> Biology is the study of life.
> Life is one god-damned thing after the other.

This was my first "scientific" encounter with the problem of inconsolability. One cannot separate the question of inconsolability from that of consolability, and there is a sufficient abundance of "one god-damned thing after the other" to guarantee, for all of us, an equally abundant supply of situations that will call for attempts at comfort and consolation. I am referring to one of those ubiquitous and hardly infrequent states of unpleasure with which all of us must cope throughout life. These states come about as a consequence of pain, loss, frustration, rejection, and a host of comparable commonplace experiences. These states of unpleasure differ in their subjective and objective manifestations and in their severity and duration; they invariably involve blows to the individual's sense of self-esteem together with some degree of anxiety and some element of the depressive affect; each person appears to utilize his or her own somewhat idiosyncratic pattern of obtaining relief from this unpleasurable state, i.e., to obtain consolation.

With some individuals, a good deal of that process depends on the comfort and solace one can receive from another person; however, some individuals seem to depend more on themselves as a source of comfort and consolation. They can and wish to be consoled, but they insist on doing the work by themselves. In this presentation I will focus on those individuals who at least consciously do not wish to be comforted and consoled, and, in fact, many of them will take a vigorous stand against any attempts to alleviate their distress or misery. I do not believe there is a discrete entity such as "inconsolability," and, similarly, I do not believe that any one individual is *always* inconsolable. It is more reasonable to adhere to the position that, on different occasions, a given person will be consolable via external or internal means, or more likely a combination thereof, and that, in different circumstances, that same person will become "inconsolable." However, there are individuals who will more or less habitually react to that particular mood by not permitting consolation or solace.

There is no one set clinical picture of inconsolability; yet certain familiar characteristics appear with some regularity. To some extent, that clinical picture is determined and colored by the event that has triggered this particular affective state. Not infrequently the inconsolable individual is capable of hiding or disguising his mood and misery to the point that no one is aware that something is very much amiss; more often the reverse is true, and the inconsolability will manifest an intrusive, invasive element which can be a conspicuous hallmark of the phenomenon, endowing the mood with a contagious quality which impinges on everyone in the immediate environment. These persons invariably demonstrate a variety of depressive affects; they tend to be withdrawn, ruminative, occupied with their thoughts and their unhappiness, and, even though they do not want to give up their unhappiness, they do not "enjoy" that unpleasure. Yet they are often quite candid in admitting to "hang on" to their misery.

Various manifestations of aggression are commonplace. These individuals are often irritable, especially if others, however kindly and discreetly, attempt to interfere with their privacy and their brooding. The disconsolate person appears to have a knack for stimulating sympathetic friends and relatives to try to alleviate his or her unhappiness by some form of humor. Invariably, these attempts fall flat or will evoke a hostile rejoinder. To accept the solace of humor would be tantamount to accepting comfort, something that the inconsolable one experiences as surrender and defeat. Some feel these gestures are an intrusion or an attack; others will react as if the consoler is trying to "seduce" them into surrendering their disconsolate state. Most patients with whom I have worked describe quite freely a definite feeling of stubbornness and of resolute determination around not giving up their misery.

I cannot claim that this more or less composite description is comprehensive or applicable to *all* inconsolable patients. The characteristics to which I have pointed and have emphasized are the ones that impressed me most in the patients I have treated in analysis. The bulk of this chapter consists of a presentation of case material in which inconsolability is an issue that came up early and frequently.

CLINICAL MATERIAL

Case 1

Mrs. D. was in her mid-30s when she came to see me, explicitly requesting analysis. She had been referred by a psychiatrist friend whose analysis I had completed about a year earlier. Later she "confessed" that the "real" reason that she selected me as her analyst was the specific wording of an interpretation that I had made to her friend and which he had related to her.

Her appearance was striking and arresting. Although by no means beautiful by conventional standards, she displayed what had to be called a "commanding presence." She was tall, slim, and, although tense and taut, extremely poised, almost to the point of aloofness. Her manner of speech was striking. Mrs. D. spoke in a low voice, carefully choosing her words with an unself-conscious and unpretentious precision. She explained that she had been considering analysis for a number of years because of her concern over the failure of two relatively brief marriages and increasing difficulties and distress in the relationship with Tom, a man with whom she had been living the past three years. Mrs. D. was uncomfortable with her 13-year-old son, but she had considerable trouble in articulating the basis and nature of that discomfort. She told me about her career as a professional actress (which suddenly seemed to make understandable her "presence"); how she had abandoned that promising career because of increasing anxiety over the possibility of making a serious error in a performance because the "whole script might suddenly drop out of my mind"; and how she had turned to teaching social sciences to junior college students. Mrs. D. described an active, diversified social life with many friends and interests but which provided her with "little comfort when I needed it"—her first reference to the inconsolability. She also described transient periods of "moodiness when

I'm not really depressed, but when I'm not really happy either and when I'd just as soon be left alone until I feel more like myself."

Mrs. D. came from a wealthy East Coast family, the youngest of three sisters. Her father was a successful physician, a handsome and glamorous figure who died of a cerebral accident when the patient was 14.

Mrs. D. painted her mother with an altogether different brush. It is difficult to recall anything positive that she could find to say about her mother. The latter was portrayed as a good-looking, vain, self-centered woman who had come from a well-to-do family that had always been preoccupied with materialistic and superficial issues; the patient felt, unequivocally, that her mother's activities and interests reflected much more these values than concern for husband, children, and home. The care of her daughters fell into the hands of a number of nurses and housekeepers whom the patient conceded were all warm and loving. Mrs. D. complained that her mother was strict, opinionated, overly concerned with good manners and proper protocol, finicky about the cleanliness and appearance of her children. However, my patient's chief criticisms of her mother centered around a whole complex of problems in trying to talk with her mother. Mrs. D.'s own terse and global summary of the trouble, "We just never talked," was a bit hyperbolic, but it accurately reflected how she felt about this aspect of the relationship with her mother. According to the patient, her mother would frequently insist, "Darling, we just have to have a nice long chat together"; but somehow these talks rarely eventuated. Or, if the almost formally scheduled talk did take place, the mother would appear disinterested and distracted, "Not there," as the patient put it, and could precipitously break off the already desultory interchange with an embarrassingly lame excuse. Often the patient had great difficulty in understanding what the mother was saying. At these moments, Mrs. D. would become hesitant and uncertain as to what she should say lest she say the wrong thing or, in turn, be misunderstood. The patient's response to some remark of the mother's might well evoke a curt "I don't know where you got that—it certainly isn't what I said." My patient would then counter with the protest that it was the mother who had been unclear, and that it was not the patient's fault that the mother had not understood. Such ripostes would infuriate the mother, who then accused the daughter of being stubborn and inattentive. These painful dramas invariably ended up in screaming fiascos punctuated by mutual accusations and the patient in despair and tears.

After these traumatic events, Mrs. D. would feel depleted, sad, and "disconnected." She would retreat to her room sometimes to cry, sometimes to mope, sometimes to try and make sense out of what appeared to her to be inexplicable. For the following two or three days, the patient would be removed and be morose, quite unapproachable by other members of the household, and feeling apprehensive about another flare-up with her mother. Except for the not terribly reassuring and relatively short-lived thought that "It wasn't just my fault," she found it impossible to comfort herself. What I have presented represents a composite of eruptions that took place as far back as the patient's sixth or seventh year and continued until late adolescence. Obviously the form and the sophistication of her own thinking and reasoning varied throughout the years, but the overall structure and sequence of the event remained constant.

Mrs. D. was reasonably successful in school, had a coterie of good friends, but was preoccupied with her acting activities which began around six. She was determined to become a famous actress and started her dramatic training at age seven and continued until she was in college, at which time she dropped out of the theater world for the reasons given above. She then married a young and already successful lawyer whom she had known for many years. The marriage was stormy from the start and ended in divorce after the birth of her son when the patient was in her early 20s. The patient remarried several years later, but this marriage also collapsed. About three years before she came for analysis, she met a divorced man with three children with whom she felt comfortable rather than "truly in love." Although their relationship has not been without its problems and pressures, Mrs. D. was quite satisfied with it and did not feel any great urge to remarry.

The major traumatic event in her life was her father's death from a massive stroke when she was 14. Mrs. D. recalled being extremely disturbed, and her description of a feeling of strangeness and "fogginess" suggested an episode of mild derealization. The events following her father's death were, to her, even more disturbing than his death itself. Soon it was revealed that the father had squandered almost all of his money, and, even though it was apparent that the bulk of the losses was the consequence of imprudent investments, the whispered allegations that a good deal of the family fortune had gone to support a series of mistresses and bookies were the items that stuck in her mind and caused her the greater distress.

The father's financial irresponsibility did not, however, lead to any alteration in the patient's standard of living. His family banded together to provide the survivors with a more than sufficient income to maintain their security and comfort. Four years later, the mother married a crotchety but conspicuously wealthy bachelor with whom the patient battled until his death when Mrs. D. was 23. The mother then became a wealthy widow who was able to offer all of her daughters considerable sums of money each year. The patient felt humiliated by her dependence on this maternal dole, and, at the same time, was not unaware of how much she coveted that money, how competitive she was with her sisters as to who was going to get the larger share of it, and how apprehensive she was lest mother remarry and have a new stepfather dissipate this fortune, as her father had done years before.

My first encounter with Mrs. D.'s inconsolability took place within the first months of the analysis. In a number of sessions, she related a series of ostensibly unconnected failures: her marriages, her career as an actress, the virtual estrangement from her sisters, the current coldness in the relationship with Tom, some difficulties she was experiencing in her teaching. Then, without making any connection to these extra-analytic disappointments, Mrs. D. began alluding to her concerns about her performance in the analysis. She made reference to her not infrequent lateness, to the fear that she was talking too much about petty issues, to her preoccupation that she might not be able to express herself clearly, and so forth. I told her that just as she felt that she had failed to do as well as she had expected in various aspects of her life outside of the analysis, she was now concerned that she might also fail to do well in the analytic work.

Her split-second response was an irate demand that I explain how I had come to *that* conclusion. She insisted that I had not really understood what she had been saying, and she complained that my "playing with words" was both unfair and confusing. She went on, as her anger gathered momentum, to let me know that she was not going to accept in a docile fashion ideas that I wanted to foist onto her. *She* was only doing what was expected of her, to say what came to mind. She was clearly deflated and discouraged, sad and hurt—and then silent.

I confess that I did not feel so good either. After a relatively brief wait, I told Mrs. D. that I did not understand all that was going on at this time and that it was not clear to me why this misunderstanding had arisen. I suggested that perhaps she had been disappointed by what I had said and that she was therefore afraid she might not be able to depend on me to help her understand what was going on. She made no reply and spent the rest of the session quiet except for a bit of muted crying, apparently oblivious of my presence. In the following session, after a period of silence, I opined that perhaps her silence and her tension were related to what had happened here in the previous hour. She suggested that it had not been necessary for me to have gone to medical school to have reached *that* conclusion. I said that she felt that it was necessary for her to remain angry and silent because she was concerned that she might become less *vigilant*—and with that word, I did luck out—and say something that I might not understand or for which, in some way, I might fault her. Somewhat to my surprise, she agreed and said that she was, indeed, quite vigilant. She added that what had happened on the previous Thursday had, indirectly, led to a quarrel with Tom. She had withdrawn from him during the entire weekend, staying by herself most of the time in spite of his apologies and entreaties. She added that for her to have in any way made up with him at that time was scary and unthinkable. Then Mrs. D. observed that there were a few times when she had tried to *console* herself with pleasant thoughts, but those thoughts would "slip away" before they could have any effect on her mood; from there, Mrs. D. launched another prolonged attack on Tom. I suggested that in this instance, at least, it was important for her to sustain her angry and disconsolate feelings in regard to Tom in order for her to sustain comparable feelings toward me.

The rest of the week was ostensibly a carbon copy of the session except that on one of those days she began to tell me more about some of her difficulties with Tom that would lead to these inconsolable moods, and once she ventured to elaborate on her frustrations around jogging and how on one recent occasion that frustration had precipitated a comparable reaction. She was still very wary, very vigilant, and very distant; but it was also evident that she was less miserable and withdrawn. Exactly what had produced these admittedly slight changes was not clear, but my own impression was that it was related to my use of the word *vigilant*. I permit myself all this detail because what took place during this first example of Mrs. D.'s inconsolability in the analysis was in general the model of similar events during the first three years of the analysis. A significant number of these episodes was triggered by some "misunderstanding" between us, be it apparent or real; but her reaction to widely diverse factors could produce the same sequence and so on.

At the same time, it became both necessary and productive to examine the inconsolability as a significant and central resistance in the analysis; as we were able to do so, we were able to learn more about the inconsolability and its constituents. The disconsolate states consequent to the "misunderstandings" served as an externalized vehicle for keeping her distance from Tom and hiding her feelings, both positive and negative, toward me. She had an uncannily acute ear for the cliché-tainted interpretation, and she experienced such lapses as evidence of my not really listening to her. Mrs. D. wanted to be special, the sole object of my interest and attention, and the cliché represented something that I could say to *any* patient. It was in the midst of trying to cope with such feelings that the patient would experience the hopelessness and what she had labeled the "disconnection" from me. It also became apparent that one of the significant determinants of being overwhelmed by the rush of these thoughts and feelings was the need to hide from both me and herself derivatives of various fantasies and their component wishes. One of the first of these to emerge for analytic scrutiny was her wish, in the period of inconsolability, to get close to or to regain the love of an object that had been lost either in reality or intrapsychically.

This was a pattern that, in different degrees and in different guises, I observed in all of my inconsolable patients. Mrs. D. could describe quite clearly the problem of not being able "to soothe myself." This is what she alluded to in what I mentioned earlier when she tried to console herself with "pleasant thoughts," which would, however, "slip away." As we were able to explore this more thoroughly, Mrs. D. was able to explain how she would plumb her mind for the reservoir of "good memories"; but feelings of guilt or uneasiness or actual contrary "bad memories" would intrude, and the "good memories" would disappear from consciousness.

A particular variant of the above deserves special comment. As stated above, in the first episode of inconsolability within the analysis Mrs. D. had alleged that my "playing with words was unfair." I had recognized that although my patient was almost obsessive in her precise and punctilious choice of words, it was also true that she never really "played" with words. For her, it was all work, and very hard work at that, and it *was* true in a sense that it was "unfair," because it was something that she would have liked to do, tried to do, but never really could do so in the fashion that she envied in others. The same was true for other kinds of play or in her sexual life. Although she would find herself indulging in daydreams, Mrs. D. never felt altogether comfortable in doing so; she could never rid herself of the suspicion that she was doing something forbidden. The main exception to this had been the acting. While rehearsing or performing, she could simultaneously abandon herself to fantasies of being great and being admired, and it was only in mid-adolescence that she began to feel uncomfortable with these gratifying fantasies. It was this conflict that eventually manifested itself in the intrusive thought, "The whole script might drop out of my mind." This interfered with both her fantasies and her acting and brought her theatrical career to an unhappy end. All of these phenomena are, of course, highly overdetermined; therefore I will focus only on those elements that are particularly relevant to the inconsolability.

In the third year of the analysis, Mrs. D. began her session by rather breezily telling me of how she had crossed the street to my office against the red light. In some detail, she described the situation, by no means minimizing the fact that her little prank was not an altogether innocuous one. In what probably was not my wisest intervention in the analysis, I asked her if she had any ideas about why she would take any chances at all; there was therefore some justification for the blast that followed. Mrs. D. was furious. I recognized immediately that my question was, at least in part, motivated by my irritation with the teasing and provocative nature of her recital; what I had missed was that the teasing also contained a genuine playful quality. This was exactly the point on which she focused her barrage. She accused me of being a wet blanket and a spoilsport, and she went on to harangue me for not wanting her to play, to have fun, to fool around. She added her conviction that I enjoyed spoiling her fun and depriving her of play.

Before withdrawing into an angry silence, she pointed out that I was behaving like her mother who could never tolerate anyone playing or having any fun, not even her husband whom she claimed to have loved very much. Mrs. D. started to tell me about an early memory but thought better of it, and, with ill-concealed disgust and discouragement, said, "Ah—what's the use," and became withdrawn and silent for the rest of that session. The next two weeks were very difficult for her, both in and out of the analysis. Mrs. D. was obviously angry with me but offered no explanation for those feelings. She was being very circumspect and very vigilant but made little effort to hide the fact that she was withholding something from me. This could be interpreted to her, and Mrs. D. explained that on the day of the red-light incident she had started to tell me about the earliest clear memory she had in regard to her father, one she assumed was from the age of five or six. She recalled the family at dinner with the father being unusually ebullient and garrulous. She could not remember the substance of the conversation, but, at one point, her mother suddenly interrupted him and, quite sternly, said, "Not in front of the children, Larry." The patient conjectured that the mother's rebuke had been in response to his using "bad words."

As we discussed this memory, over a period of many months, Mrs. D.'s initial emphasis was on how awful her mother had been. Her mother also was described as a spoilsport and wet blanket, and the patient railed about her mother's inability to let her father have a good time. She also told of many examples of her mother's behaving in a similar fashion with her sisters and herself and of how the mother never seemed to permit herself to be relaxed or playful. She repeated many of the vignettes of her mother's reluctance to talk with her, her mother's lack of spontaneity, and her mother's insistence on the correct words. One day, in this context, Mrs. D. complained that her mother always had to be "so *real*."

Then, in the midst of one of her exasperated harangues, she stopped short and wondered why her mother was like this. Almost as soon as the patient asked herself this question, her whole demeanor and focus shifted, and an altogether different set of observations began to emerge. She recalled that her mother had not always been this way. There had been a time, probably before the patient was five, when the mother had been more relaxed and playful. Further, the patient had to recognize that, although her fundamental portrayal of her mother was *essentially* correct, it was also exaggerated and even a bit distorted. Mrs. D. was chagrined to realize that all along there had been times when the mother had even been fun and that there had been occasions when they had been able to laugh together. From here the patient was able to realize that a certain aspect of her mother's behavior had been in reaction to the father's irresponsibility and infidelity and that the mother's killjoy approach to life must have been determined, at least in part, by the need to bring some semblance of order and control into what was a chaotic household. Mrs. D. could now look back on the "Not in front of the children" memory with a much more sympathetic eye and acknowledge that her father's behavior was more than a little inappropriate. After the first burst of enthusiasm for her new insight and her remorse over the scapegoating of her mother had waned a bit, the patient was able to arrive at a considerably more balanced image of her mother; but it took another 18 months of analysis before my patient was able to recognize how a significant portion of her own perceptual and mnemonic distortion of mother's character was the product of the vicissitudes of her oedipal conflicts.

In the analysis a more immediate fallout from the revised understanding of her mother was a much greater availability of what took place in her periods of inconsolability. Again this touched on Mrs. D.'s attempts to console herself, not just with "good" and happy thoughts but with more elaborate fantasies as well. She experienced these fantasies as a form of "playing with words," something that was forbidden not only because of content but because they were fantasies, i.e., not real. These potentially healing, soothing fantasies reflected, in addition to her wish for self-consolation, the wish for a daring and dangerous defiance of her mother (a part of which involved an identification with the misbehaving father). It will not come as a surprise that Mrs. D. revealed that both the fantasies and the reaction to them often involved masturbation. The patient's efforts to use fantasy, what was not real, as a means of combatting her misery would invariably be short-lived; the various repressive processes that contributed to the transience of those fantasies also contributed to the patient's inconsolability by interfering with the self-consoling mechanisms.

One of the principal reasons for her vigilance, her stubborn refusal to "give in" to any gesture or offer of consolation, was the fear that such efforts on the part of others represented an implicit or actual promise that would not be honored. This reaction derived, at different times in different proportions, from her fear of disappointment and its subsequent depressive feeling, her humiliation at the expectation of being pleased and then being ungratified, and her anxious concern in regard to the rage that often accompanied such disappointments. Although Mrs. D. was hypersensitive to almost any type of promise, three groups were particularly prominent: those related to her mother's promises to have talks with her; those related to her father's implied promises of approval and admiration; and those related to her nursemaids' less implicit promises of the rewards she would receive in the future if she was a good girl in the present.

I have already discussed the impact of the mother's unfulfilled promises around the prospect of "nice, little chats." Mrs. D.'s father was a prolific promiser and an equally profligate promise-breaker. The patient learned to tolerate his habitual promising since his failure to carry out these seriously undertaken vows was such a commonplace in the household and he was so indiscriminate in his choice of victims that, after a while, the patient just accepted these numerous derelictions.

More complex and insidious were the unspoken promises from her father that the patient brought up later in the analysis. These emerged first in the transference when Mrs. D. accused me of violating certain "promises." In her list of complaints, she included such items as my being late, the phone ringing, or changing my appointment schedule. She "knew," of course, that I had not in fact ever made promises about these issues, but, at the same time, she "felt" that she was quite justified in drawing such inferences from my behavior and some of the things that I had said. Further discussion disclosed what she called her "crush" on me and her conviction that I must entertain comparable feelings about her. Thus she could interpret my listening to her, tolerating her bouts of inconsolability, being "nice" to her as incontrovertible evidence of my being in love with her; therefore all of this was also evidence of my promising her that I would never be late, never permit the phone to ring, never change the hour of our meeting. I do not believe that this "unilateral contract" phenomenon is rare or limited to patients with inconsolability, and I have not found that it represents a significant defect in reality testing. With Mrs. D. it became an important element in the transference neurosis and replicated comparable experiences with her father.

When Mrs. D. was about five or six, her interest in acting manifested itself in her amateur performances around the home. She was not unaware of her wish to show off for her father and to gain his attention and admiration. He became a most appreciative audience and an enthusiastic admirer, praising her skill and her beauty. All of this was both exceedingly gratifying and exciting to the patient, and she chose to interpret his response as evidence of his love for her and also as evidence of a promise that when she grew up he would abandon the mother and marry his daughter. This somewhat illusory conclusion already had its basis in the previous phases of development, which I will relate below.

The third area of concern about promises, those centering around experiences with her nursemaids, also entered the analysis via the transference and the patient's persistent uneasiness over the basic rule to say whatever came to mind. She could not convince herself that I really meant that she could say what came to mind with impunity and retained many reservations about "letting myself go." As the analysis proceeded, Mrs. D. justified her suspicions and her caution with an impressive piece of casuistry. She conceded that it was true that I did not blame her, hold her *culpable*, for the secrets she revealed, but, she argued, I did hold her *responsible* for that material. Thus she concluded, with more than a trace of triumph, my implied offer of impunity was not genuine, and I had, in effect, broken my promise to her.

Eventually these same issues entered into her associations regarding her nursemaids and various derivatives from her anal phase of development. The nursemaids would urge her to busy herself with her toys and were complimentary when she occupied herself with these games, but they were irritated and critical when she left her toys in disarray, when she had made a mess. Further, the nursemaids would encourage her obediently to move her bowels; but then they would be annoyed and unhappy with her at those times when she might make a mess of it. For Mrs. D., this apparent inconsistency represented another betrayal and another example of broken promises. These very useful analytic data and the memories the data contained helped to demonstrate her sensitivity to apparently broken promises, but it also made more evident a certain "hunger" for promises and an uncanny capacity for eliciting them from significant others; in turn, she could then utilize them as defenses against a variety of forbidden wishes.

The latter became clearer as the analytic work progressed. During that period in the analysis when Mrs. D. recognized that her oedipal aspirations were not going to be gratified, her frustration and depression were commingled with indignation and rancor. Gradually we were able to reconstruct specific interactions with her nursemaids that, around the age of three or four, became somewhat elaborate bedtime rituals. She would ask the nursemaid if she had been a good girl, and the latter would invariably respond that indeed she had. The patient then would inquire about the specific ways in which she had been good, and the nursemaid would enumerate all of the virtuous acts her charge had carried out that day. Most of these centered on being clean and neat and obedient. Then my patient would carefully interrogate her nursemaid about the rewards she might anticipate for such exemplary behavior, and the nursemaid would reply to the effect, "When you grow up, you will have all the things you want." The patient would then cross-examine her nursemaid with some species of "Are you sure?" and the answer was always an unconditional affirmative. This "game" would, over a period of many months, be enacted almost every night before the patient went to bed. The elaborations could become quite complicated, and, for the patient, the whole event was a source of satisfaction and reassurance.

What was for the nursemaid only an innocent game was for Mrs. D. a serious and sacred vow, a promissory note that she expected to be redeemed at some future date, a contract that was to be fulfilled at her bidding. Further, it was the confidence in this fulfillment that for her at least—gave substance and reality to her father's multiple promises, and at the same time these expectations intensified the pain and bitterness of her disappointments when those promises were not honored. This whole panoply of fantasies and feelings resurfaced in adolescence, at the time of her father's death, when her marriages dissolved in disappointment, and in the transference. In less dramatic fashion, derivatives of these traumas played a not insignificant (if not always entirely conscious) role in many of her episodes of inconsolability.

Any attempt to console carries with it at least the implicit promise that solace and succor will be forthcoming. For my patient no such attempt was to be trusted. Such gestures merely loomed up as insincere or completely treacherous maneuvers to trick her, to lull her into a sense of security, which would prove to be false or insubstantial. She was frightened by these however ostensibly warm approaches that she was certain would lead to traumatic disappointment, humiliation, and despair, and, as a consequence, she had no recourse but to repel the offer of consolation and to withdraw into herself.

I wish to say a few words about those instances of inconsolability that presented themselves around her tendency to come late for the analytic sessions. This tendency manifested itself shortly after the beginning of the analysis and persisted for a large portion of it. My attempts to deal with this problem as a resistance based on anal phase conflicts were accepted readily, maybe too readily, by the patient, and while Mrs. D. began to control her tardiness outside of the analysis much more effectively, there was no change within the analysis. If anything, her lateness and the feelings of despair connected with the lateness—and the resultant disconsolateness—became much more marked.

One day, while talking about these issues, Mrs. D. started to say that something was unconscious, but, instead, she stated that it was "unconscionable." She was embarrassed; then, after a brief silence, she confessed that she used to steal. From here the patient was able to reveal how much the analysis and the analyst meant to her and how *eager* she was to come to the session each day. She was concerned that this would make me both uncomfortable and angry and could lead to my terminating the analysis. I will only summarize that which is somewhat apparent but which took a number of years to unravel. Beneath Mrs. D.'s eagerness were not only her budding positive feelings for the analyst but a variety of incorporative and competitive fantasies—and underlying these more specific wishes were the more proximal derivative of her oral incorporative impulses and the more general feelings of greed.

These tendencies and wishes played a significant part in her inconsolability. Not only did they contribute to the feelings of badness and unworthiness that made it difficult for her to accept some form of consolation, but there was frequently the conscious apprehension that, if others observed that she *was* consoled and *was* satisfied, they would also recognize the illicit basis on which she had obtained that gratification and consolation—her greediness would be exposed, and she would be punished.

Summary. In this lengthy description of Mrs. D. and her analysis, I have not attempted to give a comprehensive picture of her pathology or of her analysis; I have focused, rather, on the problems of her inconsolability, how those problems manifested themselves in the analysis, and what understanding we achieved about the inconsolability and its genesis and meaning. I should also point out that Mrs. D., like most of us, was also *capable* of letting others console her, and she was also *capable* of consoling herself. When, for whatever concatenation of circumstances at the moment, neither self-consolation nor consolation from others was possible, her inconsolability became evident. In my discussion of Mrs. D. I have presented analytic material that bears on her difficulty in permitting others to offer her solace (i.e., her fear of promises being broken, her fear that her feelings of greed might be exposed, and her fear that, in her case, at least, via breaks in verbal communication, contacts with others could lead to further loss of love or even loss of object—what Mrs. D. called "disconnected") and I have also presented material that bears on the patient's difficulty in providing solace for herself (i.e., the problem she had in making use of her reservoir of "good" memories, an issue related to the concept of what has been called the "loving" superego, and her problem in making use of fantasy, play, and illusion). I do not pretend that these factors are by any means the only or the necessary ones in the evolution of inconsolability, and I recognize that these factors cannot really be seen as isolated and independent; they are all interdependent. In a more general sense *anything* that interferes with an individual's ability to obtain solace from others and *anything* that interferes with the individual's ability to provide solace for himself must contribute to the vulnerability to and the tendency toward the state of inconsolability.

Case 2

Mrs. K., a 30-year-old married mother of two, presented numerous episodes of inconsolability both in the analysis and at home. She was preoccupied with her role as a woman, her feelings that women were treated unfairly, and her angry competitiveness with men. One day, she spoke of her concern that she was not as "logical" as I was, and she went on to say that this inferiority in being logical was one of the reasons women were not treated as well as men. Driving to her hour, Mrs. K. had tried to "console" herself by thinking about her relatively new baby and how "good" she felt about being a mother.

These consoling thoughts were not sustained for a very long time. They were replaced by thoughts about her baby. She recalled that when she first became pregnant, she had the fantasy that when the pregnancy was over, her body would be quite different; she had been very disappointed when, after her baby was born, her body was "still the same." Her concern about the analysis was that it could not change her body. Then she said (not for the first time) that her mother had promised her repeatedly that when she grew up, she would be altogether changed; but since she had not changed, her mother had broken her promise. She could not accept any compliment her husband offered about her body. She felt that he was lying, and the thought made her feel worse. She wanted to "crawl away and die" and she felt "unapproachable."

In the session Mrs. K.'s mood became worse. She was sad, angry, and very soft-spoken; but she continued to speak. Her five-year-old daughter had announced her intention to marry her uncle, and she had been openly seductive with him. My patient was concerned with how the daughter might be spared the humiliation of an oedipal disappointment, and she recalled her own, comparable, disappointments. Mrs. K. wanted me to help her advise the uncle on how to deal with his niece; she wanted to know some way that he could "go along with the 'make-believe' without really making her believe that she could marry him." This led to her concern that her feelings toward me were so much more intense than mine toward her. She wanted so much from me; it made her feel greedy and ashamed.

DISCUSSION

This clinical material throws some light on the role of penis envy (or other "loss") in inconsolability. The feelings of loss and deprivation per se do not cause the inconsolability; they produce an internal situation that necessitates consolation. The other factors (here her feelings of greed, her concern about broken promises) interfere with the process of restitution and reparation and lead to the inconsolable state.

The best known examples of inconsolability, and the situation to which the word is most frequently applied, are those related to the loss of a beloved person: parent, close friend, lover, spouse, or child; this is more strikingly so in the latter two instances. In my own work I have had the opportunity of analyzing a number of patients who have suffered the loss of a child or who have undergone abortions, and in these cases (especially when a child died), a significant, protracted period of inconsolability was observed. Without suggesting that other factors were not also operative, I have been impressed with a particular set of data that emerged in these analyses. These patients were burdened with a specific form of guilt and the fantasy that the loss of the child (or fetus) was their fault. This conviction was derived from oedipal guilt, and the fantasy that the dead child was the consequence of the product of an incestuous union. These women saw themselves as guilty of the crime of infanticide and their disconsolate state as evidence of a well-deserved punishment.

Although there are many more variants that could be described, I will mention only one final group that, for want of more precise criteria, I have labeled unconsolables. These are patients whose inconsolability was so intractable and so unrelenting that I have separated them from those with inconsolability. As far as I can tell, the factors that produce the painful state that requires consolation and those that interfere with the process of consolation are the same as in those whose inconsolability is less severe and of shorter duration; but either these elements are quantitatively greater or other factors must be operative. These patients not only seem to suffer more and for a longer period of time, but they produce more archaic material which at times suggests a psychotic substratum. Also, these patients frequently are not able to tolerate the pain and pressure of their disconsolation by withdrawal, rumination, or brooding alone, and, often in desperation, they may resort to various forms of action: drinking and drug taking; compulsive, repetitive masturbation, which may be free of any accompanying fantasies; bouts of eating, often in extreme amounts and in bizarre patterns; head-banging and hair-pulling, self-mutilation, and so forth. I do not feel comfortable in offering any kind of precise formulation, but it would appear that these manifestations are evidence of regressive processes in which the more highly organized, cognitive, affective, and defensive patterns are replaced by more primitive action processes. I do not presume to have even touched on all of the clinical issues related to inconsolability; even on the clinical level, there are many questions that remain to be answered. For instance (and this is true of moods and other complex affective configurations in general), it is not always crystal clear what factors or group of factors are capable of precipitating such reactions, and even more enigmatic is the process whereby the inconsolability gradually diminishes and then disappears. From the clinical perspective, I have tried to demonstrate that the analytic work can best be maintained by dealing with the inconsolability as a resistance and dealing analytically with those factors that at least appear to contribute to the interference with the process of consolation. I have been impressed with the frequency and the clarity of the role that both pregenital and oedipal components play in the evaluation and maintenance of the inconsolability. A further understanding of these interrelationships may provide us with a better knowledge of a number of "atypical" clinical pictures that often frustrate our attempts at diagnosis and classification. In that vein, it is not easy to define precisely *what* inconsolability is. At times, it appears to have the structure and genesis of a symptom; at other times that of a mood or the mourning process. In some cases, the defensive elements are most conspicuous; in others, the inconsolability seems to be the nodal point of a complex character structure. In most of my cases, the clinical picture suggests a mixture of a number of the above.

Similarly, we are still relatively ignorant of why some individuals are much more prone to becoming disconsolate than others. Studies of the neonate and very young infants demonstrate differences at birth in terms of their enjoyment of being cuddled, proficiency at self-consolations, approachability, and relative ease of satiability, but, to the best of my knowledge, no systematic follow-up studies are available that might demonstrate how, and if, these variations play a part in later vulnerability to inconsolability. There is considerable clinical evidence to suggest that these individuals who have not received "good enough mothering" or who have otherwise in the course of early development suffered early trauma may not have sufficient inner resources to utilize efforts at consolation and may also in adult life suffer more frequently from problems of inconsolability.

REVIEW OF SELECTED LITERATURE

I do not intend to offer a comprehensive review of all of the analytic literature that may contribute to our knowledge of these phenomena. There are only a few systematic contributions that focus, primarily, on inconsolability, although fragmentary allusions to it are scattered through the literature. Quite arbitrarily, I have chosen to limit myself to brief comments on those contributions which stimulated my own thinking on the subject.

1. The 1955 paper, "Say You're Sorry," by Kubie and Israel, contains a poignant report of the case of a five-year-old girl whose withdrawal, remoteness, and sadness can be viewed as manifestations of inconsolability. Although the clinical data are limited, the patient's intense feelings of guilt, her preoccupation with whose "fault" it was, and her inability to accept (or to make use of) solace, all seem similar to what is observed in adult patients with inconsolability. Particularly interesting was the patient's refusal to respond to the author's approaches until the precisely correct words were utilized. I believe that this almost magical reaction is tantamount to a game where one individual expects another individual to "guess" what he is thinking.

2. David Milrod's (1972) paper, "Self-Pity, Self-Comforting, and the Superego," is a pioneering effort to delineate some special problems relating to consolation and its vicissitudes. Milrod's focus is on patients whose self-pity as a major vehicle of consolation "may constitute a persistent major characteristic of a person who uses a grievance, even if imagined or provoked, as the stimulus to withdraw for a long spell of feeling sorry for himself" (p. 505). He stresses the narcissistic withdrawal in these patients and suggests that they may suffer from significant defects in ego boundaries and the tendency to use projection as an important defensive operation. Milrod also emphasizes what he calls a "unique bittersweet gratification" which these patients derive from "a narcissistic orgy, tinged with masochism" (p. 507), and he attributes much of the comforting obtained in the self-pitying to the "rewarding" function of the superego.

3. Herbert Schlesinger's two papers, the 1978 article on "Developmental and Regressive Aspects of Making and Breaking of Promises" and the unpublished essay on "The Nature and Regressive Determinants of the Keeping of Promises" constitute a comprehensive source of information and observations on the phenomenon of the promise. He points out

that the earliest precursors of the promise are related to "the primitive experiences of regularity in wish fulfillment" (1978, p. 30) and gratification; and he stresses that for younger children, the promise has a different meaning and significance than it does for adults. This is especially pertinent in regard to the solipsistic manner in which children may hear and experience parental assent, half-promises, and offhand promises as serious and sacred vows. He also discusses the way in which the child "rather than renouncing the [forbidden] wish . . . renounces certain possibilities of realistic gratification in the hope of thus assuring ultimate gratification of the infantile wish sometime in the indefinite future" (unpublished). Schlesinger also notes the importance of promises in the analysis; he points out that although analysts carefully avoid making promises, nevertheless, it is inevitable that the patient will feel that promises have been offered.

4. Roy Schafer's well-known contribution on "The Loving and Beloved Superego in Freud's Structural Theory" (1960) is a thorough, insightful exegesis on Freud's ideas regarding the loving and protective aspects of the superego, ideas which he never developed as comprehensively as its critical and punitive aspects. Freud always stressed that the superego had access to libidinal as well as aggressive energies. Thus, the ego could be loved as well as hated by the superego. This "loving" encompasses a guiding, protecting, taking care of, soothing of the self functions that are crucial in the processes of consolation and inconsolability. Freud (and Schafer) point to the special need for such "loving" in situations of "overwhelming danger" of a real order where feelings of helplessness may ensue. Schafer reminds us that these same feelings of helplessness and the dread of "traumatic helplessness" are involved in all levels of Freud's genetic series of "danger" situations. At these times, there may be a need and a longing for the loving, protective parents, but there is also a dependence on the loving aspects of the superego. All of these considerations are of great importance in coping with frustration and disappointment, with obtaining consolation, and the process of inconsolability. I need hardly add that one of the major factors that deter the superego from acting in a benevolent fashion in these situations is the aggression the individual may direct toward the love objects or the superego itself. This aggression, whether it is overt or whether it operates internally, is invariably involved in the blocking of consolation efforts and the emergence of inconsolability.

5. The contributions of Winnicott to this topic warrant far more space than is available. He has devoted a good deal of his writings to the

issues of consolation, inconsolability, soothing, holding, aloneness, and the capacity to be alone. Most of his principal conceptual contributions are well known, so a summary of his work is not necessary. I would, however, remind the reader that many of those concepts—the transitional object, the "good enough" mother, the idea of the facilitating environment, and the concept of "holding" were developed around the issues of the need for consolation, the ways in which consolation occurs, and the state of what I am calling inconsolability. I will focus on one point only: what Winnicott (1953) refers to as the

> intermediate area of experience, between the thumb and the teddy bear, between the oral erotism and the true object-relationship, between primary creative activity and projection of what has already been introjected, between primary unawareness of indebtedness and the acknowledgement of indebtedness.., an intermediate area of *experiencing,* to which inner reality and external life both contribute . . . the perpetual human task of keeping inner and outer reality separate yet inter-related . . . therefore studying the substance of illusion, that which is allowed to the infant, and which in adult life is inherent in art and religion [pp. 89–90].

Winnicott sees illusion as a creative, productive, adaptive process that brings together inner and outer reality and that the child can use—he would say *needs* to use—to deal with anxiety and states of the depressive type. It is a process that "may reappear" and be utilized at later ages.

Winnicott argues that the mother has the responsibility gradually to disillusion the infant, but this is impossible unless she first has been able to provide sufficient opportunity for illusion. I think that you will recognize a parallel with the work of Mahler, Pine, and Bergman (1975) on the rapprochement phase and the danger of the precipitous deflation of the child's sense of omnipotence.

What Winnicott is saying is that, after all, life is hard and that the "intuitive" parent recognizes that making the child face and conform to every bit of "objective" reality is too much of a strain. Part of that recognition entails illusion, fantasy, religion, creativity, and play; all of these modalities are crucial to the process of consolation. Where these modalities have not been "allowed" to the child, that child has been deprived of powerful weapons against all of those "one damned things after the other" with which I began this presentation. It may well be that blessed is he who can appropriately make use of illusion in just the way that Mrs. K. hoped that her brother could "go along with the 'make-believe'" without *really* making his niece believe that she could marry him.

REFERENCES

Kubie, L. S. & Israel, H. (1955), Say you're sorry. *The Psychoanalytic Study of the Child,* 10:289–299. New York: International Universities Press.

Mahler, M. S., Pine, F. & Bergman, A. (1975), *The Psychological Birth of the Human Infant.* New York: Basic Books.

Milrod, D. (1972), Self-pity, self-comforting, and the superego. *The Psychoanalytic Study of the Child,* 27:505–528. New York: Quadrangle.

Schafer, R. (1960), The loving and beloved superego in Freud's structural theory. *The Psychoanalytic Study of the Child,* 15:163–188. New York: International Universities Press.

Schlesinger, H. (1978), Developmental and regressive aspects of making and breaking of promises. In: *The Human Mind Revisited: Essays in Honor of Karl A. Menninger,* ed. S. Smith. New York: International Universities Press, pp. 21–50.

_______ (n.d.), The nature and regressive determinants of the keeping of promises. Unpublished manuscript.

Winnicott, D. W. (1953), Transitional objects and transitional phenomena. *Internat. J. Psycho-Anal.,* 34:89–97.

118 there is no discrete entity like "inconsolability" & his pts were not always inconsolable.
this avoidance of conceptualization & reductive explanations is [illegible]

120 or even that his composite description is true for all inconsolable pts.

135 lack of adequate mothering confirmed in my own material.

PART 2: THEORETICAL PAPERS

Introduction to Part 2

Theoretical Papers

The following sequence of eight theoretical papers (again two of them coauthored with Victor Calef) represents the counterpart thinking within the framework of the American mainstream ego psychology metapsychological paradigm of which Weinshel and Calef have been strong adherents throughout their careers. Unlike the collection of selected clinical papers in this volume, which adhered more to the British tradition of inextricably embedding any offered theoretical perspective or advance within the clinical phenomena in the consulting room which gave rise to them, this sequence of theoretical papers is more within the American tradition, given great gravitas by the writings of Heinz Hartmann, of being logically argued theoretical expositions with no or only rare and incidental clinical illustration. They cover approximately the same two decades, the beginning of the '70s through to the beginning of the '90s, as the clinical contributions included here (Calef died on October 12, 1983).

The first paper in this sequence—and the longest by far—"The Ego in Health and Normality" (1970), by Weinshel alone, is an extraordinarily comprehensive book essay written for the *Journal of the American Psychoanalytic Association,* reviewing a collection of volumes by (alphabetically) Erikson (1964), Glover (1968), Hartmann (1964), Jacobson (1964), Loewenstein (1966), Modell (1968), and White (1963)—almost a pantheon of the regnant voices within the Anglo-American mainstream at that time. Though it covered intensively the works of such a large group of major psychoanalytic contributors, it stands also as an overarching statement of homage to Heinz Hartmann and his central role in articulating the ego psychology theorization that embraced more or less each of the others being reviewed, though each in his or her own very individual exposition. What is incisively discussed in this long essay includes such central ego psychology conceptions as psychoanalysis as an aspiring general psychology, adaptation, the nature and role of (external) reality, the average expectable environment, the conflict-free sphere, secondary ego autonomy, drive neutralization, enduring values and psychological relativity, social compliance, and all in all the constant shifting blending of the rational and the irrational in creating optimal (or not) mental functioning within ever-varying exigent circumstance. And blended into this (seeming) potpourri are Erikson's psychosocial approach, together with his signature concepts of identity, intergenerational cogwheeling and psychological-social mutuality; Glover's developmental approach and his conception of embryonic ego nuclei in the growth and evolution of mature ego integration; Jacobson's thinking on the roles of ego and of self in psychic development; Frosch's views on the development of reality constancy as the counterpart to evolving object constancy; White's conception of the striving for effectance with drivelike power alongside traditional conceptions of libido and aggression; Modell's beginning introduction of Winnicott's views into the corpus of American ego psychology, along with consideration of the contributions of Gitelson, Tartakoff, Lampl-de Groot, and others still into the ego psychology matrix. And along with all this, consideration of what can be meant by ego strength (or weakness), by the synthetic function of the ego, by the place in theory of ego interests and of self-interests, by the place of acting (with its line of distinction from acting-out) in altering reality, by the cohesion or separateness of ego and superego functions, and all this in relation to the ever-important evaluation issue of analyzability. Surely this array covers almost everything that can be promised in the essay's title, "The Ego in Health and Normality."

The next article in this series, also by Weinshel alone, "The Transference Neurosis: A Survey of the Literature" (1971), was presented in an abbreviated form at a panel on the transference neurosis at the May 1968 meeting of the American Psychoanalytic Association in Boston, and previously, at the meetings of the West Coast Psychoanalytic Societies in October 1966. It is a comprehensive overview of the literature to that time on this central technical and conceptual vehicle of psychoanalysis as a therapy.

The essay is built around three questions raised about the transference concept by Willi Hoffer in 1955: (1) What does it mean? (2) How does it develop? (3) What role does it play in the therapeutic process? After citing most of the contributors to this focused topic—among them Gill, Glover, Greenacre, Greenson, Loewald, Macalpine, Rangell, Stone,

Strachey, and Zetzel—Weinshel concludes that the template laid down by Sigmund Freud still provided—again, until that time—the essential framework of our understanding of this central psychoanalytic conception. And within this Weinshel considered such issues as the transference as resistance, as regression, as an expression of the repetition compulsion, as something induced rather than a spontaneous development (Macalpine), as something to be "resolved" (?) by "interpretation alone" (?), as well as the Alexandrian notion of "the insoluble transference neurosis" vis-à-vis the deployment of the "corrective emotional experience." Altogether a heady mix, though we are aware, of course, that since this 1971 overview our understanding of the transference neurosis has been radically transformed, if it serves as a heuristically useful conception at all anymore.

The next, the third, paper in this sequence, "Reporting, Nonreporting, and Assessment in the Training Analysis" (1973), this one written with Victor Calef, is, like the immediately previous article on the transference neurosis, a significant marker of its era, and thus of special interest as a historical chronicle of that period's intellectual wars, but no longer a live issue. The Calef–Weinshel piece, in powerful support of the position on this issue long spearheaded by the then very influential psychoanalytic educator, Joan Fleming, articulates very persuasively, the rationale (and in their eyes, the value) of ongoing assessment, and judicious reporting, on the part of the training analyst, of the candidate's progression as someone potentially qualified to assume the analyst's professional role. It goes without saying that such reports do not reveal any of the content of the analytic material (of the real or the fantasy life of the analysand) but only of the development of those qualities and capacities critical to being a proper analyst. Nonetheless, this article can be viewed as one of the last hurrahs (and a vigorous one at that) in a losing battle that has since given way to the contrary position, the exclusion of the personal (training) analysis from the psychoanalytic educational process as far as is humanly possible.

The next, and the second in this theoretical series, of the articles coauthored with Calef, "The Analyst as the Conscience of the Analysis" (1980), is probably their very best known, and most widely remarked, collaborative paper. It was written for a Festschrift in honor of Paula Heimann, herself a prominent psychoanalytic educator—in the British Society—at the time. Like the preceding article it is about the training analysis, this time from the perspective of the tasks of the two participants in this process. Though clearly both parties bring their personalities, including of course their own ongoing conflicts and neurotic propensities, to the psychoanalytic interaction, it is the analyst's responsibility (and only the analyst's) to be the ever vigilant "keeper of the analytic process." And this is to be done by a constant self-observational process, or self-inquiry—and this focus was so forcefully propounded by these authors at least a decade before the burgeoning conceptions of the "two-person psychology" centered around the interaction and mutual influencing of two subjectivities (each with its psychological propensities and biases built on previous, not fully metabolized life experience) penetrated significantly into the American psychoanalytic mainstream educated within the ego psychology tradition. But as staunch adherents of this same ego psychology paradigm within which they were educated, Calef and Weinshel put their considerations within ego psychological language, of the necessary desexualization of certain assessment functions of the ego, of the capacity to inculcate in the analysand the qualities and functions essential to the proper maintenance of the analytic process, and so on.

The following, and final, four articles in this sequence mark the special focus that has been most identified with Edward Weinshel, as the expression of his major contribution to the conceptual debates that have marked our psychoanalytic history: this is the issue, which has so preoccupied American psychoanalysis, of the nature of the psychoanalytic process. These four papers were all written after Victor Calef's death, and in the first of the four, "Some Observations on the Psychoanalytic Process" (1984), which had been presented as the 33rd Freud Anniversary Lecture of the New York Psychoanalytic Institute on April 12, 1983, Weinshel has a footnoted reference to Calef's recent death with his attribution of much of the thinking embodied in this article to the many years of constant discussion in "that most fruitful collaboration."

One central emphasis occupies the first of these articles by Weinshel on the psychoanalytic process. It is his special conception that it is, "the resistance, together with its successful negotiation by the analyst (most often by interpretation) [which] is the clinical unit of the psychoanalytic process" (chapter 11), and he then spends the bulk of the article explaining and justifying his conviction that this "analysis" of the resistance, not its overcoming or destruction, constitutes the central task of analysis, not withstanding his acknowledgment that any number of colleagues thinking and writing simultaneously about the nature (or the essence) of the psychoanalytic process would put their chief focus elsewhere (the transference, the defenses, etc.), though clearly not in contradiction. Since Weinshel's conception is that termination of the treatment comes to the fore when the analyst is no longer necessary to sustain the psychoanalytic process (i.e., the patient has introjected and incorporated the self-analytic, or better, self-inquiring, function), it follows that the analytic process does not end with the end of the analysis. How long it then goes on, and what the evidential markers are that it is still ongoing, are, however, not really addressed.

Weinshel returned to this theme vigorously in the next, the sixth of this series of articles on theoretical issues, "Further Observations on the Psychoanalytic Process" (1990). There he begins with a recap of his prior statement, culminating in the assertion that the properly carried out psychoanalytic process leads to the gradual internalization of those psychic structures which subserve that process, thus leading to the analysand's enhanced capacity for critical self-observation, which marks the appropriate termination point. Although again acknowledging the wide range of differing foci among like-minded and similarly trained colleagues on what constitutes the essence of the psychoanalytic process, and while acknowledging as well the elusiveness of the conception as a distinct psychic construction—including some who feel the concept to be superfluous since they feel it to be just another way of talking about the whole work of analysis, not a separate conception within it—Weinshel stoutly calls the concept both feasible and useful; and seeks to persuade us as to why. In this paper he also links the properly ongoing psychoanalytic process to the accumulating evidences of what he calls *psychoanalytic* change—which to Weinshel is a more substantial concept than the often deployed conceptions of psychic structure and *structural* change, which to him are too ambiguous and not amenable to clinical demonstration.

That same year, 1990, Weinshel published the seventh in this theoretical sequence, a very much linked paper but wider in its range of considerations, "How Wide Is the Widening Scope of Psychoanalysis and How Solid Is Its Structural Model? Some Concerns and Observations," which had been the invited plenary address to the Annual Meeting of the American Psychoanalytic Association in Montreal, Canada, on May 8, 1988. The paper began with a "counsel of modesty" for the position of psychoanalysis as a therapy, a statement of the growing awareness over the most recent decades of the limitations of all efforts to alter lifelong inbred psychic structures and an effort to set a more realistic framework for what our cumulated clinical experience could lead us to expect from good-enough psychoanalytic treatments. This

Weinshel strongly felt to be a major needed swing of the pendulum away from the overidealization of psychoanalysis as a therapy that had characterized the ebullient decades of the '50s and '60s, the era of the full installation and the sweeping hegemony in America of the ego psychology paradigm architected so confidently by Hartmann and his many collaborators and colleagues. Here Weinshel acknowledged the, by then, widespread acceptance of psychoanalytic theoretical diversity, or pluralism as we had come to call it, and all the corresponding lesser certainties about what indeed psychoanalysis could accomplish, both in its reach and in its limitations, and also the far lesser certainties about how it does bring about the changes that are achieved.

But then Weinshel rebounds with his spirited and even passionate (albeit in a properly modulated way) defense of, and indeed reaffirmation of, modern (ego psychological) structural theory, identifying in that regard with the transformations effected by Charles Brenner in ego psychology theory into what many of its continuing adherents have renamed modern conflict theory and compromise formations. And as a counterfoil to the growing emphasis in our practice and in our literature on the widening scope of psychoanalysis built upon the clinical possibilities facilitated by the ramifying array of diversifying theoretical positions, Weinshel opts instead for deepening, rather than widening, and deepening preferentially, of course, within the transformed modern structural theory of which he was a steadfast lifelong proponent.

And finally in the last article in this theoretical series and in this volume, "Therapeutic Technique in Psychoanalysis and Psychoanalytic Psychotherapy" (1992), which had been presented on a panel at the Fall Meeting of the American Psychoanalytic Association in New York on December 16, 1989, Weinshel offered his most evolved thinking on the perennial issue, at least within American mainstream analysis, of the similarities and differences between psychoanalysis proper and the linked and derived psychoanalytic psychotherapies, and brought these concerns squarely into the orbit of his own idea on the psychoanalytic process. He started the article with the by then quite uncontested view that these issues of similarity and difference between the two modalities which had seemed so clearly defined in the immediate post–World War II decades, at this time, three and four decades later, were decidedly unsettled and very problematic. Previously clear and sharp distinctions were now inextricably blurred, and whatever linkages, similarities and differences were now posited were inescapably problematic, and if existing at all, were all matters just of degree and of emphasis.

Within this framework, and within the now pluralism and widened scope and modesty of clinical and theoretical aspirations, Weinshel returned to his convictions about the nature of the psychoanalysis process (the systematic and unremitting analysis of resistance) as the uniquely distinctive characteristic of proper psychoanalysis that would distinguish it from any modified psychoanalytic modality (no matter how psychoanalytic in conception and understanding) where a "psychotherapeutic process"—however that would be understood—would hold sway. This was in the end the expression of Weinshel's committed—and lifelong—belief in the psychoanalytic vision in which he had been educated and to which he devoted his professional lifetime.

Chapter 7

1970

The Ego in Health and Normality

I

It would, perhaps, be somewhat fulsome to label as monumental the collection of volumes which provides the basis for this essay (Erikson, 1964; Glover, 1968; Hartmann, 1964; Jacobson, 1964; Loewenstein, 1966; Modell, 1968: White, 1963); but it would be much more difficult to deny that—as a collection—these books represent an imposing and influential body of psychoanalytic writing. The names of the authors and contributors are among the most illustrious and respected in our literature; and the topics which are covered would seem to approach all of the crucial theoretical issues which engage us as psychoanalysts. Although the chief focus of most of the work centers on the ego and on ego psychology, there is in fact little pertaining to human behavior and its vicissitudes which is not at least touched on by the various authors. There are contributions on the psychological aspects of the very earliest periods of development, on the psychological aspects of old age; on genetics and physiology, and on some of the most esoteric aspects of ego psychology; there is material on the "normal personality," on the pathology and treatment of schizophrenia; contributions on the psychological aspects of ethics and "virtue," and a number of excellent pieces of psychological biography. Neither id nor superego is neglected; and all the metapsychological points of view are amply represented. The breadth and diversity of the subject matter contained in these works is, by itself, an impressive argument for the concept of a general psychoanalytic psychology.

When the editors of the Hartmann Festschrift entitled it *Psychoanalysis—A General Psychology* (Loewenstein et al., 1966), I do not believe that they intended to imply that psychoanalysis has already achieved that status or that even all the blueprints for such a model were already available. It seems to me—and I trust that the editors, as well as

Hartmann, would agree—that what we have at this time is an "idea" and a direction; there are still many aspects of human behavior which are not readily translatable into psychoanalytic conceptualization or concerning which psychoanalytic data is still regrettably sparse. Certainly, we bare more than just the beginnings of a scaffolding upon which to erect such a general psychology, and certainly the greatest credit for the progress we have made in this area must go to Hartmann.

Following Freud, Hartmann has emphasized—it would not be amiss to say that he has "cherished"—the hope that, with the evolution of ego psychology and the psychology of adaptation, psychoanalysis would one day be able to offer a comprehensive, general psychology of human behavior. In a sense, Hartmann has played the role of a Cato; his *delenda est Carthago* has been the need and the advantage of such a systematic general psychology. In virtually every one of the ego-psychology papers (Hartmann, 1964), he has managed to insert his message and do battle for his cause; and, of course, even more important has been the scope of his contributions which have provided us with ideas, observations, and suggestions which have immeasurably extended the range of our knowledge and its potential applications.

For the reviewer of such a collection of psychoanalytic writings, the temptation is great to approach the material from the overall vantage point of psychoanalysis as a general psychology. This is particularly so in view of both the range and the excellence of the various contributions. However, I have limited myself to a much more modest task; I have elected to focus my attention on the issues of health, normality, and ego strength. Obviously these are topics which have a special pertinence in the project for a general psychoanalytic psychology; but I believe that, although they are subjects which have in many ways been neglected by psychoanalysts, these topics are also relevant to the everyday practice of psychoanalysis. I would also state at the outset that I have not attempted to set forth an all-inclusive, comprehensive psychoanalytic psychology of these topics. For one thing, I have pretty much limited myself to material that has been dealt with and discussed in this collection of books; and, even here, I have not stressed (or, in some respects, even mentioned) some of the more significant items connected with these subjects. My approach and selection have been personal and subjective; and the results will, in many ways, be somewhat piecemeal and desultory. However, my justification for such an uneven approach is that a good deal of the material which I have extracted for review and collation has not received the attention it has warranted in the psychoanalytic literature. Furthermore, not only have I limited myself, by and large, to the work of the authors represented in this collection of volumes, I have made no systematic efforts to include the contributions of a given author outside of this collection. I recognize the inevitable gaps that must occur as a result of such omissions, especially in the case of Hartmann, Jacobson, and Erikson. On the other hand, the scope and depth of material that is available in just this group of contributions is in itself most impressive.

Both the nature and the range of this collection of volumes makes the traditional critique and review somewhat unwieldy. Although the publication dates of the various books cover a span of some five years, a good deal of the material consists of papers which have been reprinted or expanded; and some of the original work dates from 1958 (Erikson), 1930 (Glover) or as early as 1924 (Hartmann). A not insignificant portion of the basic ideas in Jacobson's monograph can he found in her long article of a decade earlier (1954). However, this constitutes neither a complaint nor a shortcoming; the material is by no means dated or outmoded. On the contrary, reading it imparts the rather comfortable feeling of mellow familiarity and established solidity; and—particularly in Hartmann's case—he also has the opportunity of following the development, continuity, and refinement of many of these fundamental contributions.

I am cognizant of the fact that the topics I have chosen for discussion are not always a crucial part of the central theme of a particular piece of work. I am also aware that I have glossed over some of the most significant and provocative psychoanalytic contributions in recent years. It is a partial balm to my conscience that most of these contributions have been widely aired and discussed during that period.[1] Nevertheless,

---

[1]In addition to the factors cited for not writing a "traditional critique and review" of these books, I should also acknowledge the sheer awe on being confronted with such a task. I take considerable comfort, therefore, in the opening sentence of Gitelson's review of Hartmann's *Essays on Ego Psychology:* "It is one of the impossible tasks: to review a book which, in fact, has been written over the course of a major career. The impact and the influence of the papers assembled in this volume have kept them under continuous review as each has appeared" (Gitelson, 1965). I can only agree and say, "amen," merely adding that the "impossible task" becomes uncomfortably compounded when simultaneously dealing with comparable works by Jacobson and Erikson. I should add, however, that Gitelson has managed to convert the impossible into

the fact remains that I have somewhat cavalierly ignored a large hulk of the substantive content contained in these 2000-odd pages (some first-rate papers have not even been mentioned); such an omission by no means reflects a lack of appreciation for the significance of such material, and for such an omission I apologize to both the authors and the readers.

II

Anna Freud (1966, p. 25) notes that the "concept of health . . . like the study of normality, is a neglected area in the psychoanalytic literature." Hartmann (1939, p. 3) begins his essay on "Psychoanalysis and the Concept of Health" with the observation that "Perhaps it would be true to say that we attach less importance in analytic circles to differentiating between healthy and pathological behavior than is often done outside those circles." Tartakoff (1966, pp. 223–224) also comments on the fact that the "normal character has received considerably less attention than the more pathological states." Aware of the difficulties attendant on arriving at a definition and criteria for psychological health and normality, she insists that "Nonetheless, we cannot abandon the concept of health and illness, and some working basis for what can be classified as normal remains implicit for purposes of analysis."

However, it is important to point out that the psychoanalyst's neglect of the concepts of health and of normality has been a relative rather than an absolute one. As Hartmann (1939) very carefully puts it, "the concepts of 'health' and 'illness' always exert a 'latent' influence, so to say, on our analytic habits of thought . . ." (p. 3). It is difficult to imagine that any analyst operates completely independently of these values. By and large, however, the basis for such values and value judgments is implicit rather than explicit; and it remains one of the formidable tasks for psychoanalysts to formalize and to make more explicit the criteria upon which such judgments are made.

It does not seem necessary to review the various historical factors which have been responsible for this neglect of health and normality and for our emphasis on the pathological. However, if we seriously do aspire toward the establishment of a general psychology, some redress of this

a penetrating and productive essay. The same should be stated with regard to Rangell's comprehensive survey of this book in his "The Scope of Heinz Hartmann" (Rangell, 1965), which very effectively covers Hartmann's contributions.

imbalance is in order; and whereas we have accumulated a good deal of data about specific areas of healthy functioning and have begun to obtain some understanding of the so-called "nonconflictual spheres," we are still far from being able to define health in terms of the total personality organization. At the same time, we should not lose sight of the fact that the need for the expansion of such understanding is not only for the sake of constructing a sound general psychology. Hartmann, in particular, has pointed out repeatedly the reciprocal enrichment of our understanding of the normal and the pathological. And while it is true that so much of what is known about the functioning of normal behavior has been derived from the observations and study of pathology, "it is also true that in order to understand neurosis and its etiology, we have to understand more completely the psychology of the healthy person, too" (1956b, p. 293). The role which healthy functions play in conflict solution, in the (temporary or even permanent) avoidance of conflict, in the choice of defense and of neurosis, are just a few of the areas in which an increased knowledge of health and normality could be of value.

Those who have addressed themselves to these issues seem agreed that simple answers and formulations will not suffice; and Hartmann, in fact, comments on the severe standards psychoanalysts insist on with regard to the concept of health. Both Anna Freud and Hartmann point out that health cannot be viewed only as the obverse of neurosis. Nor is the concept of health to be seen as the absence of specific conflicts, symptoms, or mechanisms of defense. In a more general sense, the absence of suffering in itself is no guarantee of overall psychological health; Hartmann and Anna Freud (see also Zetzel, 1965 and 1949) would look on suffering, anxiety, and depression as inevitable concomitants of normal living, and the capacity for their toleration as one of the indices of health. Hartmann alludes to health in terms of freedom, not in its philosophical sense, but in the ability to perform a given task and in the relative freedom from anxiety and affects (1939, p. 10). Yet, however valid such observations may be, they are somewhat vague and general and do not permit a more precise and "objective" definition of health and normality; and the same must be said of such terms as the "capacity for sublimation" or the "mobility or plasticity of the ego."

There is frequently the tendency—and the temptation—to equate health with adaptation; certainly Hartmann's contributions in that direction have provided us with some of the most useful leads in trying to conceptualize health and normality. However, Hartmann himself warns against reductionistic tendencies in this respect; and while he makes clear his conviction that "it is obvious that what we designate as health or illness is intimately bound up with the individual's adaptation to reality" (1939, p. 15), he makes it equally clear that he does not feel the relationship is a simple one-to-one affair.

As Hartmann adds, not only is the concept of adaptation still "in many respects too ill defined," but there are numerous instances of adaptive behavior which do not necessarily permit the parallel designation of health, at least in an overall sense. For instance, Hartmann is careful to point out that successful adaptation in one area or direction may in itself lead to maladaptive patterns in another area or direction. Adaptation can be either progressive or regressive: and the latter may involve consequences which are not harmonious with the individual's psychological health. The adaptation of an individual to reality may be in opposition to the interests and demands of the group and community; and the evaluation of health in such situations may well differ, whether one looks at the behavioral patterns from the point of view of the individual or of the community. Nor can the means that the individual utilizes in achieving a particular adaptation be ignored in such an evaluation. These issues would seem to be especially pertinent and timely as psychoanalysts attempt to understand the behavior of minority groups, including the poor, and the difficulties that one has in making assessments of "adaptive" behavior in certain environmental conditions. Hartmann goes to some pains in stressing, "adaptation is only capable of definition in relation to something else, with reference to specific environmental settings" (1939, p. 15). Here is where his concept of the "typical average environment" becomes so crucial, particularly with respect to the formulation of a concept of health.

In the face of these complexities, Hartmann would emphasize the very close connection between adaptation and synthesis (he has come to prefer the term "organizing function," which subsumes both the synthetic and differentiating functions of the ego). The evaluation of a given piece of behavior must he looked at in terms of the overall "organization of the organism," with regard to the function that behavior serves both "from within" and "from without," as well as the efficacy of that behavior in reconciling the demands of both. Obviously the relationship to Waelder's principle of multiple function is important. Glover also focuses on the role of adaptation in the conception of health; and he too is aware of the dialectic aspect of adaptation in the sense that a given adaptation may produce problems and "weakness" in other areas. Glover, too, sees the need for viewing the overall adaptation of the organism as the ideal criterion for health, and he speaks of the "relation of the total ego to crises in external stimulation and the *balance of adaptation* that ensues" (1968, p. 46).

One question not easily laid to rest has to do with the extent to which psychoanalysis can come up with a truly comprehensive and reliable understanding of the individual's relationship with reality. Again the question does not deal with absolutes; it is obvious that psychoanalysis and psychoanalytic data have contributed tremendously toward an illumination of the process of adaptation. The issue rather is a relative one: can the psychoanalytic method, the data obtained from that method or from its applications in cognate fields, provide us with the information necessary to construct a theory which would encompass all aspects of the relationship with reality? Or does the psychoanalytic method have intrinsic limitations which more or less preclude such a systemization? Robert White, whose monograph "Ego and Reality in Psychoanalytic Theory" (1963) deals essentially with the problems of action in the external world, would emphasize the latter, and takes a somewhat skeptical attitude about the usefulness of psychoanalytic thinking in coming up with at least the ultimate and penultimate answers in this area. The details of White's arguments cannot be pursued here; my own impression is that he overstates his case and overstresses the limitations of analysis in this regard at the expense of its contribution. However, the questions he raises cannot be readily dismissed, particularly in the light of the central role that the concept of adaptation must play in any general theory of psychology and, in this more limited sense, of the role of adaptation in the evolution of a concept of health and normality.

III

There is the temptation, against which even the psychoanalyst is not immune, to equate psychological health "with the ideal of a rational attitude," or in a more general way with the highest level psychological processes and functions. Here again, we are indebted to Hartmann for his exposure of this oversimplification and his clarification of what might constitute optimal functioning in a given situation. He grants that some relationship must exist between reason and successful adaptation, but "the most rational attitude does not necessarily constitute an optimum for the purposes of adaptation" (1939, p. 9). In fact, observes Hartmann, "the picture of a 'totally rational' human being is a caricature; it certainly does not represent the highest degree of adaptation accessible to man" (1947, p. 59). I could offer a score of such quotations from Hartmann's works, inasmuch as this is a theme which recurs frequently and conspicuously in his writings. Hartmann certainly subscribes to Kris's concept of "regression in the service of the ego," which is recognized as an important aspect of many adaptive—as well as creative—processes; but Hartmann goes beyond and expands Kris's significant contribution. The healthy ego, argues Hartmann, "should be able to make use of the system of rational control and at the same time take into account the fact of the irrational nature of other mental activities" (1939, p. 10).[2] In a given situation, functioning only at the highest psychological level would be inappropriate, ineffective, and essentially maladaptive. In these situations (because of external factors, internal conditions, or a combination thereof) more primitive and/or more undifferentiated processes would be necessary for successful adaptation. In discussing another aspect of this issue at a Panel on Affects at the December, 1967, meeting of the American Psychoanalytic Association, I pointed out that Hartmann

> has skillfully demonstrated that optimal psychic functioning does not necessarily depend on the most highly differentiated, highest level psychic processes and activities. On the contrary, he has shown that such optimal functioning is dependent on a scrupulous blending of the archaic with the highly developed, the irrational and the rational, the primary process with the secondary, the

[2]Loewenstein offers an intriguing example of this phenomenon in a footnote in Frosch's paper "A Note on Reality Constancy." Loewenstein argues that it is not necessary to assume that a maximum independence from animistic or anthropomorphic reactions to inanimate or nonhuman reality is always optimal. "An optimal in some people, for instance, writers, poets, painters, is to preserve remnants of a somewhat anthropomorphic view of nonhuman nature. It is possible that for some descriptive biologists the same might be true; whereas in other people, the remoteness from an animistic view of nature goes beyond the usual . . . All these various types of approach to nature should not be considered as pervading the whole of the personality; for instance, a theoretical physicist might nevertheless possess a very animistic approach to some aspects of reality, and, conversely, an artist, painter, or poet may have perfectly well developed functions of reality constancy" (Frosch, 1966, p. 357n.).

undifferentiated with the differentiated. Such a blending, or 'juggling' if you will, of such diverse elements must enlist the services of the various higher-level regulatory mechanisms, particularly what Hartmann calls the organizing function of the ego.

There is much concerning this "blending" about which we still are relatively ignorant. I would submit that it is particularly difficult to predict, in any reliable way, those situations—together with their specific components—which both evoke and necessitate the utilization of such more primitive and lower-level psychological activity; and it is equally, if not more, difficult to spell out the optimal level of activity for a given situation. Nevertheless, a concept of health and normality must take into account the necessity and the capacity for such a blending of diverse psychological elements, together with its relation to the processes of adaptation.

IV

One of the major deterrents to the elaboration of a psychoanalytic concept of health and normality is the recognition that subjective factors and subjective evaluations must inevitably play a significant part in such a formulation. The judgments which go into such an evaluation and formulation are influenced both by personal values and biases and by cultural and social conditions (Hartmann, 1939, p. 5). Hartmann points out that in a relatively uniform society, these judgments will at least "exhibit a far-reaching similarity"; but even under such conditions one must still contend with the subjective elements. "Health," says Hartmann, "is generally one expression of the idea of vital perfection; and this itself implies the subjectivity of the judgments concerning it." Actually, any serious analysis of the concept of health and normality must devote special attention to the valuations embodied in the different conceptions of health. Even if we discount the impact of the inevitable personal biases and values in necessary judgment-making that must accompany the "diagnosis" of health and normality, there is the further question of the relativity of normality and health in different cultures and subcultures and at different periods of history. For the analyst, the latter question is of particular significance, not only in terms of the acknowledgment of varying values and value systems, but also in terms of how different cultural and social systems may either facilitate or interfere with certain instinctual gratifications. This is certainly not a new problem in psychoanalysis, and Freud (1917) had already described how varying cultural situations tend toward the formations of varying super-ego contents and prohibitions (pp. 352–353). The whole question of the "conditions for repression" and how these different "conditions" influence both the culturally permissible instinctual gratifications and the subsequent form and content of psychoneurotic difficulties is a most cogent one in light of the frequently made assertion that "the neuroses have changed."

Hartmann (1944, pp. 26–27; 1950a, pp. 94–95) has provided us with the concept of "social compliance," by which

> . . . we understand the fact that social factors must also be described psychologically in such a way as to demonstrate their selective effects; they operate in the direction of the selection and the effectuation of certain tendencies and their expression and of certain developmental trends, among those which, at any given moment, are potentially demonstrable in the structure of the individual. These selective processes are present at every state of human development.

Hartmann asks about the manner and the degree in which a given social situation brings to the surface, provokes, or reinforces certain instinctual tendencies or certain sublimations; facilitates the solution of certain intrapsychic conflicts; promotes the circumvention of certain intrapsychic conflicts or the anxiety emanating from them. On the other hand, different social situations make quite different demands on the individual; and we certainly know that a given individual can appear quite disturbed and "sick" in one situation and quite healthy in another. (Perhaps the most egregious example of this is the manner in which relatively well "adjusted" individuals do well in the military service and poorly in civilian life, and vice versa.) Hartmann states:

> . . . the relation between the individual and society can be characterized for specific types of people and for specific systems and strata of society, not only as to the effect which the system exerts on the individual, but also as to the social functions which the system requires of him. The former consists of a coming-to-the-fore, suppression, and displacement of psychological impulses of the individual, insofar as these are being conditioned by society's influence.

> In the latter case one could speak of a kind of social selection and understand this as the displacements in the social environment which are accessible or forbidden to a given type of individual [1944, p. 28].

Although Erikson would use different terminology, the issue of social compliance has been one of the basic planks in his psychosocial approach. His concepts of the dynamic interdigitation of the individual and his social milieu, the cogwheeling effects between mother and child, the whole idea of mutuality are both well-known and central to his point of view. The recognition of the significance and validity of the observations of both Hartmann and Erikson makes the acceptance of any relatively simplistic concept of normality (or of abnormality) difficult for the psychoanalyst and necessitates the inclusion of such observations and concepts into any plan of health and normality. And, again, while it is not incorrect to state that we must view such judgments from the point of view of the overall adaptation of the individual to his society, such a statement does not in itself avoid the danger of the tendency toward glib oversimplification.

Tartakoff's clearly thought out and beautifully conceptualized paper "The Normal Personality in Our Culture and the Nobel Prize Complex" (1966) is an admirable example of the avoidance of oversimplification. She deals, in a more general way, with some of the issues raised by Gitelson in his paper "Therapeutic Problems in the Analysis of the 'Normal' Candidate" (1954) wherein he maintained that "so-called normality" was the façade of a narcissistic character disorder promoted by our culture. Tartakoff is concerned not only with psychoanalytic candidates (although some of her most valuable material bears on problems which come up in the analyses of these candidates), but with a broader group of individuals who by and large would have to be considered "successful" and "well-adapted." Although most of these people were not entirely free of psychological complaints and difficulties, they

> had not experienced the crippling effects of the acute or chronic symptom neuroses; neither did the majority of them suffer from severe disorders of mental functioning bordering on the psychoses . . . and only if one takes the view that no one is normal, since all men are subject to conflict and harbor neurotic mechanisms, could these patients be categorized as neurotic [1966, p. 224].

Tartakoff leans to some extent on the contributions of sociology (such as Merton and Parsons) in delineating the relations between the social structure and its goals and values on the development of the personality structure. Society has established a variety of cultural goals and has also provided various institutional means for the achievement of these goals. She underlines the particular prominence of success, optimism, and activism in the hierarchical scheme of goals and values in our culture; and how our society rewards and reinforces those attitudes and characteristics in the developing individual. Certain social situations and institutions not only facilitate the gratification of given instinctual tendencies, they enhance the possibility of achieving specific narcissistic trends and the implementation of certain self- and ego-interests. She describes the development of these adaptational patterns in regard to both the more circumscribed family situation and the broader social interactions; and she stresses that particular outlets are provided and permitted even if that pattern is not conflict-free, especially if there is the anticipation of success or the pattern is otherwise consonant with highly-valued cultural goals. These were people who shared the "optimistic anticipation that their virtues, their talents, or their achievements would be rewarded by success if they took appropriate steps toward this goal," but, on the other hand "these patients had become remarkably dependent upon the fulfillment of their expectations of life and saw in therapy a means to this end. Furthermore, the accomplishment of their goals, whatever direction or configuration they took, had become essential to the maintenance of their psychic harmony" (1966, p. 225). I cannot dwell on all the "interrelated hypotheses" developed by Tartakoff in this rich and rewarding paper: the vicissitudes of object relations in some of these patients, particularly when their narcissistic orientation interferes with "mature object love and object-directed ego interests"; the minimization and denial of their phase-specific oedipal fantasies; the failure to make optimal use of even unusual capacities if unduly preoccupied with success; the delineation of the "Nobel Prize Complex," an extreme and special variant of the need for success and acclaim that can be observed so readily in our culture; the details of the technical problems associated with the dealing of the resistances presented in the analysis of such patients; the clinical manifestations in the "decompensation" of these individuals. What I found most impressive was Tartakoff's judicious, balanced portrayal of a group of complicated personalities who obviously harbored significant intrapsychic problems and "weaknesses"—and yet had achieved a remarkable degree of successful adaptation and "health."

It would be of great interest and value to be able to compare Tartakoff's patients with a group who—to the best of our knowledge—started life with innate gifts and capacities essentially equal to the individuals she describes, but whose upbringing did not provide the same reinforcement from either the mothering object or the more immediate outside environment. In trying to understand more about the concept of "health," it would be of importance to know in some detail to what degree these special aptitudes require such reinforcement and nurturance; to what extent can the individual apply these special gifts and capacities in articulation with the particular values of society in the service of an optimal adaptation; and to what extent, if there is not in the course of early development a reasonable interdigitation of these innate qualities with the patterns and reactions of the child-rearing object, will these special gifts predispose toward the development of neurotic conflict or some other psychological disequilibrium. (See Keiser, 1969, in connection with "gifted" individuals whose gifts appear to have enhanced rather than decreased the possibility of neurotic conflict.)

One can look at the material Tartakoff has presented in terms of the importance of the "fitting together" of the individual and his society, of the inner and the outer (a point Hartmann had already elaborated in his 1939 monograph) for successful adaptation. Where the "fit" is fortunate, the relative success of the adaptation (and I do not believe it is necessary to think here in terms of "pseudoadaptation") may often be greater than might have been hypothetically anticipated from a detached assessment of that particular individual and his psychological strengths. On the other hand, where the fit may not be so fortunate, the adaptation of a given individual to his society may be much less successful than that individual's strengths may have led one to predict. (I don't believe that anyone has really exploited in any reasonable detail Freud's suggestion that Fate played a not insignificant role in man's psychological life!) I realize that when I speak of adaptation in this way, the discussion becomes generalized and somewhat vague; but I believe that the same statements can be made—and defended—in terms of neurosogenesis and manifestation of neurotic symptomatology. In those individuals in whom we can speak of a relatively good "fitting together" with the external world, the opportunities—at least as a generalization—for gratification of instinctual needs are better than for those whose adjustment is impaired because of some disharmony with the values and value systems of the culture. I realize, of course, that this is not entirely or always so, that in many individuals such a disharmony may indeed become the basis and vehicle for the discharge of certain instinctual needs (aggression particularly) and the rationalization of not facing up to internal conflict.

Yet when we come to making those evaluations and judgments having to do with normality and health, these situations can be most vexing, as any of us who deal with the younger members of our society well know. The distinctions between successful adaptation and passive conformity are not always clear-cut; and perhaps to view conformity only from the pejorative point of view is not entirely objective. In a footnote, Hartmann alludes to the fact that "the inability to conform is very often of a pathological nature" (1956a, p. 258). Nevertheless, it is hard to disagree with Lampl-de Groot's distinction between adaptation and conforming behavior. She sees adaptation as "behavior directed by a creative assessment of inner and outer factors and leading to equilibrium and constructive action"; while conformity is defined as "behavior characterized by passive surrender to inner and outer demands and norms and motivated by inner anxieties or social anxiety" (1966, p. 347).

However, all else being equal, adaptation is much easier to achieve if there is some degree of harmony between the value systems of the individual and his social scene. When such harmony is minimal or absent, the chances of either conformity or rebelliousness taking place are obviously increased. Under the latter set of circumstances, the evaluation of health and normality becomes particularly difficult. In his paper "On the Reality Principle," Hartmann (1956a) takes the—somewhat guarded—position that rebellion, and particularly rebellion against conventional accepted reality, may indeed be an indication of the individual's overall strength, an indication of his independence and autonomy. I need not belabor the importance of such assessments in making a "correct" interpretation of the rebellious behavior of many of today's youth and their rejection of many of our conventionally held—and cherished—values. Obviously, no general rule of thumb and no broad dictum is possible; but it is both vital and vexing to differentiate between those outwardly rebellious manifestations which are the product of neurotic conflict and those which are the product of health and adaptation. I do not believe that I am guilty of careless stone-throwing in saying that frequently we are guided by subjective as well as by objective factors in making such assessments and evaluations; and certainly it is not uncommon to have our own values and standards play a pre-emptive role in making judgments about such "rebellious" behavior. Nor is it necessarily true that *all* rebellion is a reaction formation against the wish to conform and submit. The acceptance of diversity, however honored in principle, is still more honored in the breech than in the deed; and the task of objectively viewing behavior divergent from our own is never an easy one.

All this is a topic of great concern to Erikson (1961), who, in his humanistic rather than strictly "scientific" approach, comments,

> An attempt to construct a ground plan of human strength, however, could be accused of neglecting diversities, of contributing to the fetish of deadly norms, and thus to the undermining of the individual as a hero or a rebel, an ascetic or a mere person of singularity. Yet the life process will always lead to more diversity than we can comfortably manage with our insights, our cures and our aspirations. And so will man's reactions to the diversity of conditions. In the process of sociogenetic change we can ascribe a long-range meaning to the idiosyncratic individualist and to the deviant as well as to the obedient conformist. True adaptation, in fact, is maintained with the help of loyal rebels who refuse to adjust to 'conditions' and cultivate an indignation in the service of a to-be-restored wholeness without which psychosocial evolution and all its institutions would be doomed. When Camus says that faith is a sin, he says it in a form and in a context which forcefully suggests that he 'cares' to relive and to restate faith beyond any compromise which, as a child, he was forced to accept [p. 156].

All of which brings us back again to the issues of subjectivity in the evaluation of health and normality and the problems posed by the assessment of how an individual "fits in" with his social and cultural environment. That both rebellion and conformity can, under given circumstances, represent either health or illness is a well-known indication of the impossibility of assessing "normality" from the vantage point of manifest social behavior alone.

V

Although it is undoubtedly true that psychoanalysts have, as a rule, generally avoided the concepts of normality and health as such, it is also true that they have—at least indirectly—attempted to cope with some of the same substantive issues under a different label—ego strength; and there is a certain reasonableness in such an approach. There is the familiarity of terminology and conceptualization in dealing with "ego strength" rather than health and normality; and, at least theoretically, focusing on "ego strength" offers the possibility of avoiding the pitfalls of more subjective judgments or implied statistical determinations. Nor is it an idle rationalization that an assessment of the efficiency of various ego functions (which can be observed, if not directly at all times, or at least inferred with a certain degree of assurance) is potentially more objective and verifiable than many of the constituents of the concept of health or normality. On the other hand, in terms of psychoanalytic psychology, the attempt to construct "a key to the problems of mental health" (Hartmann, 1959, p. 17) via "the psychology of the id" has not been very successful or useful; and it is apparent that many of the variables discussed under the rubric of mental health are best conceptualized by psychoanalysts in terms of the operation of various ego functions, and particularly those acting in certain combinations and ensembles.

However, we must—somewhat ruefully—acknowledge that the concept of "ego strength" is, as yet, a rather vaguely conceived entity. It means many things to many people; and often the term is used so loosely and so broadly that it becomes virtually meaningless. In a sense, we are caught in a kind of trap. On the one hand, if we speak of "ego strength" in a general way, such usage fails to indicate what specific strengths of what specific ego functions are being considered; and we know quite well that the presence of strength in one ego function (the most frequently quoted example, of course, is that of the defense mechanisms—and even this is imprecise, inasmuch as at different times different defense mechanisms exhibit varying degrees of "strength") may well be accompanied by the presence of impaired strength in another ego function (such as perception or the executant function). Empirically, we recognize that when applied in this way, the term ego strength is at best often impressionistic and at worst often a meaningless cliche. On the other hand, the description of a large number of the items in the ego-function repertoire and the attempt to indicate some of their qualitative evaluations may become discouragingly sterile and altogether miss the flavor of a living ego operating as a cohesive, active unit.

It is not surprising, therefore, that the idea of the strength of the ego has frequently been dealt with in very visceral terms by equating it with "grit" or "guts," while it has also become increasingly fashionable to seek for more objective criteria in the forms of scales, charts, tests, and other methods of qualifying—especially in a comparative way—the efficiency of ego functions and functioning. Glover spends a number of pages (1968, pp. 45–47) bewailing the vagueness of the concept and the difficulty of its application—and ends up by discarding the term "ego strength" in favor of what he believes is the more accurate and satisfactory concept of "psychic strength." (Glover is not just enmeshed in carping or semantics when he points out that "the ego is only a part, system, or aspect of the total psyche or mental apparatus.") White (1963) on the other hand, in discussing some data from psychological testing studies, insists that "ego strength is not an esoteric quality open only to the intuitive third ear" (p. 137).

Obviously the last word has still to be uttered on this subject. In terms of a psychoanalytic theory of health, it would be virtually impossible not to approach the subject from the point of view of not only the ego's various component activities but also from its synthetic and organizing functions. It is the latter group of ego activities which are more difficult to delineate clinically; and this is probably why Glover finds the term ego strength so frustrating and why—because in a sense he glosses over these activities of the ego—White takes a much more sanguine attitude towards the problem. If we discount White's somewhat derogatory terms such as "esoteric" and "intuitive third ear," we are—at least at the current level of our understanding—still very much dependent on our clinical judgments, "intuition" if you will, for an assessment of the degree and quality of the ego's synthetic and organizing functions. And yet these are the kinds of judgments psychoanalysts are forced to make daily. In many ways, our decisions on "analyzability" are often predicated on just these subjective and intuitive grounds—and, after all, not infrequently such judgments are anything but groundless. What many of the authors in this collection of writings have been doing is to attempt to make more explicit and more readily available the basis on which some of these "intuitive" decisions are made; and a good portion of the remainder of this essay will be devoted to reviewing some of their contributions in these areas, although this has not as a rule been the major thrust and focus of their writings.

VI

Glover emphasizes that a given psychological formation must be estimated in terms of its developmental significance. In searching for criteria of "strength" and "weakness," he recognizes the significance of the role of control of instincts and of the affects these instincts engender; but "this same factor of mastery may give rise to over-rigid defenses leading to over-inhibition of both instinct and affect and to interference with adaptation." Further, he feels that the utilization of unconscious defense mechanisms cannot serve as a criterion for strength of the ego unless the impact of that mechanism is viewed in the context of the overall adaptation of the individual. As far as Glover is concerned, "the search for decisive factors determining psychic strength or psychic weakness . . . must be pursued in the structured development of the ego." His focus, then, is essentially a genetic one. Glover (1968) alludes, of course, to the whole process of the development of ego nuclei and his well-known theory of psychic development based on the formation and condensation of ego nuclei. That theory cannot be reviewed in any detail here (Glover provides a succinct summary of his ego nuclei concepts, pp. 48–49); but suffice it that Glover envisions the ego-nucleus as representing a "memory precipitate of reactions between the post-natal, primitive psyche (largely id) and the objects of its instincts . . ."; that each nucleus—which is concerned with both "appetitive" and reactive responses to the instinctual interaction—develops in relation to the reduction or avoidance of anxiety and represents primitive signs of inner differentiation; that these nuclei have dynamic and in some degree autonomous functions; that, as development proceeds, they condense with the formation of more complex structures; and that these more complicated structures are "subject to a varying extent and at different times and occasions to structural regression." Because these regressions tend to reactivate some of the original ego nuclei, "the original state of nucleation of the ego is fateful for its later strength or weakness." This is, I believe, the way in which Glover uses the term "dissociation" in which there is an "isolation of nuclear elements, regaining through regression some of their former autonomous function, occupying for varying periods of time the approaches to consciousness and modifying other mental elements of instinctual representation as they pass through these approaches."

Nor is all "ego weakness" dependent on the process of regression. Glover points out that "early ego nuclei are both scattered and weak in function" (p. 30); and therefore this "flaw in function" can exert its effect by a persistence through life as well as by being reinforced through regression. The ultimate strength (or weakness) of the ego (or the psyche) will depend, then, on the degree to which the primitive ego nuclei retain their energy "and are capable of a degree of autonomic function"—either via "persistence" or "regression"—and "in this way preventing mental energies and reactions to them from being distributed among more integrated layers." I realize, of course, that this highly condensed synopsis of Glover's views does violence to the richness and complexity of his overall formulations; what I find lacking in his exposition is a more detailed and convincing explanation of what leads to the regressive processes which reinstitute the sovereignty of the old ego nuclei. It would seem reasonable that one of the indices of "ego strength" is the resistance of the newer, more highly differentiated and complicated structure to the process of regression and dedifferentiation. Again, there are implications of this problem in Glover's work, but I do not believe that he tackled the issue as directly as, for instance, has Hartmann in his concept of autonomy. In many ways—and I have a hunch that Glover would take vehement issue with this—the parallels between some of his concepts and those of Hartmann are greater than the differences. Glover, who delights in referring to Hartmann and his associates as "neo-Freudians," sarcastically takes Hartmann to task for his concept of secondary autonomy, referring to it as "a comforting narcissistic myth." Unfortunately, the argument cannot be pursued here, but it seems to me that Glover is indulging in what eventually become rather amusing polemics.

On the other hand, Glover has relatively little to say as to why these "early ego nuclei are both scattered and weak in function." Here I would surmise that he is not lacking in speculation or hypotheses; rather he is demonstrating his own fidelity to the conviction that "fantasy," however inspired, cannot replace careful clinical observation and sound introspection in the elaboration of scientific theory; and while Glover is ready to defend both the necessity and the value of "imagination" in psychology and psychological theory, he is also very much concerned with the difficulties inherent in the psychoanalyst's attempt to "trace mind back to its early beginnings." And, further, while Glover does not reject out of hand either the necessity for or the value of the observations of trained informants or of hypothetical reconstructions, he is probably much more skeptical and circumspect in these areas than most. "Needless to say," states Glover (p. 8), "this latter device is sometimes subject to gross error, for the proportion of phantasy to reality increases rapidly the farther back in mental history the observer seeks to penetrate." Therefore, while Glover concedes the inevitability of "hypothetical reconstructions" in trying to achieve some understanding of the earliest phases of psychic life, he is indeed quite parsimonious in making such reconstructions and can be scathing of those who do so more liberally. Here again—and I recognize that it is anything but an either–or situation—it is sometimes difficult to know whether Glover's polemics derive primarily from his obvious pleasure in intellectual combat or from the depth of his conviction of the presence of crucial substantive issues. In this volume, for instance, Glover has nothing to say about Jacobson's "The Self and the Object World"; but his essay on "Metapsychology or Metaphysics" (1966), in which he deals at length with both Jacobson's methodology and her ideas, must rank as one of the more devastating critiques of a major modern psychoanalytic thinker. Certainly one cannot find fault with his fundamental stance of insisting on scrupulous clinical observation, careful introspection, and an uncompromising adherence to the utilization of "basic mental concepts" in the formulation of psychoanalytic theory. By the same token, however, one wonders if Glover's acknowledgement of the need and value of "imagination" in this task is—at least in regard to the work of those with whom he is not in complete agreement—a kind of perfunctory lip service. Few of the people he attacks so violently—i.e., Hartmann, Jacobson, Erikson—have stubbornly held that their theoretical formulations represent the last-word blue prints on how the mental apparatus has evolved; yet one gets the impression that Glover sees some of this work as a rather nefarious attempt to foist a heretical anti-Freudian cosmology on an unsuspecting psychoanalytic audience. This is not to say that I do not find any basis or substance in some of Glover's specific criticisms; it would be most unlikely that in the attempts to envisage "the birth of the ego," there would not be occasional license taken with the facts of hard observational data, but I also find it unfortunate that Glover's valuable position in the matter of a rigorous methodology has to be compromised by the rather uncharitable vehemence of his assessments of the work of his colleagues.

VII

No psychoanalytic writer has been better able than Hartmann to portray the complexity of the ego. This complexity encompasses both its more archaic elements—in terms of its derivation from "genetic determinants in the id" and from defensive processes as well—and its higher-level, more "sophisticated" aspects. But Hartmann (1952) also stresses, as did Freud before him, that as the ego system becomes more differentiated and more complex, it also tends to become more labile. "However, we find that various functions of the ego may achieve various degrees of virtual independence from conflicts and from regressive tendencies in various individuals. What I have in mind here is the question of their reversibility or irreversibility, the question of their relative stability *vis-à-vis* inner or outer stress" (p. 176). The phenomena Hartmann is describing probably constitute his most fundamental contribution to psychoanalytic thinking and—depending on the emphasis of the moment—can be conceptualized either in terms of the principle of secondary autonomy, of the conflict-free sphere, or of the process of neutralization. Hartmann points out that there are "relevant differences in the degree to which ego functions maintain their stability, their freedom from those potential regressions to their genetic antecedents"; and he feels that this secondary autonomy, "this resistivity of ego functions against regression," is not only closely linked up to the concept of ego strength but also is "probably the best way to assess it" (p. 177. See also Hartmann, 1950b, pp. 139, 140; 1951, p. 146; 1955, p. 218).

Hartmann's secondary autonomy concept is well-known and need not be recapitulated here. In his discussion of the relation between the autonomous aspect of the ego and ego strength, Hartmann is characteristically careful and modest in his observations. In the context of that discussion, he reminds us that ego-strength concepts are "ambiguous unless we add a differential consideration of the ego functions actually involved in the situations we want to describe," that they "can be formulated only in terms of a set of specific relations" (1950b, p. 139). Yet there is more than an implication that a positive—if not general—correlation exists between the ego as a central regulatory organ and its "peripheral" manifestations in terms of the specific ego functions. I would certainly agree that the autonomous aspect of the ego and the ego functions represent one of the more dependable criteria for ego strength; I would also underscore the admonition which Hartmann has made repeatedly that autonomy is a term which should not really be used except in tandem with its modifier, "relative." This becomes particularly pertinent when we enter the clinical realm and attempt to make clinical assessments. It is difficult, for me at least, to visualize a viable ego function that is completely autonomous except in a hypothetical vacuum.

Concerning the question of ego strength, Hartmann (as does A. Freud, 1966, pp. 20–22) emphasizes the significance of the intrasystemic approach, a concept and contribution which is probably not as widely understood as that of autonomy. The question of "intrasystemic correlations and conflicts in the ego" takes on particular importance in regard to the relation between the defensive functions and the various nondefensive, relatively autonomous ego functions. This relation no doubt plays a significant role in adaptation, in conflict solution, in the achievement of drive gratification—all of which bear directly or indirectly on the question of ego strength. The degree to which the defensive activities of the ego pre-empt the ego resources at a given time or under a given set of conditions must also determine the "strength" of the ego at that time or under those conditions. As Hartmann (1950b) remarks, "Whether defense leads to exhaustion of the ego's strength is determined not only by the force of the drive in question and by the defenses at the ego's frontiers but also by the supplies the hinterland can put at its disposal" (p. 140). Obviously, what has been stated with respect to the relation between defenses and the other ego functions is of equal importance with respect to the "hypertrophy" of any other ego activity. Hartmann (1951), therefore, would not consider any definition of ego strength as "complete which does not refer to the intrasystemic structures, that is, which does not take into account the relative preponderance of certain ego functions over others; for instance, whether or not the autonomous ego functions are interfered with by the defensive functions, and also the extent to which the energies the various ego functions use are neutralized" (p. 146).

VIII

Hartmann also examines the problem of ego strength from the other side of the mountain, namely in regard to ego weakness as it is manifested in schizophrenia. His paper "On the Metapsychology of Schizophrenia" (1953) is a strikingly creative approach to some of the most vexing clinical problems and phenomena with which we are confronted. In this paper Hartmann, although acknowledging the role of the instinctual processes in the overall picture of schizophrenia, is primarily concerned with the "predisposition" to that clinical entity from the point of view of the weakness of certain ego functions. Again, his conclusions are modest and tentative; and he is more concerned—and more definite—about specific ego functions than about the ego as an overall structure. Although the paper encompasses a discussion of a large number of specific ego functions, the areas which are of particular interest for the conceptualization of a theory of ego strength center on the relation between Hartmann's theory of the primary autonomous apparatus and the predisposition to schizophrenia.

Hartmann's concept of primary autonomy need not he reviewed here; I want only to emphasize the correlation he makes between the apparatuses of primary autonomy and the "hereditary core" of the ego (1953, p. 204; 1952, pp. 169–170; 1950b, pp. 119–126). Obviously, there is still a great deal we must learn about the role of constitutional and hereditary elements in the development and maturation of psychological structures and functions. The clinical data from which to draw inferences about these influences are still most sparse. Yet the implications raised by Hartmann's hypotheses are most intriguing. In relation to schizophrenia, the predisposition to schizophrenia, and the impairment of certain ego activities that can be observed in many schizophrenics, Hartmann is concerned chiefly with two "anomalies of primary autonomy"—the impaired capacity for neutralization and the deficiencies in the precursors of defense. Hartmann skillfully demonstrates the potential effect of the impaired capacity for neutralization on a wide variety of crucial ego functions: i.e., stable object relation, relations with reality, countercathectic organizations, and subsequent superego formations. He also emphasizes the role that various primary autonomous functions play in "the first countercathectic structures" and the likelihood that such structures, in turn, may play a significant part in the evolution of the later defense mechanisms. Defects in these precursors of defense structures, suggests Hartmann, may well compromise the integrity, efficiency, and stability of the more definitive countercathectic organizations. He also points to the central role of the aggressive drives in schizophrenia, particularly to the impaired neutralization of these impulses and the defective defensive organizations available to cope with such drives. He makes clear that these various deficiencies have a mutually deleterious effect and compound the "predisposition" to schizophrenic illness; i.e., the impaired capacity for neutralization will interfere with the formation of stable object relations, which in turn are potentially necessary for the "building up" of stable countercathexes—and since the reverse is also potentially true, the process becomes a circular and deleterious one.

Hartmann does not attempt to fit all the symptoms of schizophrenia or even all the ego function deficiencies into the framework of the primary autonomy "anomalies"; and he acknowledges that the preservation of specific ego functions is not entirely dependent on the degree of secondary autonomy these functions have attained. But in this delineation of the possible types of "hereditary core" or "constitutional differences" deficiencies in those prototypical structures which will eventually become the more adult ego structures and substructures, he does offer a way of understanding—at least from the metapsychological point of view—the predisposition to schizophrenia; that is, why some individuals when subjected to certain stresses react with the ego regressions and dedifferentiations which characterize that process. (For a somewhat less sanguine view of Hartmann's concept of primary autonomy, see Glover, 1968, pp. 110–113.) In a certain sense there is a parallel between Hartmann's concept of the primary autonomous ego apparatus and Glover's concept of ego nuclei (I am also acutely aware of the many obvious differences between these conceptualizations) at least apropos of looking at the question of eventual ego strength: both concepts put considerable weight on the strength and efficiency of the very earliest psychic formations as the most crucial factor in determining the strength of the adult ego function. One might say that both are describing, in their own way, a genetic point of view concerning ego strength. It would seem reasonable, after all, that if Hartmann's hypotheses about the "predisposition" to schizophrenia have any validity, the same kind of "hypotheses" could be established in relation to other levels of ego functioning or even in relation to more specific forms of neurogenesis. One can only agree with Hartmann (1953) when he says, in a related context, "that this question has not been sufficiently studied" (p. 191).

IX

The one point on which there appears to be a reasonable degree of consensus is that the strength of the ego cannot be equated or even correlated with the strength of any one individual ego function. When talking about ego strength, one must look to the context, to the situation, in which an evaluation is being made or evaluate the ego in terms of its capacity to deal with a given task or problem. Yet there is also the inclination to deal with the strength of the ego as an overall structure; and here, too, there is some consensus that one must evaluate the ego as a whole in order to assess its strengths and weaknesses. Such an evaluation would, of course, take into account not only the strength and weakness of individual ego functions but also "how" the various functions are "put together." Thus, there is a good deal of interest in the synthetic, the integrating, the organizing functions of the ego; and, if one could concede that ego strength can be connected with one single ego function, there is a tendency to connect it with the strength of this synthetic or organizing function. This is not a particularly recent idea;

the crucial role of the synthetic function of the ego in relation to the strength of the ego has, either explicitly or implicitly, already been indicated by Freud (1926), Nunberg (1930), and Waelder (1930).

Hartmann, as I have already stated in other sections of this essay, has always underscored the role of synthesis (and as I have also mentioned, he prefers to use his concept of organizing function) as an index of ego strength or health. This has been a cardinal precept in his thinking about such matters as action, adaptation, and conflict solution. In describing the effect of analytic treatment, he points to the role of the strengthening of the ego in successfully integrating within its own organization both irrational elements and ego interests. This is one aspect of what Hartmann refers to as "the supremacy of its organizing function," when he speaks of the "ego's taking over in its own organization certain functions that have previously been executed by the other substructures of the personality" (1947, p. 67).

The significance which so many of our more prominent psychoanalytic thinkers attribute to the role of the synthetic function is reflected in the frequency with which this concept is discussed in the collection of papers presented in honor of Hartmann's seventieth birthday, *Psychoanalysis—A General Psychology* (Loewenstein et al., 1966). To mention just a few: Provence (1966, p. 118) describes a six-month-old girl's ability to deal with and coordinate multiple stimuli and comments that this "ability probably reflects the biological organization that is the somatic prerequisite for the development of the synthetic function of the ego. . . . This quality can be considered a particular area of strength in the developing ego . . . this capacity for integration later became a prominent and continuing characteristic of her ego functioning." Lampl-de Groot (1966) states that "In addition to the necessity for some kind of adaptation . . . to the environment, the individual maturing under the impact of internal conflict must bring into equilibrium the various tendencies emerging from the different structures of the mind. The synthesis required for a 'healthy' outcome is one of the functions of the ego organization." Throughout her article, she points to the need for "harmony" between "the various interests and needs of the different areas in the personality" (pp. 345–347). Spitz (1966) discusses the formation of the first rudiments of ego structure from ego nuclei as evidence that

> . . . a synthetic tendency is at work, a tendency which assembles, arranges, and links phylogenetically preformed nuclei so that they gradually form a coherent entity. However, this structure is not yet

> an ego—not even a body ego as envisaged by Freud. We are still fully in the soma, in physiology . . . this synthetic tendency which has linked the nuclei with one another is an attribute of all living organisms. It is equally present in psychic unfolding as in the course of somatic embryonic development before the existence of the psyche. . . . Synthesis is one of the most important functions of the ego and its importance in psychic life cannot be over-rated [pp. 133–134].

Lustman's (1966) highly sophisticated paper on the development of impulse control focuses on some of the aspects of the integration and synthesis of both ego and superego aims in a hierarchical superordinate structure dealing with such controls. While Anna Freud (1966) does not deal in so many words with the question of synthesis, she does allude to the role of the "intactness" of certain developmental trends in the evaluation of psychological health in children.

Allusions to synthesis and organization abound in all of Erikson's work; and, of course, it is central to his concept of identity. In *Insight and Responsibility*, he speaks, for instance, of

> . . . the human ego, the guardian of individuality . . . the inner "organ" which makes it possible for man to bind together two great evolutionary developments, his inner life, and his social planning. . . . The ego was gradually seen to be an organ of active mastery, not only in defending the inviolacy of the person against excessive stimulation from within the organism or from the environment, but also in integrating the individual's adaptive powers with the expanding opportunities of the "expectable" environment [1961, p. 148].

In her meticulous and carefully detailed exposition of the development of "self," Jacobson (1964) does not devote herself to an explicit discussion of the role of the synthetic or organizing functions, but utilizes the concepts time and again. She speaks of the importance of the organization of self and object representations into some kind of unity; of the role of "increasing differentiation and hierarchic organization" of object relationships, ego interests and identifications with objects of both sexes; the need for superego as well as ego integration; of the significance for the reconciliation and integration of opposing goals and identifications; the crucial role that the modification, stabilization, and integration of old identifications and object relations play in postadolescent identity formation; of the function the superego, when once formed, exercises in regulation and organization.

I recognize that I have taken most of this material out of a much broader and more complex context. But I believe the excerpts presented reflect a number of issues which relate to the concepts of synthesis and organization. I think I am not subjectively reading into the material when I conclude that invariably the operations of the synthetic function are viewed as "good," as evidence of constructive and healthy functioning on the part of the ego; conversely the failure of the synthetic function is seen as a significant weakness of the ego. Second, the concept is invoked to cover an impressively wide array of psychological phenomena; synthesis is seen as an integral part of the most primitive psychological processes (even, as Spitz has it, in regard to quasi-physiological activities) to some of the most intricate and elegant manifestations of the psychic apparatus. Nor do I find fault with the ubiquitousness of the synthetic function manifestations; it would appear difficult to escape evidence of such manifestations. Thirdly, the concepts of synthesis and organization are utilized both in a descriptive and explanatory fashion, more often in a somewhat vague and taken-for-granted manner. There is the tendency to assume that there "is" such a tendency, and yet disproportionately little is known or understood about its sources, its modes of operation, or even its more specific clinical manifestations. When one compares the relatively loose and extensive recourse to the concept of synthesis with the relative infrequency with which that same set of concepts is utilized with regard to specific clinical phenomena, with specific clinical data, it is both impressive and disquieting. Rosen (1961) has attempted quite effectively to apply the concept to his work on "style." Waelder has some interesting material in his paper (1930) on the relation between content and form; in a general way, the idea of synthesis plays a central role in any elaboration of character formation. I realize I can add further items to my list; but it is, all in all, a skimpy list compared to the frequency and the unquestioning enthusiasm with which the idea of "synthesis" is accepted. Certainly there are many issues related to these concepts which need clarification or at least reconciliation. Is the synthetic function a manifestation of instinct, as Freud and Nunberg described, or is it more effectively conceptualized as an autonomous ego function? Or are the two ideas readily reconcilable? What is the relation of the synthetic function to other regulatory mechanisms, especially to the more "basic" ones like the unpleasure–pleasure principle and the reality principle? Is there an independent fragmentizing principle and function which is independent of (or antagonistic to) the synthetic function (Peto, 1961)? Or are all the manifestations of decomposition (Glover, 1968, p. 64) or fragmentation merely the consequence of the failure of synthesis? Can we hypothesize a hierarchical relationship involving the various regulatory functions—and how could such a hierarchy help in an understanding of ego strength and health? In the light of these as yet unanswered questions and their significance, it is of interest to hear what Glover has to say about the concept of "synthesis."

Glover (1968) acknowledges that "it cannot be denied that the case for a 'synthesizing tendency' inherent in the mental apparatus is a plausible one."

> Instinctual drives . . . can be shown to fuse; affects can exist in a state of psychic symbiosis . . . mental mechanisms can operate in distinguishable combinations or groups . . . dreams or neuroses prove on examination to be "constructions" in which antithetical drives meet on the common ground of compromise "formations": in addition to which symptoms tend to be encapsulated in and presumably by the ego; by the process of introjection, objects are psychically incorporated in the appropriate crypts or interstices of a spongelike ego and once linked to the ego or to different parts of the ego are extremely difficult to modify, even more to disentangle; reality thinking systematizes; phantasy thinking proliferates and at the same time condenses its multifarious elements into systems; neologisms abound; and by popular assent, "character" provides a continuum from "unformed" to "formed" varieties [p. 63].

The case for a tendency to synthesis or a synthesizing function is certainly a strong one; and when we remember that Freud, writing of the "desexualized energy" at the disposal of the ego remarked, with that simplicity of which he was a master, that this energy "still shows traces of its origin in its impulsion to bind together and unify, and this tendency to synthesize grows stronger in proportion as the strength of the ego increases." What could be more plausible than to say that if instincts fuse and mental mechanisms congregate or commingle that the third and structural element in the fundamental metapsychological triad (finally represented by the ego) is not only the result of synthesis but, some think, becomes when fully formed the master or director or organizer of synthesis?

The irony, I would submit, is not too difficult to detect; and I will not reproduce the details of the devastating scrutiny (and self-scrutiny) with which he examines these various propositions. He is concerned, and rightfully so, that in dealing with the concept of synthesis, we do not "canonize the term and leave it on a dogmatic level." He reminds us of the danger that "once primary concepts are formulated, some of them at least tend to gain unquestioned currency, passing from journal to text-book to be finally apotheosized in psychoanalytical lexicons and encyclopedias without any very searching scrutiny" (p. 69). He insists that we should be able to follow the clinical manifestations of the synthesis concept from "any stage from birth to the latency period or for that matter, adolescence, and adult life down to the last period of senile decay." He deplores the extension of "theoretical postulates beyond their legitimate scope, to extenuate them, as it were, with the help of axioms that are not self-evident truths" (p. 66). Therefore, he also insists that the concept of synthesis must be submitted to investigation in terms of the basic mental mechanisms. I devote what may appear to constitute an inordinate amount of time and space to these arguments which Glover advances and which are never too far removed from contentiousness and at times seem to hover on the brink of ad hominem attacks. Nevertheless, the rigorousness which he promulgates is exemplary—albeit an example which must be difficult both to follow and adhere to—and not infrequently warranted.

When all is said and done concerning synthesis, Glover confesses that he "may seem to have turned a jaundiced eye on the concept" (p. 101). And, for Glover, when all is said and done, the basic question is "what in fact does synthesis synthesize?" Glover's answer to that question is not unexpected. Since, "as Freud maintained, the ego is developed from primary systems of memory traces then the existence of ego-synthesis supports the concept of unsynthesized ego-nuclei. What else can they synthesize?" Further, he suggests that the earliest nuclear formations become linked together "by the identity of affective experience, the root-factor, I think, in so-called 'synthesis'" (p. 100).

Certainly the concepts of synthesis and organization have been useful and potentially germinal for analysis. Yet I would agree with Glover that the concepts are beguiling and constitute a temptation toward simplification and premature closure. Even if one follows, at least in part, Glover's rigorous standards for the application of such concepts, the evidences of some kind of synthesizing activity will not be difficult to apprehend; but, on the other hand, it would be both short-sighted and erroneous to assume that *all* clinical manifestations of psychological processes coming together or acting in harmony must of necessity reflect the influence of such a synthesizing tendency. This is an area of considerable theoretical and clinical promise for further psychoanalytic understanding—including the question of ego strength, health, and normality; but it is also an area which is in need of reconsideration and further scrutiny.

X

Although Erikson's (1961) interest in the concept of ego strength can be discerned throughout a good deal of his writing, his most explicit contribution on the subject is contained in his essay, "Human Strength and the Cycle of Generations" (pp. 11–157). The paper is a typical Eriksonian *tour de force:* far-ranging, speculative, catholic, and even a bit moralizing. The latter ingredient is reflected in the very word Erikson uses to designate his particular conceptualization of ego strength: Virtue. And although Erikson offers a brief etymological explanation as to why "virtue" is the most appropriate word for his purpose, he also makes the point that the opposite of virtue is not vice, but weakness. He defines virtues as "human qualities of strength, and . . . relates them to that process by which ego-strength may be developed from stage to stage and imparted from generation to generation" (p. 113). Erikson delineates eight of these virtues, each of which is more or less related to one of his "Eight Stages of Man." They are: hope, will, purpose, competence, fidelity, love, care, and wisdom. In the elaboration of the virtue concept and the description of these eight virtues, Erikson tries to integrate the idea of ego strength with his theory of the life cycle and epigenetic development. He is concerned with those inherent strengths which emerge at specific phases of the life-cycle in relation to the phase-specific tasks, and problems with which the ego must cope at the various nodal points in that cycle. He demonstrates that, although each of these virtues arises in specific phases of the life cycle, these human strengths continue to manifest their role and influence throughout life and that they also influence and interpenetrate with each other. Further, he insists that these virtues do not develop out of a psychological vacuum; rather they emerge with and depend on other segments and aspects of development, such as the psychosexual stages, the psychosocial crises, and cognitive maturation.

Erikson does not ignore the constitutional basis for these strengths and speaks of the "minimum genetic acknowledgement necessary to assume inborn disposition ensuring and negotiating sequences of generations living in organized societies" (p. 142). Nor does he portray a simplistic, pollyannalike state of affairs where the built-in strengths mysteriously come into operation. Each stage of development has its own problems, its own vicissitudes, frustrations, and possibilities of fixation; however, Erikson points out, in spite of the crises and vicissitudes with which the individual must contend in the course of his own life-cycle, some strengths will emerge, "provided only that growth and development have enough leeway to present new issues; and that, all in all, expectable reality proves more satisfactory and more interesting than fantasy." Erikson's rambling, somewhat discursive style makes paraphrasing difficult; and I find it anything but easy to convey the flavor of the fluid and multifaceted development and emergence of these virtues. However, he is able to demonstrate that each stage of development involves a crisis, a crisis which is not necessarily a catastrophe, but rather a "turning point," one possible outcome of which is the emergence of the human strength which Erikson calls "virtue." At any one point, the strength of the individual is relative; it is based, in part, on the old strengths which have emerged from previous crises. "In an epigenetic development of the kind here envisaged, each item (virtue) has its time of ascendance and crisis, yet each persists throughout life . . . what thus grows in steps is part of an ensemble in which no part must have missed its original crisis, its further metamorphoses, and its reintegration into each later stage" (p. 140).

The "emergent virtues," Erikson would remind us, "are not external ornaments easily added or omitted according to the fancies of esthetic or moral style" (p. 135). The virtues are anchored, in addition to the epigenetic patterns of individual development and the growth of the ego, to the sequence of generations. Erikson has always stressed that the cogwheeling stages of childhood and adulthood are a system of "generation and regeneration—for into this system flow, and from this system emerge, those social attitudes to which the institutions and traditions of society attempt to give unity and permanence" (p. 152). And it is here, in turn, that Erikson sees the "most immediate connection between the basic virtues and the essentials of an organized human community." For human strength, he adds, is dependent on that total process which simultaneously regulates "the sequence of generations and the structure of society." To the individual, the ego regulates this process. The basic virtues which emerge from the interactions between the generations "have their counterparts in the spirit of those human institutions which attempt to formalize and to safeguard such dealings" (p. 155). Erikson concludes his argument with the reminder that human strength can be strong "only through a mutual guarantee of strength given to and received by all whose life-cycles intertwine" (p. 157).

Because, as I have noted above, it is so trying to paraphrase Erikson, I have—to the extent to which it is feasible—attempted to let Erikson speak for himself in connection with much of what I have extracted from his kaleidoscopic essay. For me, at least, Erikson is trying; and I do not intend this only in its pejorative sense. The difficulty is not alone in what Esman (1965) has referred to as the "occasional floridity of his style" (p. 119) or even the idiosyncratic nature of his idiom. There is an elusive "soaring" quality to so much of his writing; so often he appears to be reaching for explanations and truths which at the same moment seem to be both self-evident and yet mysterious. When Erikson deals with human strengths, with "virtue," what he says may for that moment appear commonplace and even pedestrian; but both Erikson and the psychoanalytic reader are—for better or for worse—aware of the elusiveness of so much of what is seemingly so commonplace.

XI

A definitive treatise on the psychology of ego strength would surely feature a conspicuous chapter on those aspects of identity and the "self" pertinent to health and normality. For a number of reasons, I have elected to gloss over this area in my essay. Inasmuch as these are topics which are dealt with so extensively—particularly by Erikson and Jacobson—in this collection of volumes, a review of the material which has been presented would necessitate an entire article in itself. The ideas presented in these books are well-known to the psychoanalytic community and are certainly crucial to the overall conceptualization of current ego psychology. Suffice it that any concept of ego strength must include the notion of a reasonably stable sense of self and/or the notion of the sense of one's personal identity.

However, one component of the Self concept has not received a great deal of attention. I am referring to the subject of self-interest. Actually, the self-interests are one of the subcategories of ego interests; and it is from the larger point of view of these ego interests that I would like to discuss the relation of these "interests" to the question of ego strength.

Hartmann (1950b, p. 135) speaks of a "special group of ego tendencies" which Freud (1917, pp. 414–417) labelled "egoism" and attributed, at that time, to the self-preservation tendencies of the ego instincts. Freud described the cathexes proceeding from these drives as "interests" and contrasted the latter with the libidinal cathexes of the sexual drives. Hartmann (1950b), however, would place both the self-preservation tendencies and the "interests" within the realm of the system ego, even though he acknowledges that the latter "are often rooted in id tendencies." These ego interests comprise strivings for what is "useful," egoism, self-assertion, the seeking for wealth and social prestige, the search for power and intellectual attainment, etc.—obviously a wide and disparate array of behavioral patterns. These patterns are genetically determined, at least in part, by the various instinctual tendencies which "either continue in modified form the direction of these drives or are the results of reactions against them" (p. 157). Hartmann also points out that a given component instinct may contribute to a variety of ego interests; and, that, on the other hand, a given ego interest is determined, in addition to its instinctual component, by contributions from the superego, different areas of ego functioning, by other ego interests, the relations with reality, the individual's mode of thinking, his synthetic capacities, etc. Both Hartmann and Jacobson stress that the ego interests utilize primarily neutralized energy and belong to the field of secondary autonomy. Hartmann also suggests the possibility that these interests may have at their disposal neutralized energy other than that derived from the instinctual energies from which they have developed. Jacobson stresses the intimate connection between the emergence of the ego interests and the processes of desexualization which proceed with the formation of the superego.

These tendencies, says Hartmann (1950b),

> . . . are interests of the ego; their goals are set by the ego, in contradistinction to the aims of the id or of the super-ego. But the special set of tendencies I am referring to is also characterized by the fact that their aims center on one's own person (self). I may add that this is true of their aims only. They obviously also use or serve ego functions that are directed toward the outer world, and, among the factors that lead to the change, by man, of external reality, ego interests of this kind play unquestionably a decisive role [p. 136].

Jacobson also reminds us "that we are not entitled to define (successful) ego activities simply as narcissistic gratifications. Even if they do not pertain to personal objects, their essential and central purpose is normally the pursuit of object-libidinal gratifications." Certainly, the role of these ego interests in the overall pattern of adaptation has still to be explored in further detail and more fully exploited in understanding the ways in which these interests can and do facilitate the gratification of instinctual needs.

Hartmann (1950b) further suggests (although, at the same time, admonishing against "overemphasizing terminological questions in this field so little known to us") that it might prove practical to include within the realm of the ego interests, in addition to those centering primarily on the self, those tendencies, which affect "the outer world not only indirectly . . . but whose aims are centered around other persons or around things; or those which are striving toward aims, originating in the superego but taken over by the ego, aims that center around values . . . and finally, interests of the ego in mental functioning itself . . ." (p. 136).

In *The Self and the Object World,* the development of the ego interests is one of the threads which Jacobson follows. I have already alluded to the emphasis she gives to the process of sublimation; but she also points to the relationship of the development of ego interests with the overall increase in autonomous ego functioning, with the growing independence of the child, the identification with the interests and values of the parents, the burgeoning of the repertoire of interests during latency, and particularly the role of the superego in the determination of values which in turn influence the ascendance of certain ego interests over others. It is somewhat unfortunate that Jacobson's observations and insights in this area are scattered throughout her tightly-packed volume; a more sharply delineated presentation of her ideas on this neglected area would be both welcome and useful.

Hartmann (1950b) indicates that the self-directed ego interests may operate either in collaboration with other ego functions, or in antagonism to them; and he points to the importance of the organizing function and the intrasystemic approach in assessing the role and contribution of these interests in the mental health of the individual. However, he also warns that

> . . . the subordination under this group of ego interests of the other ego functions is no criterion of mental health (though it has often been said that the capacity to subordinate other tendencies to what

> is 'useful' makes the difference between healthy and neurotic behavior). These ego interests are, after all, only one set of ego functions, and they do not coincide with those, more closely correlated with health, that also integrate the demands of the other psychic systems (synthetic or organizing function) [p. 138].

In another essay, Hartmann (1947, pp. 64–65) describes certain patients whose behavior represents a caricature of these ego interests, particularly in their emphasis on a hyperrealistic attitude towards life. Hartmann understands such behavior as an attempt to deny inner conflicts and to protect oneself from anxiety; "its defensive character is obvious."

That the whole area of ego interests is one which has been poorly understood and sadly neglected by psychoanalysts is obvious. The role they play in the assessment of ego strength, health, and normality is especially tenuous. When Hartmann argues that mental health cannot be equated with the preeminence of the influence of ego interests, I do not believe that he simultaneously wishes to discount completely the role which these tendencies do exert. Their part in adaptation and in the facilitation of "object finding" in relation to potential instinctual gratification would indicate that efficiently operating and effectively coordinated ego interests may constitute a much more significant part of that psychological composite we call ego-strength than has previously been recognized.

Even more uncertain and more difficult to catalogue is the position played by those ego interests which are more directly concerned with the self (what Kanzer [1962] has referred to as the self-interests). These self-interests, while not entirely divorced from object-directed activities, are primarily concerned with ". . . self-centered, egotistic-narcissistic strivings and pursuits of the ego" (Jacobson, 1964, p. 78n). This brings us into that very complex and stormy area of how narcissism influences the overall strength of the ego, a topic which will not yield to simple explanations and cannot he pursued here. (For Freud's attempt to differentiate "egoism" from narcissism, see Freud, 1917, p. 417.) Again, the issue would appear to involve matters of balance and integration. Jacobson underscores the point that "the normal pursuit of ego interests presupposes sufficient awareness of the differences between grandiose narcissistic strivings and corresponding wishful self-images on the one hand, and realistic ego goals based upon sound notions of the own self's potentials, i.e., one's own abilities, on the other" (1964, pp. 79–80).

Unless one takes the rather untenable and extreme stand of viewing narcissistic strivings only from the pejorative point of view, then it would seem reasonable that the "healthy" individual would have available a sufficient investment in the self-interests to promote the gratification of certain narcissistic needs and to implement at least a modicum of self-assertion. Nor am I unaware that many other influences emanating from all three psychic systems must play a significant role here. On the other hand, the narcissistic investment in the self-interests must not be so predominant as to interfere with effective object relationships. All in all, this is an area of clinical and theoretical research which, although perplexing, could be most rewarding.

XII

In his "Formulations on the Two Principles of Mental Functioning," Freud (1911) sketches the distinction between "motor discharge" and "action." He says,

> A new function was now allotted to motor discharge, which, under the dominance of the pleasure principle, had served as a means of unburdening the mental apparatus of accretions of stimuli, and which had carried out this task by sending innervations into the interior of the body (leading to expressive movements and the play of features and to manifestations of affect). Motor discharge was now employed in the appropriate alteration of reality; it was converted into *action* [p. 221].

While, to my knowledge, no one has seriously challenged this distinction, it is also of interest that few analysts have demonstrated very much interest in the extension and elaboration of this central, seminal suggestion. Hartmann's attitude is much more sanguine than mine; he states:

> "Since its beginnings psychoanalysis has made important contributions to the psychology of action that clearly reflect the consecutive levels of analytic experience and thought," but he also concedes that "we still have no systematic presentation of an analytic theory of action, to which I could refer here as to an accepted or at least generally known body of facts and hypotheses" [1947, p. 37].

Hartmann's (1947) paper "On Rational and Irrational Action" is, at any rate, an oasis in what is generally a barren territory. I have personally found it to be one of his most useful and challenging contributions. (I would also recommend Jacobson's [1964] excellent vignette on the intrapsychic shifts and activities which occur in relation to the writing of a book [p. 81 ff].)

Yet, I would submit, such contributions are relatively few and far between; and the paucity of interest in this topic is the more striking in light of its potential significance. If we follow Freud in viewing action as the "appropriate alteration of reality," then it becomes for all practical purposes the tangible indication of how effectively the ego has coordinated and integrated that whole host of constituent psychological processes which go into any one "action." It is, at least to some extent, true that as analysts we are more concerned and interested in those intrapsychic phenomena which precede an action and on which that action is dependent than we are in the action per se; and, most likely, this preference is more than justifiable. But we know precious little about how those intrapsychic processes are translated into actual behavior. It would seem that just as we are relatively ignorant of that "mysterious leap" from the psyche to the soma in the conversion reactions, so we are not much better informed about the comparable leap from the psyche to "action," if I may put it that way. Further, I would suggest that some of our "formulations"—implied or otherwise—that are invoked to "explain" certain actions are sometimes naive and simplistic. The most notorious example, I believe, is the frequency with which a certain piece of behavior is formulated in terms of an identification with a significant love object. I am not questioning that identifications of this type may not play some important intrapsychic role in respect to a given action; but the identification itself would not be sufficient basis to explain the transformation of an intrapsychic "fantasy" into action.

Hartmann points out that action is an ego function; but it is an ego activity that is codetermined by the other systems and can be triggered by any of the systems. He stresses the role which certain subsidiary ego functions such as anticipation, intentionality, and objectivation play in the emergence of an action; and, above all, he would emphasize how dependent effective action is on the activity of the organizing function of the ego. Hartmann (1947) also indicates (and this is a number of years before White's monograph) the interdependence of action and the knowledge of the outside world: "Insight into the structure of reality guides action, but action is also one of our most efficient instruments for the development of insight, or knowledge" (p. 39). He also shows that "acting in the outer world may open up new avenues for direct and indirect (sublimated) gratifications of instinctual tendencies" (p. 40).

Space does not permit a detailed synopsis of all of the ways in which the synthetic or organizing functions exercise a critical role in effective action or in the distinction between rational and irrational action. One example which Hartmann offers is the task of reconciling all of the contradictory aims and goals which are determinants for a given action, and how "normally a mutual adjustment of the different sets of aims takes place in the ego, so that the aims connected with the moral demands are compatible with those connected with adaptation to the environment, or with those representing the ego interests, or so forth" (p. 43). Hartmann is most scrupulous in demonstrating the difficulty of separating out sharply, at least, rational from irrational action; and he maintains, as I have described before, that the rational must make provisions for the irrational and that the optimal level of behavior is frequently not the highest level.

In this connection I would mention that one of the more vexing problems which analysts must often face is the differentiation between action and acting out. Not infrequently there is the tendency to look upon any action in the course of analysis as a piece of acting-out; and it is a suspicion which may as often as not be well founded. However, there are situations where this somewhat "opprobious" evaluation is unjustified or at least somewhat short-sighted. As Tartakoff (1966) points out, such a "focus has tended to obscure the highly adaptive aspects of action" and she quotes Leo Berman's comment on the difficulty of determining where "acting out" ends and "real living" begins (p. 228). Erikson (1961) holds that "at each stage of life, what appears to us as 'acting out' may contain an adaptive if immature reaching out for the mutual verification by which the ego lives . . ." (p. 170); and relative to working with patients, Erikson speaks here of "a problem of general therapeutic urgency." He goes on to say that "Some mixture of 'acting out' and of age-specific action is to be expected of any patient of whatever age, and all patients reach a point in treatment when the recovering ego may need to test its untrained or long-inhibited wings of action" (1962, p. 461).

This is a subject which cannot be followed here; but it is one which requires a great deal more attention on the part of psychoanalysts. Certainly it is an area where the assessment of "ego strength" has practical clinical significance; and I suspect that an incorrect evaluation and interpretation of a specific piece of behavior as representing primarily "acting out" instead of "action" may often have a deleterious, infantilizing, and/or discouraging impact on the patient. Likewise, in a more general way, a good deal more should be known about the relation between ego strength and action. In addition to material presented by Hartmann, what specific ego functions and what specific ego strength are prerequisites for successful action? Can we appropriately think of a "strong ego" in those situations where many of the component ego activities would appear to be functioning at a relatively high level but the resultant action is ineffective and essentially maladaptive? How can we conceptualize—other than by such vague terms as "executive functions"—the process by which the intrapsychic activity is transformed into action? These are all questions which warrant considerable attention.

XIII

While Robert White does not deal directly with these questions in his monograph *Ego and Reality in Psychological Theory* (1963), he is a psychoanalytic writer who cannot be faulted with avoiding the concept of action in his work; in fact, it can be said that action is the central focus and theme of this interesting volume. White says that the purpose of this monograph is to

> . . . attempt to develop the psychoanalytic concept of independent ego energies in order to improve our understanding of the relation between ego and reality. It is based on the belief that recent research in animal behavior and child development provides the basis for a coherent conception of such energies and the contribution they make to ego development. This conceptualization, which emphasizes *learning through action and its consequences* [italics added], is held to improve our comprehension of reality testing, early ego deviations, identification as a growth process, self-esteem, and ego strength. It is held to be useful, moreover, in resolving a number of difficulties in the psychoanalytic theory of energies [p. 182].

White thinks that this independent ego energy, which he labels as "effectance," is not derived from erotic and aggressive energies, is as basic as the instincts, not related to "particular somatic sources or to consummatory patterns of discharge . . . [but] cannot be equated with the inherent energy of the nervous system" (p. 185). He conceptualizes effectance as a neutral energy which "equips the infant from the start with a kind of energy and with a kind of structure that dispose him to construct a stable, objective, real world" (p. 60). So, although White's central theoretical hypothesis is an energic one, his chief focus is on what he sees as the manifestations of this energy—namely, action. As far as I can tell, he does not make the distinction between motor discharge and action which Freud and Hartmann have elaborated; and his principal evidence is adduced as much from animal behavior and child observation as from clinical data. He stresses, as evidence of action motivated by the independent ego energy, such phenomena as curiosity, exploratory activity, and manipulative behavior. He discusses, critically, and in some detail the current psychoanalytic theories of such topics as identification, ego strength, self-esteem, knowledge of reality, and early ego deviations; and he offers his own modifications of these concepts based on his idea of the "attainment of competence through action and through learning about the consequences of action . . . an active ego serving the biological purpose of competence" (p. 2).

The various types of behavior described by White are seen "to perform the service of maintaining and expanding an effective interaction with the environment. Closely studied, such behavior repeatedly shows characteristics of activity, effort, and the production of some kind of effect" (p. 33). For these reasons, White proposes to refer to the energies in question as "effectance," and he further proposes to designate the subjective experience of satisfaction accompanying such activity as a "feeling of efficacy." This feeling, suggests White, "is a primitive biological endowment as basic as the satisfactions that accompany feeding or sexual gratification, though not nearly as intense" (p. 35). He adds, however, that this feeling of satisfaction does not have to be connected with the achievement of a specific, intended result; the "activity is satisfying in itself, not for specific consequences."

Effectance and its consequences are crucial for the formation of psychic structure. Effectance leads to the exploration of "the properties of the environment; it leads to an accumulating knowledge of what can and cannot be done with the environment; its biological significance lies in this very property of developing *competence*" (p. 186, italics added). By "competence," White refers to "a person's existing capacity to interact effectively with his environment" (p. 39). White acknowledges that "innate capacities" play some part in the development of competence, but largely it derives from learning. "Such learning may be the result of exploratory and manipulative behavior motivated wholly by effectance, but it may have also occurred under the influence of instinctual pressures or in some combination of sources of energy. Competence, in other words, is the cumulative result of the whole history of the transactions with the environment, no matter how they were motivated" (*ibid*). For the subjective side of competence, White introduces the term "sense of competence." The sense of competence, he feels, develops from the whole past history of feelings of efficacy, "including those that result purely from effectance and those that are associated with the satisfaction of instinctual drives." White would apply "feeling of efficacy" for what is experienced in an individual transaction whereas "sense of competence" would be reserved "for the accumulated and organized consequences at later stages of ego development." The sense of competence may eventually become differentiated in terms of spheres of activity; and in the course of development, it becomes an extremely important "nucleus of motivation."

I am not suggesting that this series of skeletonized excerpts from White's most provocative contribution does justice to the range or quality of all of his ideas; I do believe, however, that I have conveyed the gist of at least the framework of his hypothesis. I would again emphasize that White's chief focus is on action, especially on the impact of action in relation to the external environment and the mutual effect of such action on both the environment and the individual. A thorough critique of White's work is beyond the scope of this essay.[3] My chief criticism is that much of what he proposes is a restatement in his own idiom and terminology of much of what psychoanalysts have already stated in their own traditional language. It is a case of trying to put old wine into new bottles, or, as Rosen so elegantly puts it, of confusing a metalinguistic revision for a metapsychological one. However, I do not intend to dismiss White's work in a cavalier manner; his criticisms, both positive and negative, of many aspects of psychoanalytic theory are often sound and penetrating, nor is he a blatantly unfriendly critic so far as psychoanalysis is concerned. When he attacks the weaknesses in such areas as the instinct theory, neutralization, the knowledge of reality, and early ego deviations, he is hitting at the soft underbelly of analytic theory. These are vulnerable targets and warrant both criticism and further scrutiny; whether his proposed revisions represent a sufficiently solid

[3]For two excellent critiques of White's Monograph, see Holt (1964) and Rosen (1965).

basis for the modification of some of these concepts is quite another matter.

White does, somewhat late in his monograph, take cognizance of the fact that Hartmann had already raised the possibility of the existence of independent ego energies; but in fairness to White, Hartmann's conceptualization of the position of such energies in the operation of the psychic apparatus is a much more limited and circumscribed one. And while White does recognize the existence of instinctual energies and their effects (and while I also recognize that White is, by design, presenting a skewed picture of his version of psychic activity), his interest in the instinctual drives and their relationship to the independent ego energies seems perfunctory. Whereas most psychoanalysts have been most concerned with the derivation of ego functions and energies from the instinctual drive energy and the external world, White again pays relatively little attention to this aspect of ego development. This, at least in part. would seem to be responsible for a peculiarly antigenetic slant in his work. He portrays, both explicitly and by implication, an apparatus in which an array of ego functions are present, more or less full-grown and full-formed, at birth, ready to go into service and operation; and relatively little concern is demonstrated for the evolution of essentially primordial functions into more mature ones. I am sympathetic with the difficulties which must inevitably attend the formulation of early psychic functions; but White's overall approach has a kind of artificial, armchair quality to it. Neither will his rather facile transposition of the data from the observation of the lower animals to the human animal be entirely palatable to all psychoanalysts. Further, although his emphasis and focus on the role of action is refreshing and useful, he tends to gloss over the role of intrapsychic factors in many of the phenomena he discusses. For example, White comes close to reducing the process of identification to imitation and its effects; and, while most analysts would agree that imitation is a process which may play some part in the complicated series of events which eventuate in an identification, they would also be much more concerned with the panoply of intrapsychic ingredients which would appear to be crucial in that process. When White states that "the objective stable world is a construction based upon action, the knowledge that we gain of the environment is a knowledge of the probable consequences of action" (p. 69), he certainly is not in error; but, by the same token, is he not guilty of simplifying a tremendously complex and multi-determined activity in which action and its effects are only one of a large series of variables? And again, recognizing his purposefully one-sided emphasis on action, White's approach seems to be woefully lacking in concern for the cognitive processes and their contribution to the activities he describes, including action and adaptation in general. It would be specious to insist that psychoanalysis possesses a comprehensive and satisfactory theory of learning, but it would be equally inaccurate to ignore the importance which the laying down and organization of memory traces must play in any such theory; and while White is not entirely unmindful of these phenomena, the position which he accords them in his concept of learning appears to be quite minimal.

It is not surprising that White views ego strength "as clearly related to acquired competence and sense of competence" (p. 193). He would stress not only what the ego has learned and acquired from conflict, but also what it

> . . . learns through dealing with the environment in conflict-free situations may prove to be useful knowledge in the next scene of conflict. It cannot be said, therefore, that the strength of the ego is purely a function of past performance in situations of crisis and stress. . . . The ideal thing would be to know the whole history of explorations in efficacy and of the sense of competence which is produced by the outcome of these explorations [p. 139].

Such actions would facilitate and provide the possibility of "alternative sources of security, affection, and interest" (p. 141) which White considers an important theme in the growth of ego strength. White warns against seeing ego strength only in negative terms, such as the absence of crippling anxiety or of anticathectic processes. Such a view, he holds,

> . . . neglects the positive contributions of effectance, which is at work building up adaptive capacities that help in coping with dangers, and a sense of competence that opposes the development of anxiety. . . . This view of ego strength as an active, cumulative achievement is valuable in understanding the stages of development, in forming a genetic theory of psychopathology, and in explaining those not infrequent cases in which good adjustments have sprung miraculously from a childhood loaded with pathological influences . . . the riddle can be solved if one pays careful attention to the way in which defenses adopted in crises lead to actions of an efficacious sort which worked well upon the particular

> environment and thus became the basis for a continuing growth of competence and confidence [p. 193].

White is aware of the problems connected with explaining such a happy outcome or of the emergence of ego strength. He would not exclude altogether "such likely constitutional factors as general level of activity" (p. 149). But he would also consider two other factors: the "inherent possibility that a psychodynamic pattern can be translated into effective actions," and the possible part played by the particular responsiveness of the environment to such actions. I do not believe that these explanations are contrary to traditional psychoanalytic theory; what White would stress more than others, however, is the ultimate dependence for the effective operation of these factors on independent ego energies.

XIV

An essay on ego strength can be virtually interminable. The inventory of ego functions is an impressively long one; and each one can be scrutinized from the perspective of its contribution to ego strength or weakness. I recognize that my own emphasis has been selective and, in a sense, skewed. I have chosen to focus primarily on some of the less commonly discussed functions and attributes of the ego and have neglected—or at least glossed over—some of the more widely-known and important ones. A better-balanced presentation of ego strength would surely place more stress on such ego activities as the defensive organizations, perception, neutralization, affect control and modulation, object relationships, reality relations, and the nuances of ego–superego interrelationships; nor can I claim that these functions have not received, in varying degree and detail, consideration in the collection of books I am reviewing. My own predilection has been based, as I have indicated earlier, partly on subjective considerations and partly on the relative neglect that has been accorded some of the other, "minor" functions, in the psychoanalytic literature.

However, it would be amiss to close this discussion without a few notes on some aspects of the ego's relations with reality as they pertain to ego strength. Even sophisticated psychoanalysts are not infrequently prone to limit their thinking of the ego's relations with reality to the function of reality testing. However, it has become clear that this constitutes a rather oversimplified conceptualization of a complex and multi-faceted organization, a point which has been stressed by Glover, Hartmann, and especially by Frosch. It would appear necessary to take into consideration, in addition to the already complicated function of reality testing, such operations as contact with reality and feelings of reality. Actually, only the relative beginnings of an overall psychoanalytic theory of reality relations have begun to unfold; and much more work remains to be accomplished in these critical areas. This becomes apparent as psychoanalysts venture more and more into the field of social and sociological problems. In this respect, Hartmann (1950a) suggests that

> . . . we should obviously feel on safer ground if we could take into account the psychological meaning of the sociological data in a systematic way. We should, for instance, wish to know the significance of the sociological data not only for the egos of the persons in question, but for all three of the psychic systems of the personality. . . . And it would be most helpful if also the sociological meaning of the psychological data were known [p. 91]. . . . Since human beings are by far the most important of real objects, the structure of reality most interesting to analysts is the structure of society. Society is not a projection of unconscious fantasies, though it offers many possibilities for such projection, and their study reveals to us the influence of unconscious factors on men's attitudes to society. We must accept social reality as a factor in its own right; certainly most analysts do not attempt to interpret human behavior exclusively in terms of unconscious drives and fantasies [pp. 92–93].

The accusation has often been directed to psychoanalysis that it neglects or is not concerned with reality and reality factors, that it is a one-sided intrapsychic psychology. A detailed refutation of such unfounded charges cannot be undertaken here; if anything, psychoanalysts attempt to deal with reality and reality issues in a much more comprehensive and sophisticated manner than most psychologists. As analysts, we attempt to integrate and to comprehend the reality factors with drives, with processes of identification, with object relations in the broadest sense, with the genetic point of view, etc.; that our integration and comprehension is often incomplete does not negate either the intention or the basic approach. It must again be acknowledged that our knowledge of reality, our psychology of the real world, is still incomplete; but I would also submit that not all psychoanalysts are as scrupulously demanding of themselves and their methodology as is Hartmann. It is not unheard of, after all, for an analyst dealing with sociological issues or with some area of applied psychoanalysis to talk or to write as if there indeed were a comprehensive psychoanalytic understanding of all aspects of the real world. Without belaboring the point, I admit to concern about the activities of some psychoanalysts interested in community mental health or in other broad social issues, operating ostensibly as *psychoanalysts*, who behave in their pronouncements and recommendations as if such an understanding were already available. Although the activity and experience of such analysts may be of great potential value in providing us with data and hypotheses for the future elaboration of our psychology of the real world, a good deal of caution and deliberation are in order before premature conclusions are drawn and premature commitments are made.

XV

No one in the psychoanalytic movement has contributed more to our understanding of the psychological aspects of reality and reality relations than has Hartmann, and virtually every chapter in his *Essays on Ego Psychology* provides some additional insight or new slant on some aspect of the subject. His "Notes on the Reality Principle" (1956a) is already a classic. Hartmann is always able to see the grays in any problem as well as the blacks and whites; he stresses, therefore, the continuum between what is healthy and effective reality testing and what is pathological and distorted. He points out that distortions of reality are experienced not only in the psychotic but in the neurotic and so-called normal. He conceptualizes the function of reality testing as a multi-layered and multi-faceted one and reminds us that in a given piece of pathology not all "layers" of this function need be involved simultaneously. He points to the complexity of the reality principle stating, "It is, indeed, an ego principle; that is, the concept of the tendencies we ascribe to the reality principle is identical with that of a group of ego functions (though not of the ego as a whole)" (p. 244). He emphasizes explicitly and by implication what could be called the "relativity of reality" and the difficulty of arbitrarily designating what should or should not be considered as "real" for a given individual. He is concerned with the genesis of the sense of reality, reality testing, of the reality principle. He describes the process of the "domestication of the pleasure principle" which he differentiates from the reality principle in the stricter sense; and in this connection (somewhat parallel to the idea of a "relative" autonomy), he qualifies domestication with "partial." He talks about the role of object relations in the development of reality testing, not only in connection with the fact that the object is the most important part of the individual's earliest external reality, but also with regard to the influence "reality" and reality testing of significant objects play in the development of what he calls the "commonly accepted view of reality." He further differentiates a more "objective" world of science from the more "personal" world of immediate experience.[4] He clarifies the concept of "inner reality" (which he distinguishes from Freud's concept of psychic reality) and underlines the fact "that in a sense all mental functions, tendencies, contents are 'real'; fantasy activity also is real, though not realistic" (p. 265). His reminder that inner reality testing suffers the same compromises as external reality through problems of acceptance, distortion, and denial is obviously of concern to psychoanalytic practitioners.

Hartmann also notes that "The reality principle includes postponement of gratification and a temporary toleration of unpleasure" (p. 247), and that "stable object relations can be a basis for stable relations also to reality in general. On the other hand we know that in the nonpsychotic person, too, withdrawal of object cathexis may lead to a loosening of the ties with reality" (Hartmann, 1953, p. 200). These statements are, I believe, in accord with Glover's idea that the ultimate test of normal reality testing is the capacity to maintain effective contact with important objects. Glover's (1968) definition, in greater detail, is as follows:

> Efficient reality-testing, for any subject that has passed the age of puberty, is the capacity to retain psychic contact with the objects that promise gratification of instinct, including here both modified and residual infantile impulse. Adding as a corollary that 'objectivity' is the capacity to assess correctly the relation of instinctual impulse to instinctual object, whether or not the particular aims of the impulse are, can be, or will be gratified [p. 39].

[4]Hartmann's concept of the more personal world of immediate experience has many points in common with Erikson's ideas about "actuality" (see Erikson, 1962, esp. pp. 462–464). Unfortunately I was unable to include this material in my survey. Laing, using his own conceptual and terminological frames of reference, approaches some of the same ideas (see, particularly, Laing, 1962, p. 20).

The heart of Glover's definition is, I believe, the capacity of the ego (via its reality-testing function) to maintain contact with the object of an instinctual drive in the absence of immediate gratification from that object. Obviously this is by no means a novel conceptualization; it had already been enunciated by Freud in "Formulations on the Two Principles of Mental Functioning" (1911), "Instincts and Their Vicissitudes" (1915), and "Negation" (1925). After all, this point is the crux of Freud's work in differentiating (and tracing the shifts) from the purified-pleasure-ego to the reality-ego. From the point of view of ego strength and weakness, therefore, one can view the capacity to tolerate frustration as one of the more crucial determinants of effective reality testing; and, in many ways. we are describing the same group of phenomena, when we speak in terms of the development of object constancy.

Again, the same issues—or at least comparable ones—are discussed in considerable detail by Jacobson in her monograph (1964) and particularly in Chapter III, "The Fusions Between Self and Object Images and the Earliest Types of Identification." She traces the development of the earliest kinds of object relationships in terms of the frustrations and gratifications which the infant experiences *vis-à-vis* his interactions with the important objects, the shifts and oscillations in self and object representations, the processes of introjection and projection, the more primitive types of identification processes, the distortions that arise consequent to early frustrations, and the tendency toward reemerging and fusion which occurs during the course of development. Jacobson's work and arguments are already familiar to most analysts; but the focus on the vicissitudes of the development of the sense of self and the differentiation of the self from what is "real" and external, and the relationship of these processes to early frustration are all germane to the concept of adult reality testing. I can only add that Mahler's work on symbiosis and the separation-individuation process bears on the same questions (Mahler's [1966] paper, "Notes on the Development of Basic Moods," is one of the stellar contributions to the Hartmann *Festschrift* volume. It telescopes a good many of her seminal ideas into this one article and is replete with astute observations valuable both theoretically and clinically. I regret that the format of my essay does not permit a comprehensive review of her presentation).

Although it is not the central focus of his article, Frosch (1966) also deals with the question of tolerating frustration and painful experience in the evolution and development of what he has described as "Reality Constancy." In a series of recent contributions,

Frosch has been concerned with delineating the various subfunctions which make up the relations with reality; and in this paper, he sketches out his concept of reality constancy which he feels is closely related to, although sufficiently distinct from, object constancy. Frosch defines reality constancy as a psychic structure which "arises in conjunction with the establishment of stabilized internal representations of the environment," evolving out of a "concatenation of environmental experiences, memories, perceptions, ideas, etc., deriving from cathectic relationships with the human and nonhuman environment" (pp. 349–350). Genetically, Frosch argues, reality constancy is closely interwoven with the development of object constancy, and to a certain extent evolves from it. He discusses the interrelations of reality constancy and the other ego functions such as reality-testing, perception, delay, anticipation, intentionality, predictability, etc., both from the developmental and operational points of view.

In his review of object constancy and its relation to reality constancy, Frosch stresses the part played by these functions in facilitating the tolerance of temporary separation from the object together with the capacity to tolerate the ambivalence which must inevitably arise toward that object. He discusses the role frustration and renunciation must play in the building up of the reality principle and reality testing and how "Painful and unpleasant experiences have to be considered, mastered, accepted, and incorporated into the representation of reality" (p. 364). Frosch also holds that this process "ultimately contributes to the establishment of reality constancy, which in turn facilitates the acceptance and recognition of unpleasant ideas and experiences as part of the environment, as well as the need to 'reckon with it'" (*ibid*). The evolution of these functions, Frosch suggests, is crucial in enabling the ego to deal with unpleasant reality constructively and adaptively. Frosch's contribution is a most useful one; however, I wish that in his emphasis on differentiating reality constancy from object constancy, he had stressed even more than he did the close connection between the two. I would follow his proposal that we must pay more attention to the significance of the nonhuman environment in the development of the psychic apparatus. and I would also agree with his criticism of White's relative denigration of human environment. But I would also want to keep in focus the fact that the human environment is, at least in the earliest stages, the more critical factor, and that the differentiation of the human and the inanimate environments is a subsequent and secondary development.

XVI

In *Object Love and Reality*, Modell (1968) states as the central theme of his monograph

> . . . that the acceptance of painful reality rests upon the same ego structures that permit the acceptance of the separateness of objects . . . the ego structure whose development permits the acceptance of painful reality is identical to that ego structure whose development enables one to love maturely. In both instances the signposts that indicate whether or not such a successful historical development has been traversed is a sense of identity. If one is fortunate enough to have received 'good enough mothering' in the first and second years of life, the core of a positive sense of identity will have been formed. This core permits the partial relinquishment of instinctual demands upon the object and in turn permits the partial acceptance of separateness of objects. It is this process upon which reality testing hinges [p. 88].

Modell has put together a lively, logically and orderly presented, stimulating volume; in the careful marshaling of his arguments he utilizes evidence not only from the psychoanalytic literature on the subject (which he handles judiciously and thoroughly) but also from a wide variety of cognate fields such as paleolithic art, philosophy, and linguistics; he also provides some interesting observation on the concepts of psychic structure, identification, regression, and the theory of schizophrenia and hallucinations. Regrettably, only a small segment of his many ideas can be dealt with here, where the selective emphasis must be on those aspects of his contributions which bear on the development of reality testing. Modell's primary interest is in the elaboration of a theory of object relation; and for him the quintessential "painful reality" is the actual or potential separation from the object, especially the archaic maternal object.

Modell begins with a discussion of magical thinking which, he argues, is not only a formal category of thought, but also a "basic mode of the ego's relationship to the human inanimate environment" (p. 10). More specifically, he holds that although the dangers which might emanate from the environment may vary, the "magical methods of dealing with the sense of helplessness remain the same" (p. 17). Modell then proceeds to develop the concept of symbols, how the symbol and the object are inseparable, how symbols become a special device for dealing with objects by influencing these objects "at a distance." This in turn permits the belief in "action at a distance" (p. 20). "For the young child," asserts Modell, "the environment is narrowed down to the mother—we might say that the environment *is* the mother" (p. 21); and the danger that arises is the possibility of the loss of the maternal object, which is manifested by separation anxiety. Such a loss can be either real or intrapsychic because of ambivalence, and Modell suggests "that the capacity for magical thought mitigates the danger of catastrophic anxiety through the creation of an illusion of lack of separateness between the self and the object" (p. 23). Further, such omnipotence or magical belief represents a kind of compensation for the prolonged biological helplessness of the human individual. As Modell summarizes it, "The symbol *is* the object denoted; action upon the symbol can affect the object—a belief in action at a distance and a belief that serves the function of negating the perception of the physical separation of objects—the fact that objects can be lost" (p. 27).

Modell goes on to observe that "It is the power of the symbol to give form to the environment—to literally create the environment" (p. 32). Borrowing from Winnicott's (1953) concept of the transitional object, Modell proposes the parallel concept of "transitional object relationship." Just as the inanimate object can be converted by the child into a substitute for the maternal environment in a form determined by the child's own inner world, in a comparable fashion, the child—and, in varying degrees, the adult as well—can create from the real relationship with a human, an object relationship which again reflects the needs and the inner life of the subject.

> The transitional object . . . is a substitute for the actual environment—a substitute that creates the illusion of encapsulating the subject from the dangers of the environment. The transitional object is not a hallucination—it is an object that does exist 'in the environment,' separate from the self, but only partially so. It is given form and structure, that is, it is created by the needs of the self. The relationship of the subject to the object is fundamentally ambivalent; the qualities of the object are magical and hence there is an illusion of connectedness between the self and the object. The relation of the subject to the object is primarily exploitative, the subject feels no concern for the needs of the object and cannot acknowledge that the object possesses his own separateness and

> individuality. The transitional object relationship is dyadic—it admits no others [p. 40].

Modell distinguishes this type of object relation from a . . .

> more mature mode . . . where the object is clearly delimited from the subject. Although the transitional object relationship is in a certain sense an illusion—in that the qualities of the object are created by the subject—nevertheless, the object remains a source of gratification. Although the object is created by the subject, it is still an object; it is something which the self requires for its safety [p. 109].

The safety is in relation to the danger from the environment, separation from the object. Again, Modell emphasizes that the organization of reality cannot be separated from those structures in the mind which are concerned with relations with objects; and similarly the maturation of object love cannot be separated from the development of the capacity to accept painful reality. He postulates "two organs for the structuring of reality." One consists of the genetically determined autonomous ego structures, such as the perceptual apparatus, but which Modell feels also require the presence of an object for their development.

> The second organ for the organization of reality is that with which we are most concerned. This is a structure that is not vouchsafed by inheritance but must be formed anew in each individual. It is, as we have observed, a structure that requires for its healthy development (to use Winnicott's term) 'good enough mothering.' Autonomous structures will be impaired if there is an absence of the maternal environment; this more plastic organ for the structuring of reality will be impaired if there is a failure of the maternal environment [pp. 87–88].

Modell follows Freud in acknowledging that the ego's capacity to accept painful reality is the essential issue in the ego's relation to reality; Modell holds that "the problem of the acceptance of reality can then be reduced to the problem of accepting the separateness of objects—that they can be lost" (p. 88). Thus the fundamental aim of magical thinking is to create the illusion of the inseparateness of the object and the subject; and "The problem of reality testing is at bottom the problem of denial—the need to disavow painful perceptions and to substitute a view of the world that is more in keeping with omnipotent wishes" (p. 93). Modell, however, recognizes that reality testing is not a simple function; and he describes a variety of mechanisms whereby the individual attempts to deal with the painful reality of separation and object loss. In this connection he makes some interesting observations on the role of identification processes. He feels that one of the consequences of identification is a "magical illusion, that is, the illusion of acquiring the quality of the object itself by means of the possession of the symbol, or part of the object. . . . Although identification leads to an illusion that minimizes the difference between the object and the subject, it is an illusion without which we cannot live; it is the basis of group ties" (p. 99).

As I have indicated, I have not attempted to present the overall model of object relations which Modell has enunciated; rather I have limited my survey of his monograph to that material which bears on the issues of reality testing and ego strength. For Modell, the strong ego is essentially the one which can tolerate separateness; if it cannot tolerate such separateness, an impairment of reality testing functioning will eventuate, with a variety of regressive mechanisms being substituted for the mature task of coping with the painful reality of loss and separation. Modell's overall task is a difficult one; as he himself notes in the preface to his book, psychoanalysis does not possess a satisfactory theory of object relationships. The thorniest aspect of such a theory, it seems to me, is the collating and the reconciling of the data from object relations concepts with those of instinct theory. We recognize, in a general way, that there is no inherent opposition between the two points of view; and in fact, the two cannot be separated. Yet the working out of even the broader details of the relationships between "real" external objects representations, internalization processes, the concept of "internal objects," and how all these must be brought within the framework of instinct theory is still quite an elusive task.

I have a minor cavil with Modell. Although it is clear that he is not unaware of the fact, I do not believe that he has been sufficiently clear, at least in overall emphasis, that the threat of separation is not the only external danger, the only piece of painful reality that will have to be tolerated. I would agree that in genetic terms, the fear of loss of object is probably the most basic fear and represents the most fundamental painful reality (the same could be stated in economic terms with a somewhat different emphasis); but I believe that more must be said about the relation between such a basic danger and those which we think of as somewhat higher in the developmental hierarchy: the loss of the love of the object, castration fear, loss of the love of the superego. When breaks in reality testing follow in the wake of a conflict triggered by, let us say, castration anxiety, must we assume that there is a one-to-one relation between the regressive processes we observe in regard to reality testing and the presence of a significant defect in tolerating separation? The answer could well be yes—and in a certain sense, since everyone must have had some problems in the separation-individuation phase, at least a partial "yes" is inevitable; but it also seems reasonable that we must look to a further understanding of those intermediary factors which either implement or hold off such regressions.

XVII

One of the areas of ego strength that might be profitably explored has to do with the relation between the ego and the superego, and some allusions to this question have already been offered in this paper. I want to discuss only one aspect of this relationship in any detail, the role the superego might play in reality relations, but I want also to mention the importance that is attached to ego–superego relations by some of the contributors to the material being surveyed. Jacobson's work in particular demonstrates this emphasis, and she repeatedly underscores the influence which superego maturation and superego identifications exert on ego structures and functioning. At the same time she constantly reminds us that the maturation and development of many of the ego functions are indispensable for the emergence and establishment of an effective superego organization. And in terms of adult psychological behavior, she stresses the importance of a harmonious relation between the aims and the activities of both ego and superego for optimal overall functioning. She points out that

> . . . modifications in the superego and ego structures and functions ultimately lead to a remarkable strengthening of both systems. This enables the ego to reset and resolidify its defense organization, despite and precisely because of the fact that these modifications result in the attainment of instinctual freedom, freedom of object choice, of thought, feeling and action, and of greater freedom from external influences and from infantile id and superego pressures. In fact, all of these liberties can be gained only to the extent to which

> superego and ego acquire sufficient autonomy and strength to subject them to the necessary limitations and to establish and maintain a stable and durable control system which is in accord with adult reality [Jacobson, 1964, pp. 188–189].

Lustman (1966) pursues many of the same arguments. He indicates that

> . . . regulation of impulse is developmentally related to internalization processes and that this internalization builds restraining structures which are a stratification of both ego and superego components. This is not to say that ego and superego are the same. On the contrary, it is of the greatest utility to maintain these sets of functions as very different. What it does suggest is shared boundaries, in that certain ego elements may induce the development of superego elements and can exist side by side, sharing common developmental roots and processes [p. 215].

Here I should also mention Hartmann's oft-repeated observation of the role that the primary autonomous apparatus may exercise in the service of primitive control and the further role which these structures may play in the development of more mature control systems.

Hartmann also considers the part which the superego may take in the testing of reality, particularly with reference to internal reality. Hartmann adds that "We should not omit that the superego may occasionally influence even the testing of outer reality" (1956a, p. 256), and that the superego may contribute to the motivation for objectivity at least in regard to the character of objectivity, intellectual honesty, and truthfulness. Stein (1966) has devoted a paper, "Self-Observation, Reality and the Superego," to a further examination and elaboration of these considerations. He reviews some of Freud's ideas—and vacillations—on the subject, making it clear that it was not easy for Freud to determine whether the process of self-observation was a function of the ego or of the superego; Stein concludes that Freud was never satisfied with the answer.

Stein's own thesis is that "self-observation is an essential element in the process of reality testing . . . self-observation and self-evaluation are inextricably linked, and more intimately involved with superego functions. Therefore the superego functions play an essential, if indirect, role in reality testing and reality adaptation." Stein argues that if the superego is conceded to be the crucial factor in self-evaluation, it must follow that "it would not make sense" to think of the superego also not taking an active role in the observation of the data about the self (p. 975).

Stein, on the other hand, concedes the difficulty involved in bringing forward clinical observations which would help clarify the role the superego plays in the field of reality testing. The crucial question, he feels, is "whether the superego, like an ideal policeman . . . ever 'prompts' the ego in the direction of more adequate reality testing, as well as the reverse" (p. 281); and while he does not view the answer as a simple one, Stein thinks it is essentially in the affirmative. He points to the problems, familiar to all analysts, connected with the telling of the truth—a problem which has close connections with moral values and conscience and therefore reflecting the involvement of the superego as well as the ego. He also stresses: "As analysts we possess, and attempt to inculcate in our patients, an attitude of telling oneself 'the truth' which has the character of a moral imperative. We are anything but neutral on this subject" (p. 285).

Stein also brings up the point that with such issues as telling the truth, it is often hard to distinguish historically the influence exerted by the ego and superego in the development of certain attitudes; and certainly the degree to which moral and punitive attitudes "play a leading role in this area of childhood training" will vary considerably from individual to individual. "Moral teaching and reality testing," he says, "are hardly to be distinguished by a young child. It takes a long time for him to be impressed with the unfortunate results of self-deception and lying to others, if he ever is" (p. 285). Stein takes the position that in the adult both ego and superego functions are involved in "telling the truth" and comparable processes; but, he goes on, "it seems reasonable to suppose that the first automatic control of the tendency to lie is a well-internalized response in which superego function is dominant. It may be considered relatively archaic, although developmentally it would be traced chiefly to the oedipal or postoedipal period—that is, the phases in which superego precursors are being organized into an integrated structure." I cannot review the various deliberations and the supporting clinical evidence which he offers, but Stein's conclusion is that "Clinical observations do generally support that aspect of superego theory which allows for a blurred and readily permeable border between superego and ego" (p. 294).

Loewenstein (1966) is essentially in agreement with the main thrust of Stein's arguments. He too alludes to the difficulty encountered in trying to tease out the clinical manifestations of superego versus ego functions; he too recognizes the blurring that can occur between superego and ego activity, especially in the child. However, he also implies that with advancing age and maturation, the two areas do become more distinct. "A younger child does not distinguish sharply between them: a prohibition to cross the street has moral undertones for him. The clear separation between what is dangerous and what is 'evil' is the result of superego formation. To pursue the analogy with the ego: we are never completely free of this early equation of danger with 'evil'" (p. 302).

Loewenstein finds the interrelationships between ego and superego functions quite intricate. Concerning the phenomenon of self-observation, he would distinguish two types. The first involves "varying degrees of awareness of inner psychic processes, such as affects, thought, sensations of the pleasure–pain continuum, etc. I believe there is general agreement that self-observations of this kind are attributable to the ego" (p. 309). The second type of self-observation is a "reflective observation of inner processes; when awareness comprises both object and subject of observation. I suppose this second kind is referred to when self-observation is considered to be a superego function. In some pathological and occasionally in some normal cases, it takes the form of self-watching, self-criticizing, as if by inner observer" (*ibid*). Loewenstein concludes that in self-observation, "the superego, whose role it is to demand truthfulness, helps to maintain objectivity, but not rarely impairs self-observation due to self-critical or self-punitive tendencies. The essential elements, however, the perception of what really is observable within oneself, and its observation, are functions attributable to the ego, albeit often standing in the service of the superego" (pp. 309–310). With development and maturation, "some superego regulations are gradually replaced by concern for reality, social responsibilities and expediency, and for ego interests. These changes represent not a complete elimination of the previous superego regulations, but a subordination of superego demands in these areas to demands of the ego" (p. 310).

Loewenstein also takes up the influences exerted by the ego ideal, although not specifically in terms of the function of reality testing. However, if we were to transpose his remarks along those lines, it could be seen that the ego ideal—especially if the reality testing function were an inordinately narcissistically invested function of the parents—might encourage a closer adherence to the reality principle in terms of the narcissistic motivation involved[5]; on the other hand, the demands of the

[5]Writing this in the weeks prior to my summer vacation I came across clinical material which illustrates some of the points discussed in these sections of the

ego ideal in terms of being "realistic" may be so "exalted" that effective reality testing might be interfered with.

Jacobson (1964) takes a position somewhat at variance with that of Stein, in particular. She states,

> whereas self-perception always represents an ego function, the self-evaluation of an adult person is not exclusively a superego function. Founded on subjective inner experience and on objective perception by the ego of the physical and mental self, it is partly or sometimes predominately exercised by the superego, but is also partly a critical ego function whose maturation weakens the power of the superego over the ego [p. 130].

In summary, it is evident that reality testing (as one constituent of a superordinate organization of functions having to do with reality relations) is one of the most crucial factors in ego strength; with somewhat less assurance, we can assert that the superego does have some influence over the ego in its reality-testing operations.

XVIII

It would, at this point, be gratifying to emerge with a psychoanalytic definition of Health and Normality. I am, however, unable to do so; nor am I able either to improve or further synthesize those definitional

---

essay. In the course of working over the feelings connected with my departure and their separation from the analyst, two male patients "confessed" to fantasies and "play" which involved their continuing the analysis during the analyst's absence. One of these patients "found" himself lying on a couch, free-associating, and generally behaving as if the analyst were still present. These vignettes reflect not only the anxiety in regard to separation and loss together with the attempts at their denial, but also the shame and guilt connected with the recognition of their attempts at avoiding the facing of a painful reality. These patients, who were generally dissimilar in most respects, had in common fathers who were "hyper-realistic" and took great pride in their adherence to the cold, hard facts of reality, together with a marked contempt for anything that smacked of unreality. On the other hand, I have encountered a countertransference reaction, often of considerable intensity, in reaction to the tendency of patients to avoid reality. On more than one occasion I have heard it stated explicitly in terms of "He [the patient] can't get away with it!" Such reactions make it difficult to discount the role of the superego in reality testing.

concepts which I have reviewed and presented. And I have grave doubts that such a concept will be forthcoming in the immediate future! On the other hand, I would again support Tartakoff's (1966) admonition that "we cannot abandon the concepts of health and illness, and some working basis for what can be classified as normal remains implicit for purposes of analysis" (pp. 223–224).

The reasons for this are several, each deserving a dissertation of its own. On a technical level, try as we will to eschew normative standards and judgments, we nevertheless use them over and over again as one means of orienting ourselves to our patient's material and as one—among many—bases for entertaining specific interventions. The fact that our standards and judgments may, at times, be contaminated by subjective distortions, bias, and so forth, does not, I would suggest, alter the fact of their usefulness. No matter how neutral, scientific, or objective we try to be, a good many of our concepts cannot entirely escape the shadow of the normal–abnormal, healthy–sick conceptual axis.

Secondly, I would heartily reindorse Hartmann's emphasis on how the knowledge of the healthy and conflict-free augments our understanding of the pathological and conflictual. And, if the project for a general psychoanalytic psychology is to be extended, then also our understanding of Health and Normality must also be expanded. Last—and this is a topic which is both interesting and most tenuous—it seems to me that we are not about to surrender our inclinations toward this kind of dichotomization, at least not readily and totally. Certainly it is true that most psychoanalysts, for reasons which are not entirely apparent, assiduously attempt to dissociate themselves from such dichotomous value judgments. In part this is no doubt associated with the wish to behave in as objective and scientific a manner as possible; in part, I would suspect, it also represents a reaction against the tendency to view Health and Normality as "one expression of the ideal of vital perfection" (Hartmann, 1939, p. 5) or as the "New Morality" (Reider, 1950, p. 43). However, I am skeptical of the degree of success that most of us achieve in completely avoiding such values, judgments, and dichotomies. My own impression is that, for better or for worse, this is a fairly basic tendency; if we didn't have a concept of health and normality, my guess is that a lot of people would find it necessary to invent one—and, in fact, very shortly, I will attempt to demonstrate that psychoanalysts have already done so.[6]

---

[6]The informative volume on *Normality* by Offer and Sabshin (1966) examines

When we get to the subject of ego strength, the story is both more simple and more complicated. The ego, after all, is a construct; and, therefore, ego strength is also a construct—not pure chimera it is true, but a construct nonetheless. Ego functions, however, are quite another matter. Here we are on more solid ground because ego functions (at least by and large) are observable and even—in spite of our prejudices—measurable to some extent. So we are in a position to make certain statements, albeit cautious ones, concerning the efficacy of specific ego functions and even in regard to clusters of certain ego functions. However, here too we must take certain qualifiers into consideration, The strength, the efficiency, of a given ego function cannot be evaluated in vacuo; we view and we judge the strength of a particular ego function with respect to a given task in terms of specific relations and "on the basis of its behavior in typical situations" (Hartmann, 1950b, p. 139). This would seem to be both proper and correct; and, in doing so, we have accumulated a good deal of data about the ego and its component functions.

However, by the same token, a disproportionate amount of what analysts know about the ego and specific ego functions comes from the analytic situation and the particular ego functions which of necessity are most likely to be engaged in the analytic work. Obviously, this is not entirely so; in the course of our daily work with patients we learn a good deal about the workings of ego functions which participate in a whole host of extra-analytic activities, But—at least as a generalization—what we know best are those functions which the analytic situation itself invokes. If this proposition is reasonably valid, then I believe it is also not unlikely that our concepts of what constitutes ego strength must inevitably be skewed in the direction of that ensemble of ego functions which come into play in the analytic work. I don't think that I am offering anything very striking. After all, most of us would concede that the ensemble—and operational quality—of ego functions required for a successful analysand are quite different from those required for a successful creative artist, an anchorite priest, a business tycoon, or a community mental health worker. I am not suggesting that these functions are necessarily better or worse for any one calling; they are just different.

Nevertheless, one consequence of this (necessarily) one-sided emphasis has been, I submit, the introduction of a rather private and

---

the concept of Normality from many different points of view, including the psychoanalytic; and Chapter II includes the synopses of the approach to this problem by a number of psychoanalysts.

perhaps solipsistic psychoanalytic concept of Health and Normality, a "New Normality" if you will; it goes by the name of Analyzability. It seems to me that for psychoanalysts, who almost unanimously would accept the ubiquity and inevitability of conflict, defensive distortion, and so forth, the individual whose pathology has not incapacitated him to the extent that he can still participate in the psychoanalytic process, that individual has taken on some of the aura of, at least, relative health and normality. I am not suggesting that this tendency is necessarily justifiable or that it would be vehemently defended by the majority of analysts; but I do believe that the tendency is discernible and at least understandable from the perspective of our work.

I vividly recall the first panel discussion I attended at a meeting of the American Psychoanalytic Association and how that meeting was temporarily "broken up" when one of the speakers, an analyst of great renown, declared with marked feeling, "that whatever else, I'm sure that my son can be analyzed in a classical analysis." I would submit that, whatever else, this analyst was conveying, by his feeling and by his words, the hope that his son was indeed both normal and sufficiently healthy to undergo classical analysis. For many, if not all analysts, to be analyzable is to be "normal" and that is "good!"

One last note. I think it is extremely difficult to determine with any degree of certainty how much direct value all this material about ego strength and the strength of the various ego functions has for the day to day clinical work of the analyst; and, to some extent, the same question applies to many areas of ego psychology. That the study of the ego and its components—and I am referring here to the post-1939 developments, as well as those earlier innovations proposed by Freud—have immeasurably enriched our psychological knowledge would appear to be beyond doubt; obviously, however, there are some who do harbor these doubts (Glover, 1968, is replete with attacks on the "neo-Freudian" ego psychology; see also Zelmanowits, 1968, for a vitriolic attack on the work of Rapaport and Hartmann). On the other hand, the specific and concrete ways in which the broadening of our science by the incorporation of the data and insights from ego psychology has produced alterations and modifications in psychoanalytic technique is, I believe, another matter. Not infrequently we hear or read about the technical aspects of the "ego-psychological approach" which often implies so much in the way of innovation but often specifies relatively little. The contributions of Hartmann (1951) or Loewenstein (1967) tend to he much more circumspect and cautious in outlining the degree of technical changes brought about by ego psychology. This is consistent with the conclusions of Lipton (1967) and Kanzer and Blum (1967) who in recent reviews of psychoanalytic technique hold that little fundamental changes have occurred with the advent of ego psychology. Lipton (1967), in his discussion of the developments of Freud's position on psychoanalytic technique from 1920 to 1939, feels that Freud's "central preoccupation was not so much the development of a psychoanalytic technique as its *preservation*" (p. 90, italics added) and concludes, "Freud considered that by 1920 the fundamental premises of psychoanalytic technique were established and that he devoted his efforts to theoretical expansion, to technical refinement, and to the stabilization and preservation of the basic premises against the numerous forces that jeopardized them" (p. 91). Kanzer and Blum (1967) have surveyed technical changes in psychoanalytic technique since 1939; and, while giving full recognition to the many contributions in ego psychology and the way in which these contributions have enhanced our understanding and point of view, conclude that "Nevertheless, classical analysis, as the innermost core of analytic theorizing and therapy, has undergone relatively little change— one that is to be measured more in the analyst's outlook and use of his techniques than in their formal aspects" (pp. 138–139).

What is hard to spell out, particularly for those of us who were not practicing psychoanalysis before 1939 and therefore do not have the advantage of the historical perspective of one who has participated in analytic work in both periods, is the extent to which that "outlook" has been transformed and translated into specific clinical operations. Calef's (1966) epigrammatic formulation on psychoanalytic technique would appear most germane here; he has stated that "Psychoanalysts do not have a technique; we have only a theory of technique," and that theory of technique, in turn, derives from our overall theory of psychic functioning and the theory of neurosis. Therefore, however difficult it may be to trace explicit changes, it is reasonable to assume that whatever influences our overall theory must inevitably also alter, however slowly and indirectly, some of our technical procedures. The precise degree and nature of such change is not clear; different analysts undoubtedly view the matter quite differently depending on their own inclinations, biases, and theoretical positions. As so often happens in our science, *non liquet.*

REFERENCES

Calef, V. (1966), Personal communication.

Erikson, E. (1961), Human strength and the cycle of generations. In: *Insight and Responsibility*. New York: Norton, pp. 111–157.

_______ (1962), Reality and actuality. *J. Amer. Psychoanal. Assn.*, 10:451–474.

_______ (1964), *Insight and Responsibility*. New York: Norton.

Esman, A. (1965), Review of Erikson, E., *Insight and Responsibility. Psychoanal. Quart.*, 34:117–119.

Freud, A. (1966), Links between Hartmann's ego psychology and the child analyst's thinking. In: R. M. Loewenstein, L. Newman, M. Schur & A. J. Solnit, ed. (1966), pp. 16–27.

Freud, S. (1911), Formulations on two principles of mental functioning. *Standard Edition*, 12:215–226. London: Hogarth Press, 1958.

_______ (1915), Instincts and their vicissitudes, *Standard Edition*, 14:111–140. London: Hogarth Press, 1957.

_______ (1917), Introductory lectures on psychoanalysis. *Standard Edition*, 16. London: Hogarth Press, 1963.

_______ (1925), Negation. *Standard Edition*, 19:234–239. London: Hogarth Press, 1961.

_______ (1926), Inhibitions, symptoms, and anxiety. *Standard Edition*, 20: 77–175. London: Hogarth Press, 1959.

Frosch, J. (1966), A note on reality constancy. In: R. M. Loewenstein, L. Newman, M. Schur & A. J. Solnit, ed. (1966), pp. 349–376.

Gitelson, M. (1948), Problems of psychoanalytic training. *Psychoanal. Quart.*, 17:198–211.

_______ (1954), Therapeutic problems in the analysis of the "normal candidate." *Internat. J. Psycho-Anal.*, 35:174–183.

_______ (1965), Review of H. Hartmann, *Essays on Ego Psychology. Psychoanal. Quart.*, 34:268–273.

Glover, E. (1966), Metapsychology or metaphysics. *Psychoanal. Quart.*, 35: 173–190.

_______ (1968), *The Birth of the Ego*. New York: International Universities Press.

Hartmann, H. (1939), Psychoanalysis and the concept of health. In: Hartmann (1964), pp. 3–18.

_______ (1944), Psychoanalysis and sociology. In: Hartmann (1964), pp. 19–36.

_______ (1947), On rational and irrational action. In: Hartmann (1964), pp. 37–68.

_______ (1950a), Applications of psychoanalytic concepts to social science. In: Hartmann (1964), pp. 90–98.

_______ (1950b), Comments on the psychoanalytic theory of the ego. In: Hartmann (1964), pp. 113–141.

_______ (1951), Technical implications of ego psychology. In: Hartmann (1964), pp. 142–154.

_______ (1952), The mutual influences in the development of ego and id. In: Hartmann (1964), pp. 155–181.

_______ (1953), Contribution to the metapsychology of schizophrenia. In: Hartmann (1964), pp. 182–206.

_______ (1955), Notes on the theory of sublimation. In: Hartmann (1964), pp. 215–240.

_______ (1956a), Notes on the reality principle. In: Hartmann (1964), pp. 241–267.

_______ (1956b), The development of the ego concept in Freud's work. In: Hartmann (1964), pp. 268–296.

_______ (1964), *Essays on Ego Psychology.* New York: International Universities Press.

Holt, R. (1964), Review of R. White, *Ego and Reality in Psychoanalytic Theory. Contemp. Psychol.,* 9:433–434.

Jacobson, E. (1954), The self and the object world: Vicissitudes of their infantile cathexes and their influence on ideational and affective development. *The Psychoanalytic Study of the Child,* 9:75–127. New York: International Universities Press.

_______ (1964), *The Self and the Object World.* New York: International Universities Press.

Kanzer, M. (1962), Ego interest, egoism, and narcissism. Panel abstract. *J. Amer. Psychoanal. Assn.,* 10:593–605.

_______ & Blum, H. (1967), Classical psychoanalysis since 1939. In: *Psychoanalytic Techniques,* ed. B. Wolman. New York: Basic Books, pp. 93–144.

Keiser, S. (1969), Superior intelligence: Its contribution to neurosogenesis. *J. Amer. Psychoanal. Assn.,* 17:452–473.

Lipton, S. (1967), Later developments in Freud's technique. In: *Psychoanalytic Techniques,* ed. B. Wolman. New York: Basic Books, pp. 51–92.

Laing, R. D. (1959), *The Divided Self.* Baltimore: Penguin Books, 1963.

_______ (1962), *The Self and Others.* Chicago: Quadrangle Books.

_______ (1968), *The Politics of Experience.* New York: Pantheon Books.

Lampl-de Groot, J. (1966), Some thoughts on adaptation and conformism. In: R. M. Loewenstein, L. Newman, M. Schur & A. J. Solnit, ed. (1966), pp. 338–348.

Loewenstein, R. M. (1966), On the theory of the superego. In: R. M. Loewenstein, L. Newman, M. Schur & A. J. Solnit, ed. (1966), pp. 298–314.

_______ (1967), Defensive organization and autonomous ego functions. *J. Amer. Psychoanal. Assn.,* 15:795–809.

_______ Newman, L., Schur, M. & Solnit, A. J., ed. (1966), *Psychoanalysis—A General Psychology.* New York: International Universities Press.

Lustman, S. (1966), Impulse control, structure, and the synthetic function. In: R. M. Loewenstein, L. Newman, M. Schur & A. J. Solnit, ed. (1966), pp. 190–221.

Mahler, M. (1966), Notes on the development of basic moods. In: R. M. Loewenstein, L. Newman, M. Schur & A. J. Solnit, ed. (1966), pp. 152–168.

Modell, A. (1968), *Object Love and Reality*. New York: International Universities Press.

Nunberg, H. (1930), The synthetic function of the ego. In: *Practice and Theory of Psychoanalysis*, 1:120–136. New York: International Universities Press, 1960.

Offer, D. & Sabshin, M. (1966), *Normality*. New York: Basic Books.

Peto, A. (1961), The fragmentizing function of the ego in the transference neurosis. *Internat. J. Psycho-Anal.*, 42:238–245.

Provence, S. (1966), Some aspects of early ego development. In: R. M. Loewenstein, L. Newman, M. Schur & A. J. Solnit, ed. (1966), pp. 107–122.

Rangell, L. (1965), The scope of Heinz Hartmann. *Internat. J. Psycho-Anal.*, 46:5–30.

Reider, N. (1950), The concept of normality. *Psychoanal. Quart.*, 19:43–51.

Rosen, V. (1961), The relevance of "style" to certain aspects at defense and the synthetic function of the ego. *Internat. J. Psycho-Anal.*, 42:447–457.

_______ (1965), Review of R. White, *Ego and Reality in Psychoanalytic Theory. Internat. J. Psycho-Anal.*, 46:256–258.

Spitz, R. (1966), Metapsychology and direct infant observation. In: R. M. Loewenstein, L. Newman, M. Schur & A. J. Solnit, ed. (1966), pp. 123–151.

Stein, M. (1966), Self observation, reality, and the superego. In: R. M. Loewenstein, L. Newman, M. Schur & A. J. Solnit, ed. (1966), pp. 275–297.

Tartakoff, H. (1966), The normal personality in our culture and the Nobel prize complex. In: R. M. Lowenstein, L. Newman, M. Schur & A. J. Solnit, ed. (1966), pp. 222–252.

Waelder, R. (1930), The principle of multiple function. *Psychoanal. Quart.*, 5:45–62, 1936.

White, R. (1963), Ego and Reality in Psychoanalytic Theory [*Psychological Issues*, Monogr. 11]. New York: International Universities Press.

Winnicott, D. W. (1953), Transitional objects and transitional phenomena. *Internat. J. Psycho-Anal.*, 34:89–97.

Zelmanowits, J. (1968), Review of *The Collected Papers of David Rapaport. Psychiat.*, 31:292–299.

Zetzel, E. (1949), Anxiety and the capacity to bear it. *Internat. J. Psycho-Anal.*, 30:1–12.

_______ (1965), Depression and the incapacity to bear it. In: *Drives, Affects, Behavior*, ed. M. Schur, 2:243–274. New York: International Universities Press.

Chapter 8

1971

The Transference Neurosis

A Survey of the Literature

It has become a virtual tradition for the member of the panel who is to present a review of the pertinent literature to begin his presentation with that somewhat melancholy statement that, owing to the limitations of time and to the overabundance of excellent papers, only a small segment of the important material could be included and a sizable proportion of the significant contributions would have to be passed over. For better or for worse, I am not in a position to offer such an apology; and although I have no intention of presenting an encyclopedic summary of everything that has been published in the psychoanalytic literature on the transference neurosis, that decision has not been dictated only by the pressures of scheduling. It is both of interest and of significance that the number of papers in the psychoanalytic literature dealing specifically, in a systematic fashion, with the concepts and the theory of the transference neurosis is remarkably small; and if I had so desired, I probably could have included at least a cursory review of all such articles in the literature. I would also suggest that this apparent lack of interest in the transference neurosis, as reflected by the relative poverty of scientific papers, is paralleled by a comparable relative disregard of the concept by psychoanalysts in their case reports and discussions. In his textbook, Glover (1955) lamented the fact that the transference-neurosis concept has fallen into "relative desuetude" and has been upstaged by generalizations, rules of thumb, pseudoscientific slogans, and a fetishistic attitude about transference (p. 123).

Yet what is quite paradoxical about this state of affairs is that no one has seriously challenged the position of the transference neurosis as—in the words of Wallerstein (1967) "the central technical and conceptual vehicle of psychoanalysis as a therapy" (p. 551). Virtually every definition—such as Rangell's (1954), Gill's (1954) or Stone's (1954)—of psychoanalysis as a therapy revolves around the concept of the transference neurosis, its development, analysis, and ultimate resolution in the treatment situation; and similarly the most sophisticated attempts to differentiate psychoanalysis from the psychoanalytically-based psychotherapies look primarily to the differences in the ways in which the transference neurosis is permitted to unfold and then handled. On the other hand, those analysts who have promulgated significant deviations from classical psychoanalytic technique have conceptualized those technical variations in terms of the management of the transference neurosis. It is not clear, therefore, why a topic like the transference neurosis—a topic which is of such central importance both theoretically and clinically—should have attracted so little attention in our literature.[1]

The 1955 International Psychoanalytic Congress featured a symposium on the problems of transference at which Hoffer (1956) delivered a brief paper on "Transference and Transference Neurosis." In this paper, Hoffer listed three questions about the transference neurosis which I would like to borrow and utilize as a framework for my review. These were Hoffer's questions: What does it mean? How does it develop? What role does it play in the therapeutic process? (p. 378). By and large, in my attempts to summarize the answers to Hoffer's questions, I will give priority—both in space and position—to the works of Freud, and I will present the contributions of other authors somewhat more briefly.

Two final introductory notes: First, while it is true that the number of papers dealing with the transference neurosis in a limited, specific, and organized fashion is quite small, it is also true that the amount of material dealing with closely related topics is virtually inexhaustible. Obviously I cannot consider in any detail such global subjects as the theory of psychoanalytic technique, the goals of analytic therapy, the concept of neurosis formation, or of the whole problem of transference in general. Nor will I be able to review such issues as the therapeutic alliance, the transference reactions in psychotic characters, transference psychosis, or the splitting of the ego in analytic therapy. I trust that many of these questions will come up for discussion in the course of the panel; but I will have to eliminate them from the purview of this presentation. Second, while I will try to organize my material around Hoffer's three questions, you will recognize that it is not always feasible to extract isolated passages from a larger context without distorting the overall meaning of that passage. Therefore, some of the quotations which I have

[1]Three relatively recent exceptions of this trend are the contributions of Kepecs (1966), Nagera (1966), and Stone (1967).

selected may have relevance for one, two, or all three of these questions. I trust that the inevitable overlap and repetition will not be unduly confusing.

WHAT DOES IT MEAN?

To return to Hoffer's questions. You will recall that Freud used the term, transference neurosis, in two different, albeit related, ways. First he spoke of the transference neurosis in distinction to the narcissistic neurosis. As a nosological term the transference neuroses (namely the hysterias and the obsessive-compulsive neuroses) referred to those psychopathological conditions in which a transference with the physician could be effected; and Freud distinguished these illnesses from those wherein he felt no such relationship could be established. In the latter narcissistic neuroses, therefore, Freud felt that the patient was not amenable to psychoanalytic influence and was not a proper candidate for analytic treatment.

Second, Freud used the term in the technical sense to designate the revival of the infantile neurosis in the analytic situation. It is with the second of these two usages that we will be primarily concerned. Freud has given us a number of excellent descriptions of his concept of the transference neurosis and what it is. The one he offered in the Introductory Lectures is probably the most succinct and useful. Freud (1917) points out that the neurotic process is not stable and inert; rather it is constantly "growing and developing," and this flux is continued into the analytic experience.

> . . . when, however, the treatment has obtained mastery over the patient, what happens is that the whole of his illness's new production is concentrated on a single point—his relation to the doctor. . . . When the transference has risen to this significance, work upon the patient's memories retreats far into the background. Thereafter it is not incorrect to say that we are no longer concerned with the patient's earlier illness but with a newly created and transformed neurosis which has taken the former's place. . . . All the patient's symptoms have abandoned their original meaning and have taken on a new sense which lies in a relation to the transference; or only such symptoms have persisted as are capable of undergoing such a transformation . . . [p. 444].

Earlier, Freud (1914) had declared: "Provided only that the patient shows compliance enough to respect the necessary conditions of analysis, we regularly succeed in giving all the symptoms of the illness a new transference meaning and in replacing his ordinary neurosis with a 'transference neurosis'. . ." (p. 154).

What should be underscored in this description is not only the obvious elements of the displacement, the transference onto the "relation with the doctor," or of the repetition of aspects of infantile conflicts, but also the element *of transformation.* Freud stresses—and I would submit that this is a point which is not infrequently misunderstood and misinterpreted—that the transference neurosis is a newly-created product. It is not a simple replication of the old or infantile neurosis in a new setting; it involves symptoms which "have taken on a new sense," or as Freud (1917) puts it, "new editions of the old conflicts" (pp. 444 and 454). He stresses that the original symptoms are divested of libido and, "In place of the patient's true illness there appears the artificially constructed transference illness . . ." (p. 454).

But Freud also felt that it was important

> to give a warning that we can draw no direct conclusion from the distribution of the libido during and resulting from the treatment as to how it was distributed during the illness. Suppose we succeeded in bringing a case to a favorable conclusion by setting up and then resolving a strong father-transference to the doctor. It would not be correct to conclude that the patient had suffered previously from a similar unconscious attachment of libido to his father. His father transference was merely the battlefield on which we gained control of his libido; the patient's libido was directed to it from other positions . . . Not until after the transference has once more been resolved can we reconstruct in our thoughts the distribution of libido which had prevailed during the illness [p. 455].

By and large the contributions of those analysts who followed Freud represent clarifications and extensions of the substance of his original formulations. Some have focused on the distinction between the transference neuroses and the narcissistic neuroses or other clinical entities in which the classical transference neurosis is not clearly encountered; and Glover (1955), in particular, has carefully paid attention to those clinical situations wherein transference neurosis did not occur. He pointed out that transference neurosis may fail to develop, not only in the classical narcissistic neurotic conditions (what we would now more likely designate as the psychotic, the psychotic character, or the borderline), but also in many character disorders, perversions, certain psychosomatic conditions, the psychopathies, cases of marital difficulties, and what he labeled as the "almost normal character." He stressed the fact that it is both a theoretical and a technical error to assume that a transference neurosis must inevitably develop in every case; but he also cautioned against the possibility of overlooking its presence and manifestations. Glover thought that the latter was particularly liable to occur in certain cases where the analysand was able to hide his ambivalent attitudes toward the analyst via an identification with him and also in certain cases where an apparent stalemate in the analytic work was in itself the crucial but unrecognized indication of the transference neurosis. When a transference neurosis develops, Glover pointed out, then the patient is involved with the analyst "as a person" (pp. 135–136). Greenson (1965) emphasized that "the transference neurosis is in effect when the analyst and the analysis become the central concern in the patient's life" (p. 157); and Loewald (1960) dealt in some detail on how "The transference neuroses are characterized by the transfer of libido to external object as against the attachment of the libido to the 'ego' in the narcissistic affections"; as well as by "the transfer of libidinal cathexes (and defenses against them), originally related to infantile objects, on to contemporary objects" (pp. 27–28).

Anna Freud (1954) described an interesting situation where a patient developed a transference to the analysis rather than the analyst, and distinguished such a process from a true transference neurosis (p. 616). Fleming (Panel, 1958) suggested the term "negative transference neurosis" to designate certain cases which failed to develop a transference neurosis and where the failure could be attributed to the fear of re-experiencing early oedipal rage reactions in the analytic situation (p. 564).

The bulk of analytic attention has been directed toward the fate of instinctual impulses in the transference neurosis and the defenses against these impulses; but it is also recognized that the transference neurosis reveals a great deal about vicissitudes of the patient's ego and superego. Strachey (1934, 1937) in particular has emphasized the latter, whereas Glover (1937, 1955) has stressed the complexity of the transference neurosis situation and warned about a simplistic concept of the phenomenon.

Loewald's (1960) careful study demonstrates some interesting and important parallels between the process of ego development and the transference neurosis. In both situations, he postulates the presence of a "differential" between psychic systems of lower and higher levels of organizations. "The analytic process," says Loewald, "in the development and resolution of the transference neurosis is a repetition . . . of such a libidinal tension-system between a more primitively and a more maturely organized psychic apparatus" (p. 30). The interaction which occurs when such a differential exists is responsible for some of the "integrative experience" which may result. Loewald also demonstrates how this differential in the transference neurosis can be compared to the interaction which can be said to occur between primary and secondary processes or between the unconscious and the preconscious.

Zetzel (1956) has suggested that the transference neurosis be conceptualized as a compromise formation, structurally not unlike that of a symptom or a dream (p. 369). Greenacre (1959) has reminded us that the transference neurosis is not a static and homogeneous structure but is, rather, fluid and fluctuant and "varies markedly in texture." Since they are in part historically and dynamically determined, there is a constant panoramic procession of transference pictures merging into each other or momentarily separating out with special clarity, in a way which is frequently less constant than the symptoms and other manifestations of the neurosis itself. She considered, therefore, that the "blanket term" transference neurosis may be a bit misleading; and she preferred, instead, to speak of the "active transference-neurotic manifestations." One might question the necessity of introducing the new nosological category, but it seems that Greenacre's observation is a valuable one and bears on another misconception of the transference neurosis. Not infrequently one hears or reads about the transference neurosis—either explicitly or more often by implication—as if it were a discrete, stable entity, which, after proper and sufficient dissection by the analyst, emerges full-grown and constant from the analytic situation—like Athena from the head of Zeus. Greenacre's emphasis on the "constant panoramic procession of transference pictures" (p. 485) helps dispel such a misconception.

HOW DOES IT DEVELOP?

Again let me begin with a statement from Freud (1917). "A capacity for directing libidinal object-cathexes onto people must of course be attributed to every normal person. The tendency to transference of the neurotics I have spoken of is only an extraordinary increase of this universal characteristic" (p. 446). Freud (1917) repeatedly emphasized that the intense feelings transferred onto the doctor are justified neither by the latter's behavior nor by the actual situation that has developed during the treatment (p. 441). At the same time, Freud insisted that the development of these feelings could not be viewed only as a "chance disturbance," but was a phenomenon "intimately bound up with the nature of the illness itself" (p. 442). Essentially, Freud saw the development of transference as the consequence, in neurotic individuals, of the frustrated demand for love. ". . . if someone's need for love is not entirely satisfied by reality, he is bound to approach every new person whom he meets with libidinal anticipatory ideas . . ." (1912, p. 100). Therefore, it is to be expected, reasoned Freud, that some portion of this libido be directed at the analyst.

But whereas Freud insisted that transference was a universal phenomenon, he also held that what was observed in analysis—and particularly in the transference neurosis—was, indeed, an "extraordinary increase" of the kind of feelings that could be ordinarily observed. And whereas he held that the ultimate explanation for these feelings lay in the "nature of the illness itself," he also recognized that the "extraordinary increase" was made possible by the "especially favorable conditions" (1914, p. 154) of the analytic situation, by the "opportunity offered by the analytic treatment" (1917, p. 442).

I would understand "especially favorable conditions" to refer to those conditions which exist when the analysis is conducted in a reasonably correct and appropriate manner. Obviously this is not the appropriate place to discuss the details of the theory of psychoanalytic technique; but, in a highly condensed way, this is what I think Freud had in mind: Characteristically, the patient begins his analysis with positive feelings for the analysis and for the analyst, which, Freud states, provide "the most powerful motive" for the advance of analytic work. Gradually, the feelings for the analyst intensify; more and more libidinal demands are directed toward him. These demands are, essentially, frustrated by the analyst—but in a specific way. The analyst does not "yield to the patient's demands deriving from the transference; it would be absurd for us to reject them in an unfriendly, still more in an indignant, manner." Rather the analyst persistently attempts to demonstrate to the patient that his feelings and wishes derive not primarily from the current situation, but from the past—he is "repeating something that happened to him earlier" (1917, pp. 443–444). This leads to a more acute revival of the pathogenic conflict.

> The longer an analytic treatment lasts and the more clearly the patient realizes that distortions of the pathogenic material cannot by themselves offer any protection against its being uncovered, the more consistently does he make use of the one sort of distortion which obviously affords him the greatest advantages—distortion through the transference. These circumstances tend towards a situation in which finally every conflict has to be fought out in the sphere of transference [1912, p. 104].

As this struggle is taking place within the analysis, there is the tendency for some of the repressed, pathological material to approach consciousness, and "the portions of that complex which is capable of transference is first pushed forward into consciousness and defended with the greatest obstinancy" (1912, p. 104). Essentially, the patient attempts to "put his passions into action without taking any account of the real situation" (1912, p. 108). The patient, in brief, wants to stop working on his problems, wants to stop remembering, and he tries to act them out in his relationship with the analyst by, in effect, repeating in the transference some aspect of the forgotten past. "He [the analyst] is prepared for a perpetual struggle with his patient to keep in the psychical sphere all the impulses which the patient would like to direct into the motor sphere; and he celebrates it as a triumph for the treatment if he can bring it about that something the patient wishes to discharge in action is disposed of through the work of remembering" (1914, p. 153). The transference neurosis, therefore, is a resistance; and its particular manifestations represent obstacles to the analysis, and to its principal task—as Freud clearly delineated it—namely, that of remembering, of making that which is unconscious conscious. As a vehicle for the re-enactment of old conflicts with old objects, it becomes, as Freud stated, "*the most powerful resistance* to the treatment" (1912, p. 101); but at the same time Freud, of course, realized that it was also the most powerful tool available to the analytic work. We shall deal with this other side of the coin in the last section of the paper; but it is paramount to keep in mind Freud's statement that "the part transference plays in the treatment can only be explained if we enter into its relations with resistance" (1912, p. 104).

Two other facets of Freud's explanation of "How does it develop?" warrant further mention, although, in a sense, they are implicitly contained in what has already been described. I am referring first to the role which Freud ascribed to the repetition compulsion in the evolution of the transference neurosis. As you recall, he elaborated on this in considerable detail in *Beyond the Pleasure Principle* (1920), but he had already stressed the point in the earlier papers on technique (1912, 1913, 1914). Related to the role of the repetition compulsion is the part played by regression in the formation of the transference neurosis, a part whose significance may not infrequently be glossed over by many analysts.

In his paper on "Further Recommendations on the Technique of Psychoanalysis," Freud (1913) makes a brief allusion to the handling of strong transference resistances in the very early stages of the analysis. I am not completely certain whether or not Freud specifically had in mind the transference neurosis, per se, but his comment does bear on a question which Hoffer did not include on his list, namely "When does the transference neurosis occur?" One of the many misconceptions about the transference neurosis is that it occurs only at a specific phase in the analysis usually relatively late in the analytic work, and it arises only in conjunction with the emergence of the nuclear oedipal conflict. I would submit that such a "timetable" concept is misleading, that the transference neurosis and its manifestations can be observed at virtually any stage of the analytic work, and that its presence is dictated by a complex of dynamic-economic considerations rather than temporal ones.

By and large there is little in the literature which takes serious issue with Freud's formulation that the transference neurosis develops from the interaction of "the nature of the illness itself" and "the especially favorable conditions" of the analytic situation. Nevertheless, there have been some interesting elaborations and extensions of this explanation. Virtually all psychoanalysts would agree that the transference-neurosis phenomena have their basic source in the ungratified instinctual demands of the analytic situation. This has been discussed by, among others, Glover (1955), Hoffer (1956), Strachey (1934, 1937), and Zetzel (1956). The latter further specifies that "the transference neurosis develops, as a rule, after ego defenses have been sufficiently undermined to mobilize previously hidden instinctual conflict" (p. 371).

Somewhat more attention has been directed to the "especially favorable conditions," particularly the ways in which the formal aspects of the classical psychoanalytic milieu (the couch, free association, the analyst's not being visible to the patient, etc.) facilitates the evolution of the transference neurosis and especially its regressive aspects. Glover (1955), Greenacre (1954), Lagache (1953), Spitz (1956), Stone (1961), and Strachey (1937) are among those who have contributed to this aspect of the subject. Macalpine (1950) takes a somewhat different stance, holding that the transference neurosis does not arise so much in a spontaneous fashion in the analytic milieu, but rather that it is actively induced by the analyst. She states, ". . . that analytic transference is induced in a 'transference-ready' analysand *actively,* and from the analytic environment. The analysand is exposed to a rigid infantile setting to which he has gradually to adapt by regression . . ." (p. 537; italics added).

I have already alluded to some of the ideas from Loewald's 1960 paper "On the Therapeutic Action of Psychoanalysis," and his carefully worked out formulations deserve something better than the short shrift they must inevitably receive in such a review as this. As mentioned in the previous section, Loewald conceptualized the transference relationship as a dynamic interaction between psychic systems of higher and of lower levels of psychic organization. In this connection, the analyst "offers himself as a contemporary object"; and, in doing so, plays a crucial role in mobilizing "ghosts" from the patient's unconscious. When the analyst promotes the transference neurosis, he is

> promoting a regressive movement on the part of the preconscious (ego regression) which is designed to bring the preconscious out of its defensive isolation from the unconscious and to allow the unconscious to re-cathect, in interaction with the analyst, preconscious ideas and experiences in such a way that higher organization of mental life can come about. The mediator of this interplay of transference is the analyst who, as a contemporary object, offers himself to the patient's unconscious as a necessary point of attachment as a transference. As a contemporary object, the analyst represents a psychic apparatus whose secondary process organization is stable and capable of controlled regression so that he is optimally in communication with his own and the patient's unconscious, so as to serve as a reliable mediator and partner of communication, of transference between unconscious and preconscious, and thus of higher interpenetrating organization of both [p. 31].

In these painfully truncated excerpts from Loewald's stimulating essay, there is not only a useful addendum to the earlier concepts of the role of the "especially favorable environment" of the psychoanalytic treatment situation but also some cogent hypotheses regarding the role of the transference neurosis in the therapeutic process.

While it is generally recognized that the transference neurosis presents the analyst with his most potent therapeutic weapon, there is also a comparable unanimity about its role as a resistance to the analytic process. Ferenczi in 1909 noted this resistance significance prior to Freud's somewhat later technical papers. It is a point that has been described by Glover (1955), who attributed these resistance manifestations to the operations of the infantile ego: by Hoffer (1956), Nacht (1957), Stone (1954), Waelder (1956), and Zetzel (1956), as well as by many others; while Lagache (1953), and Nunberg (1937) have underscored the workings of the repetition compulsion (the resistance of the id) in the manifestations of the transference neurosis.

WHAT ROLE DOES IT PLAY IN THE THERAPEUTIC PROCESS?

We now come to the final section of this review and to the third of Hoffer's questions. As before, I open with Freud's contributions. His (Freud, 1917) formulations on this topic cannot be separated from what he consistently saw as the fundamental task of the analytic process.

> What we make use of must no doubt be the replacing of what is unconscious by what is conscious . . . we lift the repressions, we remove the preconditions for the formation of symptoms, we transform the pathogenic conflict into a normal one for which it must be possible somehow to find a solution. All that we bring about in a patient is this single psychical change; the length to which it is carried is the measure of help we provide. Where no repressions (or analogous psychical processes) can be undone, our therapy has nothing to expect [p. 435].

The part, then, that the transference neurosis must play in the therapeutic process is clearly and simply that of facilitating the undoing of repression. Actually Freud went a step further. He suggested that the fundamental distinction between psychoanalysis and other psychotherapies should be made on the basis of the management and resolution of the transference neurosis. It is, then, the undoing of the internal resistances—the repressions and the "analogous psychical processes"—that constitutes the hallmark of psychoanalytic therapy.

However, the transference neurosis itself becomes the major vehicle of these resistances. As the patient becomes more involved with the analyst, there is a mobilization of old conflicts and their recasting into the symptoms, attitudes, and behavior which characterize the transference neurosis. The patient does not want to remember the old conflicts and their painful affects; instead, as Freud (1914) stated, "the compulsion to repeat . . . replaces the impulsion to remember" (p. 151). The task of the analyst, Freud (1917) insisted, is to "oblige the patient to transform his repetition into a memory" (p. 444). This transformation is carried out in the arena of the transference neurosis; and then what could constitute the greatest threat to the analysis "becomes its best tool, by whose help the most secret compartments of mental life can be opened." If the transference neurosis is properly handled, the analyst, and the patient, have a unique opportunity to observe the working of the neurotic process at first hand. "We have followed this new edition of the old disorder from its start, we have observed its origin and growth, and we are especially well able to find our way about in it since, as its object, we are situated at its very center . . ." (1917, p. 444).

Freud was always quite cognizant of the powerful tendency toward repetition in action. Nor was there ever any ambiguity in Freud's (1914) conceptual principle regarding the handling of this thorny problem.

> The main instrument, however, for curbing the patient's compulsion to repeat and for turning it into a motive for remembering lies in the handling of the transference. We render the compulsion harmless, and indeed useful, by giving it the right to assert itself in a definite field. We admit it into the transference as a playground in which it is allowed to expand in almost complete freedom and in which it is expected to display to us everything in the way of pathogenic instincts that is hidden in the patient's mind. . . . From the repetitive reactions which are exhibited in the transference we are led along the familiar paths to the awakening of memories, which appear without difficulty, as it were, after the resistance has been overcome [p. 154].

The therapeutic task, Freud (1917) pointed out

> consists, therefore, in freeing the libido from its present attachments, which are withdrawn from the ego, and in making it once

> more serviceable to the ego. . . . In order to resolve the symptoms, we must go back as far as their origins, we must renew the conflict from which they arose, and, with the help of motive forces which were not at the patient's disposal in the past, we must guide it to a different outcome. This revision of the process of repression can be accomplished only in part in connection with the memory traces of the processes which led to repression. The decisive part of the work is achieved by creating the patient's relation to the doctor—in the 'transference'—new editions of the old conflicts; in these the patient would like to behave in the same way as he did in the past, while we, by summoning up every available mental force [in the patient] compel him to come to a fresh decision. Thus the transference becomes the battlefield on which all the mutually struggling forces should meet one another. . . . In place of the patient's true illness there appears the artificially constructed transference illness . . . the new struggle around this object is lifted to the highest psychical level; it takes place as a normal mental conflict. Since a fresh repression is avoided, the alienation between ego and libido is brought to an end and the subject's mental unity is restored. When the libido is released once more from its temporary object in the person of the doctor, it cannot return to its earlier objects, but is at the disposal of the ego [pp. 454–455].
>
> It cannot be disputed that controlling the phenomena of transference presents the psycho-analyst with the greatest difficulties. But it should not be forgotten that it is precisely they that do us the inestimable service of making the patient's hidden and forgotten erotic impulses immediate and manifest. For when all is said and done, it is impossible to destroy anyone *in absentia* or *in effigie* [Freud, 1912, p. 108].

In subsequent writings on the role of the transference neurosis in the therapeutic process, most of the contributors have focused on this problem of "making the patient's hidden and forgotten erotic impulses immediate and manifest," of converting that which is "in absentia or in effigie" into a process which is vivid and viable. If the psychoanalytic experience is to constitute anything more than a detached intellectual exercise, it is recognized that the infantile conflicts together with their accompanying memories and appropriate affects must be re-experienced *in viva;* only then will this experience and the analytic interpretations provide sufficient impact and conviction to serve as a lever for effective intrapsychic changes.

> Strachey (1934) points out that the transference neurosis gives us our great opportunity. Instead of having to deal as best we may with conflicts of the remote past, which are concerned with dead circumstances and mummified personalities, and whose outcome is already determined, we find ourselves involved in an actual and immediate situation, in which we and the patient are the principal characters and the development of which is to some extent at least under our control. But if we bring it about that in this revivified transference conflict the patient chooses a new solution instead of the old one, a solution in which the primitive and unadaptable methods of repression is replaced by behaviour more in contact with reality, then, even after his detachment from the analysis, he will never be able to fall back into his former neurosis. The solution of the transference conflict implies the simultaneous solution of the infantile conflict of which it is a new edition [p. 132].

In another paper, Strachey (1937) pursued the same theme.

> For the prime essential of a transference interpretation in my view is that the feeling or impulse interpreted should not merely be concerned with the analyst but that it should be in *activity* at the *moment* at which it is interpreted. Thus an interpretation of an impulse felt towards the analyst last week or even a quarter of an hour ago will not be a transference interpretation in my sense unless it is still active in the patient at the moment when the interpretation is given. The situation will be, so to speak, a dead one and will be entirely without the dynamic significance which is inherent in giving a true transference interpretation [p. 141].

True transference interpretations under controlled conditions and in limited doses permit a patient to employ his sense of reality for the purpose of making a comparison "between archaic and imaginary objects and his actual and real ones; and I have argued," continues Strachey, "that the small scale correction which he can thus make in his attitude towards the external world is the first step towards the internal re-adjustment which is our ultimate aim" (p. 141).

Like Strachey, Nunberg (1937) also underlines the particular opportunity for the enhancement of pieces of reality testing in the transference neurosis work. This experience, declares Nunberg,

> . . . allows the ego to obtain direct access to the past, to earliest childhood. That part of the patient's ego which has remained intact now has an opportunity of confronting the infantile reality with the actual one and of comparing them so to speak, on a single plane, namely, in the present; it can assess its infantile wishes and anxieties in terms of its mature strivings, thereby devaluating the dangers threatened from their realizations. This, of course, leads to a more precise discrimination between within and without, to better reality testing [p. 107].

Greenacre (1954) characterizes the transference neurosis experience as "the most convincing medium of demonstration and interpretation to the patient," which she feels, "permits a greater degree of relief, probably because the memories are thus being actually experienced with their *full* emotional resonance and not being merely reported and talked about with a *partial* reliving" (p. 674). Gill's (1954) emphasis on the need for the development of a regressive transference neurosis is related to his conviction that only such a situation provides the opportunity for the patient to "feel his most deeply irrational and infantile transferences (p. 782). Stone (1954) also pointed to the importance of the transference neurosis in helping to effectively demonstrate the "inappropriateness to current reality" of disturbances from the past. Furthermore, the sense of reality or of vividness of the past is largely dependent, he added, "on the therapeutic transference experience; and there are many instances where the dissolution of amnesias or of the emotional isolation of memories only follows adequate emotional experience in the transference" (p. 572).

Particular emphasis was given to the recapitulation and analysis of the oedipal situation in the course of the transference neurosis by Ferenczi and Rank (1925), by Zetzel (1956), and by Glover (1955). The latter has also described the significance of the transference neurosis phenomena in observing and studying those events which had, in the past, a specific connection with the process of symptom formation. Zetzel (1956), among others, pointed to the changes which could be observed in various ego functions; these alterations, in turn, result she feels "from a change in object relations through interpretation of the transference situation" (p. 370).

My final remarks have to do with material which perhaps more appropriately belongs to the province of the theory of psychoanalytic technique, per se. I am referring to the question of the resolution of the transference neurosis and the implications this issue has for the whole question of psychoanalytic therapy. If the essence of psychoanalysis as a therapy is the development, analysis, and resolution of the transference neurosis, then, in the same vein, it would also hold that the essence of the resolution of the transference neurosis is that it be effected solely by means of interpretation. Actually, as Gill (1954) wryly noted, such a statement is redundant, inasmuch as any other vehicle of resolution constitutes a manipulation which would, in effect, only perpetuate and complicate the transference neurosis and the relationship to the analyst. The maintenance of this technical principle has been one of the cardinal tenets of psychoanalysis as a therapy, was first promulgated by Freud (1917), and has been elaborated on by a host of analysts among whom I would just mention Greenacre (1954, 1959), Hoffer (1956), Rangell (1954), Ferenczi and Rank (1925), and Stone (1954).

It would be erroneous and short-sighted, however, to ignore the fact that a significant number of analysts do not accept this fundamental principle. In his definitive paper on "Transference and Countertransference," Orr (1954) offered some remarks which I feel are as pertinent now as they were a decade and a half ago. "The development, interpretation, and resolution of the transference neurosis in the transference relationship is still the hallmark of psychoanalysis for perhaps a majority of analysts today; but for a considerable minority this is by no means the case, or at least not without considerable attenuation and modification" (p. 646).

It is true that Orr's statement came at a time when a powerful effort was being made by a sizable group of relatively influential psychoanalysts to attenuate and modify this concept of resolving the transference neurosis. I am, of course, referring to the work of Alexander and his associates (1925, 1950, 1954; Alexander and French, 1946; Silverberg, 1948; Weiss, 1946; and Nacht, 1957) who argued, essentially, that a full-blown transference neurosis was often unnecessary and frequently undesirable and detrimental. They were particularly concerned with the development of the regressive, dependent relationship to the analyst and the complications which would inevitably follow such a development. They suggested—at least in selected cases—that this regressive transference neurosis be controlled and limited by means of specific interpretations, interventions, and manipulations. It was further advocated that not all of the transference manifestations need be analyzed and resolved; but that—again in selected cases—certain aspects of the transference be utilized for the "corrective emotional experience" without necessarily attempting to free the patient from his ties to the analyst. It is also true, at least in a certain sense, that much of the furor over these conceptualizations and innovations has by now subsided, and the issue is no longer the burning one it was in the early fifties. It is not, however, entirely a dead issue, and today one hears a good deal about the crucial importance of the patient's identifications with the analyst which at least in some instances must raise both theoretical and technical questions which are not entirely distinct from those raised by the work of Alexander, et al. Obviously, the present summary is hardly the proper place to dissect out and evaluate all the nuances of these various, complicated issues; but if it is indeed true that the transference neurosis is the "central conceptual and technical vehicle of psychoanalysis as a therapy," then it is also true that whatever alters our concepts of the development, handling, and resolution of that transference neurosis must simultaneously alter our very concept of what psychoanalysis is. It is in this connection, therefore, that I found Hoffer's (1956) statement particularly impressive. He says:

> I know of course that the transference neurosis and its analysis may have limitations to be looked for in the structure of the case as well as in the comprehension of the analyst. Many patients today are satisfied with achieving less than the analysis of their transference neurosis, which is a painful process and which they manage to cut short. And still 'nothing has a greater force of conviction' for the patient than what he acquires in this way. . . . What could prevent us from not letting him invest his image of us with any quality of his past object relationship? I cannot see how not to permit the transference neurosis to take its course except by disengaging myself from the analytic task [p. 379].

Hoffer goes on to say that the analyst could, in fact, make life a lot easier for himself by carefully selecting as patients only those who do not have the tendency to act out too much,

> but once he has made his choice, he can only adhere to his conviction regarding the method of dealing with urges coming from within the patient . . . or renounce the relationship. . . . The analyst will then have to seek a compromise between these social motifs

> and the analytic goal, which is to knit together the lost connections between the past and the present. In such a case he will not find it too difficult to change over to one of those psychoanalytic techniques which foster 'transference relationships' that do not lead to the *transference neurotic* episodes but deprive the patient in his analysis of the spontaneous, transference neurotic experiences and effects [p. 379].

If one follows the history of the psychoanalytic movement, one certainly is impressed by the not infrequent—and also not very effective—pressures to bring about significant modifications in psychoanalytic technique. It may well be that the majority of such efforts have involved technical methods which have impinged on the development, analysis, and resolution of the transference neurosis; and such an impingement threatens to distort the fundamental therapeutic model on which our science rests. I would suggest that the failure of most analysts to adopt these new techniques represents neither a captious insistence on or an adherence to psychoanalytic orthodoxy nor a stubborn refusal to change with the times; it represents, rather, a response to a realistic appraisal of psychoanalysis and what it can offer. Psychoanalysis as a treatment it would seem, must best be viewed as a specific technical procedure which has therapeutic potential for a limited array of psychological disorders; as a part of that procedure the transference neurosis still occupies the crucial, central position. I trust that this review may help us to clarify and to focus on that crucial and central position.

REFERENCES

Alexander, F. (1925), A metapsychological description of the process of cure. *Internat. J. Psycho-Anal.*, 6:13–34.

_______ (1950), Analysis of the therapeutic factors in psychoanalytic treatment. *Psychoanal. Quart.*, 19:482–500.

_______ (1954), Psychoanalysis and psychotherapy. *J. Amer. Psychoanal. Assn.*, 2:722–733.

_______ & French, T. (1946), *Psychoanalytic Therapy*. New York: Ronald Press.

Ferenczi, S. (1909), Introjection and transference. In: *Sex and Psychoanalysis*. New York: Basic Books, 1950, pp. 35–93.

_______ & Rank. O. (1925), *The Development of Psychoanalysis*. Washington: Nervous and Mental Disease Publishing Co.

Freud, A. (1954), The widening scope of indications for psychoanalysis: Discussion. *J. Amer. Psychoanal. Assn.*, 2:607–620.

Freud, S. (1912), The dynamics of transference. *Standard Edition*, 12:99–108. London: Hogarth Press, 1958.

_______ (1913), Further recommendations on the technique of psychoanalysis. *Standard Edition*, 12:122–144. London: Hogarth Press, 1958.

_______ (1914), Remembering, repeating, and working through. *Standard Edition*, 12:146–156. London: Hogarth Press, 1958.

_______ (1917), Introductory lectures on psychoanalysis. *Standard Edition*, 16:431–463. London: Hogarth Press, 1963.

_______ (1920), Beyond the pleasure principle. *Standard Edition*, 18:7–64. London: Hogarth Press, 1955.

_______ (1925), An autobiographical study. *Standard Edition*, 20:7–70. London: Hogarth Press, 1959.

_______ (1938), An outline of psychoanalysis. *Standard Edition*, 23:141–207. London: Hogarth Press, 1964.

Gill, M. (1954), Psychoanalysis and exploratory psychotherapy. *J. Amer. Psychoanal. Assn.*, 2:771– 797.

Glover, E. (1937), Symposium on the theory of the therapeutic results of psychoanalysis. *Internat. J. Psycho-Anal.*, 17:125–132.

_______ (1955), *The Technique of Psychoanalysis.* New York: International Universities Press.

Greenacre, P. (1954), The role of transference: Practical considerations in relation to psychoanalytic therapy. *J. Amer. Psychoanal. Assn.*, 2:671–684.

_______ (1959), Certain technical problems in the transference relationship. *J. Amer. Psychoanal. Assn.*, 7:484–502.

Greenson, R. (1965), The working alliance and the transference neurosis. *Psychoanal. Quart.*, 34:155–181.

Hoffer, W. (1956), Transference and transference neurosis. *Internat. J. Psycho-Anal.*, 37:377–379.

Kepecs, J. (1966), Theories of transference neurosis. *Psychoanal. Quart.*, 35: 497–521.

Lagache, D. (1953), Some aspects of transference. *Internat. J. Psycho-Anal.*, 34:1–10.

Loewald, H. (1960), On the therapeutic action of psychoanalysis. *Internat. J. Psycho-Anal.*, 41:16–33.

Macalpine, I. (1950), The development of the transference. *Psychoanal. Quart.*, 19:501–539.

Nacht, S. (1957), Technical remarks on the handling of the transference neurosis. *Internat. J. Psycho-Anal.*, 38:196–203.

Nagera, H. (1966), *Early Childhood Disturbances, the Infantile Neurosis, and the Adult Disturbances.* New York: International Universities Press.

Nunberg, H. (1937), Symposium on the theory of the therapeutic results of psychoanalysis. *Internat. J. Psycho-Anal.*, 17:161–169.

Orr, D. (1954), Transference and countertransference: A historical survey. *J. Amer. Psychoanal. Assn.*, 2:631–670.

Panel (1954), Psychoanalysis and dynamic psychotherapy—Similarities and differences. *J. Amer. Psychoanal. Assn.*, 2:153–166.

Panel (1958), Technical problems of transference. D. Leach, reporter. *J. Amer. Psychoanal. Assn.*, 6:560–566.

Rangell, L. (1954), Similarities and differences between psychoanalysis and dynamic psychotherapy. *J. Amer. Psychoanal. Assn.*, 2:734–744.

Silverberg, W. W. (1948), The concept of transference. *Psychoanal. Quart.*, 17:309–321.

Spitz, R. (1956), Transference: The analytic setting and its prototype. *Internat. J. Psycho-Anal.*, 37:380–385.

Stone, L. (1954), The widening scope of indications for psychoanalysis. *J. Amer. Psychoanal. Assn.*, 2:567–594.

_______ (1961), *The Psychoanalytic Situation.* New York: International Universities Press.

_______ (1967), The psychoanalytic situation and transference: Postscript to an earlier communication. *J. Amer. Psychoanal. Assn.*, 15:3–58.

Strachey, J. (1934), The nature of the therapeutic action of psychoanalysis. *Internat. J. Psycho-Anal.*, 15:127–159.

_______ (1937), Symposium on the theory of the therapeutic results of psychoanalysis. *Internat. J. Psycho-Anal.*, 17:139–145.

Waelder, R. (1956), Introduction to the discussion on problems of transference. *Internat. J. Psycho-Anal.*, 37:367–368.

Wallerstein, R. (1967), Reconstruction and mastery in the transference psychosis. *J. Amer. Psychoanal. Assn.*, 15:551–583.

Weiss, E. (1946), Manipulation of the transference relationship. In: *Psychoanalytic Therapy*, ed. F. Alexander & T. French. New York: Ronald Press, pp. 41–54.

Zetzel, E. (1956), Current concepts of transference. *Internat. J. Psycho-Anal.*, 37:869–375.

Chapter 9

1973

Reporting, Nonreporting, and Assessment in the Training Analysis

Victor Calef and Edward M. Weinshel

> There are currents of moral ideas which are partly philosophical and partly something less precise, changes in public consciousness. . . .
>
> It is certainly not easy, and perhaps it is not possible, to calculate the real effect upon men's lives of any new system of moral ideas and of any new philosophy. . . .
>
> The more fundamental and overriding *assessments,* in relation to which all other assessments of persons are *subsidiary and conditional,* we call moral assessments, just because we count them as *unconditional* and *overriding.* . . . When we assess ourselves or others in some limited role or capacity, as performing well or ill in that role or capacity, the assessment *is not fundamental and unconditional;* the assessment gives guidance only to someone who wants to have that role or to act in that capacity or who wants to make use of someone who does. —Stuart Hampshire (1973; italics added)

Just as we were sending our manuscript to the *Journal,* we read Eli Marcovitz's paper, "On Confidentiality in Psychoanalysis," in the *Bulletin of the Philadelphia Association for Psychoanalysis,* 23:1–7, 1973. In that paper, Dr. Marcovitz expresses many views with which we are in agreement.

The authors are indebted to the members of the Subcommittees on Training Analysis of COPE and of Commission I of COPER. We have received many stimulating ideas from both groups, but the responsibility for the paper and its contents rests with the authors.

Apparently it has become more frequent in recent years for a candidate to openly object to the fact that his analyst sends reports about his analysis to the education committee. It is not difficult for the analyst to understand the candidate's fear of exposure, censure, and disaccreditation or to discern the narcissistic resistances and the inhibited exhibitionism that play significant roles in the determination of such objections. If the analyst has not, in fact, abused his reportorial function, analytic work with such complaints and the demand that the analyst should not so report can be exceedingly fruitful.

Perhaps most training analysts are somewhat more familiar with another version of those same resistances; namely, an unquestioning overidealization of the analyst and the analysis. In these instances, there is a persistent tendency to conformity, an overweening urgency to "succeed" in one's own analysis or in the supervised analyses, and the desire to protect the narcissistic needs of candidate and analyst alike. We think such tendencies demonstrate the attempts to hide the negative aspects of the transference and that, as a rule, such resistances are deeply buried in the unconscious and difficult to expose.

There is no question but that the issue of the analyst's reporting or not reporting to the education committee is a most important one, and we think it imperative that these issues be aired and examined. Certainly, the conflicts and resistances mobilized by either position and the ways one deals with such manifestations must play a significant part in the analytic work and its outcome. It would be specious to deny that some abuses of reporting—inadvertent or otherwise—must occur in every institute; and, similarly, it must be acknowledged that the training analyst does have "real" power and an important influence in the progression of his candidate through the latter's educational sequence. What is less clear is whether or not the exercise of such power and such influence is, indeed, in the best interest of the candidate's analysis and his over-all analytic training, or whether they should (and can) be done away with as unwelcome "real" contaminants which are antithetical to analysis and those best interests of the candidate.

More and more, the role of the training analysis and the training analyst in the education of the candidate has become a core and controversial issue. Much has been said and written that is critical—and, in some respects, condemnatory—of that role and of the atmosphere in which the training analysis has been conducted. A great deal of dissatisfaction and skepticism has been expressed about the therapeutic results of the training analysis; this is certainly reflected in the widely circulated and only half-facetious complaint that "the first analysis is for the institute, the second one for myself." Yet, few objective data have been offered to substantiate these views. Recent investigation by a subcommittee of COPE (Stein, 1972) and by Shapiro (1972a, 1972b) would indicate that the therapeutic results of the training analysis are not anywhere as dismal as many analysts have assumed. Furthermore, these studies also indicate that many of the issues connected with the "realities" of the training analysis are neither so insoluble nor so one-sided as some of the critics of the training analysis would portray. Certainly, more data—especially psychoanalytic data—are needed to supplement the varying impressions that have been reported in regard to the role the personal analysis plays in the candidate's training and (conversely) in the manner in which the over-all training situation affects the candidate's analysis in either a positive or negative way.

Nevertheless, despite the many objections and questions regarding the value and validity of the training analysis (at least as it is currently incorporated in the training system), it would appear that most, if not all, analysts still consider the personal analysis to be an integral part of every future analyst's experience—a view shared by the nonreporting training analysts. We would certainly concede the need for a continuous, persistent (and even "radical") examination of that position, but we do hold that the experience of analysand (patient) is a necessary one for that future analyst. Furthermore, implicit in such a position is the corollary that the analyst must himself be, in some degree at least, analyzable. This is a postulate that calls for careful elaboration; although it is one to which we will return, it cannot be dealt with exhaustively in this essay.

Various suggestions have been advanced for circumventing the ostensible conflict between the therapeutic and the educational needs of the candidate. Some have questioned the traditional inviolability of the tripartite system and would eliminate the personal analysis as a formal requirement of psychoanalytic training, asking only that the future analyst demonstrate his proficiency in the didactic seminars and in his own analysis of supervised cases. Others would require a personal analysis, but completely separate from the institute and from the training situation, thereby simultaneously doing away with the somewhat controversial and too easily glorified title of training analyst. The more frequent and more "conservative" position (in the sense of attempting to maintain the connection of the personal analysis with the institute and the training situation) for resolving the so-called "syncretistic dilemma" is best exemplified by those who call for a policy of nonreporting to the education committee on the part of the training analyst or even a relatively rigorous intra-analytic noninvolvement of the training analyst in the progression of his candidate. Dr. McLaughlin's paper, we believe, is a careful and judicious presentation of the arguments in behalf of nonreporting. He points to the need to guard the confidentiality of the analytic relationship and also the need to protect and to foster that atmosphere of trust which is a *sine qua non* for effective psychoanalytic work. We would not disagree with the goals of Dr. McLaughlin's thesis in this regard, although we do not necessarily agree with his over-all position or the methods by which he would implement such a position.

We would state our conviction that the whole problem of the position of the training analysis and the role of the training analyst have been to some extent skewed—and, perhaps, confused—by what we see as certain preconceptions and misconceptions. One of these is the very term "syncretistic," which as often as not is used as an adjective in the increasingly popular phrase "syncretistic dilemma." This is not the place to review the observations and the thinking that persuaded the authors of the "Rainbow Report" (its less well-known title is "Report of the Survey Steering Committee to the Board on Professional Standards," 1955) or *Psychoanalytic Education in the United States* (Lewin & Ross, 1960) to emphasize what they portrayed as the essentially antithetical roles of the training analysis and the educational development of the candidate; nor do we wish to involve ourselves in the somewhat ambiguous dictionary meanings of the word "syncretistic," but there is, at least in some of those definitions, more than an implication that syncretism involves the "attempt" to reconcile that which is basically irreconcilable. We do feel, however, that this somewhat pejorative label and connotation has been too uncritically accepted as a fact by a not insignificant number of analysts and has, as a result, colored their attitude on the entire subject. We would further submit that the issue is by no means so clear-cut and that it is by no means an irrefutable given that the training analysis and the education of the candidate cannot proceed side by side. It is, of course, idle speculation, but one cannot help wondering how different some of our thinking and our investigations might have been had Lewin and Ross continued to use their more neutral phrase, "trying to find acceptable ways of synthesizing their aims" (1960, p. 45), rather than emphasizing the much more slanted (as well as "catchy") term "syncretistic." Relatively little has been said, at least in print or in public, about the possibilities and the potential usefulness of such a "synthesis,"[1] and certainly a good deal more effort has been devoted to support the idea of a potentially impossible task.

Secondly, we would submit that there has been the tendency, wittingly or unwittingly, to equate too literally and too loosely the process of reporting with the violation of confidentiality. The constant and vigorous need to respect the confidential nature of the patient's personal material and his willingness to share his inner life with the analyst requires neither elaboration nor justification. Although we recognize the various dangers associated with intrusion into the analytic work by the giving and receiving of extra-analytic information, we are nevertheless not able to follow the contention that reporting *must of necessity* violate such confidences. We would propose that it is neither impossible nor even difficult for the training analyst to share material with the education committee concerning the analytic progress of the candidate without revealing specific secrets, conscious or unconscious content, fantasies, behavior, or personal historical data. We are not suggesting that abuses of confidence do not and can not occur; but we would also raise the question of the extent to which the possibility and the fear of such abuse have been utilized (both by analyst and analysand) as a source of displacement and erotization.

Thirdly, we would take issue with the frequently raised objection to the analyst's reporting on the basis that such reporting constitutes a piece of reality and is therefore "not analyzable." We recognize, of course, that as analysts our principal concern and focus are with the internal life of our patients. We would nevertheless contend that at times there may be the tendency to an oversimplified distinction between what is "real" and what is "psychological" (i.e., internal, fantasy, etc.). As analysts we are always dealing with the patient's realities *and* his fantasies and internally determined distortions of that reality. Further, a not insignificant aspect of the actual analytic work centers around and springs from "realities" that are part of the structure of the analytic situation and that, in fact, are determined by the analyst. We refer to such garden-variety items as the use of the couch, the delimited duration of each session, the adherence to a specific schedule, the necessity to pay, and to pay within a reasonable time. Analysts not only work with these realities and the

---

[1]A singular exception to this trend has been Fleming's work. See particularly her recent contribution to the *Second Conference of the Chicago, Pittsburgh, and Topeka Institutes* (1973).

patient's reactions, fantasies, and conflicts to them, but also recognize that such realities become the arena in which significant resistances are mobilized and can be dealt with in the course of the analytic work in order to uncover crucial intrapsychic material. Moreover, as analysts we are also aware that when patients are not able to accept such "realities" and to deal with them analytically, the possibility for successful psychoanalytic work is relatively remote. It is our contention that reporting, or at least the training analyst's prerogative to report, is a reality to be dealt with in the same fashion as those conditions characterizing the "ordinary" analysis.

This brings us to our central point and our central disagreement with the position of the *categorical* nonreporting training analyst. We see the debate over reporting versus nonreporting as masking the more important issue of assessment and the role of assessment in all analyses, training and nontraining alike. Obviously, assessment is an integral part of every analysis; and a significant portion of our analytic intervention deals with our assessment of how a particular function is distorted, our assessment of the meaning of such distortion, and our assessment of the derivation of such distortions. The point, however, is that such assessments—such judgments—are not, and should not be, moral ones. In the analysis of a psychoanalytic candidate, it is both necessary and inevitable that there will be assessments with regard to that candidate's capacity to be analyzed and—directly or indirectly—with regard to his capacity to analyze. It would, indeed, be a rare candidate who is not concerned about these questions and these judgments; and it would be somewhat less than accurate to claim that a candidate's concern has its origins in the knowledge that his analyst is sending reports to the appropriate training committee. We agree with Greenacre's statement that the candidate ". . . insofar as he undertakes it [the analysis] with the intention of becoming a student and in most instances is being analyzed by a training analyst, the shadow of the institute still intrudes itself both on the aspiring student and on his analyst" (1966, p. 722). We think that part of that "shadow" involves the knowledge that he will be assessed, that he will be judged, and that these assessments are crucial to the analysis and his future work; and we also think that the resistances that arise are not determined qualitatively or quantitatively by the facts of the "reality" per se. It seems to us, therefore, that for the candidate-analysand, "reality"—both external and psychic—encompasses the recognition that he will be assessed at all three levels of his training, and that his becoming an analyst is dependent on his being analyzable and being analyzed. For the training analyst to deny this reality by entering into a pact with the candidate not to report can be collusive, is in the direction of an abdication of this reality, and represents a potential undermining of the importance of the role of specific assessment in the analysis of that candidate. We suggest that the future analyst must understand and accept this "reality" in order to participate in the working alliance of the training analysis, just as all patients must accept the "reality" of time, money, vacations, and assessments. At the same time, the training analyst must be willing to accept his responsibility for those assessments which bear on the candidate's capacity to be analyzed and to do analysis.

There is considerable reluctance on the part of most people to be assessed. In the analysis, this reluctance becomes evidenced by various resistances which could be expressed by the focus on the "reality" of reporting (although we are not certain of the precise frequency of such occurrences). It is also evident that making assessments is by no means an easy task for analysts and becomes a particularly distasteful and burdensome one for many. The discussions of the participants at the Fourth Pre-Congress on Training of the International Psycho-Analytical Association (Calef, 1972) indicate some of this reluctance just in terms of spelling out the criteria for progression and the assessments which would have to be made to establish such criteria. The fact that such reluctance is probably relatively universal would seem to make it more imperative for the analyst not to enter into any agreement that could foster collusion or provide the locus for certain enclaves that are—at least silently, implicitly—"out of bounds" for analytic investigation, a *cordon sanitaire,* if you will, which the analyst should not enter because he is impinging on a territory that is not really his province.

Even if the promise not to report can be adhered to with the most admirable scrupulousness (and there is much to indicate that this is by no means a readily achieved goal) and even if the promise not to make explicit reports does not at times lead to the much less desirable reporting by implication and indirection (which, there is much to indicate, occurs more than rarely) it remains a potentially complicating intervention. Such a promise is at least or at best an inadvertent encouragement to the candidate-analysand to enter into other collusions and to facilitate resistances for which every training analysis already offers considerable potential. It is a rare training analysis in which the student's involvement in seminars and in supervision does not lead to splits in the transference that are often extremely subtle and disguise important areas of conflict. These problems in the course of training may pre-empt the analytic work for long periods of time and not necessarily because, as far as the analyst is concerned, they represent the important conflictual areas. They usually function as resistances, prolonging and obstructing the analysis, rather than facilitating it. It is also possible that progression to seminar attendance and to supervision supplies narcissistic satisfactions of the professional goals sufficiently to dilute and disguise the underlying conflicts and render them unavailable to analysis during a major portion of the training. In the preceding circumstances (of which there seem to be many variations), the very facts of training collude with the forces of resistance, whether or not the analyst reports. The analyst cannot hope to escape the implication of being the witness, if not the perpetrator, of such collusion; and we cannot avoid the conclusion that such events are abetted by an initial promise not to report and to permit the student to determine his own progression. (For a more detailed discussion of the latter point, see Fleming, 1973, especially pp. 30–31.) We are further concerned that such "promises" may promote a relatively transitory pseudo trust and pseudo confidence in the training analyst if they are experienced as an assurance of the fulfillment of the candidate's unconscious strivings and a reassurance that certain narcissistic needs are valid and realistic and, therefore, outside the purview of analytic work. Such assurance and reassurance (however sincerely and honestly rendered by the analyst) must inevitably prove hollow and lead both to resistances during the analysis and significant disappointments after it.

It is by no means infrequent (if it is not altogether universal) that candidates come to analysis with the history of certain delinquencies committed early in life or with certain latent perversions that are covered by reaction formations or other quasi-sublimations. These defensive formations may seem to be relatively effective forms of "mastery" or "cure," but these patients are nevertheless plagued with the feelings of being imposters, dishonest, or perverts. We are not referring here to actual perversions, but to neurotic fears and fantasies which negate their pregenital nature and which have to be dealt with in every analysis. Dealing with such psychological structures may become much more difficult and their exposure in the analysis more problematical when the analyst has promised not to report; and even if the patient permits such structures to become part of the analytic work, what will be his reaction to the analyst who has vowed not to report on his progress? Will the promise of the analyst's secrecy truly reassure him of the latter's concern, judgment, and integrity? Or will it again encourage him to seek for a haven in which to store certain secrets? We are concerned that the promise not to report will, in a significant number of instances, strengthen the candidate's illusion that all is well, while he simultaneously harbors unconscious doubts about both himself and his analyst.

The ways in which critical evaluations—assessments—can be utilized as constructive and effective educational tools have not, so far as we can determine, been developed by anyone or by any one field; yet the utilization of such evaluations is a task that no educational group can avoid entirely. Analysts have always struggled with this problem and continue to do so. (One of us has addressed himself to a comparable issue in regard to the question of normality; see Weinshel, 1970, pp. 729–731 [this volume, pp. 205–208].) By and large, analysts have been both cautious and self-critical about their rights and their abilities to assess. They have been aware of the potential impact of such assessments on the lives and careers of their analysands; this has also been true of training analysts vis-à-vis their candidates. The philosopher Stuart Hampshire (1973), whom we quoted at the beginning of this essay, has correctly and succinctly pointed to one of the roots of such a dilemma. In his terms, psychoanalysts want to avoid assessments that may be—or may be construed as—overriding, unconditional, or *moral* judgments. Out of such a legitimate wish, there has been an increasing tendency to nonreporting, to separating the training analysis from the training, and to eliminating assessments with regard to training by the training analyst. Those who hold to these views are convinced that all the necessary assessments can be obtained from the seminar instructors and from the case supervisors. Considerable data and observations can certainly be obtained from these sources to serve as the basis for some of the assessments we feel are crucial in the course of analytic training. But does not the elimination of the training analyst as a source of appropriate information deprive the training group of data and observations that are unique and are also consonant with what we want to know about the candidate as a future analyst? This brings us back to the question of analyzability and the question of what may and should be assessed and reported.

It may well be true that an analyst need not be analyzed to do analytic work with patients, and it may be true that—as some would say—the analyst is the "last to know" whether his candidate is capable of doing analytic work; suffice it that we do not agree with such assertions. We believe that we speak for many analysts when we include among the criteria for analyzability of the candidate the capacity to develop and to utilize certain ego functions that are relatively free of neurotic conflict and of inordinate libidinal investments, and also the capacity to develop a particular kind of professional conscience capable of distinguishing between making (again in Hampshire's terms) moral judgments and assessing specific functions. We cannot here elaborate on the specific details of these criteria, but hope to do so in a future communication.

It may also be true that course instructors and case supervisors can contribute a good deal to understanding and assessing these ego and superego functions in a given candidate; but potentially at least, the analyst has data of particular relevance and usefulness available for these assessments. The understanding of the development and "operation" of those functions, together with their assessment by the analyst with his candidate, must become a core part of the training analysis—a process that should be investigated with the candidate's knowledge and participation, and reported first and foremost to the candidate. The analyst should, however, have the prerogative of reporting on those *professionally relevant functions* if, in his judgment, he thinks it is necessary and useful for the continuation and enhancement of the candidate's over-all training experience. (This would then also include the personal analysis.) To forfeit this prerogative would not be in the best interest of either the analysis or of the educational experience, for the reasons we have outlined above. We reiterate that such reports need not include anything about the details of the candidate's past or present behavior, nothing of his secrets or his personal life. It would be sufficient to report—when and if the analyst feels that such reporting is in order—on whether or not the analytic development is or is not taking place, whether a transference neurosis is emerging, whether the candidate can free associate, tolerate the emergence of unconscious derivatives, or understand the realities of the analytic process.

We do not feel competent to explain with any degree of assurance the evolution of differing attitudes about the so-called training analysis. It would be of interest and of value to be able to trace those changes in philosophy and "public consciousness" which first influenced the establishment of the training analysis as a part of the process of becoming a psychoanalyst and those subsequent changes in "consciousness" which seem to press toward modifications in the philosophy of the over-all training experience and the training analysis so that the latter becomes solely a therapeutic venture similar to any other analytic experience. Finally, there is a more current trend that attempts to reconcile the educational and therapeutic aspects of the training analysis. With the "widening scope of psychoanalysis" and the development of ego psychology and character analysis, it does appear somewhat more feasible to be able to observe simultaneously both the differences and the similarities between the training analysis and the nontraining analysis; but it is only as we have been able to better understand and appreciate some of the special aspects and particular demands of the training analysis that we are better able to treat the training analysis as any other analysis. By that, we mean simply that, as we are able to delineate the special and distinctive resistances that tend to appear in the course of the training analysis, we can deal more and more effectively with the special problems of the candidate in the analysis without separating the analysis from the rest of the educational process.

It is in this vein that we view the whole issue of reporting. All candidates in analysis come into that situation with the fears and fantasies of having certain defects and deficiencies relating to their capacity to be analyzed and to being analysts, and of having these defects and deficiencies exposed. Obviously, these fears have much more complex and archaic roots; but in the immediate analytic situation they foster certain resistances, among which are those which relate to reporting. These resistances and their underlying fantasies and conflicts cannot be resolved merely by promising not to report. On the contrary, such a pact might tend to enhance the resistances and interfere with their ultimate resolution. We would also contend that the confusion between the moral, unconditional judgment and those judgments which would assess certain functions of the ego and superego of the future analyst have made the entire task of reporting murkier and more complicated. The so-called moral judgment has no place in psychoanalytic therapy; the assessment of functions is valid and legitimate and is, we believe, critical in both the analysis and the education of the future analyst. We acknowledge that our position is a personal one; and we do not and cannot wish to insist that this position be followed by every training analyst. We recognize that for many valid reasons a given analyst may not wish to submit reports—especially on a routine basis—on the progress of his candidate in analysis. Certainly, this is and should be his prerogative. The assessment of that candidate in terms of the evaluation of specific functions is and should be a responsibility of the training analyst. The training analysis, when properly applied, provides a particularly valuable and specific instrument for implementing such assessments, and the prerogative to report is an integral part of the training-analysis situation. It is a prerogative that should not be surrendered lightly.

REFERENCES

Calef, V. (1972), A report of the 4th Pre-Congress on Training, Vienna 1971, to the 27th International Psycho-Analytic Congress. *Internat. J. Psycho-Anal.*, 53:37–46.

Fleming, J. (1973), The training analyst as an educator. In: *Second Conference of the Chicago, Pittsburgh, and Topeka Institutes;* I. Ramzy, Coordinator, pp. 11–38.

Greenacre, P. (1966), Problems of training analysis. In: *Emotional Growth.* New York: International Universities Press, 1971, pp. 718–742.

Hampshire, S. (1973), Morality and pessimism. *New York Review of Books,* 19:23–33, January 25, 1973.

Lewin, B. D. & Ross, H. (1960), *Psychoanalytic Education in the United States.* New York: Norton.

Report on the Survey Steering Committee to the Board on Professional Standards (1955).

Shapiro, D. (1972a), The dual role problem and the results of analysis during training. Unpublished manuscript.

_______ (1972b), The silver lining: Facilitation of analysis by the training situation. Unpublished manuscript.

Stein, M. (1972), in Calder, K., Report of the Committee on Psychoanalytic Education to the Board on Professional Standards, November 29, 1972.

Weinshel, E. M. (1970), The ego in health and normality. *J. Amer. Psychoanal. Assn.*, 18:687–735.

Chapter 10

1980

The Analyst as the Conscience of the Analysis

Victor Calef and Edward M. Weinshel

Receipt of the invitation to participate in the Festschrift honouring Dr Paula Heimann's seventy-fifth birthday, was a fortunate coincidence. We were, at that time, involved in the preparation of a 'position paper' on the role of the training analysis in the so-called tri-partite system of psychoanalytic education as part of Commission I's contribution to the Conference on Psychoanalytic Education and Research (Coper, 1974), which was scheduled for October 1974 under the sponsorship of the American Psychoanalytic Association. The manuscript on which we were working had to be replaced with a shorter contribution whose emphases differed from those on which we focus in the present essay. The invitation was a reminder that the topic was one to which Dr Heimann had devoted a considerable amount of her professional interest and energy: the questions of psychoanalytic training, the problems of transference and countertransference, and the complexities of psychoanalytic technique. A re-reading of her contributions '*en bloc*' demonstrated the extent to which our own thinking has been influenced by the ideas she has put forward during the past thirty years. At the same time, it is most gratifying to find that so much of what we have attempted to delineate in our paper is consistent with the positions Dr Heimann has staked out in so many of her contributions (Heimann, 1942, 1950, 1954, 1955, 1956, 1962, 1966, 1968, 1970). We are indebted for her provocative and illuminating expositions; and, similarly, we want to express our gratitude to our colleagues on Commission I (especially to its

---

This paper was written for a Festschrift in Honour of Paula Heimann.

sub-committee on the training analysis) for their stimulation, critiques, and suggestions. The responsibility for what follows, however, resides entirely with the authors.

I

In the ongoing analytic work, the analyst assumes a function which is super-ordinate to the more specific component activities which he carries out; namely, that of serving as the 'conscience of the analysis'.[1] In this sense, the analyst is the 'keeper of the analytic process' who has the responsibility of maintaining the psychoanalytic work and process in the face of the resistances which inevitably arise (in himself as well as in his analysand) in the course of such an endeavour. Paradoxically, he can assume that function only by way of suspending, in part, his personal conscience (which is necessarily full of bias). In carrying out that work, the analyst uses an ensemble of skills mediated by certain ego functions which constitute the 'tools' with which he can operate effectively as the keeper of the analytic process.

Those ego functions have been variously described and conceptualized with some important consensus (although not necessarily to the satisfaction of all concerned) while they continue to be explored. Many will agree that some of those functions are givens, the products of constitutional endowment and the processes of early ego development, and whose absence will not be significantly altered by the analytic process. However, there are other ego activities whose optimal functioning in respect to analytic work have been infringed upon by a variety of psychopathological processes. It is the *relative* resolution of those conflicts and the freeing of those functions for effective analytic activity which constitute the principal goal of the so-called training analysis. Certain aspects and experiences of the psychoanalytic candidate's personal analysis are critical to the development of the effective utilization of his working tools and to the development of that set of attitudes which permits him to function as the 'conscience of the analysis'.

---

[1]Many years ago Erik Erikson, perhaps in a somewhat different context, in a supervisory hour suggested that perhaps the analyst had to serve as the conscience of the analysis.

II

If presented in sufficiently general terms, it is not too difficult to outline the goals of the training analysis. Various levels of conceptualization have been utilized to formulate these generalizations, beginning with Freud (1937, p. 248), who used a primarily descriptive mode in asserting that the training analysis had fulfilled its task when: (1) It permitted a firm conviction of the existence of the unconscious. (2) It enabled, when repressed material emerged, the perception in oneself of things which would otherwise be incredible. (3) It showed a first sample of the technique which was proved to be the only one effective in analytic work. (Freud is here referring to what is, in effect, an assessment for further training and, therefore, to a very brief and limited training analysis.)

As psychoanalysts have attempted to move from the general to the more specific, the list of goals and functions have become much longer and more complex. In fact, at times that list becomes so extensive and encompasses so many requirements that it appears that only a superhuman figure could comply with such demands or that a superhuman figure would emerge from a successful training analysis. It does seem at times that there is (both with regard to candidates and to analysands in general) a tendency to look and 'hope' for an impossible ideal. Practically, there is ample recognition that such an ideal is both unnecessary and unattainable. Nevertheless, the dissatisfactions and the disappointments constitute a not-insignificant element in the professional lives of many analysts. They represent areas of conflict which can influence the analytic work; and it is a commonplace observation that there may be a tendency to react to such disappointments by a 'giving up' of the analytic position in favour of extra-analytic interventions. While many analyses may have to stop short of what might be considered optimal terminations, realistic 'compromises' should be distinguished from those situations where, because of his own frustrations and disappointments, the analyst abdicates his analytic functions even transiently and no longer serves as the 'conscience of the analysis'.

It does not serve the complexity of this phenomenon to dismiss it as only a manifestation of unresolved (and unanalysed) infantile omnipotence, although such a label contains more than a modicum of truth. The various facets of the candidate's narcissism and his narcissistic resistances (including the idealization of the analyst) have a variety of sources. The impact of various derivatives of the 'doctor game', of rescue and restitutional fantasies, and other elements of the motivation for psychoanalysis as a career choice require close scrutiny and analysis. While it would be unreasonable to claim that the personal analysis is a guarantee that the analyst will not abdicate the 'analytic conscience' in favour of non-analytic compromises, it should provide more than a minor contribution to the acquisition of a conviction of the ubiquity of intra-psychic conflict and the potential for the amelioration of that conflict by psychoanalytic methods. The candidate will inevitably be influenced by both the overall attitude of the specific interventions of his analyst in regard to the realities and limitations of the analytic method and of the psychic apparatus itself.

One simplified way of stating the goals of the training analysis is to say that the development of an analysing instrument is facilitated (Isakower, 1957). It is axiomatic that the analyst's primary tool in his own unconscious, his intuition, which is made more available to consciousness and intellectual controls and is, therefore, more cognitive and relatively easily accessible to the secondary process (Heimann, 1968). Obviously, this so-called analysing instrument is not conceived as a concrete structure involving a single function or even a single set of functions. We conceptualize this instrument as having three principal components: (1) An observing, listening set of functions which carries out its activities in conjunction with a certain group of hypotheses, while simultaneously aware of the influence which the latter might exert. (2) An integrative set of functions which permits free play between primary and secondary process thinking without the loss of control and which leads to certain, at least tentative, conclusions (assessments) about what has been perceived (Olinick et al., 1973). (3) A translating set of functions which can meaningfully convey to the analysand certain information about these assessments which will permit a particular cathectic shift in the mental economy of the observed.

III

The analyst may be presented with certain limiting psychopathology which may preclude the analytic process from being instituted (despite the application of an appropriate psychoanalytic approach and technique) or interfere eventually with that individual's doing significant psychoanalytic work. It is our impression that today relatively few analysts would arrive at such a conclusion solely on the basis of manifest psychopathy, perversion, acting out, or even on the basis of a presumed psychotic or paranoid core. Such judgments are much more likely to be made upon a careful assessment of the relative immutability of fixations and/or the degree of control over the impulses which are involved; in other words, greater emphasis would be placed on the degree to which certain capacities and functions necessary for doing adequate analytic work had been compromised by that personal pathology. It is theoretically conceivable that specific, circumscribed areas of psychopathology could, in a given candidate, facilitate his doing psychoanalytical work—a topic sorely in need of further theoretical elaboration and clinical documentation.

However, those limitations on the training analysis which are imposed by the candidate's individual psychopathology only begin to describe the problems which confront both the analyst and his candidate. There appears to be an impression (at least in a not-insignificant segment of the analytic community) that since the training analysis is done within the 'fishbowl' of the institute, breaks in analytic confidentiality are inevitable, can contaminate the analytic situation, and make it impossible to carry out a successful personal analysis which is conducted under the umbrella of the training situation. Although the concerns over the impact of the breaks in confidentiality, the complications subsequent to doing analysis within an 'institution', and the relative failures of many training analyses should not be dismissed, it may also be true that the frequently circulated idea that the 'first analysis is for the institute, and the second for myself' may be a canard and a rationalization rather than an established fact. Recently, Stein (1972) and Shapiro (1973a, b) have offered material which suggests that the results of the training analysis are considerably better than might be inferred from the dissatisfactions expressed by many analysts.

In the past decade considerable focus has been placed on those problems emanating from the multiple functions, the syncretistic activity, of the training analyst. Some analysts view this issue as critical; others as essentially chimerical in nature; and it would seem that these differing viewpoints reflect different emphases on varying aspects of analytic theory, the goal of analysis in general, and the educational elements in the training analysis. Elsewhere (Calef and Weinshel, 1973 [chapter 9, this volume]) we have addressed ourselves to this issue; and here we would reiterate what we have previously stated in a somewhat different way: that the so-called examination aspect of training becomes an impossible obstacle only when that 'reality' disguises and is used as a vehicle for more deep-seated pathology and resistances which are not necessarily amenable to analysis under non-training conditions (Heimann, 1968). Of necessity, all analyses are 'examinations'. In every analysis, the analyst must make assessments and judgments of the integrity of the analysand's ego and superego functions; and it is not unlikely that since the training analysis is more explicitly an 'examination', many aspects of the analytic work will therefore be facilitated rather than impeded. It seems most unlikely that any analysis can be conducted without the examination of the questions of analysability, whether that examination is carried out explicitly or simply as a relatively implicit theme which can be detected throughout the analysis.

None of this is intended to denigrate the well-known difficulties encountered by the adult who finds it necessary to assume once more the position of a student. The narcissistic hurt engendered by such 'enforced' regressions should not be belittled; but, additionally, the narcissistic satisfactions which can be derived from the 'successes' inherent in achieving professional goals by progression ('promotion') to seminars, supervision, and unsupervised status can readily become the locus around which conflicts of ambition and competition will find formidable hiding places. In such instances, it is likely that the personal pathology of the candidate and the realities of the training situation will intertwine and impinge on the ongoing analytic work. It is imperative to find effective methods of gathering specific psychoanalytic data which would permit a more accurate dynamic formulation of the ways in which the 'realities' of the institute (in respect both to the problems of institutions in general and the operational milieux of individual institutes) foster specific resistances which might either interfere with or actually defeat the analytic work. Is it true that we observe such interferences with the training analysis only in those instances when the individual pathology and the realities of a given institute inadvertently reinforce each other? Or, is it inevitable that these realities of training must produce significant disruptions of the personal analysis? Or, is the 'reality' of training an issue which has been used as a displacement of the difficulties (and frustrations) which accompany every analytic undertaking?

As is well known, the hazards of the training analysis are not limited to the pathology of the candidate or to the realities of the training situation; obviously, any attempt at understanding these problems must also include the difficulties which are contributed by the shortcomings of the training analyst. This is, however, an area about which only a minimal amount of 'hard data' has been reported, permitting the question whether a good deal of what has been said is impressionistic, unjustifiably generalized, and the product of mythology and shibboleth. This is not to imply that training analysts, because of their own limiting psychopathology and countertransferences, may not interfere with the successful outcome of the candidate's personal analysis; but it is at least worth considering (until more reliable clinical data are available) whether some of the concern and some of the emphasis on the difficulties of training analysis may not be related to other issues; i.e. the disappointments with not turning out a 'perfect product'. Nevertheless, these are factors which warrant careful scrutiny. It would appear inevitable, at least for most training analysts, that the training situation will mobilize many of their own narcissistic concerns. These may become manifest in an inordinate degree of therapeutic zeal or an excessive sharing of the candidate's ambitions and competitive strivings. There is evidence to believe that some training analysts defend themselves against such narcissistic and competitive struggles by a pessimistic condemnation (and what becomes a kind of obstructionism) directed against students in general or, more particularly, against their own work and their own candidates (Greenacre, 1966, pp. 557–559). The need to be considered one of the 'good' analysts (i.e. successful) by the candidate group and by fellow training analysts or, conversely, the need to be 'tough' (i.e. not unduly soft in providing transference gratification) certainly may contribute to the problems of the training analyst and the training experience. We have already alluded to the marked sensitivity some analysts might have, working in the 'fishbowl' atmosphere of the training situation, and such a tendency will no doubt interfere with the optimal functioning of the training analyst. We know something of the unfortunate reverberations of struggles, splits, and cliques among the training analysts in an institute. Although we still know little of the impact of such reverberations on the training analyst's work, the potential for the creation of intractable analytic situations brought about by the unresolved transferences and countertransferences of the training analysis is staggering and disconcerting. This raises questions about the selection and evaluation of training analysts.

IV

In the face of all these potential pitfalls, it is true that we do expect a rather large yield from the training analysis. We ask that the candidate come to the analysis with at least the makings of a professional conscience, with a sense of responsibility which can develop into an analytic responsibility. He will have to learn to differentiate between 'taking care of patients' and 'a care for patients' (i.e. which is part of the 'keeping of the analytic process'); and he will learn to differentiate the '*furor therapeuticus*' from the more realistic physicianly attitude (Stone, 1961). However, the demands on an analyst go beyond the ability to establish an adequate doctor–patient relationship, an ability which in itself requires that he operate within the bounds of an analytic relationship while simultaneously concerning himself with the patient and the patient's illness. The 'conscience of the analyst' includes that which is demanded by any other 'healing' profession; but it is both different and more specific, since it is the process of analysis which becomes internalized rather than simply an identification with the analyst (Joffe, 1973).

As the analyst is confronted with the resistances of his patient, he will recognize and be able to withstand, for example, the power of the transference (together with the understanding and the conviction of its unconscious sources) and thus maintain an optimal distance from the patient and the analytic material without becoming indifferent to either. Similarly, he becomes able to withstand the fluctuations of both the patient's and his own active and passive wishes, to tolerate the regressive tendencies and actual regressions which accompany free association and free-floating attention, and to develop the capacity to handle appropriately the impulses which are stimulated by the analytic work; impulses which press forward both from his own unconscious and from that of his patient.

Above all, perhaps, the analyst must learn to recognize the presence or relative absence of resistances (and especially their less obvious, more subtle manifestations) to the process of free association and to understand the meaning of these resistances for the patient and for the analysis. Having experienced and understood his own resistances in his own analysis and having learned about his own idiosyncratic 'style' of resistances, he is then better able to recognize them in his patient and to differentiate his patient's style from his own.

In terms of the integrating and communicating functions, the analyst is able to translate the patient's (and his own) secondary process productions into primary process equivalents and then back again into a form of secondary process which can be transmitted to the patient in an effective way. A central aspect of this task is the development of the capacity to look for and to discover those sequential dynamic and genetic links which tie the primary and secondary processes to each other. It is the utilization of such linkages in communication with the patient that constitutes one of the elements which distinguishes psychoanalysis from a wild 'game' wherein the attempt is made to render the secondary into the primary process by the simple translation of symbols. Connected with this is the capacity to differentiate the content and the form of the associations from the psychoanalytic process; and it would appear crucial that the candidate both experience and appreciate the significance of these distinctions in his own analysis.

The ability to function in the manner which we have described demands of the analyst the capacity for persistent though unpressured self-observation while working with patients (Bibring, 1954). Related to such a capacity is a contribution from the superego: the acceptance of the *responsibility* for such self-observation, a term which we would differentiate from and prefer to the concept of self-analysis (especially when the latter is thought of as self-conscious, deliberate effort). The product of such an attitude and such functioning is the achievement of an ego-state which is neither solely an affective nor an intellectual one. We would describe it, rather, as a state of readiness to hear and to experience and to do that which is necessary to engender and maintain the analytic process in the patient. It implies, to be sure, the willingness to live and to work with ambiguity for long periods of time without resorting to actions which might prematurely reduce that ambiguity. It also necessitates the ability to articulate at the appropriate time conceptual material (from varying levels of thought) into every day language which avoids the pitfalls of psychoanalytic cliches.

The interferences and the resistances inherent in the candidate's first and early identifications with his training analyst have been explored in detail, while there has been an increasing recognition by analytic educators, of the significance and the critical impact of imitations and identifications for the development and integration of an individual style of analysing (Freud, 1912, p. 111). Nevertheless, we have yet to understand how and at what points in the educational sequence the identificatory processes are converted into a different form of learning and a 'personal style' (Calef, 1972a). Analysts have conceptualized that development as the achievement of a relative autonomy of certain ego-functions, and emphasize thereby that some degree of freedom and mobility of the instruments of perception, comprehension, integration, and communication are required for the analyst to do his work. Although we do not wish in any way to minimize the therapeutic tasks which are a necessary part of any analysis, our focus is on the functional and not on the therapeutic aspects of the training analysis.

Irrespective of the therapeutic success of the personal analysis, the candidate can never be entirely free of conflict created either by internal or external stresses and 'pains' originating from physiological and/or psychological sources. The analyst learns to understand the inevitable reality of living and functioning as an analyst in the face of such pains and conflicts while maintaining his particular attitude toward his work (Heimann, 1968).

The analyst utilizes the 'tools' necessary for the maintenance of the analytic work, precluding exploitation of the patient and avoiding the misuse of the analytic process as a means of obtaining irrational gratifications of his own needs. However, just as the 'rule of abstinence' does not imply that the analysand does not enjoy any gratifications during the course of his analytic experience, it would be a caricature of the analyst's task to insist that he should not derive gratifications from his work or his patients. It is the hidden gratification of narcissistic and pre-genital aims that interfere with the analytic work and to which the analyst remains alert in his conduct of the analysis and in his interactions with the patient. Each analyst must differentiate (and then deal with it in an appropriate manner) between those of his gratifications which do not interfere with the work and those which 'exploit' his patients and the analytic situation for the satisfaction of his irrational needs: a task which is not made easy by the fact that the analyst depends almost entirely on his own responses and his capacity to become aware of them to make those determinations.

The emphasis in the training analysis (and, more specifically, in understanding the work of the analyst) is on the achievement of an optimal degree of desexualization of certain ego-functions and not so much on the therapeutic goals *per se.* We have not yet exhausted the explorations of the functions which are involved and how they become de-sexualized by the analytic process. Freud's generalizations (1937, p. 250) are still applicable: 'The business of the analysis is to secure the best psychological conditions for the functions of the ego: with that it has discharged its task.' When ego-functions are *relatively* free from libidinal conflict, they are most apt to escape the hazards of inhibition and neurotic alteration and distortion. Such a relative freedom from conflicts (Hartmann, 1958) is perhaps the most direct way for the analyst to delineate the optimal psychological condition for those ego-functions which permit the individual to work, to play, to love—and to analyse!

It is the task of the psychoanalytic work to free those ego-functions *as much as is possible* from their primary libidinal investments. When the individual's object-ties are divested of their pre-genital elements (either by fortuitous events of maturation and development or by the process of analysis), he becomes capable of love relationships which are more satisfying, emotionally and intellectually; and similarly, when motor controls, intellectual activity, and the synthetic and integrative functions are no longer bound predominantly to their infantile precursors (to their relation to masturbation, for instance), then the individual is able to work and to play without the abandonment of the demands of his conscience. It is that freedom of the ego which permits the maturation and development of which the ego is capable. On the behavioural level, the evidence of that freedom may be found in the ways in which one deals with ambitions, jealousies, ambivalence, passivity, activity, etc. in his daily performances. It may not be necessary to spell out clearly which of the ego-functions needs to be operative in a relatively conflict-free state for most patients to achieve the maximal therapeutic benefit from analysis. However, if our assumptions are correct that the analyst, in his daily work, operates in a somewhat different fashion than do the majority of people in their every day activities, then it is incumbent on us to attempt to describe those specific factors which become the focus and a significant target of the training analysis, since they are the functions which go into the analyst's work and which he utilizes as the keeper of the analytic process (Fleming, 1973). The state of mind in which the analyst operates—what has been called 'evenly suspended attention'—deserves more than a cursory description.

V

Freud's (1912, p. 111) recommendation that the analyst, as he listens to his patient, is expected to place himself in a state of 'evenly suspended attention' has become a commonplace, but one which has been the subject of relatively little investigation. The so-called evenly suspended attention can be described as one of an altered state of consciousness. It is a position which favours bursts of insight which are in many ways similar (if not completely comparable) to the activities of creative artists or scientists, who reach for and discover new relationships between the various elements with which they deal. The altered consciousness has been compared to the dream state (Lewin, 1955; Stein, 1965; Olinick et al., 1973). The comparison is useful although not altogether accurate inasmuch as the analyst does not actually permit himself to dream. It would perhaps be more accurate to say that he places himself in the position of being ready to dream without actually dreaming (Fliess' [1942] concept of 'conditional day-dreaming') or without permitting himself the luxury of uninhibited fantasy. The analyst tries to maintain a state of being able to dream while still awake and simultaneously controls, to a degree, both fantasy and dream—a control which precludes both inattention and sleep.

The exploration of the theoretical relationships of the ego to the id and to the superego in the analyst at work was a subject of interest before Freud made his 1937 statement on the goals of analysis for the future analyst. Although Freud saw these operations taking place in what may be conceptualized ideally as an ongoing self-analysis, he also recognized—and warned—that at times something different and less desirable could occur. The 'something different' consisted of those internal situations within the analyst wherein the predominant influence of various defensive mechanisms allowed 'analysts to divert the implications and demands of analysis from themselves (by directing attention to other people), so that they themselves remain as they are and are able to withdraw from the *critical* and corrective influence of analysis' (Freud, 1937, p. 249; our italics). Freud's comments are portrayals of the analyst's ego and superego as they function either adequately or inadequately, a state of affairs also noted by Fliess (1942) and Heimann (1968) in economic terms. In this connexion, Fliess designated the appropriate functioning of the analyst's superego as a therapeutic conscience.

For the analyst to achieve that state of suspended attention and to serve as the conscience of the analysis, it is not sufficient that he simply renounce the gratification of certain impulses by the avoidance of motor discharge; it is also necessary that he be able to avoid such gratification in self-stimulative dream- or fantasy-formation and, in addition, to forego the externalization of these impulses upon his patients. The analyst's impulses are sufficiently available to him so that they can be recognized without the expenditure of unusual effort and can be controlled without the usual manifestations of defensive manoeuvres. This set of capacities may well be at the core of what is meant by the 'knowledge of the unconscious', of the so-called 'psychological-mindedness' and the process of identification and empathy. From a position of passivity, the analyst listens without a particular focus and without surrendering his capacity for attention. At the same time, however, this attention *is* selective wherein the analyst chooses, sometimes only preconsciously, but often consciously, those cues and clues which can lead him to the unconscious content and processes in a patient's verbalizations. Furthermore, the analyst listens to these verbalizations with his own brand of 'benign scepticism' knowing that both the content and the form of the patient's material may simultaneously be the product of meaningful analytic work and yet be utilized in the service of resistances to that very work.

The analyst (especially with his increased understanding of ego-psychology and its application to psychoanalytic technique) does not immediately transmit his information and assessments to his audience. Rather, he re-translates the unconscious back into secondary process terms and then, eventually, and in the language of the patient, makes his 'interpretive remarks'. These operations involve the analyst's incorporation of and identification with the patient but also the capacity to separate himself from the patient and the latter's associations, the ability to withstand regression, the ability to recognize and utilize the links between the secondary and primary processes, and at appropriate times, to help supply some of these links for the patient without actually pre-empting the analytic work of the patient.

'Evenly suspended attention' is only a partial description of that altered state of consciousness which characterizes 'the mind of the analyst at work'.[2] Just as we recognize that the patient cannot maintain constantly an optimal level of 'free association' the analyst cannot remain in the frame of mind that has been conceptualized as 'evenly suspended attention' during the entire length of time he sees his patient. There are times when the analyst's attention becomes focused too sharply on irrelevant details, and his preoccupation and responses to such diversions may well interfere with his following the flow of the analytic material. At other times, the analyst's attention flags; and the danger then arises of the development of fantasies, dreams, or sleep, which—no matter how much these phenomena may be the consequences of the patient's associations and style of associating and can be used in subsequent interpretive work—often are co-determined by the idiosyncratic dynamics of the analyst himself (Calef, 1972b). This altered state of

[2]The topic of 'the mind of the analyst at work' has had an increasing focus of attention. See, for example, the recent contributions by Gray (1973) and Olinick et al. (1973). Their emphases may be somewhat different from our own, but they deal with identical issues.

consciousness of the analyst depends on the willing suspension of those habitual characterological integrations which are so crucial to the maintenance of his personality. This is not to say that the analyst changes his personality and assumes a new and spurious 'role'; rather, when the analyst is hurt, angry, embarrassed, disgusted, jealous or shocked, or when—in contrast—he is pitying, satisfied, flattered, propitiated, approving or loving (all of which, and more, he can expect to experience in the course of any analysis), he will not respond in the same way that he is accustomed to do with his friends and his family. We do not believe that this implied reserve and control indicates that the analyst must become a detached and uninvolved mirror; we know, on the contrary, that the analyst's affective 'involvement' and the particular way in which this involvement is utilized, constitute a necessary element for the analytic work. It may be that the utilization of these idiosyncratic emotional responses becomes the crucial element in the evolution of the necessarily individual and varying styles of analytic work.

The clinical descriptions of evenly suspended attention are probably of greater value than the theoretical expositions. All of Freud's various phrases to describe the matter, Bion's (1970) concept of the analyst as container and Winnicott's (1960) of the analyst as a good mother, Lewin's (1955) comparison of the analytic situation to a dream state, and Fliess' (1942) therapeutic conscience are additive descriptions of the same phenomenon although there may be some important differences in the various conceptualizations of the observations. In addition, however, the descriptions do imply, at least, some technical advice whether intended or not by the various authors, which would tend to make a caricature of the analyst and the analytic situation. It is doubtful that what was intended was that the analyst permit his mind to become an empty container for whatever a patient had to place in it. Nor is it likely that the analyst was intended to assume the position of being the good mother. Despite the fact that any metapsychological view (Freud's 'witch') is limited, it does have value for differentiating the various conceptual views from one another and will perhaps also avoid certain misconceptions which may be derived from certain descriptions. Obviously, the metapsychological rendition will also imply certain technical corollaries; while, at the same time, it will avoid others. This will be especially true in this instance if we approach the matter (with Fliess and Lewin) from the quantitative, or more correctly, the economic, aspect without ignoring the qualitative issues (explicit as well as implied) in the clinical descriptions. The qualitative descriptions may be misinterpreted to imply that evenly suspended attention requires the analyst to involve himself in some form of conscious ego-splitting, whereas the economic view addresses itself to the relative distributions of energy; the latter would not be the same as 'splitting' (Heimann, 1966).

We believe that the analyst's intermittent altered state of consciousness permits a cathectic shift in which the specific aspects of the censorship functions are transiently 'put to bed'; to rest, but not to sleep. However, since sleep and dreaming (including day-dreaming) are approached but yet avoided, it may be somewhat misleading to use the term, 'censorship', to describe the functions which are inhibited. It is probably more appropriate to utilize a comparable, if not identical, concept which analysts use for those functions which operate during wakefulness, namely 'resistances' and we would like to examine in greater detail this idea: that it is some of the analysts' resistances which are suspended during the phase of evenly suspended attention. Looking at these issues in cathectic terms and from the point of view of resistances (rather than censors) which are momentarily de-cathected, leads us to examine those resistances which the analyst has to set aside, put to bed so to speak, as he works by the very act of a willing alteration of consciousness, a change in attention-cathexis and/or withdrawal of certain hypercathexes. We have already alluded to those narcissistic resistances which the analyst controls in order to avoid the secondary gains comparable to those obtained by the neurotic from his illness; similarly, we have also discussed those resistances within the analyst which permit him to use the analytic work as a vehicle for the primary gratification of the 'perverse' pre-genital core of his own neuroses and to hide from himself the existence of such a latent core.

Furthermore, while he firmly maintains his hold on his ideals, on his own superego functions, the analyst simultaneously finds a way of freeing himself from the pressures and the fears of censure from both the outside world and from his patients. Not only can he not permit himself the indulgence of confession and of absolution; he must, in addition, acquire an attitude which allows the expression of censure, dislike, and disapproval from his patients and from others in his environment. The analyst who operates under the inordinate fear of such disapproval during his work with patients will, we suggest, have particular difficulties in maintaining the analytic process.

We would emphasize that the partial withdrawal of cathexes from those structures which maintain specific resistance functions does not imply the parallel withdrawal of cathexes from other ego- and superego-functions. On the contrary, we believe that it is not unlikely that the withdrawn cathexes are put into the service of those observing, evaluative, judgemental, and critical faculties of which both the ego and the superego partake and which are required for psychoanalytic work; and while it is likely that some well-established links and connexions are rendered temporarily inactive by these processes, this does not mean that *all* links and connexions are so sundered. A variety of judgements, not only moral judgements about the patient, are put to one side; and it is anticipated that the analyst will be able to demand of himself that he differentiate those assessments which relate to the operations of certain of the patient's ego-functions from various moral judgements which anyone is bound to make. It is incumbent on the analyst that his moral judgements should not interfere with the effective assessment of the patient's function and activities or of other aspects of his work with the patient (Calef and Weinshel, 1973 [chapter 9, this volume]).

In such a state, which facilitates these cathectic shifts, the analyst is then prepared to 'hear' his patient's free associations. The latter can be conceptualized as serving the same functions as the day residue of a dream in providing the 'stimuli from above' which trigger internal processes and associations within the analyst. It is an especially useful stimulus if it meets with some impulse-derivative from the analyst's unconscious. It is difficult to reconstruct precisely what takes place in the mind of the analyst as he begins to perceive the links in his patient's associations, discovers insights about his patients, and endeavours to convert those insights into potential interpretations; so here, even more than usual, some speculative interpolations are necessary. We refer here not so much to the dramatic, sudden, and intuitive insights, but rather to the everyday work of the analyst which eventuates in those occasional 'good hours' so well described by Kris (1956).

When the free associations of the patient touch on some counterpart in the analyst, that material optimally becomes more available to the analyst on both the conscious and pre-conscious level. What also becomes available to the analyst is a way of comparing how he and the patient resist and defend against such impulses and their derivatives. Unless the analyst is quite aware of his own resistances and defences *vis-à-vis* such material, it is more difficult for him to recognize and appreciate the significance of his patient's productions and to evaluate them in terms of the current analytic work. It is this very opportunity which is provided to the analyst for making such comparisons that contributes very significantly to his conviction, or at least the sense, that he is on the right track. Certainly, one of the fundamental experiences of the training analysis is the opportunity of being confronted with and learning about one's own resistances and defensive operations—an experience which can become the basis for continued post-analytic self-observation and self-scrutiny.

We have attempted to describe in theoretical terms the (primarily) economic relationship between the ego and the superego in the work of the analyst. More attention to the analyst at work could be given to capture more accurately (and from a more clinically oriented point of view) those moments in which the interpretive insights of the analyst are formulated. Here we stress the readiness to permit such events to occur automatically without conscious control. It is not likely that attempts to perform these functions consciously will be effective. In the meantime, some confirmation of our formulation may be found, as an example, in the contrast offered by the pre-analytic work-ego of the candidate, especially one whose character has unknowingly been forged from the many, frequently observed, obsessive-compulsive determinants which lead to rationalizations and intellectualizations in the form of isolations, undoings, and reaction-formations. Such candidates come to the training analysis with well-formed work habits which they attempt to maintain with their patients. These ego-syntonic structures are held with pride and a high degree of conscientiousness, even recognized intellectually by them as the product of a harsh superego. The recognition by the candidate of the restrictions and inhibitions of such a work-ego will be minimal and could be easily overlooked by his analyst, especially in the face of the absence of anxiety on the part of the candidate and/or the analyst's tendency to approve of such laudable patterns. The trainee will work with despatch and efficiency and even with a high degree of productivity and creativity. Such work is nevertheless determined by reaction-formations, much like symptoms, and thus will be protected against any encroachment on the part of the analysis which might threaten these structures. The forces of resistances are powerful; and not infrequently these resistances are enhanced in a trainee by his unconscious rejection of the role of the patient, even though he may consciously accept it. That force of 'belief', dependent on a split in the functions of the ego, is practised in the analysand's own analysis and in his work with patients. The range of what might be rejected by the concomittant reaction-formations is large, and the effective work-ego of the analysand is impaired.

In the analysis of candidates, it sometimes happens, despite (or because of) the defensive systems described briefly in the previous paragraph, that a trainee begins to report a series of parapraxes related to the conduct of his work, i.e. missed appointments, lateness, slips of the tongue in the presence of patients, peculiarly worded interpretations, etc. These are usually incidents not previously experienced before analysis and which readily reveal rejected unconscious impulses, impulses which the perpetrator of these breaks in the usual work pattern did not believe existed. Yet these are welcome experiences in the analysis because as substitutes for, and perhaps precursors of, the transference neurosis, they contain the hidden pre-genital impulses with which the trainee protects himself by utilizing (in the form of reaction-formations) these habitual work patterns. The successful analysis of the parapraxes unveils the defences against unwanted impulses as defences which are antithetical to analytic work.

We realize that a condensation of clinical vignettes, especially when abbreviated and disguised to serve the needs of confidentiality, does not adequately serve the purpose of unveiling the process of analytic work. Nevertheless, we have juxtaposed a theoretical description of the relationships of the superego to the ego in the work of an analyst by a partial and condensed clinical portrayal of a number of cases in training. The altered ego precludes the capacity to serve as the conscience of the analytic work. If analysis deals successfully with the reaction-formations involved, the work-ego of the trainee will be influenced to a remarkable degree to permit that candidate the affective functioning necessary to work as an analyst.

If the above considerations have validity, then we must take them into account in our discussions of the selection and progression of candidates in the psychoanalytic institutes. Short of analysis, we are too often limited to educated guesses and intuitive hunches about whether the candidate will be able to develop the particular superego of the analyst. The usual selection procedures of the institute cannot predict that potential with any degree of accuracy. In our opinion, the progression of a student should be heavily dependent upon whether such a development is possible and is in evidence in the personal analysis and during supervision. Whether or not that development can be detected may be *the* appropriate subject of reports to the institute by the training analyst (Calef and Weinshel, 1973 [chapter 9, this volume]).

With any degree of success of the personal analysis, the future analyst should be able to assume the role of a Doctor Watson to his patient's

Sherlock Holmes, and thus be able to avoid the pre-empting of the analysing functions of his patients while retaining the position of the conscience of the analytic process. To maintain that role, he needs to keep a constant vigilance, to be constantly ready to alter his views about himself and/or his patient as analytically determined evidence emerges from the unconscious of the observed and the observer by way of dreams, free associations and the transference. The danger of relinquishing that responsibility carries with it the danger of using analysis as a tool to be directed against others instead of for them and for oneself.

SUMMARY

The analyst assumes the superordinate function of 'the keeper of the analytic process' in the face of the resistance against it (in himself and his patient). To do so he suspends his personal conscience (biases), paradoxical though it may be. Avoiding the over-estimations and over-expectations for the personal analysis, it is nevertheless expected that it will provide a relative resolution of conflict to permit certain ego functions sufficient freedom (secondary autonomy) for the development of the analysing instrument which includes listening, observing, integrating and translating functions and allowing a mobile translation of secondary into primary processes and then back again to secondary process thought and language. It is in the evenly hovering attention (an altered state of consciousness) which the analyst consciously permits himself that his resistances are temporarily suspended, old connexions held in abeyance to potentiate the possibility for new ones to occur. It is a state of readiness to sleep and dream though precluding inattention, sleeping, and dreaming while permitting limited fantasy formation.

REFERENCES

Bibring, G. (1954), The training analysis and its place in psycho-analytic training. *Internat. J. Psycho-Anal.*, 35:169–173.

Bion, W. R. (1970), *Attention and Interpretation.* London: Tavistock.

Calef, V. (1972a), A theoretical note on the ego in the therapeutic process. In: S. Post (ed.), *Moral Values and the Superego Concept in Psycho-Analysis.* New York: International Universities Press.

_______ (1972b), 'I am awake': Insomnia or dream? *Psychoanal. Quart.*, 41: 161–171.

______ & Weinshel, E. (1973), Reporting, non-reporting, and assessment in the training analysis. *J. Amer. Psychoanal. Assn.*, 21:714–726.

Coper (1974), Commission I. *The Tripartite System of Psychoanalytic Education.*

Fleming, J. (1973), The training analyst as an educator. *The Annual of Psychoanalysis*, 1:280–295.

Fliess, R. (1942), The metapsychology of the analyst. *Psychoanal. Quart.*, 11:211–227.

Freud, S. (1912), Recommendations to physicians practising psycho-analysis. *Standard Edition*, 12.

______ (1937), Analysis terminable and interminable. *Standard Edition*, 23.

Gray, P. (1973), Psychoanalytic technique and the ego's capacity for viewing intrapsychic activity. *J. Amer. Psychoanal. Assn.*, 21:474–494.

Greenacre, P. (1966), Problems of training analysis. *Psychoanal. Quart.*, 35: 540–567.

Hartmann, H. (1958), *Ego Psychology and the Problem of Adaptation.* New York: International Universities Press.

Heimann, P. (1942), A contribution to the problem of sublimation and its relation to the processes of internalization. *Internat. J. Psycho-Anal.*, 23:8–17.

______ (1950), On counter-transference. *Internat. J. Psycho-Anal.*, 31:81–84.

______ (1954), Problems of the training analysis. *Internat. J. Psycho-Anal.*, 35:163–168.

______ (1955). A combination of defence mechanisms in paranoid states. In: M. Klein, P. Heimann & R. Money-Kyrle (eds.), *New Directions in Psychoanalysis.* New York: Basic Books.

______ (1956), Dynamics of transference interpretations. *Internat. J. Psycho-Anal.*, 37:303–310.

______ (1962), Curative factors in psycho-analysis. *Internat. J. Psycho-Anal.*, 43:228–231.

______ (1966), Comments on Dr Kernberg's paper. *Internat. J. Psycho-Anal.*, 47:254–260.

______ (1968), The evaluation of applicants for psychoanalytic training. *Internat. J. Psycho-Anal.*, 49:527–539.

______ (1970), Opening remarks of the moderator—'The non-transference relationship in the psycho-analytic situation'. *Internat. J. Psycho-Anal.*, 51: 145–147.

Isakower, O. (1957), Problems of supervision. Report to the Curriculum Committee of the New York Psychoanalytic Institute. Unpublished manuscript.

Joffe, W. (1973), Personal communication.

Kris, E. (1956), On some vicissitudes of insight in psycho-analysis. *Internat. J. Psycho-Anal.*, 37:445–455.

Lewin, B. (1955), Dream psychology and the analytic situation. *Psychoanal. Quart.*, 24:169–199.

Olinick, S., Poland, W., Grigg, K. & Granatir, W. (1973), The psycho-analytic work ego: Process and interpretation. *Internat. J. Psycho-Anal.*, 54:143–151.

Shapiro, D. (1973a), The dual role problem and the results of analysis during training. Unpublished manuscript.

_______ (1973b). The silver lining: Facilitation of analysis by the training situation. Unpublished manuscript.

Stein, M. (1965), States of consciousness in the analytic situation: Including a note on the traumatic dream. In: M. Schur (ed.), *Drives, Affects, and Behavior, Vol. 2.* New York: International Universities Press.

_______ (1972). In: K. Calder (ed.), Reports of the Committee on Psychoanalytic Education to the Board on Professional Standards, November 29, 1972.

Stone, L. (1961), *The Psychoanalytic Situation.* New York: International Universities Press.

Winnicott, D. (1960), The theory of the parent–infant relationship. *Internat. J. Psycho-Anal.*, 41:585–595.

Chapter 11

1984

Some Observations on the Psychoanalytic Process

I

In 1968 Greenacre (p. 211) decried the fact that the gradual emergence of the concept of a psychoanalytic process was not accompanied by a "very compact" literature on the subject. References to the concept were scattered throughout numerous papers on theory, technique, and clinical findings. She also pointed to the critical "interdependent roles of technique and theory" in the evaluation of the concept. If one accepts that very basic and reasonable hypothesis (which Greenacre did not explicitly pursue), then one should also accept the parallel hypothesis that as psychoanalytic theory developed and changed, there should have been parallel shifts in the theory of psychoanalytic technique—and in the conceptualization of a psychoanalytic process, however inchoate that conceptualization might be. Freud's (Breuer and Freud, 1893–1895) earliest concept of a psychoanalytic process would therefore be viewed as something quite unlike (though with some parallels to) that which we would delineate in the period since the enunciation of the dual instinct theory (1920), the elaboration of the tripartite system (1923), and the concept of signal anxiety (or signal affects) (1926).

Victor Calef, M.D., died on October 12, 1983. He was an outstanding psychoanalytic clinician, teacher, and author, and this paper is dedicated to his memory. While I am indebted to many colleagues for direct and indirect help in writing this paper, most significant has been my collaboration with Dr. Calef over a period of many years. During those years, the topic of the psychoanalytic process was a persistent one in our discussions. I know that Dr. Calef planted the seed for many of the ideas I have incorporated in this essay, and I have borrowed shamelessly from a number of his unpublished papers. I shall always be grateful for both his assistance and for that most fruitful collaboration.

In the past quarter of a century, there has been increasing interest in the idea of a psychoanalytic process; in fact, the term has achieved a certain vogue and has taken on an aura with a positive connotation. It is "good" for there to be a "psychoanalytic process" in an ongoing analysis; and it is even better to be able to demonstrate it. Indeed, the Committee on Certification of the Board on Professional Standards of the American Psychoanalytic Association has indicated that a significant criterion for gaining full membership in the Association is the capacity of the applicant to demonstrate the presence of this process and its appropriate management in his or her case reports.

Nevertheless, references to the psychoanalytic process, although more frequent, still remain somewhat scattered in our literature; discrete, organized dissertations on the process are still far from numerous. More striking is the fact that, while everyone seems to talk about the psychoanalytic process, there is little evidence to indicate that there is anything close to a consensus on how we might define the term. There is more than a little confusion about the relation of the psychoanalytic process to the psychoanalytic situation, psychoanalytic technique, the therapeutic or working alliance, the transference neurosis, the development of insight, "being *in* analysis," and so on. The distinctions are not easily formulated in an abstract theoretical fashion, let alone from specific clinical data, especially when the data are limited and circumscribed.

According to the *Concordance* (Guttman, et al., 1980, p. 1013), Freud used the word "process" 1297 times. I confess that I have not examined each of these references, but a more than cursory scan of the many columns of citations, together with a limited but judicious sampling of them, has persuaded me that only a few of these references are connected with the psychoanalytic process in the sense that I will use it here. One of these almost 1300 references to the word "process" is probably familiar to most psychoanalysts, coming as it does from the essay, "On Beginning the Treatment," written seventy years ago. In his discussion of the problems around the patient's "justifiable wish" to shorten analytic treatment, Freud (1913) said:

> When patients are faced with the difficulty of the great expenditure of time required for analysis they not infrequently manage to propose a way out of it. They divide up their ailments . . . and then say: 'If only you will relieve me from this one (for instance, a headache or a particular fear) I can deal with the other one on my own in my ordinary life.' In doing this, however, they over-estimate

> the selective power of analysis. The analyst is certainly able to do a great deal, but he cannot determine beforehand exactly what results he will effect. He sets in motion a process, that of the resolving of existing repressions. He can supervise this process, further it, remove obstacles in its way, and he can undoubtedly vitiate most of it. But on the whole, once begun, it goes its own way and does not allow either the direction it takes or the order in which it picks up its points to be prescribed for it. The analyst's power over the symptoms of the disease may thus be compared to male sexual potency. A man can, it is true, beget a whole child, but even the strongest man cannot create in the female organism a head alone or an arm or a leg; he cannot even prescribe the child's sex. He, too, only sets in motion a highly complicated process, determined by events in the remote past, which ends with the severance of the child from its mother [p. 130].[1]

Let me underscore a number of key points in Freud's analogic statement:

1. He sets forth a goal for the analytic work, that of the resolving of existing repressions.
2. He calls attention to limitations of both the analyst and the analysis. Certainly, the analyst cannot predict the outcome of the analytic process.
3. He sketches out what the analyst *is* capable of doing. The analyst sets in motion a process aimed at resolving repression; he can supervise the process, further it, and remove obstacles in its way, which will "vitiate most of" the repressions.
4. He argues that the process, once initiated, must run its own course, a course determined by events in the remote past.
5. He asserts in this analogy that this "highly complicated process" comes to an end only when the patient is separated from the analyst.
6. Although he does not spell it out explicitly, Freud presents us "with a notion, however loosely defined, of a progressive development over time in a definite direction" (the words are from Kris [1956, p. 253]).

[1]I am indebted to Samuel Hoch for calling this passage to my attention a number of years ago.

I am not optimistic about the prospects of constructing a concise definition of the psychoanalytic process which will be congenial to all colleagues, let alone be accepted by all of them. Whoever proffers such a conceptual definition would of necessity present a formulation which would reflect his own editions of the basic postulates of psychoanalysis, his elaboration of those postulates into various levels of theory, the ways in which he translates that theory into practice, and his conscious and not-so-conscious goals of analysis.

My point of departure will be Freud's phrase, "the resolving of existing repressions." But my discussion will focus more on the whole idea of a "dynamic unconscious" and the work that needs to be carried out in order to deal with those forces which maintain the repressions—all the mechanisms of defense and resistance,[2] not just the specific mechanism of repression. I will emphasize those external observables, the resistances, which from many sources become the obstacles to that work, for both analyst and patient. I recognize, not entirely with equanimity, that I will most likely achieve only a portion of my goal. I anticipate that my work will, however, permit a considerable exploration of a wide variety of both conscious and unconscious psychological activities.

I would concede that one might discuss the phenomenology of the process, but I do not believe that a narrative version of that phenomenology really tells about *the* process, although some fragments of the story may afford us some hints of and access to the process and "lead" us to it. Similarly, our interest in the genesis and the development of the "psychology" of each analysand permits each analysis to become "a sort of self-played dramatic play in and by which the history of the individual is reexperienced, restructured, acquires new meanings, and regains old meanings that were lost" (Loewald, 1979, pp. 372–373). Such a "history," the product of a great deal of analytic labor, of many insights, of careful reconstruction, may provide us with an important and fascinating document; but it is not the process.

The psychoanalytic process is a *special* interactive process between two individuals, the analysand and the analyst. There may have been a time when the "process" was seen as something taking place only within the patient. The psychoanalytic process requires that there be two people working together, that there be object relationships, identifications, and transferences.

[2]For an excellent general description of resistance, see Stone's (1973) "On Resistance to the Psychoanalytic Process."

I recognize that it is somewhere between whimsical and quixotic to try to subject the concept of the psychoanalytic process to a metapsychological scrutiny; I would like to be able to do so, but I cannot. I would, however, like to borrow the framework developed by Rapaport and Gill (1959) as a point of departure for some observations on the process:

1. *The genetic-developmental point of view* was invoked in Kris's (1956) statement "of a progressive development over time" (see also, Calef, 1976, 1982b) and in Freud's phrase "determined by events in the remote past." It is also reflected in the assumptions we entertain about the capacity of the human psyche for change and for growth (Loewald, 1980, pp. 281–283) and about its capacity as well as its propensity for regression; and, of course, we divide the analysis and its "process" into the opening, middle, and end stages.

2. *The adaptive point of view* is useful in observing how the patient deals with and adapts to the analytic *situation*, the structured understanding of the ground rules and the mutual responsibilities that serve as a framework for the analytic venture. This is not to say that there is a set of rules for all analyses; but for each analysis, there evolves a sometimes tacit and sometimes more explicit agreement in regard to a set of activities and boundaries that will guide that particular psychoanalytic relationship. Neither the structure nor the governance is in itself *the* process; but the manner in which the participants react to those rules, the way in which each experiences his particular task and carries it out, and the way in which those tasks and rules are disregarded do play a significant part in the emergence and effective maintenance or in the disruption or stagnation of the analytic process (see Spruiell, 1983b). For the patient the basic tasks are free association and a fealty to thinking and talking, in distinction to action; for the analyst, the principle of abstinence and serving as the guardian of the analytic process (Calef and Weinshel, 1980 [chapter 10, this volume]; Weinshel, 1982).

Again, the rules and the structure of the situation are not to be equated with the process or *directly* related to what occurs in the analysis (notwithstanding the assertions of Macalpine [1950]); rather, they represent, in Calef's (1976) words, which form an extension of what I quoted earlier from Freud, "an attempt to control a small number of variables as best we can, knowing that they can be controlled only minimally in a very complex situation. Rather than rules of technique, they serve simply as background for comparisons against which we may witness the various ways in which patients and analyst alike repeatedly fail in the fulfillment of the implied ideals" (p. 2). However, it is the detection and recognition of these repeated failures that permit the analyst to make certain specific interventions and then to observe and to follow the responses of the patient which constitute what we can designate as the crux of the analytic process. I am referring, of course, to resistances and their interpretation.

All patients and all analysts will "adapt" to the analytic situation in their own characteristic fashion. For both patient and analyst, that adaptation will be determined by the totality of their assets and liabilities, their conflicts and anxieties, the vicissitudes of their drives, their overall defensive repertoire, their motivations for the analytic work, and much more. Inevitably, there will be some impingement on their analytic work, on their capacity to carry out their analytic task, and this will be reflected in that observable we call a resistance. The resistance, together with its successful negotiation by the analyst (most often by interpretation), is the clinical unit of the psychoanalytic process. Hartmann's (1939, p. 51) concept of the "state of adaptedness," especially in relation to the idea of "an average expectable environment," provides us with another way of viewing the manner in which the analysand deals with the analytic tasks and situation as the process unfolds and develops. Ideally, we anticipate that, as the analytic work progresses, the patient will gain new resources which are reflected in a new state of adaptedness and an increased capacity to participate in the analytic work and in the analytic process. These changes can be observed clinically.

3. *The structural point of view* is implied and reflected in our study of behavior and our assessment of psychological functions. Assumptions about structure and structure formation form an integral element in our concepts of the tripartite psychic apparatus, of defense and resistance, of character and habitual patterns of drive discharge. "Structural change" has become not only a highly prized goal but also a kind of slogan and shibboleth; it is also difficult to demonstrate and explicate.

4. *The dynamic point of view* concerns itself with psychological forces, with their direction and their magnitude. (Some aspects of dynamic considerations have already been alluded to in my discussion of "adaptation".) In relation to the psychoanalytic process, we view these forces as organized according to those elements which move in the direction of supporting and pursuing the analytic work and those elements which serve as obstacles to the work, the resistances. Our understanding of the resistances is certainly more sophisticated than the concept Freud advanced in 1894, but there are as yet many gaps in our knowledge about

these phenomena. Our classification of resistances, based primarily on Freud's (1926) discussion in *Inhibitions, Symptoms and Anxiety,* has been of tremendous value, both theoretically and clinically, but relatively little has been added to that contribution. Similarly, we have only an incomplete understanding of those factors which contribute to the initiation and support of the process.

I have not been able to discover a more satisfactory explanation for the "primary motive force" for the analytic work than that offered by Freud in "On Beginning the Treatment." Although some of his remarks may be questioned or revised, they remain the basic hypotheses for these considerations. Freud (1913) began by asserting, "The primary motive force in the therapy is the patient's suffering and the wish to be cured that arises from it." He then acknowledged the inadequacy of this ingredient alone:

> By itself, however, this motive force is not sufficient to get rid of the illness. Two things are lacking in it for this: it does not know what paths to follow to reach this end; and it does not possess the necessary quota of energy with which to oppose the resistances. The analytic treatment helps to remedy both these deficiencies. It supplies the amounts of energy that are needed for overcoming the resistances by making mobile the energies which lie ready for the transference; and, by giving the patient information at the right time, it shows him the paths along which he should direct those energies. Often enough the transference is able to remove the symptoms of the disease by itself, but only for a while—only for as long as it itself lasts. In this case the treatment is a treatment by suggestion, and not a psycho-analysis at all. It only deserves the latter name if the intensity of the transference has been utilized for the overcoming of resistances. Only then has being ill become impossible, even when the transference has once more been dissolved, which is its destined end [p. 143].

I do not think that Freud persisted in his belief that "only then has being ill become impossible"; but his position in regard to the centrality of overcoming the resistances never wavered. He added that "yet another helpful factor is aroused," the patient's intellectual interest. But he noted that due to the "clouding of judgement that arises from the resistances," this factor is only of limited value. This intellectual interest, however, should be differentiated from gradually increasing pieces of "insight" that become available as a result of the analytic work. This insight (utilized by both the analyst and the patient) and the process are related to each other in a circular (Blum, 1979, pp. 41, 45; Kris, 1956, p. 269), a helical, and a dialectic fashion. Blum's (1979) contribution, "The Curative and Creative Aspects of Insight," not only offered a comprehensive exposition of insight from many different vantage points but demonstrated repeatedly the interdigitating relationship between insight and the process.

We recognize that the motive forces leading to an individual's entering analysis include not only the pain and the wish for cure, but the primarily unconscious anticipation that the cure will come about as a consequence of receiving from the analyst the libidinal gratifications which had not been received from the original love objects. We know that the frustration of that wish becomes, in turn, another painful experience for the patient as well as an opportunity for his deeper and more significant involvement in the analytic process.

I should add—only for the record, so to speak—that the transference not only provides us with a most significant motive force for the analysis; it also becomes a significant resistance against the analytic work and process (Freud, 1912, p. 101). It is futile to argue which is most crucial to the analysis, the process or the transference; both are obviously vital. I see them as phenomena on somewhat different levels of conceptualization: the process-resistance issue is closely connected to the energic-biological-quantitative postulates of our science; the transference and its vicissitudes become the principal (although not the only) vehicle by which we can observe, study, and deal with the resistances.

The discussion of the "dynamics" of the process should include a word or two about the "quantitative" relationship of the conflicting forces operative in that process, especially as that relationship is influenced by the analyst's participation—particularly by his interpretations of the various aspects of the resistances. Those interventions help shift the balance of forces (the "equilibrium"), which permits a loosening of the resistances and assists the patient in the continuation of the analytic work. Arlow (1979, p. 194), in his discussion of interpretation, referred to a comparable sequence.

5. *The "quantitative factor"* could perhaps be considered just as well under the rubric of the economic or energic point of view. The economic viewpoint is, of course, a highly controversial one. If it is true that metapsychology is Freud's "witch," then the energic concept must represent the queen in the coven. Suffice it to say that we do not possess *a*

comprehensive energy theory that is satisfactory and convincing. It is nonetheless very difficult to see how we can dispense with an energic point of view. In terms of the process, those economic assumptions are basic to an understanding of the various shifts, displacements, countercathexes, hypercathexes, transformations, etc., that take place at any point in the process. It is true that we could alter the labels for these various phenomena, but we are still left with energic phenomena.

The questions are often asked: When does the analysis *really* begin? How does it start? How do we know that a patient is *in* analysis? Less frequently, comparable inquiries are made in regard to the psychoanalytic process as such. None of these questions are answered readily or without some resort to personal preference or arbitrariness.

I do not believe that a psychoanalytic process exists at the very beginning of the treatment (except, perhaps, under most unusual circumstances), nor does it start necessarily with the first manifestation of a clear-cut resistance. Most analysts probably follow a personalized variant of Freud's advice not to communicate to the patient "the hidden meaning of the ideas that occur to him [or initiate] him into the postulates and technical procedures of analysis . . . . until an effective transference has been established in the patient, a proper *rapport* with him" (Freud, 1913, p. 139; see also, 1912, pp. 101–105; 1913, pp. 137–140). In those early analytic hours the analyst will tend to deal with the patient and his productions with some care and caution, and with special consideration for the viability of the patient's budding involvement with the analyst and the analysis. The analyst will assess the possible impact on the patient of his interventions, particularly the effect those interventions may have on the analytic relationship. The analyst may delay for the moment the interpretation of a particular resistance, if he feels that the patient's tie with the analyst is not sufficiently solid to bear the impact of such an intervention. Conversely, the analyst will direct many of his early interpretations toward the elucidation of those resistances whose primary purpose is to ward off that attachment and/or transference. I would suggest that this is the thrust of Freud's caveat about waiting for the "proper *rapport*." Freud went on to say,

> It remains the first aim of the treatment to attach [the patient] to it and to the person of the doctor. To ensure this, nothing need be done but to give him time. If one exhibits a serious interest in him, *carefully clears away the resistances that crop up at the beginning* and avoids making certain mistakes, he will of himself form such an

> attachment and link the doctor up with one of the imagos of the people by whom he was accustomed to be treated with affection [1913, pp. 139–140, italics added].

I emphasized Freud's phrase, "carefully clears away the resistances that crop up at the beginning," because I believe that it is the appropriate interpretation of those early resistances that "sets in motion a process." That process may flicker and fade if the patient cannot respond—if the resistance does not yield sufficiently—in a way which permits the resumption of the analytic work. The interpretation and the response constitute the basic unit of the process; it is *evidenced* by shifts in the patient's material, his affects, his overall behavior, and by an increased interest in and focus on the analytic work—albeit most often in minuscule degrees. We know, however, that as soon as the work is reinstituted, another resistance will appear, often as the consequence and product of the previous analytic work. At times, the "new" resistance may be of the same genre as the previous one—a reality resistance, a superego resistance, a narcissistic resistance, a character resistance, a transference resistance; more often, the resistance changes to another from the patient's repertoire. It appears that individual patients (or the combination of a given patient and a given analyst) develop characteristic patterns and sequences of resistance. This is an area that needs further investigation and offers considerable promise of enhancing the efficacy of our analytic work (Calef, 1976, 1982b).

This process, this clinically demonstrable interaction of resistance and interpretation, continues throughout the analysis. There are times when the force of the resistance seems diminished and when the interval between the manifestations of resistance is increased, but neither the process nor the resistance ever entirely disappears. Our exposure and exploration of the resistances provides both analyst and analysand with the opportunity of discovering the connections and the content of the patient's mental life, both conscious and unconscious. (My focus is on the mental life of the patient, although comparable phenomena are, of course, operative in the analyst.) Even when presented in a sketchy fashion, such a conceptualization of the analytic process will help us to better comprehend the discontinuity of the analytic activity and the analytic work. The establishment of an effective analytic process in which the patient demonstrates the so-called working or therapeutic alliance—when the patient may be said to be "*in* analysis"—is not a once-and-for-all achievement. That very complex concatenation of ego functions, superego influences, and instinctual drive derivatives which permits the patient to work cooperatively with the analyst is constantly prone to impingement by conflict, regression, anxiety, sexualization, etc. The "working alliance" is a relatively transient rather than constant structure and for this reason alone becomes a potentially confusing rather than useful concept, especially when viewed as a discrete psychological entity (Brenner, 1979; Calef, 1976, 1982b; Curtis, 1979; Hanly, 1982).

The patient, after all, enters analysis with his symptoms, his miseries, and—notwithstanding his disclaimers to the contrary—the anticipation of a magical fulfillment of his infantile wishes. He will more often than not attempt to comply with the analytic rules; his heart, however, will really not be in *this* project. One of the tasks the analyst must pursue sedulously and patiently is the diversion of the patient's interest and focus from the symptoms to the analytic work. This cannot be achieved by kindness, sympathy, or empathy alone—let alone by fiat. This gradual weaning of the patient to a genuine interest in his own psyche and its activities is best accomplished by the appropriate interpretation of those resistances which present themselves in the earlier stages of the analysis (although "early" is often a relative term). Those interpretations, most often quite "bland" and even ostensibly simple, will produce a fleeting sense of understanding and of being understood. They probably also contribute to the formation of that well-known split of the ego into experiencing and observing functions and to the identification with the analyst qua analyst (Sterba, 1934; Strachey, 1934). In addition, they are instrumental in helping the patient to shift his interest from his miseries to his psyche and the analysis. These shifts and transformations reflect, I suggest, shifts in the mental economy and are best conceptualized in our economic metaphors. What occurs is consistent with the *idea* of the "working alliance" but without the connotation of a fixed and stable structure.

In the next section of this paper, I will present these same schemata from a somewhat different vantage point and in a different idiom, but first a few words about the resistances of repression and the resistances of the id. Both groups of resistances share the qualities of being difficult, obstinate, and frustrating—frustrating in the sense that they confront us with the limitations of ourselves as analytic instruments, with the limitations of our current analytic techniques, and with our limitations in controlling and influencing the course of the analytic process.

The loosening and undoing of the resistances of repression remain *the* goal, or at least one of the principal goals, of most analysts. Yet it is a goal which is never reached in its entirety. I am by no means referring to a goal as ambitious as the one which evoked the somewhat ironic aside by Anna Freud (1968): "I myself cannot help feeling doubtful about trying to advance into the area of *primary* repression" (p. 147, italics added). Even after assiduous and careful reconstruction, we must settle so often for only a partial "softening" of the resistances and a limited clarification of the nature and genesis of the "existing repressions." I would hold, however, that the work of both the analyst and the patient in the *efforts* to deal even partially with these obdurate and sometimes recondite resistances brings about internal energic shifts which produce psychological changes, if not insight (Kris, 1956, p. 268). Therefore, working through, no matter how thorough and how persistent, should never be equated with "working through to conclusion." These are, I believe, instances of the activity of the psychoanalytic process in which concurrent evidence of observable change is not available. These somewhat sober reminders, however, should not distort our view of what the patient, piecemeal, and persistent interpretive efforts to expose and explain the resistance of repression can accomplish. Even with our limitations, and in addition to the "silent" changes alluded to, we do succeed in exposing a great deal about the genesis of symptoms, the history of fixations and regressions, the impact of trauma, the roots of the development of relations with objects, the nature of primary process activity, and the interrelationships of the various elements of the psychic apparatus.

The workings of the resistances of the id are even more mysterious (probably because of their close conceptual connection to economic and quantitative factors) and more impervious to our direction and control. It is very difficult—perhaps impossible—to formulate meaningful interpretations dealing with such phenomena as the repetition compulsion, the adhesiveness of the libido, or the channelization of various instinctual discharge patterns. We try, as best we can, to point out repetitive patterns and repetitive dynamic configurations. We have much to learn here.

II

In 1941 Bernfeld published his version of the psychoanalytic process in an almost forgotten paper, "The Facts of Observation in Psychoanalysis."

A group of us in San Francisco, most of whom never knew Bernfeld personally, have been influenced and intrigued by Bernfeld's formulations. Because of this, together with the fact that this infrequently read contribution is not easily available, I would like to review some of its principal ideas. Bernfeld (1941) proposed that "the scientific methods [in this instance, of psychoanalysis] are nothing more than everyday techniques, specialized, refined, and made verifiable" (p. 290). The "everyday techniques" on which Bernfeld built his presentation come from ordinary conversation; their application is "specialized, refined, and made verifiable" in accordance with the basic tenets of psychoanalytic theory and with the basic facts of the observations of clinical psychoanalysis.[3]

Bernfeld offered what at first glance might appear to be an oversimplified model of the psychoanalytic process, but its seeming simplicity is deceptive. It is a jargon-free, highly sophisticated model of what takes place in a clinical analysis, presented in everyday language. His framework is what transpires in a conversation between two individuals. Focusing on the "patient," Bernfeld first described what he labeled as "ordinary conversation." The analytic parallel is, of course, free association. At certain points, an obstacle to that conversation will arise. Bernfeld referred to this as "the *state* of hiding a secret" (p. 298, italics added), what we conceptualize as a resistance. This "state" may be followed by what Bernfeld called the "confession." The "confession" is facilitated and abetted by "an interference" from the second individual: in analysis, the analyst's intervention or interpretation. The "interference" (intervention, interpretation) is what Bernfeld referred to as "actively influencing" the patient. With the confession of his secret, the patient is then able to resume his ordinary conversation. However, the same process and cycle will repeat itself, a phenomenon which is a source of potential frustration but also a source for both patient and analyst of increasing and accruing knowledge of the patient's psychological functioning. This enhanced familiarity with the patient's patterns of "conversation," especially those shifts from "conversation" to the "state of hiding a secret," permits the analyst (and eventually the patient) to

[3]It could be argued that such a hypothesis derives from a kind of circular thinking. I do not agree with this argument. If nothing else, Bernfeld's hypothesis has the virtue of an internal consistency in its interdependence of theory and clinical practice.

recognize more effectively the clinical differences between the two "states" and to evaluate, with increasing degrees of confidence, the distinctions between a genuine and a bogus "confession."

Bernfeld's very interesting discussion of the "verification of the confession" (pp. 296–303) is a persuasive one that can only be touched upon here. He stressed that what is at issue is not whether that confession is realistically or ultimately correct but whether "the patient has told precisely and correctly the story which for some time he has withheld" (p. 297). Bernfeld reminded us as well that "a lie can be a confession" (p. 296). Most of all, Bernfeld's assessment depended on the clinical material and evidence, "the life history of the confessing person" (p. 299) and the "advantageous position" of the psychoanalyst who "does not have to deal with one single confession" and who "observes [the patient] confessing in various emotional and physical states." Thus the "risk of deception is not excluded although minimized" (p. 300). Bernfeld emphasized again and again the role of the clinical data, the "facts of observation," and put a good deal of faith in the potential value of "intersubjectivity"—"because a relevant group of people can reach an agreement as to whether or not the predicted effect takes place" (p. 302). In a recent critique titled "Kuhn's 'Paradigm' and Psychoanalysis," Spruiell (1983a) suggested with considerable cogency that the small case conference among psychoanalytic peers may represent a vehicle for demonstrating the presence or absence of such intersubjectivity.

Bernfeld (1941) stressed that if one "uses the rules of the psychoanalytic method . . . [the] patient will show resistance, will confess, etc." (p. 302), but he also warned that "the pattern of secret-confession does not occur if you do not actively produce it. . . . Thus this technique is equivalent to the use of a new observation instrument" (p. 303).

Thus Bernfeld saw the removing of obstacles as the analyst's chief function. The analyst establishes an "encouraging atmosphere" which minimizes distrust and shame in the psychoanalytic situation and which "creates the conditions under which the patient is likely to confess secrets" (p. 296). Bernfeld repeatedly stressed "the incorrect assumption that the psychoanalyst's interpretations aim exclusively at *the* secret" (that is, the specific content of what has been repressed) (p. 295). In fact, argued Bernfeld, it is not necessary that the analyst know, or even possess more than a clue about, the specific secret content. What the analyst needs are "observations . . . of indications of *a state of mind* which he assumes to be due to an effort to keep secret a part of the material . . ." (p. 295) and a conjecture (very often an intuitive one) about the nature of the secret. When the latter is available, the analyst is "able to act," i.e., to interpret the obstacles to confessing the secret. Although he did not elaborate this in any systematic way, Bernfeld's immediate interpretive focus was on those affective states, such as distrust and shame, which are responsible for the intrapsychic events which lead to the formation of resistances. In this connection, Bernfeld hinted at a critical distinction between psychoanalysis and other therapies. The latter may use suggestion to elicit certain *content;* in psychoanalysis, "that which is *suggested* to the patient by the analyst are those conditions necessary for the removal of shame, distrust, or other impediments to 'confession'" (Calef and Weinshel, 1975, p. 39). In this way Bernfeld also unveiled the important affective core of the resistance (Calef [1976, 1982b] discussed the "affective core" concept in more detail) and demonstrated that the *facts of analytic observation* are patterns of "resistance" *and* "confession" rather than the confession per se (Calef and Weinshel, 1975, p. 39). The pattern of resistance and confession, then, constitutes, as I have submitted, the basic unit of the psychoanalytic process as well as the basic fact of observation in psychoanalysis. Bernfeld's paper also "focuses on the essential dialectic nature of the psychoanalytic process and at least inadvertently points to its inherent 'interminability'" (p. 39).

Among the contributions contained in Bernfeld's relatively brief paper is one that we may too readily take for granted: the recognition that the psychoanalytic process, best actualized by the psychoanalytic *work*—and here I mean "work" in the sense of persistent labor—is the essence of the psychoanalytic endeavor. What Bernfeld told us, both directly and by implication, is that this frequently inconspicuous, almost silent labor (Abrams, 1980; Calef, 1983, p. 97; Kris, 1956, p. 270) may be obscured by the more dramatic and more readily communicated product of that work—insight. Abrams (1981), in discussing the various meanings of "insight," called our attention to the lack of a transitive verb "to insight" and the need for a "form that would connote mental *work.*" He went on to speak of "insight-producing *activity*" (p. 953, italics added). Shengold used Freud's (1900, p. 195) famous and felicitous "Karlsbad Journey" as the central, ongoing metaphor in his poetic dissertation on insight as metaphor, and he concluded that essay with an observation that is significant both philosophically and psychoanalytically. Speaking of the limitations inherent in reaching our analytic goals, Shengold (1981) noted, "We try to get as close as possible, and perhaps the journey matters more than the attainment of the goal" (p. 304). In a panel discussion on developmental concepts and adult analysis

(Panel, 1977, p. 226), I suggested that a useful way of distinguishing the differences in how individual psychoanalysts conceptualize the psychoanalytic process is in terms of those whose chief clinical emphasis is on the goal (in this panel, the reconstruction of early psychic life) versus those whose chief emphasis is on the work necessary to achieve that goal. I believe that this distinction may be helpful in a better understanding of our colleagues whose point of view may not always coincide with our own. My own bias in this regard, and that of Bernfeld, must be clear.

III

I am not qualified to sketch out in any detail or with any degree of certainty a blueprint of the structural and economic underpinnings for those behavioral components and sequences which I have labeled the basic psychoanalytic process unit (Bernfeld's "facts of observation"). Those structures and that organization would depend upon and originate in a variety of givens. They would develop in relationship with the ongoing analytic activity, primarily the analyst's interpretations vis-à-vis the patient's resistances and the activity of the patient in response to those interpretations.

What I have in mind is a complex organization comparable to what Abrams (1981, p. 253) described as the "specific coordinated activity, the expression of an achievement in the mental organization, which yields psychological discoveries." I would suggest that this organization and these structures—the psychoanalytic process—remain as permanent products of the reasonably successful analysis and that their presence is reflected most immediately and most tangibly in the operation of a more effective and more "objective" capacity for self-observation. I am aware of a certain amount of oversimplification in what is at best a "tangled bank" (Hyman, 1962) of psychological structures and activities, and I am also aware of the limitations inherent in this self-observation. If we are to think of self-observation as an autonomous ego function, we should not ignore "the admonition which Hartmann has made repeatedly that autonomy is a term which should not really be used except in tandem with its modifier, 'relative'" (Weinshel, 1970, p. 699 [this volume, p. 168]). Kris (1956) reminded us that the goal of completely objective self-observation is "never to be reached; the temptations of denial and self-deception can hardly be conquered" (p. 267). In spite of these vulnerabilities and imperfections, the capacity for reasonably autonomous, reasonably objective, reasonably stable self-observation activity, which would include a superego component[4] that accepts the responsibility for self-observation, would appear to be the quintessential desideratum from a reasonably successful analysis, at least in the functional sense. I prefer to think in terms of self-observation rather than self-analysis; but in this context, the latter term more clearly, if not more accurately, conveys the idea and contention that the enhanced capacity for a more objective and effective self-observing activity represents both the continuation of and the heir to the psychoanalytic process.

The kind of self-observing capacity that we might conceptualize postanalytically—and perhaps this is somewhat idealized—would derive from an amalgam of the following:

1. Those elements responsible for self-observation which existed prior to the analysis and which did not alter markedly.
2. Those elements which underwent modification during the course of the analysis.
3. Those elements which represent residues of the transference with the analyst.
4. Those elements which represent a relatively stable identification with the analyst's functioning, particularly his observing functions.

You will recognize the parallels with the questions of the fate of the transference in psychoanalytic treatment, the issues of the "unresolved" transference, and the work of Arnold Pfeffer. Pfeffer's (1959, 1961, especially 1963) pioneering follow-up research challenged, in a careful and persistent fashion, the sacred-cow concept that a principal goal of the analytic work was the so-called complete resolution of the transference. Actually, Pfeffer's "challenge" involved three issues.

First, his studies questioned the concept of "resolution" of the transferences. Just as his data appeared "to support the idea that conflicts underlying symptoms are not actually shattered or obliterated by analysis but rather only better mastered with new and more adequate solutions" (Pfeffer, 1963, p. 234), it also supported the idea that there is neither a shattering nor an obliteration of the transferences.

---

[4]The role of the superego in its relationship to reality testing and self-observation in particular is discussed very thoroughly in Blum's (1981) paper, "The Forbidden Quest and the Analytic Ideal: The Superego and Insight."

Second, he questioned the idea that the incomplete resolution of the transference is necessarily evidence of some failure or incompleteness of the analytic work. Pfeffer contended: "In the course of the analysis, the person of the analyst becomes, and after the analysis remains . . . a permanent intrapsychic image intimately connected with both the regressively experienced conflicts and the resolution of these conflicts in the progression achieved" (1963, p. 238). Both aspects of this "permanent intrapsychic" image are integral constituents of Pfeffer's proposed criteria for a successfully completed analysis. In some cases at least "there may be a minimal experiencing of the conflict previously contained in the neurosis as well as the repetition of the adaptation facilitating resolution of these same conflicts" (p. 242). Pfeffer did not question that transference residues also can and do result from incomplete analyses and that

> such transference residues are observable as operative in residual psychopathology . . . . however . . . even in most highly satisfactorily analyzed patients a second type of transference manifestation with a different basis is also observable; that is, transference manifestations based on repetition—repetition of the essence of the analytic experience itself . . . as well as the repetition of the ego and superego changes that provide new solutions to old conflicts [p. 243].

In these statements Pfeffer indicated the ongoing viability and activity of the analysis, the transference, and the process, as well as the adaptive value of this "residual" activity.

Third, Pfeffer no longer dealt with residual "transference" as if it were a homogeneous entity. As demonstrated above, he delineated those residual transferences still organized around significant conflict and potential pathology from those based on "repetition" of the effective analytic work and not necessarily related to conflict or residual pathology. It could be argued that these two categories really represent quantitative differences on a continuum, but I do not believe that such a distinction alters the thrust of Pfeffer's contribution. Although Pfeffer did not indicate specifically that those transferences based on "repetition" were also closely related to an identification with the analyst's functioning and his observing functions, I have chosen to understand his text from that vantage point.

In a recent article Calef (1982a) first of all coined the eponymous "Pfeffer Phenomenon" and then extended and more sharply delineated some of the features of that phenomenon. Calef conducted a most interesting follow-up study on a series of his former analysands. From the responses of these expatients, he drew a number of impressions and conclusions in regard to (among other things) the postanalytic fate of the transference and of the psychoanalytic process. Calef was impressed with the evidence of extensive residual involvement with the analyst even though the Pfeffer Phenomenon per se was not always manifested.

Calef made a distinction comparable to the one enunciated by Pfeffer in regard to two kinds of transference. Although the emphases of the two authors differ a bit, I believe that they are dealing with identical issues: ". . . the transferences that need to be relatively resolved," declared Calef, "are those that seek libidinal gratifications (primarily those that seek pregenital aims and objects); for they are the ones that maintain the inhibitions, symptoms, and anxieties and interfere in the lives of people" (1982a, pp. 112–113). However, he continued, "Those transferences which, by analytic work, have been freed of the sexualizations find their usefulness in work and sublimations and then are no longer the same as once they were; indeed, they do not require further resolution or disappearance" (p. 113). Calef suggested that the postanalytic continuation of the analytic work may depend in part on the "aid of the transference image that is recalled under certain circumstances. . . . If so, it would be misleading to refer to such transference manifestations as evidence of unresolved transference" (p. 113). Calef's conclusion, although expressed in somewhat different terms, is again similar to that of Pfeffer. "The outcome of analysis may be dependent (not so much on the identification with the analyst per se but) on the nature and extent of the *identification with its process* and on the *nature* of the transferences that persist postanalytically" (p. 113, italics added). Calef broached the provocative question that the *absence* of such phenomena may indeed indicate areas of analytic incompleteness or failure.

My own interest in this facet of the analytic process was generated in the past three years by the return of three patients whose analyses had been completed some fifteen to twenty years ago. Their analytic treatment had been terminated with both patient and analyst reasonably satisfied with its outcome. All three had gotten along quite well since the completion of their analyses up until a brief interval prior to their coming back for further treatment. And all three mentioned very quickly after their return—each in his or her particular fashion—how they had utilized the analysis, the analyst, and the analytic working together in dealing with transient crises or anxieties postanalytically.

What struck me most was the way in which these patients got back into the analytic work so quickly and so effectively. Each of these patients commented on the feeling of "it's as if I've never been gone." Although it was evident that there were residual areas of both transference and neurosis that required further analysis, the analytic process and the analytic work did not require a significant kind of re-establishment; and although the resistances did not fail to appear, these patients dealt with them much more as partners in the analytic effort than one might have expected. In my own experience, at least, the same observation could not be made in regard to individuals who came to me after prior analysis with another analyst. It is a subject that warrants more careful investigation.

I must now question one phrase from Freud's 1913 statement quoted near the beginning of this paper in regard to the analytic process. That phrase came at the end of the statement in which Freud, in analogizing the analytic process to the process of pregnancy, asserted that the process "ends with the severance of the child from its mother." I have argued that the analytic process does not end; it may become quiescent, dormant, but not really ended.[5]

IV

My final set of "observations" could be entitled "The Pitfalls of Perfectibilism and the Elevation of the Not-So-Good Hour." The *Oxford English Dictionary* (1971, p. 684) defines perfectibilism as "the doctrine of perfectibility of human nature in this life." A perfectibilist "is one who holds this doctrine." Perfectibility is the "capability of being perfected or becoming perfect; the quality of being improvable to perfection; specifically, the capacity of man, individual and social, to progress indefinitely towards physical, mental, and moral perfection; the doctrine of this capacity."

[5]In the course of writing this paper, I made the "obligatory" investigation of what the dictionaries had to say about the word "process." I consulted the *Oxford English Dictionary*, *Webster's New World Dictionary*, and the Second Edition of *Webster's New International Dictionary, Unabridged*. Needless to say, there were several score definitions and synonyms available, but those having to do with an "end" were very rare. More often the definitions related to the concept of "course," something ongoing or continuous, a series of actions.

There is a certain amount of outward consensus among psychoanalysts that "perfection" of any kind is not a reasonable, rational goal for the human being; that any doctrinaire position is at best suspect; and that, when it comes to psychoanalysis as such, we are particularly keen on acknowledging our limitations and our distaste for doctrine. Perhaps I should modify my title to "The Pitfalls of Latent and/or Closet Perfectibilism"; but, seriously, there seems to be at least a grain or two of belief in that doctrine in most of us. There has never been a shortage of caveats and somber precautions in regard to the overestimation of the therapeutic capabilities of psychoanalysis. And Freud, especially after *Analysis Terminable and Interminable* (1937), was considered to have a pessimistic view about those capabilities. Yet, if one reads the report of the panel, "Analysis Terminable and Interminable—Twenty-Five Years Later" (Panel, 1963), one has to wonder why so many of the very competent participants on that panel deemed it appropriate and necessary to admonish quite strenuously against the dangers of therapeutic overoptimism. Certainly, those admonitions and disclaimers have not vanished in the past two decades, and here I am very scrupulously offering the same. I will not attempt any comprehensive explanation of this issue other than the obvious: we are not so confident that we all accept the principle of a very limited perfectibility.

In that 1963 panel, however, Loewenstein stressed the particular danger of the pitfalls of therapeutic overoptimism at a time when ostensibly new knowledge has become available. Loewenstein expressed his skepticism about whether "we can accomplish *that much more* now than in the past" (Panel, 1963, p. 135, italics added). I believe it is true that, with the introduction of new knowledge and insights, particularly when that which is introduced becomes the focus of a revisionist point of view or system, there is a concurrent surge of optimism over the prospect of a significant increase in our therapeutic potential. As we know, such a point of view may burgeon into a doctrine or a cult.[6] I would suggest that Gitelson's (1963, p. 343) recommendation of "a counsel of modesty" for psychoanalysis is a worthy slogan for our profession.

Actually, I would like my remarks about the pitfalls of perfectibilism (I did not spell out the pitfalls, since I assume that everyone is well acquainted with them) to serve as a kind of background music for the second part of my title, "The Elevation of the Not-So-Good Hour." As my readers might have surmised, the not-so-good hour is to be evaluated

[6]Arlow (1983) has made a comparable observation.

in juxtaposition to the so-called "good" analytic hour. Again, I need not redescribe the latter: the good hour is described explicitly in our literature; many, perhaps too many, case descriptions contain sessions that fall, at least by implication, into that category (but, ironically, this does not hold for Kris's [1956] contribution in which the term "good analytic hour" was coined). A significant portion of the vignettes we exchange with colleagues are related—not without a degree of pride—about a "good hour," and so forth. Typically, this vintage of clinical narrative tends to contain a number of ingredients: the content of the session is most conspicuous; often, a specific obstacle is confronted and overcome; an aura of the epiphany often permeates the description; diverse elements of the analysis, the transference, and the neurosis may fall together with disarming ease; and more often than not the analyst is careful to indicate that before "the" good hour, a great deal of laborious and undramatic effort was exerted in previous hours.

I am being somewhat tongue-in-cheek about all this quite purposefully and, in a sense, paradoxically, because I have a great fondness for the "good" hour. It is fascinating, exciting, sometimes humbling (especially if you are not the narrator), and potentially instructive. But are these really the good hours? There is no question that they make the analyst feel good, and they make the patients feel good. These hours provide the analyst with an indication that the analytic process is moving, and moving in a certain direction; and they help us to attach words and content to what Calef (1982a, p. 113) called the "ineffable" process.

Nevertheless, we should not permit ourselves to believe that it is those sessions which become *the* goal of our daily analytic endeavor or to confuse the product of that endeavor with the endeavor itself. I would submit that the *really* good hour is the one in which, at the time or in retrospect, we are able to detect some dent in the resistance configuration. I use the word "detect" because it is crucial that we be able to detect in a more precise manner the evidences of resistance, particularly the subtler ones, and that we be able to detect those responses and reactions in the patient which reflect his or her participation in the analytic process.[7] Martin Stein's (1981) paper, "The Unobjectionable Part of the Transference," provided an excellent example of this.

[7]Those "responses and reactions" are by no means always obvious or easy to recognize as the patient's "being in analysis." A recent discussion of these issues can be found in Baranger et al. (1983, pp. 10–11).

What I have in mind by "The Elevation of the Not-So-Good Hour" is an increased recognition of and attention to the less glamorous and exciting exchanges that take place daily at the interface of the analyst–analysand interaction, the more prosaic and "quiet" elements of that interaction, and the nuances of how the analyst and his interventions assist the patient's analytic efforts—instead of so much attention to those "frames" in the analytic work which feature the analyst in a starring role. I believe that a more even-handed focus can eventually reveal to us a good deal more about the nature of the psychoanalytic process, its manifestations, and its management. I have not attempted a tightly organized, comprehensive "definition" of the psychoanalytic process; what I have offered is a series—and, I trust, a not too desultory series—of observations regarding the process and its relationship to resistances and their interpretation. I have suggested that the process continues, although in a muted form, postanalytically, as a more objective and more effective capacity for self-observation; and I have argued that the relatively "pedestrian" analytic session focused on the exploration of a given resistance warrants closer attention.

REFERENCES

Abrams, S. (1980), The silent process. In press.

_______ (1981), Insight: The Teiresian gift. *The Psychoanalytic Study of the Child*, 36:251–270.

Arlow, J. A. (1979), The genesis of interpretation. *J. Amer. Psychoanal. Assn.*, Suppl., 27:193–206.

_______ (1983), Issues and integrations in the evolution of psychoanalysis: Criteria for change. Keynote address presented to the combined meeting of the West Coast Psychoanalytic Societies, San Francisco, March 11.

Baranger, M., Baranger, W. & Mom, J. (1983), Process and non-process in analytic work. *Internat. J. Psycho-Anal.*, 64:1–15.

Bernfeld, S. (1941), The facts of observation in psychoanalysis. *J. Psychol.*, 12:289–305.

Blum, H. P. (1979), The curative and creative aspects of insight. *J. Amer. Psychoanal. Assn.*, Suppl., 27:41–69.

_______ (1981), The forbidden quest and the analytic ideal: The superego and insight. *Psychoanal. Quart.*, 50:535–556.

Brenner, C. (1979), Working alliance, therapeutic alliance, and transference. *J. Amer. Psychoanal. Assn.*, Suppl., 97:137–157.

Breuer, J. & Freud, S. (1893–1895), Studies on hysteria. *Standard Edition*, 2.

Calef, V. (1976), The psychoanalytic process. Presented to thc meeting of the Association for Child Psychoanalysis, Kansas City, March.

_______ (1982a), An introspective on training and nontraining analysis. *The Annual of Psychoanalysis*, 10:93–114.

_______ (1982b), The process in psychoanalysis. Unpublished.

_______ & Weinshel, E. M. (1975), A neglected classic: II—Siegfried Bernfeld's "The facts of observation in psychoanalysis." *J. Phila. Assn. Psychoanal.*, 2:38–40.

_______ & _______ (1980), The analyst as the conscience of the analysis. *Internat. Rev. Psycho-Anal.*, 7:279–290.

Curtis, H. C. (1979), The concept of therapeutic alliance: Implications for the "widening scope." *J. Amer. Psychoanal. Assn.*, Suppl., 27:159–192.

Freud, A. (1968), Difficulties in the path of psychoanalysis: A confrontation of past with present viewpoints. In: *The Writings of Anna Freud, Vol. 7: Problems of Psychoanalytic Training, Diagnosis, and the Technique of Therapy, 1966–1970.* New York: International Universities Press, 1971, pp. 124–156.

Freud, S. (1894), The neuro-psychoses of defence. *Standard Edition*, 3.

_______ (1900), The interpretation of dreams. *Standard Edition*, 4/5.

_______ (1912), The dynamics of transference. *Standard Edition*, 12.

_______ (1913), On beginning the treatment (further recommendations on the technique of psycho-analysis I). *Standard Edition*, 12.

_______ (1920), Beyond the pleasure principle. *Standard Edition*, 18.

_______ (1923), The ego and the id. *Standard Edition*, 19.

_______ (1926), Inhibitions, symptoms and anxiety. *Standard Edition*, 20.

_______ (1937), Analysis terminable and interminable. *Standard Edition*, 23.

Gitelson, M. (1963), On the present scientific and social position of psychoanalysis. In: *Psychoanalysis: Science and Profession.* New York: International Universities Press, 1973, pp. 342–359.

Greenacre, P. (1968), The psychoanalytic process, transference, and acting out. *Internat. J. Psycho-Anal.*, 49:211–218.

Guttman, S. A., Jones, R. L. & Parrish, S. M., eds. (1980), *The Concordance to the Standard Edition of the Complete Psychological Works of Sigmund Freud, Vol. 4.* Boston: G. K. Hall.

Hanly, C. (1982), Narcissism, defence and the positive transference. *Internat. J. Psycho-Anal.*, 63:427–444.

Hartmann, H. (1939), *Ego Psychology and the Problem of Adaptation.* New York: International Universities Press, 1958.

Hyman, S. E. (1962), *The Tangled Bank: Darwin, Marx, Frazer and Freud as Imaginative Writers.* New York: Atheneum.

Kris, E. (1956), On some vicissitudes of insight in psychoanalysis. In: *Selected Papers of Ernst Kris.* New Haven: Yale University Press, 1975, pp. 252–271.

Loewald, H. W. (1979), Reflections on the psychoanalytic process and its therapeutic potential. In: *Papers on Psychoanalysis.* New Haven: Yale University Press, 1980, pp. 372–383.

_______ (1980), Psychoanalytic theory and the psychoanalytic process. In: *Op. cit.*, pp. 277–301.

Macalpine (1950), The development of the transference. *Psychoanal. Quart.*, 19:501–539.

Oxford English Dictionary (Compact Edition) (1971), Oxford: Oxford University Press.

Panel (1963), Analysis terminable and interminable—Twenty-five years later. A. Z. Pfeffer, reporter. *J. Amer. Psychoanal. Assn.*, 11:131–142.

_______ (1977), The contribution of psychoanalytic developmental concepts to adult analysis. P. J. Escoll, reporter. *J. Amer. Psychoanal. Assn.*, 25: 219–234.

Pfeffer, A. Z. (1959), A procedure for evaluating the results of psychoanalysis: A preliminary report. *J. Amer. Psychoanal. Assn.*, 7:418–444.

_______ (1961), Follow-up study of a satisfactory analysis. *J. Amer. Psychoanal. Assn.*, 9:698–718.

_______ (1963), The meaning of the analyst after analysis: A contribution to the theory of therapeutic results. *J. Amer. Psychoanal. Assn.*, 11:229–244.

Rapaport, D. & Gill, M. M. (1959), The points of view and assumptions of metapsychology. In: *The Collected Papers of David Rapaport*, ed. M. M. Gill. New York: Basic Books, 1967, pp. 795–811.

Shengold, L. (1980), Insight as metaphor. *The Psychoanalytic Study of the Child*, 36:289–306.

Spruiell, V. (1983a), Kuhn's "paradigm" and psychoanalysis. *Psychoanal. Quart.*, 52:353–363.

_______ (1983b), The rules and frames of the psychoanalytic situation. *Psychoanal. Quart.*, 52:1–33.

Stein, M. H. (1980), The unobjectionable part of the transference. *J. Amer. Psychoanal. Assn.*, 99:869–892.

Sterba, R. (1934), The fate of the ego in analytic therapy. *Internat. J. Psycho-Anal.*, 15:117–126.

Stone, L. (1973), On resistance to the psychoanalytic process. *Psychoanal. Contemp. Sci.*, 2:42–73.

Strachey, J. (1934), The nature of the therapeutic action of psycho-analysis. *Internat. J. Psycho-Anal.*, 15:127–159.

Weinshel, E. M. (1970), The ego in health and normality. *J. Amer. Psychoanal. Assn.*, 18:682–735.

_______ (1982), The functions of the training analysis and the selection of the training analyst. *Internat. Rev. Psycho-Anal.*, 9:434–444.

Chapter 12

1990

Further Observations on the Psychoanalytic Process

In a previous contribution, I described the psychoanalytic process as "a *special* interactive process between two individuals, the analysand and the analyst. . . . [It] requires that there be two people working together, that there be object relationships, identifications, and transferences" (Weinshel, 1984, p. 67 [this volume, p. 269]). I also suggested that

> all patients and all analysts will 'adapt' to the analytic situation in their own characteristic fashion. For both patient and analyst, that adaptation will be determined by the totality of their assets and liabilities, their conflicts and anxieties, the vicissitudes of their drives, their overall defensive repertoire, their motivations for the analytic work, and much more. Inevitably, there will be some impingement on their analytic work, on their capacity to carry out their analytic task; and this will be reflected in that [at least relative] observable we call a resistance. The *resistance, together with its successful negotiation by the analyst (most often by interpretation), is the clinical unit of the psychoanalytic process* [p. 69, italics added] [this volume, p. 271].

Further, I proposed that in the course of psychoanalytic work there occurs a gradual internalization of the organizations and structures which subserve those activities, that they remain "as permanent products of the reasonably successful analysis and that their presence is reflected most immediately and most tangibly in the operation of a more effective and more 'objective' capacity for self-observation" (p. 82 [this volume, p. 281]). During a discussion at the May 8th meeting of the COPE-PAP Study Group, Abend proposed that the broadest definition of a psychoanalytic process was "those events which occur in an ongoing analysis" (Abend, 1986a, p. 3). Such a definition is reasonable but so broad as to be essentially meaningless, other than to indicate that one can say that the psychoanalytic process is *the* analysis; and, of course, this is precisely the point that Abend was making. He makes the same point in a more detailed and substantive way in his discerning and challenging article, "Some Problems in the Evaluation of the Psychoanalytic Process" (Abend, 1986b).

Abend's essay is a searching yet sympathetic critique of the concept of a "psychoanalytic process" which extends well beyond the thorny problems related to demonstration and validation. There may be significant variations of "*standard*" *psychoanalytic technique*—situations in which we deal with the consequences of the widening scope of psychoanalysis, and situations in which there are "clinical evaluations of proposed major alterations of theory and technique" (1986b, p. 211). He argues, quite cogently, that in such situations (and many others as well) it may be exceedingly awkward to utilize the concept of psychoanalytic process that I have outlined. And Abend correctly points out that there are many other concepts of the process which may or may not share much common ground (pp. 213–215). He states that my

> approach concentrates on only one portion of the various activities constituting a psychoanalysis, albeit one all analysts acknowledge to be of critical significance, and designates it as the 'process' element of psychoanalysis. Weinshel makes no suggestion that attention to the manifestations of resistance is unique to psychoanalysis, nor that it is the only feature that distinguishes a *true analysis* from other therapies [p. 213, italics added].

These criticisms are both important and valid; they focus on some crucial current difficulties within psychoanalysis, problems which complicate any attempt to establish reasonable assumptions about a psychoanalytic process which would be acceptable to the various psychoanalytic points of view in the United States at this time.

In my 1984 paper I confessed that

> I am not optimistic about the prospect of constructing a concise definition of the psychoanalytic process which will be congenial to all colleagues, let alone be accepted by all of them. Whoever proffers such a conceptual definition would of necessity present a formulation which would reflect his own editions of the basic postulates of psychoanalysis, his elaboration of those postulates into

> various levels of theory, the ways in which he translates that theory into practice, and his conscious and not-so-conscious goals of analysis [Weinshel, 1984, pp. 66–67] [this volume, p. 269].

Those words were written early in 1983 from the vantage point of an analyst who followed the ego-psychological, structural-theory orientation, and my conceptualization of the psychoanalytic process derived from my version of that orientation. I did not expect that colleagues from other schools of thought would find my formulation of the psychoanalytic process particularly convincing; and, in fact, I was not even persuaded that all structural-theory psychoanalysts would view that formulation with enthusiasm or conviction. Psychoanalysis is a particularly personal endeavor; and the manner in which each analyst translates *his or her* version of psychoanalytic theory into clinical technique may border on the idiosyncratic. Today the degree of analytic heterogeneity is considerably greater than it was seven years ago, and it is even more perplexing now to develop a unitary concept of a psychoanalytic process than it was seven years ago.

In an era of increasingly pluralistic conceptualizations of what defines psychoanalysis and what constitutes a clinical psychoanalysis, it is no longer feasible to insist that there is *one* "standard psychoanalytic technique," let alone a "true analysis." Nor can we differentiate, with any degree of assurance, true psychoanalysis from other psychotherapies, even when the latter are designated as "psychoanalytic psychotherapy." I have not seen all of the papers presented at the four panels on Psychoanalysis and Psychoanalytic Psychotherapy at the 1989 Mid-Winter Meetings of the American Psychoanalytic Association, but it would appear that most of the panelists (as well as members of the audience) accepted the fact that those distinctions were difficult to demonstrate clinically, and the differences between the two modalities were, more often than not, of degree and emphasis rather than of kind.

In another place (Weinshel, 1990 [chapter 13, this volume]), I have developed the thesis that in the last few decades there have been impressive (albeit gradual and muted) changes in American psychoanalysis in which our claims and expectations have become more realistic, more in accord with our clinical observations, and more "modest." Many of those changes also reflect a relativistic rather than an either/or position regarding our theories, techniques, and results. I cannot review all of these shifts in this essay, but the list includes some of the central elements in psychoanalytic thought and work. For instance: we talk more of changes and of alterations of compromise formations than of psychoanalytic "cures"; we do not think about eliminating psychological conflict but hope for a favorable resolution of old conflicts; we do not believe that analyses are entirely complete, and we understand that an analysis can be helpful even if not altogether finished; we no longer demand that the successful analysis be dependent on the complete resolution of all of the transferences; and we do not anticipate that resistance will be overcome but rather that a careful and persistent analysis of the resistances will play an integral part in the overall analytic work. I could go on at some length about many other comparable shifts in our thinking and practice. In my 1990 paper [chapter 13, this volume] I also recognized that not all of my colleagues, even those who shared my general psychoanalytic positions, would necessarily agree with me.

I believe that this brief digression is relevant to how we may proceed in our efforts to elucidate a concept of the psychoanalytic process. It is difficult to visualize at this time or in the immediate future (except in the most general way) a model of a psychoanalytic process which might encompass all of the different points of view, schools of thought, and individual inclinations; and it appears much more reasonable—when it comes to constructing psychoanalytic processes—to limit ourselves to our own particular theoretical and conceptual bailiwicks. I suggest that such a necessary but also desirable limitation would help us focus more on those relatively familiar "facts of observation" rather than retreat to what Abend appropriately designates as "mysterious factors . . . magical explanations . . . invocation of a quasi-mystical 'process concept'" (1986b, p. 210). It seems quite unlikely that we can, at this time, integrate into one concept all of the differing—and even antithetical—points of view that compete so actively in our psychoanalytic marketplace. Such an attempt stands a good chance of ending up as a loose hypothetical amalgam rather than a useful cohesive proposition.

The concept of a psychoanalytic process is, I submit, feasible and useful. In reaction to some of the critiques of my 1984 paper [chapter 11, this volume], I have amended, but not really changed, the definition I offered there. I have not altered my conviction that persistent and effective work with the resistances (of both analysand and analyst) constitutes the core of the psychoanalytic work and process. However, it was an unfortunate blunder not to make explicit what I had assumed was already evident by implication; that is, that a more comprehensive conceptual definition of the psychoanalytic process should, in some way, recognize *all* of the various factors which play some role in the overall analytic work. Thus, my current concept of the process would include those more "general" factors (such as transference, the establishment of a psychoanalytic situation, free association, the reconstruction of unconscious fantasies, and a host of others—all of which have, however, been co-opted by a whole variety of psychotherapies) *and* what I consider to be the more "unique" element, the *unit* of the psychoanalytic process, "the resistance together with its successful negotiation by the analyst." The "general" factors play a significant part in any analysis, of course, and they are interdependent with the more "unique" element which I described above.

The structural theory model of analytic therapy—especially as it has been elaborated by Charles Brenner and his collaborators—is particularly well suited as a base for the sort of psychoanalytic process I have presented. Inasmuch as the concept of the unremitting presence of psychic conflict and the concept of compromise formations represent such fundamental assumptions within modern structural theory, it is inevitable that a steady, day-to-day engagement with the resistances as they arise in the course of analysis is especially conspicuous in the work of analysts of this persuasion. Resistances are relatively observable (as contrasted to the more abstract defenses) obstacles to the analytic work and can be described in ordinary language. Our work with these resistances restores the progress of the analysis. In a sense "progress" is what a "process" is all about. Note these three (among many more) definitions of "process" in Volume 8 of *The Oxford English Dictionary* (1978):

> Column l, #1, "The fact of *going on* or being carried on as an *action* or a *series of actions or events; progress, course.*"
> Column 2, #5, "Something that *goes on* or is carried on; a *continuous action* or series of actions or events."
> Column 2, #6, "A *continuous and regular action* or *succession of activities* taking place or carried out in a *definite manner,* and *leading to the accomplishment of some result*" [p. 1408, italics added; see also, Weinshel, 1984, p. 87].

I believe that the emphases added above are self-explanatory. Any psychoanalysis consists of a series of actions and activities (invariably discontinuous rather than in a straight line) aiming in a definite manner at certain (but not necessarily *altogether* certain) goals. When a resistance originating from either the analyst or the analysand arises, it poses an obstacle to the progress of the analytic work, and dealing with that obstacle becomes the central and necessary focus of the analysis. I suggest that it is our *special attitude and approach* to the resistances that serves to *organize* the analytic work and comprises the most significant and reliable distinction between psychoanalysis and so-called psychoanalytic psychotherapy or the even more vague "psychoanalytically informed" psychotherapies. I recognize the difficulty in spelling out in precise terms the special attitude and approach of psychoanalysts to resistances. Foremost is the conviction that *resistances are inevitable* in the psychoanalytic work, that they are not "bad" or necessarily an indication of trouble within the analysis, and that resistances will not "go away" or be "overcome," as Freud was wont to say. I like to think of resistances in a dialectic sense, that is, just as we feel that we have dealt with one resistance, another will soon take its place. I suggest that another aspect of the analyst's posture toward resistance is the awareness that productive psychoanalytic work and resistance can take place simultaneously (Stein, 1981). Such a realization sensitizes the analyst to look for budding and unexpected resistances both in the patient and in himself, not as a Javert on the trail of some miscreant but as an ally in an important joint venture.

It is true that a good deal of what I have just proposed is relatively subjective, but it is this complex subjectivity that plays such an important role in our clinical activities; and, at this time at least, that same subjectivity exerts a consequential influence on our attempts to differentiate psychoanalysis from other forms of psychotherapy.

The differences between psychoanalysis and psychotherapy are relative and not necessarily consistent. It is not likely that those distinctions can be determined on the basis of evaluating a single session or even a cluster of sessions. As analysts, we look for certain changes in the nature of the analytic work or in the patient's symptomatology or complaints as indices of analytic progress. For many years one of the honored criteria for such progress was evidence of so-called "structural change." It is not always possible, however, to distinguish whether changes in the course of an analysis can be attributed to the psychoanalytic work per se or to one of a wide variety of extra-analytic factors. We should at least consider that our long-held claim that "structural change" is the sacrosanct province of psychoanalysis may be a somewhat solipsistic one. Since structural change in psychoanalysis may be difficult to demonstrate in a manner that is clear and open to consensual validation, and difficult to differentiate from changes brought about by non-analytic mechanisms or therapies, I would suggest that the term "psychoanalytic change" may be more realistic and more useful (Weinshel, 1988, p. 264).

Most analysts have compiled their personal lists and criteria for clinical evidence of changes that may bespeak the presence of a psychoanalytic process. I found the paper Compton prepared for the December 1988 meeting of COPE-PAP a particularly penetrating and down-to-earth approach to the study of the process; and the "Catalogue" he assembled (drawing on some earlier suggestions from Abend) "as a sort of bill of particulars for a framework that might allow us to decide that a psychoanalytic process is or is not occurring, or, perhaps more appropriately, what it is" (Compton, 1988, p. 19). Compton does not believe that the items in his catalogue will necessarily provide absolute evidence for the unequivocal determination of a psychoanalytic process (another way of asking this is in terms of the questions, "Is this patient *in* analysis?" or "Does it appear that we can observe a 'working alliance' at this time?"); but I believe that the following items are very helpful criteria in deciding that the psychoanalytic work is progressing and that a psychoanalytic process is probably operative. The following portion of the "Catalogue" focuses on what can be observed in the patient:

1. Gradual and progressive revealing of historical material relevant to the presenting symptoms or life dissatisfaction.
2. Unfolding in the relationship with the analyst (transference) of all major aspects of the behavior patterns, feelings, and modes of relating (central conflicts) that explain the symptoms and life dissatisfactions according to the patient's individual experience (history).
3. Cooperative interest in unraveling the meaning of verbalizations, symptoms, dreams, fantasies, and behavior in and out of the session.
4. The presence or development of the ability to address and objectify the elements of immediate experience in the sessions.
5. Change for the better in psychological disposition and the conduct of life.
6. Changes in relationships, including the relationship to the analyst.
7. Appearance of new material, including memories, fantasies, and affects.
8. Appearance of symptom-like phenomena that are new and relatable to the treatment situation.
9. Shifts in the images of family members.
10. Changes in predominant thematic content.

11. An increase in tolerance for the awareness and verbal expression of sexual and aggressive affect and fantasy with relative decreases in distortion of such fantasies.
12. Changes in affect management (more control, less control); alterations in content, range and modulation.
13. Decrease in frequency and intensity of symptoms, or disappearance thereof.
14. Some sense of self-understanding.
15. Some sense of what the hidden fantasy of gratification or repair that partially motivated seeking treatment is, with some realization that it will never be fulfilled.
16. The development of some sense of the analyst as real person within the role of analyst, as opposed to a larger-than-life imago [Compton, 1988, pp. 20–21].

Compton's list reflects emphasis and activities, and especially *changes*, which involve a shift in the analysands' focus from their symptoms and immediate "miseries" to an increasing participation in and a sense of responsibility for their analysis and their mental functioning. This focus closely parallels what I described at the beginning of this paper as the

> more effective and more 'objective' capacity for 'self-observation' and for what we call insight, a term that is still the subject of considerable uncertainty and controversy; and while there is no consensus as to whether insight is a process or a product or a therapeutic instrument, there does appear to be general agreement that clinical analysis aims at symptom relief based on increased self-awareness. . . . The achievement of insight, in the sense of increased self-awareness, probably remains a primary operational objective for most psychoanalysts in their daily clinical work. Translated into somewhat different idiom, the achievement of insight (or the capacity for self-analysis, self-observation, self-inquiry, and other related terms) also implies a greater and easier access to unconscious psychological derivatives [Weinshel and Renik, 1992].

Further,

> whatever an analyst's particular orientation or emphasis, he is likely to understand analytic work as some sort of ongoing process in which the analysand's capacity for self-observation is enlarged and refined. Therefore in clinical psychoanalysis . . . when analytic work

> proceeds, *insight and symptom relief merge into a single goal.* The analysand's resistances clarify themselves as the most immediately relevant *symptoms* to be studied, and no distinctions can or need be made between investigations of the analysand's self-observational difficulties and investigations of his psychopathology.[1]
>
> From this point of view, too, it can be seen that another goal of the analytic work is to make it possible for the analysand to engage in a form of self-observation or self-inquiry that at least approximates the analytic situation. The agreement to terminate the analytic meetings, then, is best understood not as a decision to terminate the analytic process but as a judgment that the analyst's input is no longer required to adequately maintain the analytic process [Weinshel and Renik, 1992].

Compton (1988, p. 20) also believes that "the idea that the process takes place in the patient is, at this point, no longer tenable. Two people have to be present and interacting for a psychoanalysis to take place. . . ." He then offers a comparable, albeit briefer, catalogue for the analyst "that we would see as necessary to say that there is evidence for what we call a psychoanalytic process occurring" (p. 22). Compton suggests the following:

> 1. Freedom to experience a wide range of affect and thought in the clinical situation, coupled with the ability to contain and make use of such experience.
> 2. Maintenance of an attitude of non-judgmental neutrality towards the patient, coupled with consistent attentions to understand the patient's experience and to be helpful.
> 3. A consistent, or even relentless, attempt to convey that understanding of experience to the patient in ways that are within the capacity to accept, and at times when acceptance is at least possible.
> 4. Abstinence from seeking or providing gratification, advice, counsel, of forms other than the pursuit of understanding and the emotional support inherent in an attitude of helpful interest.
> 5. Non-involvement in the patient's life outside of the analysis.

[1]Spruiell (1989) cogently stresses that patients' resistance is to parts of their own minds—and "from that, flow open and disguised resistances to the analytic process."

6. Maintenance of sufficient frequency and duration of contact so that the treatment experience becomes a central matter in the life of the patient [p. 22].

If analysts are not able to function in a manner consistent with these six precepts, we believe they are encumbered with resistances against doing the analytic work, and they must recognize the necessity of dealing with these resistances in the most appropriate fashion. On the other hand the items listed in Compton's "Catalogue" reflect *changes* which take place in the course of the analysis and imply conflicts, anxieties, and resistances which have to be detected, exposed, and understood. When all is said and done (notwithstanding the efforts to classify various manifestations of resistance encountered in the analytic work), as psychoanalysts, we essentially deal with two forms of resistances: those that come from the analysand and those that come from the analyst. It is, however, the analyst who must serve as the "conscience of the analysis" and the "keeper of the analytic process who has the responsibility for maintaining the psychoanalytic work and process in the face of resistances which inevitably arise (in himself as well as in his analysand) in the course of such endeavor" (Calef and Weinshel, 1980, p. 279 [chapter 10, this volume, p. 246]).

Not all psychoanalysts, not even those who share my psychoanalytic orientation and goals, either assign the same centrality or importance to the role of resistance in the analytic work or view the work with resistances as the core of a psychoanalytic process. Many of these colleagues prefer to emphasize the ongoing analysis of the transferences as the quintessential element of the analytic work and process. These preferences may be a matter of personal style; but, in many ways, it is difficult to separate cleanly the two concepts. We are, of course, mindful of Freud's dictum that the transference is "*the most powerful resistance* to the treatment" (Freud, 1912, p. 101) as well as the treatment's most powerful tool; but in many quarters there has been a tendency to sever the connection between these two conceptual terms with an almost total emphasis on the "transference" and a virtual ignoring of the resistance component. I did not (nor would I) take issue with Willick's claim at the 1989 Panel, "Similarities and Differences Between Psychoanalysis and Psychoanalytic Psychotherapy: Therapeutic Technique," that "the criterion most often cited to distinguish the two methods of treatment for these patients concerns the extent to which there is a *mobilization* of an *intense transference relationship* and the ability of the analyst to understand and interpret it to his patient" (Willick, 1989, p. 2).

What is implied in this brief quotation from Willick's excellent exposition and made more explicit in the body of his paper is that dealing with an "intense transference relationship" is neither simple nor easy; and, certainly, the word "mobilization" indicates that effort was expended to bring those transferences to the attention of both the analysand and the analyst. What makes this portion of the analytic work so difficult for both parties are the powerful affects and the resultant resistances mobilized by those affects; and, until those resistances can be detected, exposed, and understood, work with those transferences is less effective.

I assume that what Willick describes as "intense transference relationships," others (including myself) would designate as *part* of the "transference neurosis." I submit that the terminology is not as critical as the concept itself: that is, the concept of a somewhat indeterminate stage in the course of a productive analysis at which the major transferences (some but not necessarily all of which are related to the oedipal phase) come together around the person of the analyst. I raise the issue of the transference neurosis not to defend its validity but to point to some of the not uncommon misconceptions about that concept which are related to the idea of a psychoanalytic process.

The transference neurosis is still viewed by some as a simple replication of the infantile neurosis. What Freud suggested was that the transference neurosis was a repetition in a different setting (within the psychoanalytic situation and process) with a new object (the analyst) of certain psychic conflicts (predominantly oedipal). Furthermore, the transference neurosis does not just happen, and it does not emerge suddenly or magically as a full-blown entity. It is invariably the product of a good deal of prolonged analytic labor (working through), with many transferences and the resistances associated with them.

I suspect that the most significant misunderstanding in regard to the transference neurosis is in viewing it as the goal of psychoanalytic therapy. The transference neurosis per se neither guarantees the success of the analytic treatment (as many hope) nor destroys it (as some contend). Freud stated that analysts "regularly succeed in . . . replacing [the patient's] ordinary neurosis by a 'transference neurosis' of which he can be cured by the therapeutic work" (Freud, 1914, p. 154). Today we would probably say that appropriate psychoanalytic work with a patient manifesting a transference neurosis will result in a more effective "resolution" of crucial intrapsychic conflicts, with less pathological, more adaptive compromise solutions than had been possible in childhood.

If the antecedent analytic work has made available the complex dynamic/structural situation we conceptualize as the transference neurosis, then the patient and the analyst will have a better opportunity to analyze those transferences along with the resistances to which they are so intimately related. These resistances are formidable ones, particularly because they derive from those fateful early conflicts and the effects they engendered. I would hazard the guess that it was these elements that inspired this famous statement of Freud's:

> It cannot be disputed that controlling the phenomena of transference presents the psycho-analyst with the greatest difficulties. But it should not be forgotten that it is precisely they that do us the inestimable service of making the patient's hidden and forgotten erotic impulses immediate and manifest. For when all is said and done, it is impossible to destroy anyone *in absentia* or *in effigie*" [Freud, 1912, p. 108].

If the analyst and analysand are able to negotiate these troubled waters with reasonable effectiveness, it is likely that the analytic outcome will be a successful one. If the analyst and analysand are unable to deal effectively with these powerful resistances of repression, it would be inaccurate to insist that the analytic effort is automatically a failure; but, by the same token, the outcome will probably be less positive than the ideal of the rich and particularly gratifying results we observe in those cases where we feel the "transference neurosis" has been "analyzed" more satisfactorily. Again, it is not the "transference neurosis" that is the effective *agent* in producing this salutary outcome; nor is it the "transference neurosis" that is "the source of stalemate and analytic failure" (Cooper, 1987, p. 577). It is the capacity of the psychoanalytic dyad to deal with these crucial resistances that will determine the extent to which the "transference neurosis" can be utilized most productively. Translated into the idiom of the psychoanalytic process, we could say that in the transference neurosis we facilitate the analysis of the resistances of repression and enhance the ego's capacity for more objective self-observation.

I have been defending my thesis that the effective unit of the psychoanalytic process consists of the "resistance, together with its successful negotiation by the analyst (most often by interpretation)." There is a great deal we do not know about the psychoanalytic process; and the concerns Abend elaborated in his 1986 contribution, some of which were discussed earlier in this essay, warrant continued careful and dispassionate consideration. Dale Boesky's distinguished essay in this special issue of *The Psychoanalytic Quarterly* is an unflinching yet friendly critique of the current status of the concept of the psychoanalytic process; Boesky scrutinizes a large number of its crucial elements as well as its areas of potential confusion and misunderstanding. These range from the pitfalls inherent in using the concept as a noun rather than as a verb, to speaking of *the* process rather than of the many subprocesses, to the more dangerous hazard of forgetting the significant difference between describing the various changes which occur in the course of the "process" and *really* understanding the causes of those changes.

Abrams (1987, p. 441) points to the concept's "ambiguity, controversy, and diversity of usage." He presents a list of complaints from an assortment of colleagues concerning the complexities of the "process concept." He then asks, "Is it worth saving at all?" and his response to his own question deserves quotation in detail:

> The effort seems justified for several reasons. To begin with the ambiguity, the controversy, and the diversity of usage are expectable developments. Terms, especially those that refer to hypotheses or concepts, are necessarily ambiguous. Theories are always open-ended; they serve to promote fresh discoveries and the discoveries are used to modify the theories. Scientific disciplines spiral forward in just such a manner. And because of their ambiguity, conceptual terms readily become centres of controversy; and the more central the term, the more readily. Evidence to confirm new theories of pathogenesis or the efficacy of a novel technical approach can only be persuasively drawn from the psychoanalytic situation. Consequently, views of the inherent process are regularly being reshaped so that they will be consistent with the fresh offerings. And controversy invariably leads to organized factions staking claims to the 'truth'. The presence of such expectable developments is no reason to abandon the term; rather, it is a reason to press for further differentiation so as to disembed what is useful. If ambiguity, controversy, and misuse had been sufficient reason to abandon ideas we would have long since lost transference and resistance.
>
> The psychoanalytic process is a very useful term. It draws attention to what is fundamental about the methods as well as the facts and theories of our discipline. It does this indirectly by underscoring the infra-structure of our work. All analysts

> operate out of theoretical frames of reference and basic postulates. It is better to know what those theories and assumptions are than not to know them, whether they are internally consistent or whether they are not, and if they conform to views of the psychic apparatus in general or if they do not [pp. 441–442].

I heartily endorse all of the points which Abrams has stated so clearly. It is likely that a comprehensive, clear, and convincing formulation of the psychoanalytic process will not be available in the near future. I suggest, however, that the efforts to further an understanding of the process have provided us with some exciting and potentially fruitful ideas. I will point to some contributions from the three colleagues whose criticisms of and concerns about (together with varying degrees of advocacy of) the psychoanalytic process I have just presented: Abend, Abrams, and Boesky.

In his previously quoted article, "Some Problems in the Evaluation of the Psychoanalytic Process," Abend offers the reader a perceptive (and useful) discussion of "transference cures," a topic which has pretty much escaped psychoanalytic scrutiny in recent years. Abend is concerned with a genre of the transference cure quite different from what Freud described in 1913. Abend (1986b) explains:

> We mean that a powerful beneficial impact on the patient's psychological functioning comes about as a result of the unconscious significance of the relationship to the analyst in the mind of the patient. . . . for some patients, the unconscious meaning of being in analysis and of the relationship with the analyst produces meaningful alterations in certain compromise formations involved in their disturbed functioning, which in turn leads to clinical improvement. The presumption is that it is the significance of the relationship alone that is beneficial, and not an understanding of its meaning. . . . How do we determine that a patient's desire for analysis, and his functioning as an analysand, is undertaken or maintained primarily to obtain an unconsciously gratifying relationship rather than to gain an understanding of it and of himself? . . . Every workable analysis also comprises this dichotomy of aims, as Freud recognized, and the negotiation of their incongruities is an essential feature of the analysis of the transference.
>
> Either the *persistence of unusual resistance patterns* completely hides from the analyst's view important aspects of the transference,

> which can thus never be adequately addressed, or we are forced to a less than fully satisfactory, though possibly correct, quantitative explanation . . . [pp. 223–224, italics added].

I have extracted this intriguing fragment as an example of a clinical observation which concerns the course of a psychoanalytic endeavor and its relation to whether some kind of "unusual resistance" may be interfering with the progress of the analysis and with the analytic process. It is a situation which confronts us frequently and requires more detailed study.

Abrams (1987, 1989) has formulated what he designates as a "schematic model" of the psychoanalytic process. In that impressively sophisticated model, Abrams utilizes and blends developmental, psychopathological, structural, and therapeutic considerations. He divides the psychoanalytic process into four steps (which I can do little more than quickly mention here), each of which he organizes around its characteristic *resistances.* First is the step of "The Resistance of Character," which

> is met by a systematic group of interventions designed to demonstrate the limitations and disadvantages of the patient's positions and their unconscious determinants. When this first step is properly negotiated, there follows a disequilibrating transition which leads to the second stage of the process [Abrams, 1987, p. 447].

In the second step, labeled "Resistance of Transference Consolidation (The Transference Neurosis)," the

> abnormal character traits are regressively transformed back into the childhood components from which they arose and cluster about the immediacy of the analytic situation. This is very different from the first step. Initially, the patient approached the analytic situation in the same way in which he approaches all other tasks. With the transference consolidation, the patient treats the analyst and engages the treatment task in a way that reflects a very particular earlier view [p. 448].

Abrams refers to the third step as "Resistance of the Revived Past (The Infantile Neurosis)," in which the

> nuclear conflict of childhood is revived, recalled and reconstructed. The childhood issues are encountered directly. . . . Genetic interpretations and reconstructions help lead each patient to discover the events and experiences hitherto relegated to the unconscious or transformed into structured character-traits. The pathogens are affectively returned to their origins. . . . Having vividly revived the past, some patients threaten to settle there permanently. They may be further moved to do so, because dwelling on the past sustains the analytic relationship and wards off the expected autonomy that looms ahead [pp. 448–449].

The fourth step, "Post-Analytic Consolidation," comes about with the decision to end the analysis, which

> helps shatter the resistance of the revived past. A new disequilibrating transition appears. When the prospect of truly ending is finally acknowledged any or all of the earlier resistances may be revived. Despite their intensity and vigour [all] lack the degree of organization which characterized them at the height of their dominance. . . . The time needed for post-analytic consolidation varies in length; perhaps it never ends. After a successful analysis, the potential for new discoveries and fresh integrations remains [p. 449].

Abrams warns that his schema is not a "tidy model" which unfolds in "orderly steps." Nevertheless, the model does provide the analyst with a sense of direction and with a discussion of the *resistances* which have to be dealt with all along the course of treatment so that the process will not get bogged down at any of the critical points in that journey.

Dale Boesky's paper, "The Psychoanalytic Process and Its Components," contains some particularly rich contributions to the concept. I have already indicated his concerns and caveats regarding the "process"; here, I will focus on only one item from his treasure-trove of ideas on how certain aspects of resistance influence the course of the analysis. He stresses that

> transference and resistance remain the core of any definition of the psychoanalytic process. Furthermore, I am convinced that the transference as *resistance* in any specific case is unique and would never, and could never, have developed in the identical manner,

> form, or sequence with any other analyst. *In fact the manifest form of a resistance is even sometimes unconsciously negotiated by both patient and analyst.* I am suggesting here a type of adaptive or benign iatrogenic resistance. The analyst in such cases is almost always the first to recognize the presence of the resistance, as well as her or his own participation in it. I am not referring here to cases in which the analyst acknowledges some shortcoming or some lapse in objectivity. Instead, I have in mind complex and lengthy sequences of interaction which only gradually become evident to the analyst as a resistance in the patient and to which the analyst has in some more or less subtle way contributed by his or her own behavior. The phenomenon to which I refer seems to me to include countertransference but transcends that concept. . . . it is useful to view certain behaviors of the analyst, which actually join in the creation of a "useful" resistance, as a creative contribution which is necessary only for that analyst and would not be necessary for another analyst. I do not see how we can dispense with finding a better way to account for the sense of struggle that every analyst must go through in every analysis with every patient than is afforded by our present simple views of countertransference. If there can be no analysis without resistance by the patient, then it is equally true that there can be no treatment conducted by any analyst without counter-resistance or countertransference sooner or later [Boesky, 1990, pp. 572–573].

I have let Abend, Abrams, and Boesky pretty much speak for themselves in presenting three fresh ideas on the role played by resistances in the psychoanalytic process. These contributions also provide some new perspectives and potential insights into aspects of psychoanalytic theory and practice beyond the narrow limits of the psychoanalytic process. In closing, I once more borrow from Abend and state that it was

> not my intention to offer a *clarified* conception [of the psychoanalytic process], but to help to prepare the way for a more systematic effort to do so. Because the idea of a psychoanalytic process articulates with some of the most interesting and puzzling aspects of clinical theory—the mechanism of therapeutic action, the nature of resistances, working through, and the resolution of the transference, to name just a few—it remains a problem of compelling fascination [Abend, 1986b, p. 211, italics added].

It should be of considerable interest to contemplate the product of future investigations of the psychoanalytic process.

REFERENCES

Abend, S. M. (1986a), In COPE-PAP, May.

_______ (1986b), Some problems in the evaluation of the psychoanalytic process. In: *Psychoanalysis. The Science of Mental Conflict. Essays in Honor of Charles Brenner,* ed. A. D. Richards & M. S. Willick. Hillsdale, NJ: The Analytic Press, pp. 209–228.

Abrams, S. (1987), The psychoanalytic process: A schematic model. *Internat. J. Psycho-Anal.,* 68:441–452.

_______ (1989), Ambiguity in excess: An obstacle to common ground. *Internat. J. Psycho-Anal.,* 70:3–7

Boesky, D. (1990), The psychoanalytic process and its components. *Psychoanal. Quart.,* 59:550–584.

Calef, V. & Weinshel, E. M. (1980), The analyst as the conscience of the analysis. *Internat. Rev. Psycho-Anal.,* 7:279–990.

Compton, A. (1988), The idea of a psychoanalytic process. In: COPE-PAP, December.

Cooper, A. M. (1987), The transference neurosis: A concept ready for retirement. *Psychoanal. Inq.,* 7:569–585.

COPE-PAP. Reports to the Committee on Psychoanalytic Education—The Study Group on the Psychoanalytic Process, The Board on Professional Standards of the American Psychoanalytic Association.

Freud, S. (1912), The dynamics of transference. *Standard Edition,* 12.

_______ (1913), On beginning the treatment (Further recommendations on the technique of psycho-analysis I). *Standard Edition,* 12.

_______ (1914), Remembering, repeating and working-through (Further recommendations on the technique of psycho-analysis II). *Standard Edition,* 12.

Oxford English Dictionary (1978), Volume 8. Oxford: Clarendon Press.

Spruiell, V. (1989), Personal communication.

Stein, M. H. (1981), The unobjectionable part of the transference. *J. Amer. Psychoanal. Assn.,* 29:869–892.

Weinshel, E. M. (1984), Some observations on the psychoanalytic process. *Psychoanal. Quart.,* 53:63–92.

_______ (1988), Structural changes in psychoanalysis. *J. Amer. Psychoanal. Assn.,* Suppl., 36:263–280.

_______ (1990), How wide is the widening scope of psychoanalysis and how solid is its structural model? Some concerns and observations. *J. Amer. Psychoanal. Assn.,* 38:275–296.

_______ & Renik, O. (1992), Treatment goals in psychoanalysis. In: *The Technique and Practice of Psychoanalysis: A Memorial Volume to Ralph R. Greenson*, ed. A. Sugarman, R. A. Nemiroff & D. P. Greenson. Madison, CT: International Universities Press, pp. 91–99.

Willick, M. S. (1989), Similarities and differences between psychoanalysis and psychoanalytic psychotherapy. Presented to a Panel at the American Psychoanalytic Association, December 16.

Chapter 13

1990

How Wide Is the Widening Scope of Psychoanalysis and How Solid Is Its Structural Model?

Some Concerns and Observations

Gitelson (1963) suggested, and I concur, that "The time may be appropriate to propose a counsel of modesty for psychoanalysis" (p. 343). More recently, I heard a colleague assert—without apology or qualification—that "anything can be analyzed." I confess that I reacted to this allegation as much with envy as with surprise. If that claim is anywhere near accurate, Gitelson and I have been deceived and deceptive, and psychoanalysis has little need for humility. I submit that most of us know better, and that psychoanalytic work—exciting and challenging as it is—is also difficult and demanding. Certainly, one of the qualities it demands from its adherents is the willingness and the ability to accept its limitations.

In his Presidential address, Cooper (1984) observed that "Some time during the past decade or so, when none of us were paying much attention to it, we [the American Psychoanalysts] began to be grown up. As it happens with our children and our patients, we often do not notice the early signs of change and are surprised to discover that maturational landmarks have been achieved" (p. 246). Cooper suggests that one of the significant early evidences of this nascent maturity was the evolution of what started as a "raucous battle" over Heinz Kohut's new theories into a more constructive and even-handed dialogue. Cooper also pointed to the gradual cessation of the prolonged grieving over the death of Sigmund Freud which facilitated the capacity of psychoanalysts the world over to get out from under Freud's still charismatic "shadow" and to become increasingly independent in their psychoanalytic thinking.

I believe that Cooper's comments were most timely even though I would draw somewhat different conclusions from the maturity he observed. I agree that the debate over the Kohutian theories was a significant nodal point in the recent history of American psychoanalysis, but I would suggest that the early origins of the maturity of the American Psychoanalyst go back 35 years or more. Further, I have some concerns that perhaps we may have exaggerated—at least in its duration—the role played by the collective mourning over the loss of our founder in inhibiting our psychoanalytic creativity. That Freud's death has had a fateful impact on the development of our science goes without saying; but it is also likely that, as time went on, there may have been a tendency—as new troubles came up—to invoke that influence almost automatically rather than to explore other, less conspicuous possibilities.

As an alternative, the central thesis I propose is that in the past 35 years American psychoanalysis, at least that portion of it closely associated with the ego-psychological, structural model, has been engaged in a relatively unobtrusive campaign to bring psychoanalysis within a more realistic—more modest —frame of reference. I do not believe that this campaign was organized or planned; nor did it just happen. Its motivations were undoubtedly multiple and reflected disparate interests and varying concerns. Some issues, however, were of special significance.

Although Freud's 1937 "Analysis Terminable and Interminable" is remembered by many analysts primarily for the author's emphasis on the limitations of psychoanalytic therapy and its putative pessimistic tone, it is not altogether clear that all psychoanalysts really took Freud seriously. It is striking that almost any discussion of that epic contribution seems destined to include an at least brief detour on the role Freud's pessimism and personal problems and tragedies might have played in his formulation of that paper. This is not to question the propriety of considering these extraclinical factors in an in-depth critique of "Analysis Terminable and Interminable," but I cannot help but wonder whether the persistent juxtaposition of Freud's caveats regarding the therapeutic limitations of our science and his own psychological state at the time he composed the paper may not reflect a certain reluctance to accept the validity of those limitations.

I would suggest that in 1988, or even in 1963, a conspicuous therapeutic overoptimism must reflect not so much an idealization of Sigmund Freud, as an overidealization of psychoanalysis as a therapeutic instrument. We must keep in mind that despite his 1937 focus on the limitations of the psychoanalytic method, earlier in his career Freud was not averse—as seems not to be unique among those who engender and then introduce new psychotherapeutic approaches—to at least implying somewhat extravagant claims for his nubile offspring. Freud was not altogether unaware of this tendency. He somewhat sheepishly acknowledges, "I was mistaken . . . when the Wolf Man left me in the midsummer of 1914 . . . I believed that his *cure was radical and permanent*" (Freud, 1918, p. 121; 1937, pp. 217–218; italics added). I doubt whether many of us today would be comfortably convinced that the phrase "his *cure* was radical and permanent" could apply to any psychoanalytic treatment any more than we would accept Freud's 1913 statement that when the "intensity of the transference has been utilized for the overcoming of resistances. Only then has being ill become impossible, even when the transference has once more been dissolved, which is its destined end" (Freud, 1913, p. 143). In fact, we could take issue with three elements in that brief statement: we do not really "overcome" resistances; we do not really believe we can guarantee that being ill will be "impossible"; and we do not think that the transferences will be completely dissolved. So just as it took Freud a good deal of time to recognize that some of his early optimism about the therapeutic potential of psychoanalysis had been exaggerated, it took his followers a comparable amount of time to recognize that their own clinical results were not entirely in accord with their expectations. I have always been grateful to Gill (1954) for his pithy, pungent reminder that "there is no doubt that we can still recognize our friends and colleagues, even after they have been analyzed" (p. 787). While the intrapsychic contributions to such unrealistic expectations will always be present, the external pressures in this direction appear to be considerably diminished.

For American psychoanalysts therapeutic overoptimism derives not only from our personal inclinations and temptations or from the precedents established by Freud and other psychoanalytic pioneers. It is not unlikely that we are still enmeshed in what Gitelson referred to as the "belated reckoning" for the too easy time American psychoanalysis had in ensconcing itself in the American scientific and intellectual communities. Between 1956 and 1964 Gitelson presented three incisive and provocative essays on the social, scientific, and organizational aspects of the American Psychoanalytic Association which are as pertinent, vigorous, and disconcerting today as they were when he presented them (Gitelson, 1956, 1963, 1964). They all deserve reading, rereading, and careful contemplation.

Gitelson noted that the psychoanalytic pioneers in our country did not have to face the same uphill struggle for social and scientific recognition that confronted their European colleagues. He argued that this relatively rapid acceptance and premature popularity of psychoanalysis was facilitated by massive support from a large segment of the then powerful mental hygiene movement and from a significant sector of those within the "neuropsychiatric" profession who wished "to escape from its neurological sterility and its institutional thralldom and to establish for *itself* a scientific foundation as an effective therapeutic specialty" (Gitelson, 1973, p. 393; italics added). In addition, two adventitious factors served the emergence of the unwarranted expectations of the fledgling American psychoanalytic movement. One was the forced emigration of large numbers of experienced and prestigious psychoanalysts from Hitlerian Europe who brought with them a "prefabricated" and relatively stabilized body of psychoanalytic knowledge and understanding "whose basic theories had been formulated and were being examined and extended" (p. 393). The active presence of this influential cadre of analytic practitioners and theoreticians provided a shortcut for the development of American psychoanalysis and psychoanalysts and reduced significantly the more usual painfully laborious and frequently chaotic evolution of new psychoanalytic centers.

The second adventitious factor was the dramatic—and eminently useful—role psychoanalysis played in military psychiatry during World War II. Using "only the rudiments of psychoanalytic theory" (p. 407), psychiatrists and only partially trained medical officers

> were able to improvise psychotherapeutic measures that were effective and seemed to offer a rationale that was impressive and promising. All of this led, Gitelson argued, to the striking upsurge of interest in psychoanalysis after World War II and to an even closer alliance between psychiatry and psychoanalysis. . . . However, it also led to an enhancement of the already 'overoptimistic burgeoning' of unrealistic expectations of what psychoanalysis and psychoanalysts might provide and produce [Weinshel, 1983, pp. 79–80].

All of this contributed to a tremendous popularity and an image of psychoanalysis that was grossly inflated and almost embarrassingly extravagant. The trouble was that many of the psychoanalysts themselves, as well as conspicuous segments of the general public, fell in love with that image. When the inevitable disillusionment set in, the analysts were often unprepared for the not always friendly criticisms from their erstwhile enthusiastic supporters.

The more recent history of the erosion of that inflated image is well known and is not the focus of this presentation. Suffice it that it hastened the self-examination and more realistic self-appraisal which were certainly late in coming and are probably far from complete. As I suggested earlier, the gradual movement toward a more modest conceptualization of the potential of psychoanalysis does not appear to have sprung from a single source or been instigated by a single individual or group, or derived from any single theoretical point of view. As a result, its history is far from clear. On the other hand, the products of these activities are both unequivocal and impressive. Let me enumerate some of the changes that have taken place, mostly without fanfare, in psychoanalytic theory and practice in the last 35 years. I believe that the items on this—by no means complete—list will indicate the extent to which our claims have become increasingly realistic and significantly more in harmony with our clinical observations. I have already alluded to a few of these shifts, and all of them are more or less commonplace.

1. We rarely speak any more of psychoanalytic "cures." We are much more likely to focus on changes, shifts, or compromise formations.
2. We do not, as a rule, talk about eliminating psychological conflict, and we pretty much accept the presence of conflict as one of the givens of being alive. We do hope that the analysis will result in a more favorable resolution of the central conflicts that existed prior to treatment: and I have always been intrigued with Joan Fleming's emphasis on the opportunity afforded for a "re-solution" of the old psychological conflicts in the relatively more favorable conditions of a more mature ego apparatus operating within a psychoanalytic situation.
3. We do not think about analyses being complete or finished. We can conceptualize a psychoanalysis as a dialectic process which, in a sense, could be endless but yet is not necessarily interminable. We recognize that an analysis can be terminated successfully even though more analytic work *could* be carried out.
4. We no longer insist that the transferences be *completely* resolved, i.e., analyzed. We realize that, if an effective psychoanalytic process has been established, it is unlikely that such an outcome is possible or necessarily desirable.
5. We no longer think about "overcoming" resistances. We try rather to analyze them and to learn more about their source, their structure, and the specific unpleasurable affect to which they respond. We anticipate that a product of this analytic work will provide a greater access to the unconscious derivatives associated with these resistances.

6. We do not seem to hear so much about parameters. I suspect that one reason is that we are less likely to feel that a particular intervention is *the* only correct one in a given situation and that technical errors on the part of the analyst are inevitable. With greater interest in and emphasis on the psychoanalytic process, we assume that we shall have opportunities throughout the analysis to deal with these difficulties in the ongoing analytic work.

7. Insight is still a highly valued desideratum. We aim and we look for it in our analytic work; but I do not believe that it is still considered to be the *sine qua non* for a successful psychoanalysis. The word "insight" carries with it connotations of something a bit mysterious and a bit static rather than something active and ongoing. This is why I suggested that one of the permanent products of and an indication of a successful analysis is "the operation of a more effective and objective capacity for self-observation" (Weinshel, 1984, p. 82 [this volume, p. 281]). I believe that Robert Gardner's (1983) phrase "self-inquiry" even better captures the sense of what we tend to describe—incorrectly—as "self-analysis." In some ways, the same can be said of the place of the recovery of repressed infantile memories in our analytic work. Although we are still very much (and in some ways more) concerned with relations between the present and the past and with an adequate understanding of the past, especially as it relates to the present and to current conflicts, the retrieval of old memories *per se* is no longer our principal goal.

8. The analysis of dreams is no longer "the royal road to a knowledge of the unconscious activities of the mind" (Blum, 1976, p. 316; Weinshel, 1987, pp. 184–186; Arlow and Brenner, 1988, p. 8). It is my impression that most analysts no longer carry out in a routine fashion a formal analysis of each and every element of the manifest dream content. These assertions are not to be construed as meaning that dream analysis is no longer a significant tool in the analyst's technical repertoire—far from it, but the analysis of transference and resistance, of fantasies and a variety of other psychological products has become of comparable significance in our search for the derivatives of the unconscious elements of behavior. One aspect of this shift, one which deserves more attention than it can muster here, is the gradual clarification of what Freud conceptualized as the dynamic unconscious in distinction to the so-called descriptive unconscious. For clinical purposes the dynamic unconscious is closely tied to repression and resistance and is, therefore, part and parcel of our daily work with patients. In this work, the analysis of transference and resistance is as effective as the analysis of dreams.

9. In 1984, I made an explicit plea for a more modest approach to our analytic work under the heading of "The Pitfalls of Perfectibilism and the Elevation of the Not-So-Good Hour." In that mini-sermon I argued that what E. Kris (1956) described as "the good analytic hour" had become distorted with an undue emphasis on content, dramatic changes, and "an aura of the epiphany." I suggested

> that we should not permit ourselves to believe that it is those sessions which become the goal of our daily endeavor or to confuse the product of that endeavor with the endeavor itself. I would submit that the *really* good hour is the one in which, at the time or in retrospect, we are able to detect some dent in the resistance configuration. . . . What I have in mind by "The Elevation of the Not-So-Good Hour" is an increased recognition of and attention to the less glamorous and exciting exchanges that take place daily at the interface of the analyst–analysand interaction, the more prosaic and "quiet" elements of that interaction, and how the analyst and his interventions assist the patient's analytic efforts— instead of so much attention to those 'frames' in the analytic work which feature the analyst in a starring role [pp. 89–90] [this volume, pp. 287–288].

I believe that such a position is not only technically wise, but is a very practical application of the counsel of modesty.

10. I very much agree with the statement enunciated by Boesky (1988) that: "One of the major trends in the refinement of the theory of technique in modern psychoanalysis has been the increased awareness of the importance of the participation of the analyst in the psychoanalytic process . . . Freud's image of the passive mirror has been relinquished" (p. 303). For a *clinical* demonstration of that important development, I would refer you to Spruiell's (1984) "The Analyst at Work." This shift is well known and well documented both by our experience and in our literature. Here, I stress again how much this current position differs from the one reflected in much of Freud's earlier writing (e.g., Freud, 1919, p. 161).

I'm quite sure that I have by no means exhausted the list of changes that have taken place in psychoanalytic theory and practice, which point to a less imposing conceptualization of what we should expect from psychoanalysis; nor have I included the many alterations in theory and practice not directly related to my main focus. By no means do I anticipate that all will find congenial the ten items I have presented as if they were universally accepted articles of faith. On the contrary, I would expect a good deal of disagreement with a good deal of what I have proposed. Nevertheless, I hope that at least I have persuaded you that American ego-psychological psychoanalytic theory and practice derived in considerable part from Freud's structural theory *has* changed, reflecting a more realistic assessment of psychoanalysis, an assessment more closely related to clinical experience and observation.

Of necessity my presentation has been skewed: in my concern for conveying the necessity for modesty, it is crucial that I not overemphasize the limitations of the structural theory at the expense of its many assets and strengths. In a discussion of my 1984 remarks on what Goodman (1983) called "the fantasy and fallacy of perfectionism as it is at least implicitly expressed in some conceptualizations of the analytic process," he pointed out "that the psychoanalytic process . . . is in fact a tremendously powerful instrument which, as it doesn't require perfection to be legitimized, allows us to work with greater confidence and less apology toward actually attainable objectives that are often enough confirmable as having profound personal value."

It is not clear how many American psychoanalysts still adhere to this so-called "traditional" model of psychoanalysis, I would surmise that the number is not an insignificant one, although I am less sure of the extent to which those who differ with this approach have rejected it in its entirety as compared to those who have retained the bulk of its theoretical-clinical corpus and whose differences reside in specific areas and degrees of emphasis.

Wallerstein (1988) acknowledges what had been a generally known, but hitherto essentially ineffable, fact of psychoanalytic organizational life, that not all psychoanalysts throughout the world share the identical theoretical perspectives, that, on the contrary, there is increasing diversity and "pluralism" in different areas and even within the same geographical area. He suggests that "what unites us is our shared focus on the clinical interactions in our consulting rooms" (p. 19). It is no longer possible to argue with the actualities of this diversity. The main thrust of the 1989 International Psychoanalytical Congress in Rome will be to demonstrate that which unites us: "The Common Grounds in Psychoanalysis: Clinical Aims and Process." In an article on "The Future of Psychoanalysis" Arlow and Brenner (1988) recognize the diversity within the American Psychoanalytic Association and raise some cogent concerns about the extent to which "the differences among all these theories, so apparent to every observer, may stem from the fact that the data of observation are not, in truth, the same. In fact, they are often very different. Perhaps all analysts *do not use the same technique,* even though all call the technique they use by the same name" (p. 9; italics added). Obviously this and comparable questions remain thorny issues which will require careful scrutiny.

No matter how neutral and how objective one struggles to be in this matter of "pluralism," it is inordinately difficult not to at least speculate as to which point of view may be superior: has the greatest explanatory power, the greatest degree of internal coherence, and the most convincing demonstration of correlating theoretical exposition with actual clinical data. It is hard to reject cavalierly Charles Hanly's assertion that "Multiple perspectives *per se* are not necessarily an advantage" (Shengold and McLaughlin, 1976, p. 271).

Sandler (1988) presents a relatively severe critique of the structural theory—as put forth by Boesky (1988). Sandler (1988) concludes with the somewhat startling assertion that "We may have to allow ourselves to become aware of the fact that Freud's structural theory has an important place in the *development* of psychoanalysis, but like all theories its limitations become apparent, and the examination of such limitations is an essential part of the healthy development of our theory" (p. 344; italics added).

It is neither possible nor desirable to take issue with the necessity of reexamining not just the limitations of any theory but *all* of its aspects. However, the implication that the structural theory is important currently only in a historical sense is considerably less palatable, particularly in the context of Sandler's specific criticisms which are the basis of his consigning the structural theory to "an important place in the development of psychoanalysis." Sandler alleges five "limitations" in the structural theory to justify his evaluation: (1) "The deficiencies in classical technique" which interfered with our understanding of "disturbed feelings about the self within the self–object relationship" and which led to the emergence of "the Kohutian view"; (2) our limitations in dealing with "the effects of the so-called deficit in structural development"; (3) "the tendency to equate conflict with oedipal conflict"; (4) our tendency to "view our patients' conflicts as being essentially between drives and ego; and (5) our failure to recognize that the "unconscious conflictual wishes of our patients are not always instinctual ones" (p. 343).

All of these allegations involve complex and still debatable issues. Each contains a grain of truth, but much of that truth is more applicable to the past than to the present. My response to these criticisms is designed to clarify possible misunderstandings of *current* structural theory rather than to establish its correctness.

There has been considerable controversy between the "traditional" psychoanalysts and the followers of Kohut, but I doubt that those differences center primarily on the theories of the self. It is also correct that it has not been particularly easy to incorporate the concept of the self into the structural theory. Nevertheless, it was Hartmann (1950) who first suggested the distinctions between the "self" and the "ego." As the evolving modern structural theory gradually abandoned the "notion of viewing any clinical phenomenon or specific mental function as the sole domain of just one of the three major systems," it was possible to demonstrate that the structural model could deal adequately with "experiential phenomena, for the self, or for object relationships" (Boesky, 1988, p. 305).

There have also been significant differences of opinion regarding the appropriate technical approach to dealing with the "effects of so-called deficit in structural development"; but here I would *assume* that the stance of a majority of structural theory psychoanalysts is closer to Sandler than to Kohut. The former declares, "I would only add that conflict occurs in *all* our patients and can be interpreted, even if they have substantial deficit pathology." The differences between the structural theory approach and that advocated in some of the other orientations focus on the relative emphasis on the use of interpretive versus noninterpretive interventions in the treatment of such individuals.

To equate all conflict with "oedipal conflict" would be unfortunate, but such a tendency is hardly conspicuous at this time. Certainly there has been an increasing interest in preoedipal conflict. If that interest also involves controversy, I would suggest that it concerns the inclination to dichotomize the preoedipal and oedipal conflicts and issues as if the two were totally independent rather than interrelated and interactive. Also there are many analysts (and this includes me) who would agree with Abrams (1974) that

> There has always been one group of disorders . . . that has been of central interest to analysts: disorders of the oedipal phase. During this phase, normal development is further propelled by a nuclear intrapsychic conflict. The resolution of that conflict helps to establish the fundamental framework of the mental apparatus with its

tripartite organization. The disorders that are linked to the oedipal period are of interest to psychoanalysts because they *are especially amenable to psychoanalytic treatment*" [pp. 445–450; italics added].

Sandler (1988), borrowing a phrase Boesky (1988) uses, declares that the "standard formulation of structural conflicts does at times appear to be 'simplistic, reductive, and misleading.' We can no longer view our patients' conflicts as being essentially between drives and ego." I do not believe that Sandler's version of the current structural theory of conflict is either accurate or up to date.

Brenner's (1982) elaboration of the concept of "compromise formation" has become a crucial linchpin in the structural theory. Briefly, it posits that the outcome of any psychological conflict is the product of the interaction of a hypothetically infinite series of components; and even the simplest of such conflicts involves considerably more than just the drives and the ego. We would anticipate complex contributions from various drive derivatives, a variety of affects, a whole panel of resistances, the superego and the unconscious need for punishment, the whole panoply of ego functions that mediate reality testing, and the intrapsychic regulatory agencies such as the synthetic and integrative activities. Rangell (1989) describes higher-level ego functions such as unconscious ego choices and decisions, will, accountability, and responsibility, among others. These elaborations of our theory not only suggest possible avenues for refining our clinical understanding; they also reflect the extent to which the concept of psychological conflict as developed within the structural theory is a highly complex and sophisticated enterprise about which a great deal is still unknown and which certainly cannot be viewed as a "simplistic, reductive, and misleading" confrontation of the drives with the ego.

I heartily endorse Sandler's reminder that unconscious conflictual wishes of our patients are not *always* instinctual ones. The examples he provides of the latter genre are useful and thought-provoking. This is an area which has been largely neglected by psychoanalysts; but this neglect is by no means a structural theory phenomenon. Ironically, some of the seminal work on this topic was done in the United States in the 1950's and '60's.

Hartmann spoke about a special group of ego tendencies, the *ego interests,* and attributed Freud's old concept of the "self-preservative tendencies of the ego instincts" to the ego. The ego interests involve a disparate collection of behavior patterns including striving for what is "useful," egoism, the seeking for wealth and social prestige, the search for power and intellectual attainment. Hartmann (1950) described these tendencies as "interests of the ego; their goals are set by the ego, in contradistinction to the aims of the id or of the superego" (pp. 135–150; see also Weinshel, 1970, pp. 708–711 [this volume, pp. 179–183]). It is not clear what happened to these nascent and somewhat indefinite lines of thought, although there is much to suggest a resemblance to some of the directions taken by Kohut and the self psychologists.

Some of Rapaport's work comes closer to what Sandler raised regarding a noninstinctual source of psychological conflicts. He was quite concerned about the overemphasis on the explanatory potency of the instinctual drives and "the corresponding underemphasis on the explanatory potency and study of the other determiners of behavior" (Rapaport, 1960, p. 177). He stressed that a "psychoanalytic theory of motivation must distinguish between instinctual drive motivations [and conflicts], motivations derived from and dependent on instinctual drive motivations, and motivations autonomous from instinctual drive motivations whether they are derived from instinctual drives or are of a different origin" (p. 174).

Rapaport's statements support the suspicion that these are issues to which we have not given sufficient attention, but they also hint at the difficulty in making clear-cut distinctions between the three groups of motivations (and potential conflicts) outlined by Rapaport. It is, of course, less of a difficulty if one discards completely the instinctual drives, but neither Sandler nor the structural theory analysts do so. The concept of drive derivatives already reflects a certain "taming" of the instinctual drive and implies a compromise between the peremptory quality of the drive and the control exerted by the ego, and permits the introduction of such useful concepts as the autonomy of the ego, the conflict-free sphere, the change of function, and developmental transformations. The concept of the *relative* autonomy of the ego (and that autonomy is *always* relative!) entails that any clinically observable, ostensibly noninstinctualized structure may be the subject of a regressive reinstinctualization. These by no means unusual clinical phenomena make it difficult to claim that a given conflict is incontrovertibly *not* an instinctual one. An error in the assessment of the clinical data in *either* direction could (to use Sandler's phrase) "have a distorting effect on our understanding and distortion of our patients' material" (see also Sandler, 1974, and Abrams, 1974).

I submit that clinical analysis is never altogether clear and simple, that certainty in clinical formulations can be chimerical and often be foolhardy, and that the structural theory does provide us with serviceable—if not foolproof—tools to investigate thorny clinical issues. While those tools may not provide immediate solutions for those problems, it does at least discourage us from leaping to premature conclusions. The structural theory's stress on conflict and compromise formation *virtually* guarantees an emphasis on multidetermination and a premium on searching for the unexpected.

It is difficult to pass judgment on the degree to which the structural theory has facilitated or obstructed the widening scope of indications for psychoanalysis; even among its adherents there are differences of opinion. Some like Anna Freud have felt that we have proceeded too quickly and too far; others have argued that we have lagged behind what was and is possible. Whether or not we agree with Gray's (1982) inclination to see these lags as a consequence of a "general resistance" (and there is much that is convincing in his premise) or whether the application of some of the new or modified concepts is just difficult, it has often taken us an inordinately long time to integrate them. I was surprised to see how much and in how many different ways our discipline had changed—until I prepared to write this paper.

These modifications are impressive even though "we are still able to recognize our psychoanalysis" even after we have subjected it to a fairly extensive review. One of the greatest pressures on the structural theory has been to provide more effective techniques in treating the sicker patients in our clientele, the so-called borderline and narcissistic personality disorders. It has been said repeatedly, but maybe not often enough, that there is no *one* psychoanalytic technique. What we do have is a powerful—albeit imperfect—theory of psychoanalysis which possesses the potential for myriad applications, many of which we have not even thought of. The application to which we have invested our major effort and energy is the therapeutic. If we do harbor the ambition of making psychoanalysis a "general psychology," and if we are to claim therapeutic as well as academic relevance for our theory, we have the responsibility to examine the ways in which our theory and our overall clinical experience can be employed as therapeutic agents in the treatment of our severely ill patients; this includes a clarification of the limitation of such applications as well as their possible extension.

I do not know what the *overall* experience of the "traditional" psychoanalyst has been in working with severely disturbed patients, and it is not clear what their overall response to those experiences has been. My own impression is that their stance is a somewhat "conservative" but not a necessarily negative one (see Abend et al., 1983, pp. 200–203, for a helpful discussion of this issue). I say "impression" because accurate statistics are hard to come by. I think that most analysts have undertaken the analysis of the more disturbed patients utilizing what they consider to be the so-called "classical" technique, sometimes with minor or not so minor variations, and with varying degrees of success and satisfaction. I suggest that more is "going on" in this area than we may be aware of. There may be a considerable "lag" in our overall ability to absorb, to integrate, and to apply appropriately the ideas and suggestions that have emerged in recent years. I shall mention just a few such contributions primarily as *indicators* of the various sources from which it may be possible to gather clues and cues which may help us to better understand severe pathology and sicker patients.

1. I have found the work of Hanly (1982) and Shengold (1985, 1988) on the vicissitudes of anality to be an effective bridge between the less and the more sick patients. The anal phase of development is a period in which we see crucial struggles involving primitive instinctual derivatives, intense primal affects, and still fragile control and defense structures. Further, there is a watershed or Januslike quality to many elements of those anal-phase struggles wherein some of those elements appear fixed to or pulled to the archaic and primitive, while others appear to be moving or even driving toward greater growth and individuation.

2. In their book, *Borderline Patients: Psychoanalytic Perspectives,* Abend, Porder, and Willick describe a clinical research project in which a number of borderline patients were analyzed and the results of those analyses were carefully and comprehensively studied. The conclusions are both modest and impressive. The authors claim only that a certain number of sicker patients could be analyzed successfully utilizing the "conventional analytic skills and an understanding of familiar analytic concepts" (Abend et al., 1983, p. 243). We need more studies like this one.

3. Kris's (1985) contributions on "convergent and divergent" conflict not only expand the theoretical scope of conflict, but also provide a potential for dealing with resistances which otherwise might not be available for analytic scrutiny.

4. Stein's (1981) "The Unobjectionable Part of the Transference" is another contribution that calls our attention to the problems of dealing with subtle and ostensibly innocuous resistances; and Willick's "On the Concept of Primitive Defenses" (1983) is a sage essay which warns that

the so-called "primitive" defenses used by the infant and child are not necessarily the same as those described in the borderline and psychotic. Willick offers suggestions regarding the evaluation of the ostensibly sicker patient.

I trust that these brief samples of the work of colleagues provide examples of the kind of ideas that can provide accretions to and stimuli for widening the scope of analysis. That my samples are not strikingly sensational and are admittedly "accretions" rather than "breakthroughs" may indicate that I am thinking more in the direction of deepening rather than widening; I hope that both will take place. I also have a personal "hope chest" which contains a "shopping list" of what I want from the structural theory in the near future. These are some of the problems I would like to see resolved:

1. I would like us to be able to know more about the psychoanalytic aspects of character, its development, and its relation to other aspects of the psyche and to conflict.
2. I would like us to further clarify the synthetic rather than the antithetical relations of the pregenital and the oedipal contributions to both development and conflict.
3. I would like us to eliminate the futile debate as to the primacy of conflict versus deficit in psychogenesis and to learn more about how both factors influence illness and can be dealt with in analytic therapy.
4. I would like us to know more about the development of higher-level structures and functions and their relation to the more primitive ones.
5. I would like us to learn more about many of the nuances of resistances and their relations to the other aspects of the psychic apparatus, and I would like us to know more about the analysis of resistances, especially what we blithely call the "systematic" analysis of resistances.
6. I would like us to be better able to avoid the pitfalls of tyrannization by "diagnoses." I would submit that psychoanalytic diagnosis is a necessary evil; but it can also lead to thinking about and even "treating" a diagnosis rather than an individual human being.
7. I would like us to handle more effectively all of the issues around the differences between psychoanalysis and psychoanalytic psychotherapy and the vexing questions about what to do about the latter. I suggest that we have managed to avoid facing some of the more troubling aspects of these issues and that one reason for this avoidance is that we are not unequivocally clear about what those differences really are. I would like

us to illuminate and to explicate those differences on scientific rather than political or socioeconomic bases.

8. I suspect that a principal clue to resolving the psychoanalysis/psychotherapy dilemma may be in differences in the nature of the therapeutic process of each; so I would like us to know more about the nature of the *psychoanalytic* process. A good deal has been said about the psychoanalytic process in recent years, but nothing like a consensus about its meaning has been achieved.

My "shopping list" is hardly a modest one; nevertheless I believe it is realizable. I believe I have been clear in my conviction that the structural theory is sound and strong, even with its imperfections and limitations. I am equally convinced that its scope—both in its width and its depth—can be increased, albeit gradually and prudently.

REFERENCES

Abend, S., Porder, M. & Willick, M. (1983), *Borderline Patients: Psychoanalytic Perspectives*. New York: International Universities Press.

Abrams, S. (1974), A discussion of the paper by Joseph Sandler on "Psychological conflict and the structural model: Some clinical and theoretical implications." *Internat. J. Psycho-Anal.*, 55:63–66.

_______ (1987), The psychoanalytic process: A schematic model. *Internat. J. Psycho-Anal.*, 58:441–452.

Arlow, J. A. & Brenner, C. (1988), The future of psychoanalysis. *Psychoanal. Quart.*, 57:1–13.

Blum, H. P. (1976), The changing use of dreams: Dreams and free associations. *Internat. J. Psycho-Anal.*, 57:315–324.

Boesky, D. (1988), Comments on the structural theory of technique. *Internat. J. Psycho-Anal.*, 69:303–316.

Brenner, C. (1982), Compromise formation. In: *The Mind in Conflict*. New York: International Universities Press, pp. 109–119.

Calef, V. & Weinshel, E. (1980), The analyst as the conscience of the analysis. *Internat. Rev. Psycho-Anal.*, 7:279–290.

Cooper, A. (1984), Psychoanalysis at one hundred: Beginnings of maturity. *J. Amer. Psychoanal. Assn.*, 32:245–267.

Freud, S. (1913), On beginning the treatment (further recommendations on the technique of psycho-analysis, I). *Standard Edition*, 12.

_______ (1918), From the history of an infantile neurosis. *Standard Edition*, 17.

_______ (1919), Lines of advance in psychoanalytic therapy. *Standard Edition*, 17.

_______ (1937), Analysis terminable and interminable. *Standard Edition,* 23.
Gardner, R. (1983), *Self Inquiry.* Boston: Atlantic Monthly Press/Little, Brown.
Gill, M. M. (1954), Psychoanalysis and exploratory psychotherapy. *J. Amer. Psychoanal. Assn.,* 2:771–797.
Gitelson, M. (1956), Psychoanalysis USA. In: Gitelson (1973), pp. 239–253.
_______ (1963), On the present scientific and social position of psychoanalysis. In: Gitelson (1973), pp. 342–359.
_______ (1964), On the identity crisis in American psychoanalysis. In: Gitelson (1973), pp. 383–416.
_______ (1973), *Psychoanalysis: Science and Profession.* New York: International Universities Press.
Goodman, S. (1983), Discussion of "Some observations on the psychoanalytic process" by Edward M. Weinshel. Presented to the San Francisco Psychoanalytic Society, September 17, 1983.
Gray, P. (1982), The "developmental lag" in the evolution of technique for psychoanalysis of neurotic conflict. *J. Amer. Psychoanal. Assn.,* 30:621–655.
Hanly, C. (1975), In: Shengold and McLaughlin (1976), p. 271.
_______ (1982), Narcissism, defense, and the positive transference. *Internat. J. Psycho-Anal.,* 63:427–444.
Hartmann, H. (1950), Comments on the psychoanalytic theory of the ego. In: *Essays on Ego Psychology.* New York: International Universities Press, 1964, pp. 113–141.
Kris, A. (1985), Resistances in convergent and divergent conflicts. *Psychoanal. Quart.,* 54:537–568.
Kris, E. (1956), On some vicissitudes of insight in psychoanalysis. In: *Selected Papers of Ernst Kris.* New Haven: Yale University Press, 1975, pp. 252–271.
Rangell, L. (1989), Action theory within the structural view. *Internat. J. Psycho-Anal.,* 70:189–203.
Rapaport, D. (1960), On the psychoanalytic theory of motivation. In: *Nebraska Symposium on Motivation,* ed. M. R. Jones. Lincoln: University of Nebraska Press.
Sandler, J. (1974), Psychoanalysis and the structural model: Some clinical and theoretical implications. *Internat. J. Psycho-Anal.,* 55:53–62.
_______ (1988), Psychoanalytic technique and "Analysis terminable and interminable." *Internat. J. Psycho-Anal.,* 69:335–345.
Shengold, L. (1985), Defensive anality and anal narcissism. *Internat. J. Psycho-Anal.,* 66:47–73.
_______ (1988), *Halo in the Sky: Observations on Anality and Defense.* New York: Guilford Press.
_______ & McLaughlin, J. (1976), Plenary session on changes in psychoanalytic practise and experience: Theoretical, technical, and social implications. *Internat. J. Psycho-Anal.,* 57:261–274.
Spruiell, V. (1984), The analyst at work. *Internat. J. Psycho-Anal.,* 65:13–30.

Stein, M. H. (1981), The unobjectionable part of the transference. *J. Amer. Psychoanal. Assn.*, 29:869–892.

Wallerstein, R. (1988), One psychoanalysis or many? *Internat. J. Psycho-Anal.*, 69:5–21.

Weinshel, E. (1970), The ego in health and normality. *J. Amer. Psychoanal. Assn.*, 18:682–735.

_______ (1983), Message from a past president—Maxwell Gitelson, M.D. In: *The Identity of the Psychoanalyst*, ed. E. Joseph & D. Widlocher. New York: International Universities Press, pp. 67–84.

_______ (1984), Some observations on the psychoanalytic process. *Psychoanal. Quart.*, 53:63–92.

_______ (1987), A discussion of various contributions. In: *Interpretations of Dreams in Clinical Work*, ed. A. Rothstein. Madison, CT: International Universities Press, pp. 181–188.

Willick, M. (1983), On the concept of primitive defenses. *J. Amer. Psychoanal. Assn.*, 23(Suppl.):175–200.

Chapter 14

1992

Therapeutic Technique in Psychoanalysis and Psychoanalytic Psychotherapy

Many years ago, when I was an advanced candidate, I would have been quite comfortable and even certain about the similarities and differences in technique between psychoanalytic psychotherapy and psychoanalysis. Those were the golden days of psychoanalysis in the United States, and I was convinced that once I achieved enough knowledge and experience to do "the right thing," I would have no trouble in distinguishing the two modalities, applying them appropriately, or in being clear about the impact my therapeutic interventions might have on my patients, analytic or psychotherapeutic. My own analytic training began in the wake of the exciting 1954 "debates" on this subject involving Gill (1954), Rangell (1954), and Stone (1954) as well as the related contributions of Bibring (1954) and Anna Freud (1954); and although I recognized that there was some sort of spectrum between pure psychoanalysis and a somewhat less admirable psychoanalytic psychotherapy, I was reasonably confident that in good time any problems related to those distinctions would yield to the burgeoning development of my psychoanalytic skills.

Today my certainty is limited to the recognition that those distinctions are not as clear or unequivocal as many of us once believed. After many years of clinical practice, one realizes that there is a considerable gap between what one has learned in psychoanalytic school and from psychoanalytic books and what one encounters in one's consulting room. The living patient is much more complex and distinctive than can be portrayed in even the most authentic and vivid written reports, and the actual assessment of a prospective analysand is far more perplexing and unpredictable than what had been reflected in discussions on analyzability. It was surprising that in conducting a psychoanalysis or in doing psychotherapy, we would utilize ostensibly similar technical tools and speak of ostensibly comparable concepts in ostensibly identical terms. It has become increasingly evident, however, that those tools and concepts and terms do not have the same meaning and significance for all of the people who have been using them. Nevertheless it was disconcerting trying to understand how and why a patient would emerge from a twice-a-week psychotherapy with results and changes that *appeared* to approximate our goals for a satisfactory psychoanalysis, whereas the changes we observed in a comparable patient at the end of a long and seemingly productive ongoing psychoanalytic experience might be considerably less impressive. It seems foolhardy to draw even tentative conclusions from such comparisons; and many variables can help explain those, at least apparent, enigmas. Yet such "paradoxical" findings do raise questions about the differences in the therapeutic techniques utilized, and the therapeutic process engendered by psychoanalysis and psychoanalytic psychotherapy.

Psychoanalysis in the United States has changed a great deal in the past 35 years; among those alterations, two are particularly germane to the present topic. There has been a striking shift from a relatively homogeneous adherence to the ego-psychological structural model of psychoanalysis to other analytic models and schools of thought. Among the consequences of this heterogeneity are new conceptualizations of psychic structure, psychopathology, and the nature of psychoanalytic therapy; and these alterations, in turn, have led to a broadened base of indications for psychoanalytic treatment. As a result, many cases which formerly had not been considered suitable for psychoanalysis have been appearing more and more frequently on psychoanalysts' couches. This tendency, marked by attendant confusion, became more conspicuous as analysts who no longer limited themselves to the more traditional analytic positions undertook the treatment of more disturbed patients, such as those with so-called borderline or narcissistic personalities. While the term "psychoanalytic psychotherapy" did not emerge in relation to this genre of patients, its utilization did become much more prominent in the discussions of the treatment of borderline and narcissistic patients; and at times it was not clear whether the treatment was considered to be psychoanalysis proper or psychoanalytic psychotherapy. On the other hand, that comparable cases were being treated in "analysis" called even more attention to some of the confusion and ambiguity about these two modalities of therapy.

The second significant change in American psychoanalysis I summarized in my proposal "that in the past 35 years, American psychoanalysis

. . . has been engaged in a relatively unobtrusive campaign to bring psychoanalysis within a more realistic—more modest—frame of reference" (Weinshel, 1990, p. 277 [this volume, p. 311]). I view this "modesty" as a corrective to the unrealistic goals and expectations that characterized the early history of psychoanalysis in the United States and was reflected in the gradual shifts in our attitudes and practices. Instead of talking about analytic cures, we are now more likely to talk about changes or new compromise formations; instead of "eliminating" psychological conflict, we are more content with its modification; we no longer expect analyses to be complete or all of the transferences to be completely resolved; we do not feel we can "overcome" resistances, and think rather of analyzing them; we no longer see "insight" as the *sine qua non* of analysis, and focus more on a heightened capacity for self-inquiry or self-observation; the dream is no longer *the* royal road "to a knowledge of the unconscious activities of the mind," and the retrieval of repressed memories *per se* is neither an absolute guarantee of a successful analysis nor even its principal objective.

Some of these changes and the gradual movement of the therapeutic goals and objectives of American psychoanalysis in a more realistic direction are the consequence of clinical experience and the observation that the degree of congruence between our expectations and our results was often less than anticipated. Also, as analysts became more conversant with and more sophisticated in the intricacies of the ego-psychological structural model, there was increasing appreciation of the multiple factors that contributed to psychological conflicts and the protean outcomes of those conflicts. Simultaneously, we became more aware that all of these outcomes represented "compromise formations" rather than either-or, all-or-none solutions (see Boesky, 1988; Brenner, 1982). These relativistic qualities also applied to the psychoanalysis itself, and it became more evident that what took place in the course of a given well-conducted analysis was not free of interventions and maneuvers which were usually considered to be psychotherapeutic rather than purely psychoanalytic. Further, it turned out that there was not necessarily a one-to-one connection between such "parameters" and the way the analytic work proceeded and progressed. As we hesitatingly surrendered our illusions of the perfect analysis, we also relinquished the fantasy of a crystal-clear differentiation of psychoanalysis and psychoanalytic psychotherapy. In brief, we have become considerably less arbitrary about what psychoanalysis is and how a psychoanalytic treatment should be carried out.

Difficult as it is to define psychoanalysis in a way that would satisfy all of its adherents, it is almost impossible to agree on what psychoanalytic psychotherapy is. The latter task is a particularly vexing one. I would suggest that the term is unfortunate and confusing. Psychoanalytic psychotherapy should denote a form of therapy that is psychoanalytic, but then what psychotherapy is *more psychoanalytic* than psychoanalysis itself? If it were possible, I would prefer to limit the term "psychoanalytic psychotherapy" (even *more* preferable would be "psychoanalytic therapy") to that form of psychotherapy we designate as psychoanalysis, and then label all the rest as (just plain) "psychotherapy." In spite of the considerable concern about the relation between our more abstract basic theory and our clinical practice (see Klein, 1973; Sandler and Sandler, 1984; Wallerstein, 1988), I continue to view my clinical work as a specific (albeit not necessarily direct) application of our overall psychoanalytic theory. Hypothetically, the appropriate application of that theory should warrant the appellation "psychoanalytic psychotherapy" and should produce a "psychoanalysis." We know, of course, that things are neither that clear nor that simple (see Wallerstein and Weinshel, 1989, pp. 341–373).

A clinical psychoanalysis is an excruciatingly personal, almost idiosyncratic, endeavor for both the analyst and the analysand. Even those psychoanalysts who subscribe to the same theoretical orientation and conceptualizations will not necessarily develop or apply those concepts in identical ways; and, as the degree of diversity and "pluralism" within our profession has escalated, it became increasingly difficult to describe precisely what a psychoanalysis *is,* what its appropriate goals are, and what is *distinctively psychoanalytic* in the course of psychoanalytic treatment. What I wrote in connection with a definition of the psychoanalytic process can apply as well to the definition of a psychoanalysis itself:

> Whoever proffers such a conceptual definition would of necessity present a formulation which would reflect his own editions of the basic postulates of psychoanalysis, his elaboration of those postulates into various levels of theory, the ways in which he translates that theory into practice, and his conscious and not-so-conscious goals of analysis [Weinshel, 1984, pp. 66–67] [this volume, p. 269].

It is not surprising that not all psychoanalysts accept the same criteria for deciding which cases should be "in" psychoanalysis and which in psychotherapy.

On a clinical level, I do not believe that we can readily differentiate psychoanalysis from psychotherapy *simply* on the basis of utilizing the traditional psychoanalytic appurtenances and the technical tools of our profession (see Arlow and Brenner, 1988, p. 9). Not everything a psychoanalyst does is necessarily psychoanalytic any more than the claim of being "analytically oriented" is a guarantee that the therapist does analytic work. Certainly the use of the couch or free association are not in themselves designative of psychoanalysis. The same holds true for such time-honored concepts as "interpretation," transference and countertransference, resistance and defense, the unconscious, or intrapsychic conflict. These terms and techniques are no longer part of the sacrosanct private domain of psychoanalysis and psychoanalysts. They are used and applied by virtually all varieties of psychotherapists the world over, even by those who may disagree or violently reject psychoanalysis either as a theory or as a technique. Psychoanalysis can no longer be defined either by the frequency or duration of a therapy. Even within the American and International Psychoanalytic Associations there are both individual analysts and component societies that have taken the position that a satisfactory analysis can be conducted with less than four or five sessions a week and that the whole enterprise can be completed in a relatively brief period of time. This is not to say, however, that these concepts and these techniques are not crucial components of all analytic work and of any analysis.

I question, however, if one can make a reliable determination of whether one is or is not observing psychoanalytic work if that observation is limited to a single session or a small cluster of sessions. I would suggest that analytic work can only be dependably studied and defined from the perspective of an ongoing, longitudinal examination of that work. We have to study the *psychoanalytic process*, and it is my suspicion

> that a principal clue to resolving the psychoanalysis/psychotherapy dilemma may be in differences in the nature of the therapeutic process of each; so I would like to know more about the nature of the *psychoanalytic* process. A good deal has been said about the psychoanalytic process in recent years, but nothing like a consensus about its meaning has been achieved [Weinshel, 1990, p. 294] [this volume, p. 325].

There are analysts who are not very taken with the idea of a psychoanalytic process; those who consider it a *concept* worth pursuing seem divided as to its meaning and significance. One could argue that the term and concept refer to the course of thc entire analysis and include the role of *all* factors that played a significant part in the analytic work (see Rangell, 1989); or one could hold that the concept of a psychoanalytic process should focus on those relatively *specific* analytic activities which are unique for psychoanalysis as a therapy. Although these two viewpoints appear antipodal, I believe both are useful in establishing cogent criteria for defining a psychoanalytic process: the broader definition because none of those significant individual factors (transference, resistance, free association, the reconstruction of unconscious fantasies, etc.) are completely independent of each other or completely unrelated to the more "specific" analytic activities; more specific analytic factors because they help to deline psychoanalytic work, differentiate it from other forms of psychotherapy, *and* provide a useful organizing frame of reference in following the course and status of the psychoanalytic work. Because "psychotherapy" is a more diffuse practice involving a much wider and heterogeneous array of psychopathology and therapeutic settings, I find it difficult to conceptualize a "psychotherapeutic process" that would be comparable to a psychoanalytic process in terms of cohesiveness and usefulness.

Elsewhere (Weinshel, 1984 [chapter 11, this volume]) I suggested that the patient's resistance to the analytic work, the analyst's interpretation of that resistance, and the patient's response to that interpretation represented the basic "unit" of the psychoanalytic process and the core of the analytic work. (For a somewhat different but comparable concept of the psychoanalytic process, see Abrams, 1987, 1989.)

I agree with Freud (1913, p. 130) that the analyst "sets in motion a process, that of the resolving of the existing repressions. He can supervise this process, further it, *remove obstacles* in its way. . . ." While it is clear that the analytic work is by no means *limited* to "the resolving of the existing repressions," a crucial portion of that work is centered on dealing with forces that maintain the repressions in the "dynamic unconscious." I refer here not only to repression in its limited sense, but to all the mechanisms of defense and resistance, particularly to defenses that interfere with the ego's making appropriate connections. I do not expect to be able to do away with all repressions or to recapture all of the repressed, but the persistent "pursuit of the unconscious" by way of the consistent interpretation and eventual analysis of the presenting resistances "provides both analyst and analysand with the opportunity of discovering the connections and content of the patient's mental life, both conscious and unconscious" (Weinshel, 1984, p. 75 [this volume,

p. 275]). The focus on the exposure, exploration, and analysis of the resistances cannot be separated from a comparable engagement with the recognizable transferences; and trying to decide which of the two is more crucial to the analysis invariably becomes a futile debate, since transference and resistance are more often than not different aspects of the same psychological phenomena at differing levels of abstraction and conceptualization.

A significant advantage of a resistance-centered concept of the psychoanalytic process is that resistances

> . . . are (on the whole) observable clinical phenomena. It is true, of course, that our observations may turn out to be inaccurate or their significance poorly understood; and it is also true that we may fail to detect the resistances in the clinical material, especially when the evidence for the resistance is subtle or disguised. Moreover, we are all aware that recognition and exposure of resistance do not guarantee an effective analysis of the resistance configuration. Nevertheless . . . we can and do observe: (1) the clinical evidence of the *obstacles/resistance* to the analytic work; (2) the intervention/interpretation of the analysis of the resistance . . .; (3) the response of the patient to the analyst's interventions. When that response includes some change in the patient, especially in the way he approaches the analytic work, the analysis, the analyst, or himself (self-observation), it seems reasonable to assume that some kind of structural change has taken place. If that change (an attitude or character trait, a pattern of behavior, an alteration or ostensible disappearance of a symptom, etc.) persists, that assumption seems more legitimate and convincing. [For a somewhat different but also defense/resistance-focused approach, see Gray, 1973, 1982.]
>
> This sequence of events is by no means inevitable or foolproof (but then, neither are our interpretations) even in this circumscribed and microscopic kind of observation. We can never be certain that there is a one-to-one connection between steps 1, 2, and 3; but the sequence should at least be treated with some respect and consideration with regard to a potential *causal* relation [Weinshel, 1988, pp. 266–267].

This is why I feel most comfortable in following the course of an analysis by focusing on the vicissitudes of the resistances as they are recognized and interpreted.

As the resistances emerge in the analytic work, simultaneously—almost inevitably—the "special interactive process" between the two individuals involved in that process and the various conflicts and relationships that develop in the course of that complex interaction come into focus. Even if a given resistance appears to be related primarily to the analytic situation or the patient's fears or fantasies in regard to analysis, it is impossible to separate the person of the analyst from these manifestations of conflicting attitudes and tendencies toward the analytic work; and similar conflicts and resistances to analysis are evoked within the analyst. The analysis of resistances provides a constant and inevitable reminder that *two* people are always involved in the psychoanalytic endeavor.

It follows that the course of the analysis is not determined solely by the analyst's interpretations or his general behavior. Unless the patient is able to participate in that distinctive psychological exploration we call psychoanalysis—distinctive because although it is mutual, it is also tilted—that exploration (the analytic work) does not proceed, and a psychoanalytic process cannot be maintained. This failure may be the consequence of the analyst's inability to understand the patient's problems and psychological makeup, or of his own shortcomings (countertransferential or otherwise), or of technical blunders that interfere with the patient's engagement in the analytic work. On the other hand, if the patient either does not have or cannot acquire the necessary psychological "skills" and "strengths" for a cooperative venture such as psychoanalysis, psychoanalysis may not be the treatment of choice for that person. We are painfully aware that with the most careful evaluation of a prospective analysand, even experienced and sensitive psychoanalysts may not detect or appreciate sufficiently psychopathology that will make it impossible (at least in *that* analytic dyad) for a reasonably productive psychoanalytic process to develop.

It is not unusual for such cases to end up in psychotherapy. Ideally, it will become clear to both the analyst and analysand that the analytic work is neither significantly productive nor appears to demonstrate the promise for future productivity. There is a mutual agreement to terminate the "analysis" and to shift to "psychotherapy" with either the same or another therapist. In situations where there has been a decision to continue the therapy with the erstwhile analyst as the psychotherapist, we should be able to garner some useful information and hints as to the way in which that "analyst" works (and thinks about that work) with a patient in both psychoanalysis and (in many ways with the *same* patient) in psychotherapy.

Such cases raise the question, of course, of why and how the analyst comes to the decision that it is in the best interest of the patient to abandon the analytic undertaking. The whole issue of why the patient may want to stop the analysis raises questions and issues that usually are at variance from those that concern the analyst; and it has been argued that if the analysand and the analyst can come to a mutual agreement that psychotherapy may be a more appropriate therapy than psychoanalysis, then that analysis has not been an unsuccessful one. That is another matter. I suggest, however, that the *analyst's* thinking in this regard indicates a great deal about that analyst's goals for clinical analysis and the essential criteria he employs in evaluating the progress and effectiveness of the analytic work and process. I have stressed already that these goals and criteria are strikingly personal ones with considerable differences in the way various psychoanalysts conceptualize them. I want to describe what I look for in the clinical data that would indicate that psychoanalytic work is progressing.

I have stated my preference for observing the progress of the analytic work and the analytic process by following the resistances and the changes that resulted from the analysis of those resistances. It is always very difficult to decide with any degree of certainty whether those observed changes have taken place as a result of that psychoanalytic work or whether they are the product of a variety of extra-analytic factors. Each analyst accumulates

> his own list of clinical observations that may indicate that there have . . . been intrapsychic changes due to the analytic work; and, while none of these observations and inferences drawn from them are infallible, they are of great value in assessing the course of the psychoanalytic process. Among these criteria, I would stress the analysand's capacity to be less focused on the 'symptom' or his 'misery' in general and to become more of an active participant in the analytic work; the capacity to tolerate and to utilize in the analysis drive derivatives that have hitherto been markedly disguised, or distant, or essentially disavowed—the same phenomena can be described in the idiom of alterations in the quality and nature of the compromise formations; the capacity to recognize and utilize defenses and resistances; the capacity for an identification with the analyst *qua* analyst and an increased empathy for the analytic work and the analyst; the capacity for an increasing tendency to try to 'understand' the analyst's interpretations (or silence), instead of an

> automatic rejection or perfunctory agreement [Weinshel, 1988, p. 265].

I should point out again that not any one or more of these changes in themselves are solid guarantees that an effective psychoanalytic process is operative, nor does this mean that any one or more of these changes by themselves *cannot* be attained through other than psychoanalytic therapeutic approaches. An *analysis* is the product of a large number of interacting transactions operating over a substantial period of time.

To this short list I would add: the capacity for a greater tolerance in the expression of affects; evidence of a broader repertoire of more precise and subtle affects; the elucidation and *analysis* of a transference configuration beyond the initial stage of its recognition and utilization *by the analyst* in the treatment. This provides the patient with "the opportunity to become aware of, review, and alter obsolete conclusions that underlie some current maladaptive attitudes. Analytic work, when it is productive, unveils and examines certain compromise solutions which are actively operative even though they were forged under conditions long past" (Weinshel and Renik, in press).

A significant number of items on this list deal with the analysand's increasing interest in and preoccupation with his analysis and his own mental operations in distinction to his more immediate unhappiness and symptoms. This shift in interest is frequently associated with the development of "insight," a term that is still the subject of considerable controversy. While there is no consensus as to whether insight is best viewed as a process or a product or a therapeutic instrument, there seems to be general agreement

> that clinical analysis aims at symptom relief based on increased self-awareness. . . . The achievement of insight, in the sense of heightened self-awareness, probably remains a primary operational objective for most psychoanalysts in their daily clinical work. Translated into a somewhat different idiom, the achievement of insight (or the capacity for self-analysis, self-observation, self-inquiry, and other related terms) also implies a greater and easier access to unconscious psychological derivatives [Weinshel and Renik, 1992].

My position is that the most convincing and reliable indicator of productive psychoanalytic work is the establishment of a relatively permanent psychoanalytic process together with the attitudes and psychic structure that have evolved to support it, and that "their presence is reflected most immediately and most tangibly in the operation of a more effective and more 'objective' capacity for self-observation" (Weinshel, 1984, p. 82 [this volume, p. 281]). This enhancement of self-observation is the product of the action of a large number of elements and procedures

> the sum and substance of which constitute clinical analysis as we know it. A partial list would include investigation of fantasies and dreams; gaining an understanding of the relevant traumatic past (on the basis of actual recovered memories or by reconstruction); establishing the role of drives and drive derivatives; the clarification of both intersystemic and intrasystemic intrapsychic conflict; the exposition of the content of anxieties and depressive affects (and other affects as well), including an understanding of the various ways in which these affects elicit defensive activities.
>
> Whatever an analyst's particular orientation or emphasis, . . . when analytic work proceeds, *insight and symptom relief merge into a single goal*. The analysand's resistances clarify themselves as the most immediately relevant *symptoms* to be studied, and no distinctions can or need be made between investigations of the analysand's self-observational difficulties and investigation of his psychopathology.
>
> From this point of view, too, it can be seen that another goal of analytic work is to make it possible for the analysand to engage in a form of self-observation or self-inquiry that at least approximates the analytic situation. The agreement to terminate the analytic meetings, then, is best understood not as a decision to terminate the analytic process, but as a judgment that the analyst's input is no longer required to adequately maintain the analytic process [Weinshel and Renik, 1992].

My emphasis on resistances, the analytic process, and an enhanced capacity for objective self-observation does not ignore or depreciate the role of such factors as countertransference, empathy, or the significance of a "new" relationship. I look upon these as "prerequisites" for doing psychoanalytic work rather than as an integral part of that work *per se*.

Ticho (1972, pp. 315–333) spoke of psychoanalytic treatment in terms of treatment goals, which deal with the "removal of obstacles to the patient's discovery of what his potentialities are," and life goals, which are "the goals the patient would seek to attain if he could put his potentialities to use." I find these distinctions useful, especially since the patient is usually more concerned with the hope and expectation of a happier life. The analyst, however, is likely to be more focused on a persistent pursuit of the treatment goals with the expectation that the psychoanalytic method is more effective if so employed. This bias is, of course, consistent with Freud's precept that "The business of analysis is to secure the best possible psychological conditions for the function of the ego; with this it has secured its task" (Freud, 1937, p. 250).

I feel I have neither presented a comprehensive depiction of what takes place in a psychoanalysis nor differentiated a psychoanalysis from all the other forms of psychotherapy, including what we call psychoanalytic psychotherapy; instead, I have limited myself to a portrayal of how I view and how I practice psychoanalysis.

I have not attempted to describe systematically how I view and practice psychotherapy or psychoanalytic psychotherapy—a term I do not find congenial. If I think of a psychoanalytic psychotherapy in the broadest sense (that is of any method of psychotherapy which is based on and employs psychoanalytic concepts, theories, and techniques), then that term could encompass *at least* the following clinical situations (all of which I have encountered in the last few years; see Gray, 1988, pp. 41–50): (1) psychoanalysis; (2) psychotherapy with very severely disturbed patients; (3) psychotherapy with patients who are so "well" that it would be inappropriate to involve them in a therapy as extensive and as demanding as psychoanalysis. This includes those who have had a satisfactory psychoanalytic experience, but who have, for one reason or another, returned for further therapy; (4) psychotherapy with "older" patients, i.e., in excess of 60; (5) psychotherapy with patients who cannot, for reasons of money, distance from available psychoanalytic services, health, etc., participate in four-to-five times a week psychoanalysis; (6) psychotherapy with patients who "appear" to be analyzable and have the resources to be in analysis, but whose resistances to such a psychotherapy necessitate another approach; and (7) psychotherapy with some patients with psychosomatic disorders.

The list is not complete, but it does demonstrate that it would be awkward to formulate *one* relatively discrete psychotherapeutic design, approach, and process that would be applicable to all of these categories of psychotherapy. It is my impression, however, that most psychoanalysts do treat some patients who are not in analysis; certainly, I do so myself.

I enjoy doing "psychotherapy." I find it interesting, valuable, and certainly not easier than or inferior to psychoanalysis; and I think I learn a good deal from these experiences. I confess, however, that unless the patient is so disturbed that analysis appears to be out of the question either at the moment or in the not too distant future, I am always thinking of being able to transfer that patient into what I consider to be a psychoanalytic situation; and I try, as best I can, to keep my work with that patient within the confines of what I think of as psychoanalytic. I try to think of the work from the points of view of the dynamic unconscious and the resistances, of the likely unconscious fantasies involved, and of how certain psychological manifestations came to be the way they are. The results have varied considerably. There have been times when I have been able to shift such a patient to "analysis" either with myself or a colleague; there have been times when once or twice weekly psychotherapy has produced external results which evoked pleasure and gratitude from the patient and some puzzlement and perplexity from me; there have been times when I have had to abandon such an approach and operate in a more "supportive" (a term that has always bewildered me) or "manipulative" (a term that is more clear but less palatable) approach; and, of course, there have been times when the whole enterprise was a failure or disaster. I am not able, however, to correlate around one organizing concept the various ways in which I have worked with this array of patients—and although I felt that some of what I was doing was *psychoanalytic,* I was not convinced that any of these therapies constituted a psychoanalysis. Other analysts may feel differently.

I have reviewed much of the work I have done with patients both in analysis and in psychotherapy. Although I cannot testify to the validity of my impressions, I would like to go over in a synoptic way some differences in "technique" in the treatment of patients in psychoanalysis and in "psychoanalytic psychotherapy."

1. My goals for analysis tend to be more open and more general, less time-limited. There is more focus on character than on symptoms, and the most tangible goals have to do with self-observation and self-inquiry. In psychotherapy, I am likely to *think* more along time-limited lines, with more specific goals and relatively more focus on the symptoms or other psychological distress.

2. I conduct an analysis (with rare exceptions) four or five times a week. In psychotherapy, the frequency of meetings tends to be somewhat variable and often is determined by hunch.

3. In analysis I focus on the resistances as they emerge, paying a great deal of attention to the affects which I believe to have elicited that resistance. I view the analysis of the resistances as a dialectic process in that, as one resistance has been dealt with, another will soon come forth. While I try to deal with resistances in virtually all the patients I treat, work with psychoanalytic psychotherapy patients is liable to be less systematic and persistent, and more selective. In a related vein, I am usually more concerned with the "frame" in the psychoanalytic situation than in psychotherapy, and also more observant about the ways in which both participants comply with that "frame" (Spruiell, 1983; Weinshel, 1984, pp. 68–69 [this volume, pp. 270–271]).

4. In conducting an analysis, I see my role as the Dr. Watson to the patient's Sherlock Holmes (Calef and Weinshel, 1980, p. 289 [this volume, pp. 262–263]) and try not to preempt the patient's responsibility and autonomy. I see the analyst's role primarily as the conscience of the analysis and the keeper of the psychoanalytic process, and see—generally—the analyst as less directive than in work with psychotherapy patients. Also, with the latter patients, I tend to be more concerned with the patient than the process; and this involves being more directive. I stress that I am speaking of "tendencies" rather than with either-or distinctions.

5. I accept that, for better or worse, *some* "suggestion" is an inevitable concomitant of the analytic process. Bernfeld (1941) noted, and I agree, that in psychoanalytic therapy it is more likely that the suggestions are directed toward the resistances, while in other therapies the suggestion is much more frequently utilized to elicit specific content (Calef and Weinshel, 1975, p. 39). Further, in analysis it is more feasible to deal with the impact of the "suggestion" on the ongoing analytic work.

6. In analysis, I usually utilize dreams for both their available content and for the resistances that can be discerned both within the dream and in the way the dream is dealt with by the patient. The analysis of dreams leans very heavily on the associations of the dreamer. In psychotherapy, more emphasis is placed on the dream content and how that material can be used in the current situation to make a specific point; relatively less attention is paid to the resistances and the patient's associations.

7. Reconstruction of the past, in analysis, proceeds slowly and usually piecemeal. One depends a good deal on the analysis of specific transferences in attempting to "reconstruct" how psychological patterns and

conflicts from the past developed and were transformed on the way to adulthood rather than searching for specific repressed memories or trauma. In psychotherapy, reconstruction is considerahly less stringent and less likely to be connected with a persistent analysis of transferences and, therefore, one is more prone to produce constructions rather than reconstructions.

8. I am concerned with issues of abstinence, but am likely to be more selective and circumscribed rather than global than was true in the past. In psychotherapy the therapist will probably be less concerned with abstinence and more likely (wittingly or otherwise) to provide transference gratifications. The same differences apply, I believe, to "analytic neutrality" and the analyst's "equidistant stance." This is an important subject which warrants much careful attention and evaluation.

9. The technical tasks of the analysis are mainly (but not only) concerned with dealing with the transferences and resistances. In analysis the transference is "analyzed" in terms of its source, its affective connections, the defenses and resistance with which it is associated, and the gratifications it garners. In psychotherapy, my work with a transference configuration tends to be less intense and often limited to its identification and its therapeutic use in the treatment, often without thorough analysis (Gill, 1951, p. 62). I should add that there are great variations here in both modalities.

10. The pace of an analysis tends to be slower, more deliberate, and more inclusive. The general "rule" is to allow the analysand to initiate the interchange and introduce the topic, but this is not necessarily always so. In psychotherapy, I would probably be tempted to interpret the transferences earlier than I would in an analytic situation where it would be advantageous to let the transference deepen and "ripen." In psychotherapy, the analyst will probably share in the selection of the material to be scrutinized and be less likely to maintain the neutrality of an equidistant position.

11. I consider the termination of an analysis to be one of its more consequential decisions. It is almost always a mutually agreed upon decision which is implemented carefully over a significant period of time. As I mentioned earlier, the ideal termination is one in which both analyst and analysand concur that the analytic work can continue without the presence and input from the analyst. In psychotherapy, the decision to terminate the therapeutic work is more likely to be somewhat arbitrary and influenced by the patient's life goals and his subjective improvement.

It seems that what I have stated in this essay is pretty much in line with my favorite definition of the difference between these two modalities. This exemplar of directness and brevity came from Helen Ross at a talk she gave in San Francisco about 30 years ago. When asked what *she* thought the difference between psychoanalysis and psychoanalytic psychotherapy was, Dr. Ross hesitated not a moment asserting that "Psychoanalysis lasted longer, went deeper, and came up dirtier." It may be that we shall have to live and work with *this* kind of unambiguous statement until we can come to a clearer and more convincing consensus about exactly what psychoanalysis is—and isn't—than we possess at the present time.

REFERENCES

Abrams, S. (1987), The psychoanalytic process: A schematic model. *Internat. J. Psycho-Anal.*, 68:441–452.

_______ (1989), Ambiguity in excess: An obstacle to common ground. *Internat. J. Psycho-Anal.*, 70:3–7.

Arlow, J. A. & Brenner, C. (1988), The future of psychoanalysis. *Psychoanal. Quart.*, 57:1–14.

Bernfeld, S. (1941), The facts of observation in psychoanalysis. *J. Psychol.*, 12:289–305.

Bibring, E. (1954), Psychoanalysis and the dynamic psychotherapies. *J. Amer. Psychoanal. Assn.*, 2:745–770.

Boesky, D. (1988), Comments on the structural theory of technique. *Internat. J. Psycho-Anal.*, 69:303–316.

Brenner, C. (1982), *The Mind in Conflict*. New York: International Universities Press.

Calef, V. & Weinshel, E. M. (1975), A neglected classic: Siegfried Bernfeld's "The facts of observation in psychoanalysis." *J. Phila. Assn. Psychoanal.*, 2:38–40.

_______ (1980), The analyst as the conscience of the analysis. *Internat. Rev. Psycho-Anal.*, 7:279–290.

Freud, A. (1954), The widening scope of indications for psychoanalysis: Discussion. *J. Amer. Psychoanal. Assn.*, 2:607–620.

Freud, S. (1913), On beginning the treatment (further recommendations on the technique of psychoanalysis). *Standard Edition*, 12.

_______ (1937), Analysis terminable and interminable. *Standard Edition*, 23.

Gill, M. M. (1951), Ego psychology and psychotherapy. *Psychoanal. Quart.*, 20:62–71.

_______ (1954), Psychoanalysis and exploratory psychotherapy. *J. Amer. Psychoanal. Assn.*, 2:771–797.

Gray, P. (1973), Psychoanalytic technique and the ego's capacity for viewing intrapsychic activity. *J. Amer. Psychoanal. Assn.*, 21:474–494.

_______ (1982), "Developmental lag" in the evolution of technique for psychoanalysis of neurotic conflict. *J. Amer. Psychoanal. Assn.*, 30:621–655.

_______ (1988), On the significance of influence and insight in the spectrum of psychoanalytic psychotherapies. In: *How Does Treatment Help?* ed. A. Rothstein. Madison, CT: International Universities Press, pp. 41–50.

Klein, G. S. (1973), Two theories or one? *Bull. Menn. Clin.*, 37:102–132.

Rangell, L. (1954), Similarities and differences between psychoanalysis and dynamic psychotherapy. *J. Amer. Psychoanal. Assn.*, 2:734–744.

_______ (1989), Action theory within the structural view. *Internat. J. Psycho-Anal.*, 70:189–203.

Sandler, J. & Sandler, A.-M. (1984), The past unconscious, the present unconscious, and interpretation of the transference. *Psychoanal. Inq.*, 4: 367–399.

Spruiell, V. (1983), The rules and frames of the psychoanalytic situation. *Psychoanal. Quart.*, 52:1–33.

Stone, L. (1954), The widening scope of indications for psychoanalysis. *J. Amer. Psychoanal. Assn.*, 2:567–594.

Ticho, E. (1972), Termination of psychoanalysis, treatment goals, life goals. *Psychoanal. Quart.*, 41:315–333.

Wallerstein, R. S. (1988), One psychoanalysis or many? *Internat. J. Psycho-Anal.*, 69:5–21.

_______ (1989), Psychoanalysis and psychotherapy: An historical perspective. *Internat. J. Psycho-Anal.*, 70:563–591.

_______ & Weinshel, E. (1989), The future of psychoanalysis. *Psychoanal. Quart.*, 58:341–373.

Weinshel, E. M. (1984), Some observations on the psychoanalytic process. *Psychoanal. Quart.*, 53:63–92.

_______ (1988), Structural change in psychoanalysis. *J. Amer. Psychoanal. Assn.*, 36(Suppl.):263–280.

_______ (1990), How wide is the widening scope of psychoanalysis and how solid is its structural model? Some concerns and observations. *J. Amer. Psychoanal. Assn.*, 38:275–296.

_______ & Renik, O. (1992), Treatment goals in psychoanalysis. In: *The Technique and Practice of Psychoanalysis: A Memorial Volume to Ralph R. Greenson*, ed. A. Sugarman, R. A. Nemiroff & D. P. Greenson. Madison, CT: International Universities Press, pp. 91–99.

BRIEF NOTES

On Being a Legacy

Julie Weinshel Tepper

On my 18th birthday, my parents gave me a copy of *The Joy of Cooking*. I still have it, not because I'm much of a cook, but because of its epigram by Goethe, which is often in my mind as I seek my own identity as a psychoanalyst: "That which thy fathers have bequeathed to thee, earn it anew if thou wouldst possess it" (Faust).

When this project began, collecting my father's papers into a book, Bob Wallerstein had the idea that the three family members who have followed him into his field—his stepdaughter, Dena Sorbo, his granddaughter, Caitlin Pittel Stark (my daughter), and myself—might want to share our thoughts about his influence on our professional paths.

What a task for a daughter! My father, like many psychoanalysts who prospered during psychoanalysis' "golden age," was devoted to, and passionate about his profession. His wife came first, of course, and I *want* to think his children, and later his grandchildren, followed close behind, but I wouldn't have bet on it! In our family, psychoanalysis was an extra, but much revered, family member. And, as much as he loved his profession, my father never invited my brother or me into it.

Nevertheless, in my middle age, I did follow him into it. I have frequently described myself as "crawling in his footsteps," with all that such a journey entails: the predictable conflicts, and the many pleasures of being a "legacy" candidate and psychoanalyst.

In the year before his 75th birthday, in a prophetically valedictory telephone conversation, my father told me how profoundly grateful he was to have known the people whom he had analyzed, and how privileged he felt to have been allowed to enter their lives and minds. It was an odd conversation, almost as though he felt compelled to say something aloud that had been on his mind. Perhaps he had become aware of the creeping onslaught of the Alzheimer's disease that eventually robbed him of his mind. But I knew he was telling me something important. He was announcing, for the record, how meaningful and how good his life as a psychoanalyst had been.

This book contains many of his papers and ideas, but it was not the ideas that first drew me into his field, to crawl in his footsteps. As I said, he never encouraged me or invited me in. So why become a psychoanalyst, with all the time, money, effort, and domestic sacrifice that training requires? It was his unshakeable sense of the value of psychoanalysis, and his enduring excitement about and interest in the work that pulled me. At times he was discouraged with the politics; and I know, though he thoroughly enjoyed every moment of comedy, he always carried the sorrows of his patients with him. But he was never bored. For 50 years, he saw patients six days a week, he read and wrote every night, he attended thousands of professional meetings, classes and conferences, and the man was never, ever bored. That's why I followed him into the field.

When I began my training at the Los Angeles Psychoanalytic Institute, I used my father's set of the *Standard Edition* of Freud's papers. As I read through Freud, especially in that first year, there I was, where my father had been. There, with the dust motes floating off the pages, were his penciled comments, his annotated bookmarks, his underlinings, his exclamation points. So *this* was what captured his mind, and held it for so many years!

The enduring love of one's work, the conviction that one is doing something of value, and the anticipation of a daily rendezvous with the confounding mysteries of the mind—these my father has bequeathed to me. Possessing them anew—that is my own work.

A Vision of Ed Weinshel

Dena Marshall Sorbo

Twenty-one years ago, my mother and Ed Weinshel married.

I didn't know what to make of him at first. I wondered if he could really be as generous about life, love, and work as he seemed to be. He had a leap in his step and vitality in his laugh; he'd clutch both of my hands, squeeze, and then give a robust hug. He was a great observer of those around him and would comment sparingly and with caring precision if something concerned him. I remember standing in the kitchen at dinnertime; he'd burst through the door after a long day of seeing patients and supervisees. He was full of energy. He would hug and kiss all and inquire about each of us. Then came the vitally important questions, what was for dinner and did you want "fruit" in your martini or not? His loving embrace of life and of those around him was truly remarkable. He showed me that the doors in life were open and that I simply had to walk through. If I couldn't, I needed to figure out why not. He encouraged me in so many ways; to get married, to have kids, to think about psychoanalysis, to Enjoy. I grew up in a family where the parting words were, "Be careful"; Eddie's were, "Have fun!" He was at the hospital when my sons were born; he walked them and sang to them. He crawled after them under the Thanksgiving table and would scoop them up in his arms to their mutual glee. Their foreheads and noses pressed together would create spasms of giggles and delight for all.

It was through Eddie that I became really interested in psychoanalysis. I was immediately impressed with his profound respect for the patient, and for the psychic pain the patient endured. He admired and valued their hard work to get well. I am a clinical social worker and at the time we met I was working with adolescents and families. Occasionally, he would give me a psychoanalytic book he thought might interest me. He invited me to attend talks he gave at the American Psychoanalytic Association meetings or locally at the San Francisco Psychoanalytic Institute. My appetite was whetted intellectually and emotionally. I began my own journey into the psychoanalytic world. I am now completing my third year of training at the San Francisco Psychoanalytic Institute, which he so loved and was a part of for so many years. As a candidate here I have had the opportunity to benefit from his legacy as a fine teacher and analyst.

I think of Eddie every day in my work and with my family. I feel so grateful to have had his loving influence in my life. I surely wouldn't be an analyst now if it hadn't been for Ed Weinshel. He was like fresh air and sunshine to me. It's a much less sunny world without him.

A Granddaughter's View
Caitlin Pittel Stark

Tucked away in a closet adjoining the master bathroom of my grandparents' house in San Francisco was a small metal safe with a combination lock. On visits, my sister and I waited eagerly for the time to be right—though it always caught us by surprise—for our grandfather to lead us up the winding stairway to the safe. We watched, patient, while he worked the lock with solemn intent. Then, suddenly, his eyes lit up. Our eyes lit up. The tiny door opened. Inside were Hershey's miniatures. Krackle. Mr. Goodbar. Special dark, and my favorite, milk chocolate. We were allowed as many as we could eat, no questions asked, no worrying about saving our appetites for dinner. No one made us feel more important than Papou (as we called him), more attended to. The ritual of the safe was predictable, the same every time, but it never lost its wonder. When that tiny door opened, it was magic, as if we did not know what lay behind it all along.

My grandfather had a stroke just months before I began my doctoral program in clinical psychology. Though I grew up among therapists, and studied psychology in college, it was not until graduate school that I was exposed to and developed a fascination, in earnest, for the kinds of ideas that had shaped my grandfather's career. I felt immeasurable sadness, in those first years, that I could not talk with him about Freud, about object relations, the meaning of dreams, the capacity to be alone. We never talked about my first clinical cases. Finally, I was learning the family language, too late to speak it with him.

What I remember of his wisdom, I have tried to put in place on my own. This story (as I remember it) was overheard when I was a teenager. It comes to me whenever I worry about breaking the therapeutic "frame." One of my grandfather's patients called him unexpectedly one evening to ask advice. The patient wanted to know what shirt he should wear for a date. As I listened, someone in the room remarked, laughing, that they hoped he had done the right thing. My grandfather said, "I told him to wear the blue one." I discovered later that his supervisees often quoted him as saying, "Our patients will forgive errors of technique, but not errors of the heart."

It is difficult to write about my grandfather's work, to speak about him as a psychologist, rather than as a grandchild. I can only imagine that he brought to his patients the same kind of patience, care, and unconditional acceptance that he brought to my sister and me throughout our lives. He never gave me advice about how to be a therapist, but I have learned through his example. In my own work, I try to remember that who you are is more important than what you do. I have learned to respect the many different kinds of human needs. I am anchored in the belief that human behavior always has more than one meaning, and that there is always room for wonder, even when you think you know what lies inside.

PUBLICATIONS BY EDWARD M. WEINSHEL, M.D.

(1952), The psychotherapeutic aspects of schizophrenia. *J. Nerv. & Ment. Dis.*, 115:471–488.

(1955), Some psychiatric considerations in tinnitus. *J. Hillside Hosp.*, 4:67–92.

(1960), The psychotherapeutic approach to emotional problems. *Calif. Med.*, 93:19–23.

(1963), Psychiatric considerations of the forty-year-old dental patient. *J. Calif. Dent. Assn.*, 39:3.

(1966), Severe regressive states during analysis. *J. Amer. Psychoanal. Assn.*, 14:538–568.

(1970), Some psychoanalytic considerations on moods. *Internat. J. Psycho-Anal.*, 51:313–320.

(1970), The changing identity of the psychiatrist in private practice: A symposium (with L. C. Patterson, I. Philips, L. Schwartz & D. Schwartz). *Amer. J. Psychiat.*, 126:11.

(1970), The ego in health and normality. *J. Amer. Psychoanal. Assn.*, 18: 682–735.

(1971), The transference neurosis: A survey of the literature. *J. Amer. Psychoanal. Assn.*, 19:67–88.

(1972) (with Victor Calef), On certain neurotic equivalents in necrophilia. *Internat. J. Psycho-Anal.*, 53:67–75.

(1973) (with Victor Calef), Reporting, nonreporting, and assessment in the training analysis *J. Amer. Psychoanal. Assn.*, 21:714–726.

(1975) (with Victor Calef), A paradigm and a credo. *Contemp. Psychol.*, 20: 33–34.

(1975) (with Victor Calef), A neglected classic II: Siegfried Bernfeld's "The facts of observation in psychoanalysis." *J. Phila. Assn. Psychoanal.*, 2:38–40.

(1975) (with Victor Calef), Review: *The Unconscious Today*, ed. M. Kanzer. *Psychoanal. Quart.*, 44:640–647.

(1976), Concluding comments on the congress topic. *Internat. J. Psycho-Anal.*, 57:451–460.

(1976) (with Victor Calef), Transference neurosis. In: *The Encyclopedia of Neurology, Psychiatry, Psychoanalysis, and Psychology*, ed. L. Wolberg. New York: Aesculapius Publishers, pp. 256–261.

(1977), Plenary discussion of the report of Commission IV (Child Analysis) to the 1975 Conference on Psychoanalytic Education and Research. In: *Psychoanalytic Education and Research*, ed. S. Goodman. New York: International Universities Press, pp. 85–94.

(1977), "I didn't mean it": Negation as a character trait. *The Psychoanalytic Study of the Child*, 32:387–419. New Haven, CT: Yale University Press.

(1979), Some observations on not telling the truth. *J. Amer. Psychoanal. Assn.*, 27:503–533.

(1979), A message from a past president, Maxwell Gitelson. In: *L'Identité du Psychanalyste*, ed. E. Joseph & D. Widlocher. Paris: Presses Universitaires de France, pp. 85–99. [Also in *The Identity of the Psychoanalyst* (1983), New York: International Universities Press, pp. 67–83].

(1979) (with Victor Calef), The new psychoanalysis and psychoanalytic revisionism. *Psychoanal. Quart.*, 48:470–491.

(1980) (with Victor Calef), The analyst as the conscience of the analysis. *Internat. Rev. Psycho-Anal.*, 7:279–290.

(1980) (with Victor Calef, Owen Renik & E. L. Mayer), Enuresis: A functional equivalent of a fetish. *Internat. J. Psycho-Anal.*, 61:295–305. (Also presented as the first Bernhard Berliner Memorial Lecture on April 11, 1980.)

(1981), Book review: *The Mind of Watergate* by L. Rangell. *Internat. Rev. Psycho-Anal.*, 8:121–124.

(1982), The functions of the training analysis and the appointment of the training analyst. *Internat. Rev. Psycho-Anal.*, 9:434–444.

(1983) (with Victor Calef), A note on consummation and termination. *J. Amer. Psychoanal. Assn.*, 31:643–650.

(1984), Some observations on the psychoanalytic process. *Psychoanal. Quart.*, 53:63–92.

(1984), Book review: *The Concordance of the Standard Edition of the Complete Psychological Works of Sigmund Freud*, ed. S. Guttman, S. M. Parrish & R. L. Jones. *Internat. Rev. Psycho-Anal.*, 11:494–497.

(1984) (with Victor Calef), Anxiety and the restitutional function of homosexual cruising. *Internat. J. Psycho-Anal.*, 65:45–62.

(1985), Book review: *Transference Neurosis and Psychosis* by M. I. Little. *J. Amer. Psychoanal. Assn.*, 33:146–151.

(1986), Perceptual distortions during analysis: Some observations on the role of the superego in reality testing. In: *The Science of Mental Conflict: Essays in Honor of Charles Brenner*, ed. A. Richards & M. Willick. Hillsdale, NJ: The Analytic Press, pp. 353–374.

(1987), A discussion of the various contributions. In: *The Interpretation of*

Dreams in Clinical Work, ed. A. Rothstein. Madison, CT: International Universities Press, pp. 181–188.

(1987), Foreword. In: *Halo in the Sky* by L. Shengold. New York: Guilford Press, pp. ix–xiii.

(1988), Structural changes in psychoanalysis. *J. Amer. Psychoanal. Assn.,* 36(Suppl.):263–280.

(1988), Play and playing in adult psychoanalysis. *Bull. Anna Freud Cent.,* 11:108–127.

(1988), The many borders of borderline: On the virtues of modesty in psychoanalytic diagnosis. *Psychoanal. Inq.,* 8:333–352.

(1989), On inconsolability. In: *The Psychoanalytic Core: Essays in Honor of Leo Rangell, M.D.,* ed. H. Blum, E. Weinshel & R. Rodman. Madison, CT: International Universities Press, pp. 45–69.

(1989), *The Psychoanalytic Core: Essays in Honor of Leo Rangell, M.D.,* ed. H. Blum, E. Weinshel & R. Rodman. Madison, CT: International Universities Press.

(1989) (with Robert Wallerstein), The future of psychoanalysis. *Psychoanal. Quart.,* 58:341–373.

(1990), How wide is the widening scope of psychoanalysis and how solid is its structural model? Some concerns and observations. *J. Amer. Psychoanal. Assn.,* 38:275–296.

(1990), Further observations on the psychoanalytic process. *Psychoanal. Quart.,* 59:629–649.

(1991), A discussion of the "Old woman's touch: Reflections on the treatment of a case of obsessional neurosis" by R. M. Loewenstein. In: *Psychoanalytic Case Studies,* ed. G. Pirooz Sholevar & J. Glenn. Madison, CT: International Universities Press, pp. 61–77.

(1991) (with Owen Renik), The past ten years: Psychoanalysis in the United States, 1980–1990. *Psychoanal. Inq.,* 11:13–29.

(1992), Therapeutic technique in psychoanalysis and psychoanalytic psychotherapy. *J. Amer. Psychoanal. Assn.,* 40:327–347.

(1992) (with Owen Renik), Treatment goals in psychoanalysis. In: *The Technique and Practice of Psychoanalysis: A Memorial Volume to Ralph R. Greenson,* ed. A. Sugarman, R. A. Nemiroff & D. P. Greenson. Madison, CT: International Universities Press, pp. 91–99.

(1993), Psychic structure and psychic change: A case of inconsolability. In: *Psychic Structure and Psychic Change: Essays in Honor of Robert S. Wallerstein, M.D.,* ed. M. Horowitz, O. Kernberg & E. Weinshel. Madison, CT: International Universities Press, pp. 29–56.

(1993), *Psychic Structure and Psychic Change: Essays in Honor of Robert S. Wallerstein, M.D.,* ed. M. Horowitz, O. Kernberg & E. Weinshel. Madison, CT: International Universities Press.

INDEX